# The Switch Image

Thinking|Media

Series Editors

Bernd Herzogenrath

Patricia Pisters

# The Switch Image

*Television Philosophy*

Lorenz Engell

Translated from the German
manuscript by Anthony Enns

BLOOMSBURY ACADEMIC
NEW YORK • LONDON • OXFORD • NEW DELHI • SYDNEY

BLOOMSBURY ACADEMIC
Bloomsbury Publishing Inc
1385 Broadway, New York, NY 10018, USA
50 Bedford Square, London, WC1B 3DP, UK
29 Earlsfort Terrace, Dublin 2, Ireland

BLOOMSBURY, BLOOMSBURY ACADEMIC and the Diana logo are trademarks of Bloomsbury Publishing Plc

First published in the United States of America 2021
This paperback edition published 2022

Copyright © Lorenz Engell, 2021

For legal purposes the Acknowledgments on p. viii constitute an extension of this copyright page.

Cover design: Daniel Benneworth-Gray
Cover image © Paolo Sanfifilippo

All rights reserved. No part of this publication may be reproduced or transmitted in any form or by any means, electronic or mechanical, including photocopying, recording, or any information storage or retrieval system, without prior permission in writing from the publishers.

Bloomsbury Publishing Inc does not have any control over, or responsibility for, any third-party websites referred to or in this book. All internet addresses given in this book were correct at the time of going to press. The author and publisher regret any inconvenience caused if addresses have changed or sites have ceased to exist, but can accept no responsibility for any such changes.

A catalog record for this book is available from the Library of Congress.

ISBN: HB: 978-1-5013-4928-7
PB: 978-1-5013-7737-2
ePDF: 978-1-5013-4930-0
ePUB: 978-1-5013-4929-4

Series: Thinking Media

Typeset by Deanta Global Publishing Services, Chennai, India

To find out more about our authors and books visit www.bloomsbury.com and sign up for our newsletters.

*For a long time I would no longer go to bed early. When watching television, I would continue thinking about what I was watching, but my thoughts would take a rather peculiar turn; it seemed to me that I myself was the immediate subject of what was shown: a church, a war, a quartet, a candidate. The subject of my viewing would separate itself from me, leaving me free to apply myself to it or not; and at the same time my awareness would return and I would be astonished to find myself in a state of darkness, pleasant and restful for my eyes, but even more, perhaps, for my mind, to which it appeared incomprehensible, without a cause, something dark indeed. I would ask myself what time it could be.*

*The television viewer has in a circle round him the chain of the hours, the sequence of the years, the order of worlds. Instinctively he orients himself towards them, and in an instant reads off his own position on the earth's surface and the time that has elapsed during his viewing; but this ordered procession is apt to grow confused, and to break its ranks. Suppose that he is sitting in an armchair, for instance, after dinner: then the world will go hurtling out of orbit, and the magic chair will carry him at full speed through time and space. Perhaps the immobility of the things that surround us is forced upon them by our conviction that they are themselves and not anything else, by the immobility of our conception of them.*

Adapted from Marcel Proust, *In Search of Lost Time, Volume 1: Swann's Way*

# Contents

Acknowledgments     viii

## Part I  Television 1.0

1  Switching On: The Beginnings of Television     3
2  Live Television     19
3  The Series (1)     42
4  Flow     75
5  Interconnecting     97

## Part II  Trajectories, Expansions, Intensifications

6  Instant Replay     123
7  The Space Image     148
8  Switching: Remote Control     179
9  Second Screens     213

## Part III  Television 2.0

10  The Series (2)     247
11  Reality and History     272
12  Switch-Off-Images: The Endings of Television     304

Bibliography     337
Index     359

# Acknowledgments

This book was generously funded by the *Internationales Kolleg für Kulturtechnikforschung und Medienphilosophie* of the Bauhaus University Weimar and supported by the research group *Bild-Evidenz* of the Freie Universität Berlin. My thanks therefore go to the taxpayers who made this possible. I thank the editors Patricia Pisters and Bernd Herzogenrath as well as Katie Gallof, Erin Duffy, Faye Robinson and many others at Bloomsbury Publishing. I would like to emphasize the clever work of the translator Anthony Enns. Ida Brückner took marvellous care for the English references and Marie Fernschild for the index.

I was privileged to have decisive debates with fellow scholars like André Wendler, Anna McCarthy, Antonia Lant, Antoine Hennion, Antonio Somaini, Bruno Latour, Christoph Menke, Elena Esposito, Francesco Casetti, Georges Didi Huberman, Jane Feuer, Jens Schröter, Jimena Canales, John Caldwell, Jürgen Müller, Katerina Krtilova, Katharina Niemeyer, Laura Frahm, Lisa Parks, Lynn Spigel, Markus Stauff, Mary Ann Doane, Michel Chion, Sibylle Krämer, and Wolfgang Beilenhoff. Of great importance was the work on the concept of ontography with Astrid Deuber Mankowsky, Daniela Wentz, Jane Bennett, Gabriele Gramelsberger, Michael Lynch, Michael Stadler, Sebastien Blanc, and Till Heilmann. Without the intensive discussions with Michaela Krützen at the HFF Munich, the book would not have found its form. Lisa Gotto was a close companion to the project from the beginning. Oliver Fahle has listened and given infinitely valuable and patient advice.

Everything I do not owe other people, I owe my academic teacher, Renate Möhrmann. But I am especially grateful to Christiane Voß, who not only invented and developed the key concept of the anthropo-mediatic relation, but critically and supportively guided the entire conceptual development of the switch image and of ontography. Vincent Heßelmann supported me at a crucial stage of the writing process and helped me to maintain discipline. Thank you.

This publication was supported by the Internationales Kolleg für Kulturtechnikforschung und Medienphilosophie of the Bauhaus-Universität Weimar with funds from the German Federal Ministry of Education and Research.

IKKM Books

Volume 48
An overview of the whole series can be found at
www.ikkm-weimar.de/schriften

SPONSORED BY THE

Part I

# Television 1.0

# 1

# Switching On

## The Beginnings of Television

Let's look at television at first only as a picture (consisting of image and sound). Of course, television is more than that, it is also an economic and social institution, an art, an agency of knowledge and a political space; it has a history. Nevertheless, we can consider it as a picture of image and sound for the beginning. For in all the other things that television is, it always appears in image and sound. This is true for television as art anyway, but also for television as a commodity, because it earns its money with image and sound. As an institution, television circulates images and sounds; its agency grows through images and sounds. The knowledge it processes is embodied in images and sounds, and its political space is populated by images and sounds.

So let us look at this picture with its image and sound, and for the beginning let us concentrate on the way in which the television picture shows and does the things it shows and does, instead of always looking on these things themselves, on the "what." In doing so, we follow grounding assumptions of media philosophy: The "how" of media determines the "what" of media or at least puts it under conditions. How and by what means does the television picture call up its topics, objects, people, worlds? Instead of traditionally asking: "What is television?" we therefore prefer to begin with questions like: "How does television operate, how does it come about, how does it work?," since it is through this "how" that what television shows and does and what it is itself finally comes into question.

### The Switchable Picture

To see all of this, we have to *switch on* television; otherwise the picture will not appear neither as image nor as sound. When switched on, the television set transforms itself from a mere piece of furniture to the complex apparatus at issue here (Scannell 2014: 60–77). Switching on is the conditio sine qua non of the television picture. The television picture is first and foremost a *switchable* picture, and everything else follows literally after it and exactly from it. Similarly, in order to draw a comparison, the screen image of the moving picture is tied to an inescapable condition: it has not only a frame in the surface, as many other pictures do as well, but also a mandatory course in time (and usually also a temporal limitation, namely a beginning and an end). This is precisely where the character of the film image as an image of movement and time is determined, as represented by various film theories. Also for film everything else literally follows from this ground, its temporality. The television picture, on the other hand, must above all be switched on (or switch itself on) in order to be present at all and then be able to show, call, address, and instruct the world, to touch it, to point to it and to itself and in doing so read the world and itself—and you can switch it off again at any time. In the evolution of technical images, other types of images have succeeded television in its switchability, such as video images and digital images. But the television picture is the prototype of the switchable picture—and vice versa: switching is the prototype of all televisive operations. Television, as we will see later, is even the prototype of a picture that ultimately functions as a switch itself.

The television image, along with its sound, derives from its switchability and defines itself through it. It does not, on the other hand, proceed like other images, above all via its visibility and audibility, or its frame or its duration, like film. Turning on is always the first operation of television, always its beginning. A television picture that is not switched on does not exist, nor does a picture that is switched off. The structure, aesthetics, and semantics of all kinds of pictures presuppose a capacity for discernment that they can assume as a starting point for everything else. Just as the delimitations in size and time lend the other images the ability to become distinct against their surroundings as well as to draw distinctions themselves, the television picture owes itself to switching. Of course, the television picture also has a boundary in the picture plane derived from the size and format of the screen: an outer, more or less wide frame. Early television theories drew quite far-reaching conclusions from the—at that time—tiny size of the screen (Bazin 2014: 67–74): the television image penetrated everywhere more easily, it preferred "talking heads" and set itself in the place of real interlocutors, and it made the world smaller and "philistinized" (Anders 1956: 22). Likewise, television pictures have their limits in time, especially those from the early days, when there was still the beginning and end of broadcasting activity in the course of the day. Nevertheless, television is not determined as a picture by its frame and size but by its switchability. This is equally true for the dissemination that the transmission of a television picture can attain in the geographical and sociographic spaces. Ranges and ratings are mostly (not always) limited, with considerable consequences for the picture itself. Nonetheless, even ranges and ratings depend on television's ability to switch and to be switched.

There are three reasons for this extraordinary position of switching for television. First, as we have already seen, switching primarily determines the handling of the television picture, that is, the practice of television. Paddy Scannell, in his analysis of the switching on of television, has put this in a context with the concept of "being-in-the-world" in Heidegger's sense (Scannell 2014: 62–4): The mere television furniture is just another thing through which the world around us confronts us like an outside. Switching on, however, leaves the device "on hand": it is manageable and connected to us. It now integrates us into the world, so that our existence emerges as "being-in-the-world." In terms of media philosophy this idea can be put still differently: Before we see and hear, the buttons are the points of contact, distinction, and transition between television and its outer environment, especially with regard to its human users. Undoubtedly, the screen is an interface which converts electromagnetic signals into optical signals which are perceptible to us as living beings. But even before the perceptible images appear, the purely technical process of switching converts into an—however minor—action involving the human being, a gesture (Flusser 2014: 217), in the handling of the switch buttons. In order to be switched on, to be able to be at all, television instrumentalizes a human gesture. It is precisely this intermediate point between a technical process and a human and subjective action that we call an *operation*. More precisely, it is an anthropo-mediatic operation (Voß 2010). It is first the anthropo-mediatic operation which generates the medium (here: the television picture, namely by switching it on) on the one hand. On the other hand and in the same course it articulates its human use and thus produces the television viewers as such (not as human beings at all but especially as human beings watching television). And this generative double function of the switching operation applies not only to watching but also to the production of television images.

Secondly, however, the television images among themselves without regard or relation to viewers are distinguished from one another by switching processes. Switching discerns them and relates them at one time so that they even touch one another. Television also makes these switching processes perceptible and explicit for the users ("we are now switching over . . ."), even though they are technical and functional. And thirdly, switching works not only on the macrolevel of operative anthropo-mediatic handling of television, as well as on the meso level of the structure and aesthetics of the images among themselves, but also entirely below the level of human perception and before the completion of the images, only in the technical production of the images themselves. Even the infinite, volatile flow of electromagnetic signals, which the screen converts into optical signals and to which the image owes its existence, is regulated, controlled, articulated and structured by switching processes. The television picture emerges from its switchability as an entity that is contoured at all and thus observable for us as well. Perhaps Friedrich Kittler's famous dictum: "Only what is switchable is at all" (Kittler 2017: 5) actually applies to the television picture.

Even sophistry can't change that. One can, of course, discuss whether opening the curtain in front of a stage set, whether switching on the lighting in front of a painting in a museum, whether switching on the projector in the case of projected pictures is already a form of switching on the respective pictures or would be tantamount to switching them on. But that is absurd. All these images may not be visible if they are not released by lighting (or opened to the view as with the curtain), but they are nevertheless always present as images, like the slides in their frames, the frames on the filmstrip or the paintings at night in the museum. They all do not derive their specific characteristics and even less their presence from the fact that they can be opened or illuminated with the help of switching processes. This becomes clear from the fact that all these pictures can be stored, for example archived, like objects. Not so—at first—the television picture. The television picture is created only when the device is switched on. Perhaps this could be said about the moment of movement of the moving film image, as it appears exclusively in the projected image on the screen. But even if so there remains a serious circumstance that binds television pictures to electricity and electromagnetism and thus to their switchability: the signals that the device receives are not images at all, but instructions according to which the device first generates the image. Even if today, unlike in the early days of television, it is finally possible to record and archive these signals, in themselves they are still by no way images.

Even the shutter release of the photographic camera, which could best be compared to a switch, does not have the same function for photography. The photo is the first image to be produced automatically, photomechanically. In the case of photography, the mechanics and the photochemical processes must be triggered by the push of a button; once released, they run by themselves, purely according to causal laws. The peculiarity of photography lies in this mechanical causality, and many of the aesthetics and theories of photography focused on it (Geimer 2009; Kracauer 1960: 12–23). Once shot and processed, the picture exists. The television image, on the other hand, like the digital image later, only exists when and for as long as it is switched on. It is not illuminated and not projected on a screen; it shines from within, out of itself and it only appears when it shines and while it is being produced; and this shining is also necessarily electrically induced and thus switchable—like the electric current.

## Current and Switch

In order for television pictures to pass through on the surface of the tube screen, two trivial, but momentous, conditions must be met. The television set must be connected to the world outside television in two ways: first, with the electrical power supply and, secondly, with the emission or transmission of electromagnetic signals. Even today, computer and telephone images—at least temporarily: you have to charge the device—connect to the power grid and the data network (if they are online). Since the middle of the twentieth century at the latest, both flows, electrical and electromagnetic, have spanned the entire earth with the expansion of the electricity grids and radio networks, and in some cases—think of the television satellites, which in the meantime have put their own belt around the earth in outer space—they even reach beyond it. They form the primary technical environment, milieu or *media sphere* of television. Once the television picture is switched on, they pass through, they are transformed and controlled, and in the process they generate the picture. Before it records or even depicts anything else, television does register these two currents to which it owes itself, which pass through it and connect it to the world outside television. The television picture is present when the connection to these two streams is established, and not present when this is not the case. All visible and recognizable images that television will then circulate are conversions and complications of the two streams into which television switches on.

In terms of technical history, the picture tube is actually an electrographic device at first. It serves to make visible, to optically distort and measure electrical currents and signals, comparable to an oscillograph or a radar screen (Abramson 1974: 65-9). In terms of linguist Roman Jakobson, television images are therefore initially purely "phatic" signs, that is, signs that record and display the mere flow of signals or the channel itself, without saying or expressing anything beyond that (Jakobson 1963). Only afterward, through numerous implications and complications, through relations and all sorts of further operations, which we will of course follow in detail in the later chapters, do television pictures take on other functions. To speak further with Jakobson: via the referential function the images then refer to the world, conatively and expressively they reach us and express something, through their aesthetic and metalinguistic functions they say something about themselves as images and about television. The television picture is thus part of the current and the signal circulation on the one hand, its product on the other and its visual trace on the third. It indicates the signal current to which it owes itself and of which it is a part. The image is not split off the signal and does not belong to some completely different order, but it emerges from the signal and couples itself to it. This characteristic "modus operandi" of television shall be called ontographic here—at first without discussing the term in more detail (Stadler 2014: 13–22; 31–60). In this sense, ontographic is not only what happens inside and on the surface of the picture tube but also the function that the television picture has in its much wider, global, and world-generating context, its electrographic media sphere (Débray 1991), into which it switches itself on when it is switched on.

Let us therefore take a closer look at the process of switching on. Despite all intuition and expectation, switching on television is surprisingly by no means the simple and strictly binary distinction of *on* and *off*. It is not so timeless and bodiless as it is gladly accepted in idealized and abstract ways. In the same way—for a new side glance—the framing of the film images, simply because of the camera's mobility, is not a stable and simple distinction between inside and outside (Bazin 1997: 211–19; Bazin 2005a: 76–94; 2005b: 164–9). Switching on the television set is itself an operation, that is, an intervention on the one hand and a continuous course on the other: an ontographic operation.

So what exactly happens when the television set is switched on? In its hypothetical and experimental time, from the 1880s to the 1920s, the television set was not yet a closed black box but an open and rather complex arrangement, an assemblage of numerous technical aggregates, all of which had to be connected to each other and to the power grid and individually connected in order to function as a whole, that is, to produce an image (Abramson 1974: 15–34). Quite a number of subsequent switching processes had to be carried out one after the other until the device finally worked and produced an image. This image, which finally appeared, was also tiny in size compared to the apparatus to which it was owed. Later on, this changed, with the development of the television set as a closed, compact box (shaped as a thing, and hence a marketable commodity) from the 1930s onward. Now the individual components switched on automatically, one connecting to the other. There was now a single switch that put the entire apparatus into operation at once by connecting it to the mains. Actually, one must even say more precisely: the central switch ended the interruption, which separated the device from the power supply, to which it was always connected as soon as the plug was plugged in. Switching on was the termination of the power interruption; the switch was an interrupter.

The device—we are now talking about classic tube television since the late 1940s, when the medium developed its characteristic form—could (and still cannot) show a picture immediately when switched on, just as a—today old-fashioned—incandescent lamp lit up immediately when the light switch was operated. Rather, the individual technical components had to become operational slowly and gradually. Capacitors, for example, had to charge up and the picture tube had to warm up. This took some time. During this waiting and threshold period only unsemantic traces were visible and audible, representing nothing but the gradual advance of the current and the signal flow into the components of the device, which were noticeable as picture and sound noise, as cracking or as optical wave patterns, showing no external objects.

And still today digital receivers, just like computers (they in fact *are* computers), have to start up after switching on, which takes more or less a long time. They are neither switched on nor off during this time. This is particularly impressive with internet television, which receives its signals digitally via the telephone line. The booting process takes several minutes after switching on, during which written texts and graphic signs keep us informed about the various technical phases of the process of contacting the internet. Today, however, the switch-on operation has also changed to the extent that television, like many other devices, can no longer be switched off completely, but always remains in the so-called standby mode. It is always under power, and some of its components are always activated in a kind of minimal mode. As with a computer, switching on a television set since the 1980s has also been a booting process. Switching on is therefore a question not just of the flow or nonflow of current but of the voltage and quantity of the current and its introduction into certain components.

Whether it shows a visible picture of something or not, the apparatus is now—and has been for several decades—always in operation, and it always signals this intermediate state between on and off, being and nonbeing, namely by the glow of the diode on the front of the device, which, mostly in red, signals the dimmed, but still active, operating, state of the television set. Through this diode, the sleeping appliance, which is not yet switched on, signals that it is continuously connected to the world, whether with us or without us, and that, when we switch it on, it switches itself on to a current to which it has always been connected. And as far as the electric current is concerned, this also applies, in another way, to the signal flow. It is true that the device does not actually receive any signals when it is shut down. Nevertheless, these signals are always present; they surround the device or even wait to reach it. Just like electric current, they are always there, ubiquitous and omnipresent; and the diode indicates not only that the device is already connected to the mains but also that it is ready to receive. It communicates nothing but its own ability to communicate, nothing but the mere existence or persistence of contact. The diode is the light that stands in for the receivability of dozens or hundreds of pictures and programs, which always surround the appliance and into which the TV set and into which we can interfere (Jakobson 1963).

This, of course, gives cause for reflection on this intermediate and threshold state. How can we assess the *mode of being* (Souriau 2015) of a switched-on but not yet visible image, an image that may appear somewhere else or later or never at all, that is nevertheless "somehow" present and effective, that offers itself or takes place? What is the status of reality and possibility of the signals, images, and programs that are always present but remain in a dimmed mode? They seem to exist in a kind of intermediate mode, in a mixed modality between possibility and reality, which can perhaps first of all be described by concepts of modality such as that of the *latent*—the hidden, the still pending, but nevertheless existing—and the *manifest*—the tangible, the concrete, that which encounters. Although the latent does not perceivably occur, it is there and might appear or be exposed, and it is precisely with this possibility that it becomes noticeable, for example as something still to come in the future. In engineering, latency is precisely the intermediate state between a cause (e.g., the switching on) and its effect (e.g., the emerging picture). It is therefore effective (as it were in the background) and therefore real. The diode of the device indicates the latency of a seemingly unmanageable number of images that might become present or can be realized. Still not being there, they are yet already effective and real, for example, in that they compete and set each other under conditions. They are always already there, they form the environment of television, its—as it were initially technical—milieu which is not perceptible to us but via the diode. After switching on, the images condense and become reality, and then, little by little, certain tangible images manifest themselves on the screen. The modal difference and transition between the latent and the manifest images is operationalized through the switch-on button and in the switch-on process.

## The Tube Image

Earlier we have simply said that a television picture which is not switched on would not be existing or available either. But now it turns out that this is not quite the case. Even a TV set that is not switched on shows the exact presence of available signals and latent images via the LED in standby mode. A device finally switched on and working allows the inscription or drawing of one (or sometimes several) of these signal flows on the screen and performs their conversion into visible pictures for us. Now selected, defined pictures are being generated according to the instructions of the signals. The difference between switched-on and switched-off device is therefore not absolute but a question of the degree and intensity of the current flow, of the modality of the signal flow, and of their coupling. The process of switching on and off thus in no way separates the being of the images from their nonbeing. Rather, the operation of switching on distinguishes a world of electric and electromagnetic currents and potential images, which have always presumably been present and which have always invisibly surrounded, reached and even traversed the device, from their registration, their visualization, and their becoming image through the screen; and this is not so much a sharp and fundamental difference but a relative one, according to measure, degree, and modality.

However, the transformation of the latent into the manifest has not yet been completed when the device is switched on, but has only just begun. This transformation takes place in the picture tube of classic tube television, once set into operation, incessantly and repeats itself again and again as long as the device remains switched on. After the switch-on, the electromagnetic signals are admitted into the picture tube and are present there, manifest, but they are not and as such do not yet result in an image that is perceptible to human observers and viewers and tangible in this sense. In this respect, they still remain latent, pending. Only when they hit the inner surface of the screen tube and light up the electrosensitive dots, the pixels, do they appear.

In a way, the television image never even becomes manifest: the television image consists (or manifests itself) exclusively in being drawn or written without ever being complete and present (Abramson 1974: 48–50). Fifty times a second, the cathode ray swivels the inside of the screen from top left to bottom right, line by line and point by point, and causes the pixels on the inside of the glass tube to light up, but after being touched by the ray they soon extinguish again until the ray passes again. The picture therefore resembles more the process of writing in its very execution than a traditional picture: the writing of the television picture exists like a ghost writing only in the moment of its being written; it fades away again immediately as soon as it has been written—it disappears uninterruptedly and to the same extent in which it is written. Before the screen surface has even been penned to completion, the picture writing begins to twilight again. Nothing remains. The images of television do not manifest themselves, but they persist as continuous processes of transforming the latent into the manifest. Thus, on one and the same surface of the screen, an uninterrupted stream of continuous activation and extinction, of drawing and writing, runs through, without ever leading to a completed, retrievable, or repeatable image or directory, a time-resistant graphic image or writing that would last longer than the process of drawing and writing itself. In this respect, the television picture is a continuous appearing and disappearing. Its *mode of being* is a continuous being drawn or being registered.

We now also see why the electromagnetic signals of the cathode ray do not contain any semantic image information. They do not represent anything preexisting, but merely instruct the individual pixels to light up or not to light up. The classic tube image is therefore not an image in the conventional sense. It makes something visible to us in the end, but it does not record and retain anything. Since it preserves nothing, unlike all other images, including photographic and cinematographic images, which at least exist as a fixed image frame on the celluloid strip even when they are not running through the projector, and which can be shown again and again, one can also not preserve it, not own it and not transport it.

For this *mode of being* we shall also use the term of the ontographic (Engell 2015): The television image is ontographic insofar as it consists exclusively of being drawn in one course. The televisual image is not a finished graphic, not a font and not a directory, but a writing and a drawing operation. The television picture is not a picture, but an infinite stream of electromagnetic signals, without any persistence. It exists on the surface of the screen only right now in the very process of its rising from latency. The signals transform into optical signs, into points of light, ready to manifest on the surface so that we can perceive them. But already in their manifestation they are forced to fade again and pass by. And only with the help of the inertia of our eye can we then draw them together into something like an image in a kind of synthesis or macroscopy. The images only manifest themselves in the human visual apparatus, and this in-betweeness is why they are anthropo-mediatic (Voß 2010), just like the switch-on operation. All this is set in motion at the moment of switching on.

## Beginnings on Television

Now, of course, the world does not only consist of electromagnetic signals and electric currents. As we have just seen in the example of the picture tube, television rather converts electromagnetic signals into optical signals, which in an anthropo-mediatic way condense into manifestly perceptible images (and the same applies to the sounds). Conversely, it happens during recording, which transforms light and sound data into electromagnetic signals. Once switched on, television is therefore no longer only part of its primary media sphere, the electrical and electromagnetic world of currents and signals recorded electrographically, but also of the world visible and audible to us as part of which television also appears. Television couples itself to the visible and sayable world as soon as images and sounds manifest themselves on the screen and in the loudspeaker. After being switched on, it is connected to the visible and audible world, continuously connected by a signal and event flow not only to the world of electrical currents and electromagnetic signals but also to the imaginable, affective, and epistemic worlds. Just as it enters into the latent signal flow when it is switched on, so also in what can be seen, felt, and thought of. Television is not separated from the world it shows, but affected by it. Its distinction from the world is not a strict one, operated via a semantic level or a semiotic abyss like it separates the sign from the designated, but only by a rather lateral distance according to measure, degree, and, as seen, modality.

This can be seen very clearly when one looks at the phenomenon of the beginning of something on television, similar to switching on. Every program, and every show, on television has a beginning. But everything that begins on television has already begun; it never occurs completely and does not really stop. Television does not distinguish itself sharply and in principle from what it shows, but rather gradually, with varying intensity. It switches itself into processes that have always been in progress, of which it is a part, and which it registers. We have already seen this with reference to the technical functioning by switching on the device. But it also applies to the beginnings or insertions of the manifest broadcasts and programs.

Let us take a news program as an example. On the one hand, nothing is as punctual as a news program—nothing marks a certain time as sharply and effectively as its beginning. On the other hand, however, a news program has already begun insofar as it was anticipated before it began. Most news programs have not only already been announced before as just impending, in program notes, announcements, text boards, or especially at the end of the previous news program of the same station. Often a very short preview of the most important news and headlines is given shortly before the start of the news broadcast. The most important of the eight o'clock messages are already known before eight o'clock. When the transmission finally begins it is not the welcome of the spectators which stands in the first place nor is it the first message, but the recurring opening credits of the show with often elaborate graphics, with logo and station identification, and usually with a prominent music jingle. This intermediate state, which is only a few seconds long, corresponds to the no-man's-land of the threshold and waiting time during the switch-on. In addition, news broadcasts in commercial channels are often interrupted by advertising blocks. This, in turn, requires that the current news program already provides an outlook on what will follow the advertising block, and that the second news block begins with a summary of what has been reported so far. It is not uncommon for a news program to end with another summary of the most important news items (which is usually very similar to the summary broadcast before the start) and finally with the announcement of the upcoming issue of the news show along with its main topics. On some stations, even during the news broadcast, a lettering runs through at the bottom of the screen with headlines and *breaking news*.

Individual contributions, news program, and the surrounding program are thus presented in denser and looser couplings that penetrate and replace each other. This does not only concern the distinctiveness of the show, its parts, and other programs on the horizontal level of time and program flow. It also concerns the differentiation of the semantic levels: Do the news deal with the world—that would again be the referential function according to Jakobson (Jakobson 1963)—or—as metatext—with television itself (or about both relationships, for instance, with regard to their simultaneity, their topicality)? Whether the summary at the end is the continuation of the program with a condensed repetition of the most important, or whether it is a metatext to it that deals not with the events but with the program just seen, can no longer be determined. Likewise, the announcement of the news program could be an anticipation on the same level or a view of the forthcoming program from a higher level.

And what applies to the news can also be found in other forms of beginning, such as fictional television series. Here, too, the new episode of a series is present in program notes, announcements, and text panels even before it is broadcast and before it begins, and is also shown in trailers as a shortened preview. If the episode actually begins, then three different sequences mix and overlap over the initial minutes, namely the opening credits of the series, which are common to all episodes and something like the characteristic of the series; the opening credits of the individual episode, in which their title and participants are named; and finally the fictional plot itself. So here not only the text (the episode of the series) and the context (what has happened so far) are offset against each other, but also the text and the paratext (comparable to the cover text or the author's biography of the book) (Genette 1987). Again, in this game between text, paratext, and context, the distinctiveness of the semantic stages is dissolved. Different degrees of horizontal affiliation, delimitability, and shiftability of a part of the show to another location displace the discernability of hierarchically and vertically different semantic levels. And this is exactly the way it is with the end: here, too, the reference to the next episode is given with a first preview, not to mention the complications of the cliffhanger (Fröhlich 2015)—and the wrap-up. In the extreme extension—but we cannot pursue this here—it becomes apparent that the extra-television reality, be it fictional or real, is something from which the intra-television reality could again only be distinguished gradually and horizontally, but not fundamentally and hierarchically.

To sum up: When switched on, the current and signal flows lead over into the ontographic image of television. In it, television makes its media sphere, the electromagnetic world, register itself in the television image and become visible. Likewise, the visible and macroscopic programs, the episodes and the contributions switch on and inscribe themselves into the continuously running and always preceding broadcasting events, as if they had always already begun. Through compression and detachment, they peel out within a sequence and dissolve into it again. The metatexts can no longer be sharply distinguished from the object texts on television, but all parts of the text operate on one and the same level on which they shift against each other and interconnect with each other. After all—and this is indeed the hypothesis I would like to put forward—television as a whole also behaves ontographically toward its surrounding world into which it enters and intervenes, including its anthropo-mediatic entanglement with its users (Voß 2010).

## Switching Off from the World and Switching On Into It: Stanley Cavell and Marshall McLuhan

In a famous essay on television, Stanley Cavell described television as a special relationship between the world and its observation, namely a "current of simultaneous event reception" (Cavell 1982: 85; 89), as opposed to film, which he understands as a "succession of automatic world projections" (Cavell 1982: 85). In other words, according to Cavell, through television we watch the sequence of events that occur in the world as they occur; the stream of events simultaneously travels across our screens. So with Cavell we could assume that real events and screen events are not separated by anything but are part of one and the same process. Thus Cavell's observation also attributes ontographic qualities to television.

On the other hand, however, Cavell develops a special term for television reception. This is demonstrated by a comparison of television perception with film viewing. According to Cavell, the event stream of television is not *seen or watched* as it is for film ("viewing") but *witnessed and surveilled* ("monitoring") (Cavell 1982: 85; 90). Strikingly, it is not the viewers and users who are monitored by television, as one would immediately assume today, but, according to Cavell, the human subjects themselves monitor the world through and with the help of television like a department store detective in the surveillance room. Now, as Cavell sees it, the "viewing" of the film is characterized by an inclusion and participation, an implication, participation, or immersion of the observing subjects in the projected event. In other terms, this can be understood as an anthropo-mediatic relation of mutual inclusion. In contrast, the surveillance of the world by television creates a maximum lack of participation. The "monitoring" of television leads to the greatest possible distance between the uninvolved viewers and the world and assigns to the former a more or less hermetically sealed interior of observation an unattainable "outside" to the latter. Television refers the world to a distant outside space, blocks it out, silences it, and thus suggests protection from it. It shields us and disconnects us from the world. In view of the catastrophic state and the increasingly disastrous development of the world, this is the secret both of the effectiveness of television and of the unwillingness and inability of theory formation and philosophy to take television seriously as an object of reflection.

The ontography of televisual "monitoring" according to Cavell would thus be that of the separation between subject and object or consciousness and world. In fact, some authors, such as Graham Harman (Harman 2010) and Ian Bogost (Bogost 2012), see ontography as a way of describing and contemplating the world, especially the world of things, as if there were no description and contemplation. This reality is outside and before all description and contemplation, all by itself, even before things can become objects for subjects.

Diametrically opposed to Cavell's view of television is Marshall McLuhan (McLuhan 1964). For McLuhan, television is not the medium of counter-anthropo-mediatic secession, separation, and shutdown of the world. On the contrary, it is the place of the maximum involvement with the world. McLuhan, for example, speaks of television as a "cold medium" (McLuhan 1964: 24–44) that, always incomplete, even imperceptible, integrates its viewers into the picture in a special way or, conversely, projects the picture into them. In contrast, the, film is a "hot medium" that confronts contemplation in its overwhelming over-completeness. At the same time, the medium merges with the world by contracting it into a "global village" (McLuhan 1964: 43; 106). Whether in the metaphor of the "global village" or even more in that of the "cold medium," McLuhan's idea of an immediate relation between world, contemplation, and medium always shines through. Switching on television would hence always be switching on into the world. McLuhan's ontography would therefore rather correspond to a phenomenological position that, as in Maurice Merleau-Ponty's work (Blanc 2000), takes its starting point from perception as reference, as transit and integration, as a zone of "mingled bodies" (Serres 2008) rather than from their separation.

## Switching Modes of Being

With Cavell and McLuhan we can differentiate between two televisive ontographies. One, the ontography of separation, is motivated epistemologically and ontologically. It aims at the self-drawing and self-relating of things and operations in a world that is as it is, that gets by without subjects and without human intervention, and in which we can nevertheless gain insight with the help of ontographic television. It first switches into the primary media sphere of television, into the world of electromagnetism as it operates out there. The other, however, the ontography of reciprocal inscription, is motivated aesthetically and phenomenologically. It aims at the recursive integration of drawing (in a broad sense that applies to the television image of image and sound) and the mode of being of a world that registers itself (and us). It switches into the world as we as viewers can perceive and switch it.

## References

Abramson, Albert. 1974. *Electronic Motion Pictures*. New York: Arno Press.
Anders, Günther. 1956. "Die Welt als Phantom und Matritze." In: Günther Anders. *Die Antiquiertheit des Menschen*, vol. 1: *Über die Seele im Zeitalter der zweiten industriellen Revolution*, pp. 97–211. München: Beck.
Bazin, André. 1997. "A Bergsonian Film: The Picasso Mystery." In: André Bazin. *Bazin at Work: Major Essays & Reviews from the Forties & Fifties*, pp. 211–19. New York, London: Routledge.
Bazin, André. 2005a. "Theater and Cinema." In: André Bazin. *What Is Cinema?* Vol. 1, pp. 76–124. Berkeley, Los Angeles, London: University of California Press.
Bazin, André. 2005b. "Painting and Cinema." In: André Bazin. *What Is Cinema?* Vol. 1, pp. 164–9. Berkeley, Los Angeles, London: University of California Press.
Bazin, André. 2014. "Looking at Television." In: André Bazin. *André Bazins New Media*, ed. by Dudley Andrew, pp. 67–74. Oakland: University of California Press.
Blanc, Sébastien. 2000. "L'ontographie ou l'écriture de l'être chez Merleau-Ponty." *Les Etudes philosophiques* 3: 289–310.
Bogost, Ian. 2012. *Alien Phenomenology, or What It's Like to Be a Thing*. Minneapolis, London: University of Minnesota Press.
Cavell, Stanley. 1982. "The Fact of Television." *Daedalus* 111, no. 4: 75–96.
Débray, Regis. 1991. *Cours de médiologie générale*. Paris: Gallimard.
Engell, Lorenz. 2015. "Der Film zwischen Ontografie und Anthropogenese." In: *Mediale Anthropologie*, ed. by Lorenz Engell, and Christiane Voss, pp. 63–82. München: Fink.
Flusser, Vilém. 2014. *Gestures*. Minneapolis, London: University of Minnesota Press.
Fröhlich, Vincent. 2015. *Der Cliffhanger und die serielle Narration. Analyse einer transmedialen Erzähltechnik*. Bielefeld: Transcript.

Geimer, Peter. 2009. *Theorien der Fotografie zur Einführung*. Hamburg: Junius.
Genette, Gérard. 1987. *Paratexte*. Paris: Seuil; engl.: *Paratexts: Thresholds of Interpretation*. Cambridge: Cambridge University Press.
Harman, Graham. 2010. *The Quadruple Object*. Winchester, Washington, DC: Zero Books.
Jakobson, Roman. 1963. "Linguistique et poétique." In: Roman Jakobson. *Essais de linguistique générale*, pp. 213–22. Paris: Minuit.
Kittler, Friedrich. 2017. "Real Time Analysis, Time Axis Manipulation." *Cultural Politics* 13, no. 1: 1–18.
Kracauer, Siegfried. 1960. *Theory of Film: The Redemption of Physical Reality*. New York: Oxford University Press.
McLuhan, Marshall. 1964. *Understanding Media: The Extensions of Man*. London, New York: Routledge.
Scannell, Paddy. 2014. *Television and the Meaning of Live*. Cambridge: Polity Press.
Serres, Michel. 2008. *The Five Senses: A Philosophy of Mingled Bodies (I)*. London, New York: Continuum.
Souriau, Etienne. 2015. *Les différents modes d'existences*. Paris: Presses Universitaires de France; engl.: *The Different Modes of Existence*. Minneapolis: Minnesota University Press.
Stadler, Michael. 2014. *Was heißt Ontographie? Vorarbeit zu einer visuellen Ontologie*. Würzburg: Königshausen & Neumann.
Voß, Christiane. 2010. "Auf dem Weg zu einer Medienphilosophie anthropomedialer Relationen." *Zeitschrift für Medien-und Kulturforschung (ZMK)* 1/2: 170–84.

2

# Live Television

In 1884 Paul Nipkow applied for and received a patent from the patent office in Berlin for an invention that he called the "electric telescope." This apparatus did not function according to the principle of the television tube, with which we began; rather, it was an electromechanical apparatus with two rotating perforated disks that generated light impulses. Their transformation into electrical impulses was performed by a plate made of the photosensitive element selenium. The "electric telescope" nevertheless established the basis for the production and transmission of fleeting images with the help of electrical current. However, Nipkow never actually built his device, as this was not necessary for the granting of a patent: a device only had to be functional and producible in order for it to be patentable. In the 1920s, other pioneers, especially John Logie Baird in Great Britain, adopted Nipkow's construction principle in order to build and implement experimental television sets. As television tubes were developed and tested by Manfred von Ardenne and Denesz von Mihaly in Germany and Alexander Zworykin in Russia, others continued to work with rotating perforated disks and selenium sensors. Electromechanical television competed for quite a long time with electronic tube televisions, and both systems were even used in parallel during the Nazi Olympic Games in Berlin in 1936. Nipkow's principle was subsequently abandoned in favor of television tubes, which could produce considerably denser images with more pixels and which were also less susceptible to interference.

## A Definition of Television and the Order of the Simultaneous

Even though it became technologically obsolete, Nipkow's "electric telescope" is nevertheless of vital importance and theoretical interest. The patent application contained an early definition of television, as it stated that the purpose of the apparatus was "to make an object at location A visible at any location B" (Hickethier 1998: 15). This simple definition is extremely enlightening not only for what it says but also for what it does not say. What it designates is a configuration that consists of four variables: an object, the visibility of the object, and two locations (A and B). Nipkow thus conceived of his invention in the traditional way as a physical object situated in space at location A. He also implicitly assumed the existence of a subject, for whom the thing at location A was discernible, visible, and recognizable as an object. The "electric telescope" then separated the visibility of the object for human vision—that is, its visual appearance—from the object itself and reproduced it at location B. Television was thus conceived first as a *visual dispositif* and second as a *spatial arrangement*. Countless later television theories follow Nipkow's foundational assumptions by conceiving of television using the categories of space, visibility, the gaze, and even remote viewing. In theory we could perhaps even continue to work with this definition today. Even though it involves a purely technical definition—namely, a patent application—it is thus interestingly irrelevant whether the carrier technology is electromechanical, electro-analog, or digital. One could say that the visibility of any object situated at another location always involves television, for example, even when this visibility is made possible by informatic apparatuses.

What Nipkow never considered was the multiplication of secondary locations, but this must be added if the definition is to refer to television in a narrower sense. In the case of television, for example, the object is visible not at *one* remote location but rather at *many* different locations.

Nipkow thought in the categories of telegraphy and telephony rather than broadcasting, as his television was a kind of videophone between two precise points rather than between one point (the sender) and a great variety of other points (the receivers). He thus thought about the space involved entirely differently, as it was a vectorial space that always connected two points with one another through a directional movement—namely, the movement of the signal, which for Nipkow also ran through a cable. That was not the same as the space of broadcasting or later networking, which were defined by dense spatial coverage and in which the signals were always already present.

Other determinants were not named in the definition, although they were very much implied. The first is the difference between locations A and B and their distance from one another, but this is perhaps merely a quibble. The second is the implied observer, who does not have a name or any further description; one could even say that the observer is irrelevant to this understanding of television if not for the fact that visibility always plays a central role in the conditions of human perception. The third and most crucial determinant is the category of time or more precisely *simultaneity*. The key feature of the "electric telescope" is not that it simply makes an object visible at another location, as this is true of every image, such as paintings, photographs, drawings, graphics, and diagrams (what Bruno Latour refers to as "immutable mobiles"), which can also be transported to locations other than those where the objects they depict are situated and which also make the objects visible at these other locations (Latour 1986: 7ff, 21ff). What is crucial for television, however, is that the object is visible at location B *at the same time* that it is situated at location A. This *simultaneity* is the unique feature of television. Television is less about the transmission of visibility, as emphasized by Nipkow, than the production of this *simultaneity* (of visibility). What we see is also not the object as such but rather its situatedness at location A *while* we are situated at location B, which is entirely different from cinema. The object of visibility is not only absent but also at the same time present— that is, it is not merely here but also somewhere else—at a specific or at least specifiable location.

## The Raw Materials of Television

The *simultaneity* of television is technically produced by connecting the electrical current and signal flow to both locations through a single physical *contact* or uninterrupted causal chain. It appears here at my location not only *while* it is situated somewhere else but also precisely *because* it is situated there. In this chain of remote actions, for example, a switching process at location A (such as switching over to another camera) results in an image change at location B. A sudden alteration or movement of the object becomes visible at location B not only *when* it occurs but also *because* it is happening, as its visibility is released by the object and its movement. Along with this come, though, various possibilities of a mere assertion, simulation, or pretense of *simultaneity* and a synthetic production of *simultaneity*, as we will see. Nipkow's space-bound definition of television is nevertheless closely related to its initially characteristic simultaneity, as space is, according to Leibniz's famous definition, nothing more than the order of being present together ("Spatium est ordo coexistendi") (Leibniz 1863: 18).

Television thus in its origins performs two basic transformations. First, as we have already seen, it transforms electrical and electronic impulses into light impulses, and it thereby surrounds its primary electrographic media sphere with a wider media sphere of visibility and anthropomediality. The second transformation is twofold. Visibility is charged or amalgamated with *simultaneity* by means of the mere existence and functionality of a causal relation (or its operative assertion and suggestion), and this causal relation is produced and embodied by the electrical current and signal flow on the basis of *indexicality* (Engell 2013). According to Charles Sanders Peirce and

Alfred Gell, a characteristic feature of indexical images (and indexical forms in general) is that they identify themselves as something that has been caused (Gell 1998: 13, 35ff). In other words, they not only show something but also draw attention to its causation, and they thus thematize the causal relation in which they stand. Live television images connect indexicality with *simultaneity* through the electrical and electromagnetic current. Even though it is perhaps not the object of televisual visibility, this *simultaneity* is still always its theme. At the same time, nevertheless, this *simultaneity* leads to the strict *succession* of signals, which can be seen in Nipkow as well as later tube television and in some ways also digital television. It is significant for television that this *succession* remains on the macrolevel of what is visible to us—namely, in the continuous form of image writing and in the sequence and duration of images on the screen. By means of television, we can see the being-there (Dort-Sein) and the being-as-it-is (So-Sein) of the object situated at location A. As a result, we can also see its emergence, disappearance, movement, and continuous alteration, if it happens and always precisely while it happens. This ontographic processuality is part of the transformation of visibility into *simultaneity*, which is typical of television. And the *simultaneity* that arises from *continuity*, *indexicality*, and *visibility* then results in the spatial structure of television, on which Nipkow was focused (i.e., the two locations, A and B, which are different from one another).

After electricity and electromagnetism and after light and visibility, television thus also has a third raw material—namely, *time*. Because the dominant spatial order of television only emerges from *simultaneity*, we must now also conceive of the objects described by Nipkow as *temporal objects*. They are understood not only according to their positions or locations in space but also according to their positions or locations in time. It is also possible to differentiate between *position* and *location* (Serres 2008: 236ff). *Positions* are merely defined by parameters and coordinates in empty space, as they are space-spanning but not themselves space-filling points. In contrast, objects actually mark and occupy these empty, abstract, uniform, and featureless positions in space. They thereby make them perceptible, three-dimensional, and imbued with qualities so that they eventually become space-filling and qualitative *locations*, which become detached from their positions and develop their own distinct order.

In the same way, it is also possible to differentiate between temporal *events* and merely numerical points in time. *Events* are to time what physical objects are to space, as they mark points in time and thereby make them perceptible and imbued with qualities. *Events* can also take place consecutively or simultaneously. In this sense, *events* are the *temporal objects* of television as a temporal medium that is produced through succession and simultaneity. The following will thus focus on live television and television events as temporal objects that constitute the objects of television, and we will eventually return to the question of time as both the raw material and end product of television itself.

## Live Television

In the beginning, all television involved direct transmission or live television, provided that it was not used to show films. Nothing was recorded or preserved, as it was a transmission medium rather than a storage medium. It only produced, to quote Cavell again, a "current of simultaneous event reception" (Cavell 1982: 75–96). In an American context, this early period lasted from 1948 to 1953, although according to some estimates it continued until 1956 or even 1960. This period is also known as the "golden age" of television (Marschall 1987). News broadcasts and weather reports, quiz and variety shows, as well as television plays, the episodes of television series, and even commercials were produced live in studios in front of running cameras. In the case of a television play, for example, three different stages were built in the three corners of a spacious studio, and cameras would alternate between these stages as the story was performed on them so that it was possible to represent scene changes and parallel plots. Switching from one camera to another also enabled cutting, as in the case of shots and reverse shots during dialog or variations between medium and long shots.

The stage in the fourth corner was used for commercials, which were also performed live. Billy Wilder's film *The Seven Year Itch* included a parody of such a live transmission: in the frightened and libidinous fantasy of the rather harmless film protagonist, Marilyn Monroe uses her live performance in a toothpaste commercial to warn that he is an alleged sex fiend. Television plays and series episodes were thus actually theatrical transmissions, which is why early television series often had titles like *Kraft Television Theatre* or *The Philco Television Playhouse* (which were named after the companies that purchased the airtime and the commercial breaks) (Marschall 1987: 66–75). The impression of a live transmission was precisely avoided in these formats, however, as viewers were supposed to think that they involved the transmission of a recorded event that was already fixed and thus also fundamentally repeatable. Standards, routines, and structures were established, scripts and texts were memorized, and rudimentary rehearsals were scheduled before the actual broadcasts. The ongoing show was issued as having already taken place, that is, as having been previously determined or recorded. Television then attempts to simulate an anteriority by means of simultaneity (which is exclusively at its disposal), a practice that André Bazin already made fun of in France in 1950 (Bazin 2014: 51–3).

Something else applies to live transmissions, which explicitly marks them as such and which especially constitutes the aesthetic, epistemic, and even moral core of television for early television theory (as well as for Bazin)—namely, its quality of being present (Dabei-Sein) while something is happening (Bazin 2014: 48–50). It is also possible to distinguish between countless different cases, such as live shows, live news broadcasts, live commentaries, live sports broadcasts, and live broadcasts of external events (official ceremonies, sporting events, and live reports on location, among others), which were (and are) important program items. The object of these explicitly live transmissions, which thematize and produce simultaneity, is always an event, which thus becomes a temporal object in the abovementioned sense, as it occupies and fills a previously empty temporal position.

Two entirely different phenomena were originally identified as events: glaring, disjointed, abrupt, discontinuous, and basically unexpected occurrences, which tended not to be staged, and ongoing, continuous, and in a sense always already dramaturgical or theatrical processes. In both cases, the simultaneous flow of an event (or events) and its visibility on the screen, which is typical of television, produces a special effect of mutual presence. And even though this is an image effect, it is again based less on visual observation than on participation or the sense of being present.

In a famous and at the time bold analysis, Umberto Eco reconstructed the live transmission of television using art theory by comparing it to *instant composing* in jazz (Eco 1989: 105–18).

According to Eco, the viewers of a live broadcast do not see the actual event taking place at location A; rather, they see the televisual shaping of the event, which is actually still in the process of happening. Eco's own example is a public wedding ceremony, but we could also extend this to soccer games and live shows. More precisely, Eco argues that live broadcasts transform the contingent and unpredictable into an event or what he calls, borrowing a term from John Dewey, an "experience": the witnessing and sharing of a fixed and complete form (like the "gestalt" in gestalt theory) as it emerges from the impermanent flow of events and time itself (Eco 1989: 111f; Dewey 2008). In the case of television transmission, according to Eco, the artwork emerges before our eyes and consists precisely of its own emergence and causation: "[T]he TV director must essentially invent an event that is still happening, and invent it so that it is the same as the one that is taking place" (Eco 1989: 113). It is possible to recognize here once again the essential ontographic feature of television: as soon as it evolves into a structured, organized, arranged, and meaningful flow, it immediately disappears again (and its gestalt dissolves).

Eco also identifies the switchability of the image as a prominent function, as this experience is due to two operations: selection and switching (though he refers here to "montage") (Eco 1989: 107). The monitor wall displays all of the available camera images, such as the images from various cameras positioned along a ceremonial procession or along the sidelines of a sporting event. The director then chooses one of these images, which goes on air, and switches to another image at an appropriate point in time (the television director also tells the camera operators where they should point the cameras and what they should follow). In the end, after all of these images have been assembled and broadcast and the allotted time and sequence of events have concluded, then, according to Eco, an act has taken place before the viewers that corresponds to the *formation of an experience* in Dewey's sense (Dewey 2008). For Dewey, *experience* is neither a personal possession nor a cognitive process, even if it is localized in the subject's own consciousness. It is also not a property of the real world. Instead, it is the mode in which events first become accessible, also for human subjects, and the consciousness in which they are localized is actually the organ of experiential participation. It is roughly analogous to the *openness* of the world in Heidegger's analysis of being (Heidegger 2008: 170f).

In the live broadcast, television occupies the position of consciousness. This would imply that it is only through television that a soccer game, for example, acquires the form through which it becomes accessible. Live television would thus represent the externalization and observation of an experience, which the viewing subject perceives no longer within herself but rather as a process in an exterior space—namely, on the screen. The artwork (if one chooses to see the live broadcast as such) would then no longer be the object of experience; rather, it would itself be a form of experience acquisition. And the content of the television transmission would accordingly be less important than its flowing form. Insofar as experience and subjectivity are interrelated, live television would at the same time be a subjectification without its own subject—namely, the subjectification of the viewer.

## A Side Note on Radio

At this point, it is necessary to insert some reflections on the relationship between television and radio. Radio was obviously also characterized by live broadcasts, and it also facilitated participation in events taking place in the immediate present, such as a soccer game or a royal wedding. The consistency and structure of simultaneity in these media were fundamentally different, however, and this difference was not limited to the disparate sensory channels involved (optical and acoustic), even though it arose from them. In radio, for example, there is no equivalent to the division of scenes and images in television, which are arranged sequentially by cutting or more precisely switching from one camera angle to another. Even though it is possible to switch from one microphone to another during a live event on radio, such as when a passerby or a player is interviewed, the switch itself is usually not audible (except in the case of reflexive, experimental, or comical arrangements).

The perspective of the speakers (or hearing range) and the sequence of perspectives (or sections) are also not audible. There are no spliced-in close-ups or reverse shots in radio; rather, there is only the perspective of the general overview, even when a broadcast is transmitted from the chaotic center of an event, such as a crowd of people. Everything else must be explicitly spoken. In Eco and Dewey's terms, the framework for reproducing the formation of experience is entirely different, as it is linguistic and therefore no longer immediate but rather already semantically mediated. In other words, the underlying structure of a radio broadcast is a linguistic structure, so the formation of the "live" in radio always already occurs through the subject of the speaker or commentator, which is perceptible and present in the voice that makes the experience and relays it to us.

In contrast, television is constantly switching, and the switching of the *switch image* is completely visible in the differences between the images. The fact that these switches are actually decided by a director is irrelevant, as this subject never appears. Moreover, the director is largely a functionary of the televisual apparatus as a whole and at most part of a subject that is distributed across many people as well as technical devices, processes, and even the images themselves. It is only through the visibility of switching that television produces a dramaturgical sequence of images that is synchronized with events and that leads to the formation of experience. It organizes and punctuates this sequence not linguistically but rather by means of its own switches. In the case of verbal commentary, television can thus assume two different perspectives: the perspective of radio, which tends to be all-encompassing and unspecific (in contrast to the accompanying image), and the perspective of each individual image, which is perceived as partial and assembled.

## Before Experience

Eco's analysis was based on a concluded and completed live experience, which has a successful or at least predictable form. This is not necessarily the case, however, as the "mode of life" of a live broadcast goes hand in hand with disruptions, cancellations, incompleteness, and uncertainties, and it thus transcends or traverses Dewey's concept of experience. This misunderstanding is evident in Eco's use of the concept of "montage," as the switching from one camera to another in the course of a live broadcast is precisely not comparable to the form-giving function of "montage" in film. Montage or film editing involves a fixed operation that has already taken place, whereas the cutting or switching of live television happens precisely in the present, before our eyes, while we are watching. Switching is neither repeatable nor revisable; unlike film editing, it can no longer be optimized or altered and then shown to us. In other words, film editing is temporally stable, while switching is not. In the moment of its emergence, it is already past. Switching thus does not have a fixed experiential form.

This difference becomes clearer when the ontology of the live broadcast is compared to the "modes of existence" that Étienne Souriau attributed to the artwork in the course of its production (Souriau 2015: 219–40). An artwork that is in the process of being created occupies an intermediate state, as it is neither completely "present-at-hand" nor "not-at-hand." Souriau thus imagines that from the moment when something from the nascent artwork is there, such as an initial sentence or brushstroke, whatever else follows is subject to certain conditions. The artist is not entirely free to continue or complete the work in a different way; rather, the unfinished work is already contributing to its own completion. It usurps the artist and imposes conditions on her. Artworks are thus involved in their own development, according to Souriau, which again reflects their fundamentally ontographic nature. In this sense, live television broadcasts are never truly completed, even though they eventually stop and they could eventually be recorded, archived, and played back at a later time. Even during the hundredth rerun, if it occurs, it is still possible to watch the broadcast participate in its own creation.

That might sound unusual or far-fetched at first, but Émile Zola already identified something similar in his writing on the experimental novel in the nineteenth century (Zola 1893). According to Zola, the characters in the novel impose conditions on the writer that he cannot arbitrarily change, much like the conditions placed on an experiment in a laboratory. Eco similarly argued that the work embodies its own intention, which has little to do with the divergent intention of the author (Eco 1989: 117f). It remains open whether the work is completed according to its own implicit intentions or whether it impedes, delays, or restarts its completion. It is possible that we will never learn what the work actually wanted to become, whether it became what it could have been, and which other works could have emerged in its place.

In the case of live television broadcasts, this means that the event and its televisual transformation both participate in the creation of what is still on the verge of becoming. This includes all of the participants, including nonhuman actors (according to Eco, for example, a cat that happens to be lying in a window plays a role) and, in particular, everything already done on the broadcast. The live broadcast, which dominates television, is thus always contingent; even after the transmission finally ends, it could also still have been different. The experiential form—that is, the formation of a somehow complete and meaningful shape—is thereby only one of countless possibilities. Interruptible, inconsistent processes and events that cannot be integrated into a whole are also possible, and that includes not only technical breakdowns or slips of the tongue. The possibility that a process can always be different also defines the character of the live broadcast, even when it is concluded or in the past. It is not simply the case that accidents are incorporated into the action and into our experience as we watch, as Eco assumes; rather, what finally appears as a television event is always kept in tension with what does not happen or does not happen in that way. Live television thus tends to provide not a cohesive experience of meaning but rather its constant deferral. Live broadcasts do not end; they are merely interrupted. They always remain prior to experience.

## Present, Simultaneity, Synchronicity

Reflections on the temporal figure of presence like those Eco found in Dewey's pragmatic philosophy (and thus similar starting points for an aesthetic of live television) can also be found in other historical and theoretical works, which are surprisingly contemporary to Dewey. For example, a similar idea appears in Edmund Husserl's phenomenology as well as Henri Bergson's philosophy of life—namely, the idea of an extended present in the process of "normal" lived experience. In lived time and in the representation of time in consciousness, according to Husserl's argument, time initially possesses a continuous, structureless, and unquantifiable present (Husserl 1991: 24ff). In this sense, everything present as an event may already lie in the past at the moment of its arrival, but it is still lastingly effective. Also present is that which has yet to arrive, but which already presents itself as something which has not yet occurred in relation to the events that have already been. A prime example, which appears in Husserl as well as Bergson, is musical melody (Husserl 1991: 33f). It consists of individual notes, which are played consecutively at specific points in time, yet it nevertheless emerges as a whole that is extended over time. In the process of its completion, it resounds in an extended present and is "there" as a whole. Husserl speaks here of the "retention" that holds the past sound and the "protention" that runs ahead to the next one (Husserl 1991: 33–6, 54f).

Bergson's term for this is *duration* (Bergson 1988: 9–21; 50–63), although this concept has a somewhat different rationale, as Bergson does not assume that there is always already a "consciousness" that produces the experience of an extended present in time through the operations of retention and protention. Instead, he identifies duration as a fact in the material reality of the present and the future, and he argues that consciousness, subjectivity, memory, and perception arise from the internal organization and dynamics of matter itself. In this sense, according to Bergson, the extended present of a melody or, to use another example, the flight of an arrow is "real." In contrast, the retrospective representation of this present in consciousness leads to a distortion that seeks to suspend all movement by dividing it into a sequence of isolated and quantifiable points in time. Bergson also refers to this as "cinematographic consciousness" because he sees filmstrips as precisely such a sequence of frozen now moments (Bergson 1889).

Both of these views of time are based on the tension between extended time and mere points in time. In order to talk about *simultaneity*, it is thus necessary to distinguish it from *synchronicity*, as the difference between these terms reflects different understandings of the present—namely, as a continuous present or as a point in time that already disappears the moment it arises and that never occupies time itself. Although these terms may be used differently elsewhere, *synchronicity* here refers to a concurrence between points in time, while *simultaneity* refers to a concurrence between ongoing processes. The former thus reflects an understanding of the present as intermittent, while the latter reflects an understanding of the present as extended.

This polarity is an old topos of time theory. Aristotle already cited it in his *Physics*, in which he grappled with the (even older) sophistic view that time does not exist (Aristotle 2005: 218a). According to the sophists, time consists of three elements: past, present, and future. The past includes everything that no longer exists, and the future includes everything that does not yet exist. Both the past and the future therefore do not exist. While the present does exist, it occupies a point of pure difference between the past and the future— that is, between two different forms of nonbeing—which cannot be extended. In this sense, reality also does not correspond to the present. All three of the elements of time thus do not exist, and consequently neither does time as a whole. Aristotle is of a different opinion, however, as he sees time as an operative result that always already connects extension and duration to the mere difference of the point in time. For him, both forms of the present thus belong together, as does synchronicity and simultaneity, and the operation that connects them is counting. Time, he says, refers to what is counted or countable in movement (Aristotle 2005: 219b).

This could almost already be seen as a sufficient analysis of live television's production of the present. The movement is the course of an event, such as a soccer game or a royal wedding, and the operation is the purely differential process of switching, which does not quantify movement in a strict sense but does scan, punctuate, and disassemble it into distinct and indeed countable units. Cutting always takes place at the same time as its perception in the present, yet it also produces the past and the future—that is, time as a whole—because as soon as one shot ends another always still seems to be forthcoming.

## Moment, Instant, Event

It is necessary to make a distinction regarding points in time that at least exist in the subjective perception of time. On the one hand, there is the ideal and completely extensionless point in time or the *moment*, which represents a pure, incorporeal difference between before and after. The moment itself does not take place in time; rather, it produces time by punctuating, marking, and making it measurable. On the other hand, there is the *instant* (Cassin 2004), which does not correspond to physical and measurable time in that it also has no extension that would distinguish it from the moment; rather, it is only due to the subjective experience of time through (human) perception and imagination. This does not initially happen in television, but it can be evoked by television. The instant is an intensely full and expansive temporal experience. It presents itself as a temporal overview that even applies to the horizontality and unboundedness or endlessness of time in all three temporal dimensions: past, present, and future. Although it is actually temporary, the *instant* nevertheless appears to last for a certain duration and, while it lasts, it is experienced as boundless in a present that also encompasses the past and the future. The experience of the *instant* is often subjectively connected to the experiences of rapture, ecstasy, happiness, or love (Kierkegaard 1980: 79–88). For Martin Heidegger, this threefold horizontality of the instant in the simultaneity of past, present, and future is an essential feature of *temporality*, out of which emerges the directed linearity and terminability of time as we know it (Heidegger 2008: 457–61; Heidegger 1992: 319f). Normally imperceptible, temporality is revealed to us through the experience of the instant and the threefold horizontality that Heidegger also refers to as the three "ecstasies" of time (Heidegger 1982: 264, 1992: 319f).

It is not initially relevant to our argument concerning television whether the experience of the instant can be traced back to a purely physiological or neurological effect at the microscopic level or the work of a more or less independent consciousness or whether, conversely, it reveals a prior ontological condition of the temporality of time itself, as Heidegger assumes. However, the distinction that we have just identified with regard to the point in time as *moment* and *instant* also applies to the concept of the event. On the one hand, the event is something completely incorporeal that does not take place in time but rather only marks it like a lightning bolt as a point in time (Luhmann 1995: 63). The event can thus be a technical concept, like the idea of the point in time as a moment. On the other hand, however, it can also be understood as an extended condition within time itself—namely, as the period of time within which something happens, takes place, or changes (Luhmann 1995: 78f). In terms of television and live broadcasts, the former would apply to the practice of switching from one camera to another, while the latter would apply to the transmission of an event, like a soccer game or a royal wedding, as the process of the physical and social exterior world of television. Participation in the *moment* and its organization of time takes the form of *synchronization*. When a cut is made, it takes place in the control room and on every screen at the same time. In contrast, participation in the *instant* and its horizontal extension—that is, participation in a continuous rather than intermittent process—takes the form of *simultaneity*. Viewers are then integrated into the collective and extended present of a continuous and still ongoing event through the simultaneity of experience.

Hans Ulrich Gumbrecht has beautifully demonstrated how the experience of the instant is relevant to a live broadcast using the example of sports coverage (Gumbrecht 2004). In the instant when a soccer player performs the so-called killer pass, the end result as well as the preliminary moves that made it possible are suspended as we follow more or less breathlessly the entire flight of the ball from when it leaves the player's foot to when it finally goes in the goal (or not). It is possible to apply this to many other examples, such as ski jumping and dance, as well as cases outside of sports. Like the formation of experience, which according to Eco's analysis is normally localized in the subject, presented by television, and comprehended live when viewed, television also presents the experience of the instant as an external process of the extension of time, which takes place outside our merely psychic inner world. In other words, we perceive the instant no longer within ourselves but rather as an extended form of time in the outside world or again as a subjectification (of time) that takes place without a subject on the screen or in anthropo-mediatic entanglement with it.

However, it would not be possible to produce this flow of extended instant as experience without exact technical (and aesthetic) synchronization and timing through the operations of television. Cavell's description of television as a "current of simultaneous event reception" essentially includes both forms—namely, that of the (intermittent) event as well as that of the (continuous) stream. Both of these concepts—the *synchronous* and the *simultaneous*—are also used to distinguish between technical and experiential or conscious concurrence. Television broadcasting now appears to include both forms of participation, yet it also correlates them with one another—or, even more, they are always already available in the form of their anthropo-mediatic entanglement, and it is only possible to separate them into *synchronicity* and *simultaneity* through analysis. The operation of switching, which is purely technical, is constantly intervening in the event, which is a continuously flowing process, and neither form of concurrence can take effect and thus become real without the other.

## Being-Present (Dabeisein) When Not-Being-Present (Nicht-Dabeisein)

Eco's example, which may seem strange from a contemporary perspective, is the live broadcast of royal wedding celebrations. Daniel Dayan and Elihu Katz use the sample example roughly thirty years later in their influential study on live television events, although they reach completely different conclusions (Dayan and Katz 1987). First, they assume that the process of the event has a definite form, which is indeed ceremonial, and that television imitates and follows this form in its broadcast. Television is thus to a certain extent "faithful" to the event itself. Second, they emphasize the exceptional nature of such an event, which sets itself apart from the everyday. Unlike Eco, however, they focus not on the event itself but rather on the attention it attracts and its binding force for viewers. The event is always already public and appealing, so its announcement on television produces attention of the second order. This is why the attendees and the crowds of participating onlookers are often shown disproportionately and extensively on such broadcasts. In other words, viewers at home watch not the event itself but rather the watching of the event. The difference between the direct or "real" presence of the attendees and the mediated presence of the viewers at home is also incorporated into the broadcast, as we experience ourselves paradoxically as nonattendees and nonparticipants, which precisely constitutes the shared experience of all nonparticipants. In his close examination of the attack on September 11,

Paddy Scannell updated this analysis and refuted Luc Boltanski's objections: it is not necessary to participate in a catastrophe directly "on the ground" in order to be *near* it and especially its victims precisely through not-being-present (Scannell 2014: 208; Boltanski 1999). It is no coincidence that this idea recalls Niklas Luhmann's observation that television provides a "non-consensual reality," as individual viewers consider what they see—at least initially—as unreal and perhaps manipulated, but at the same time they also believe that other viewers believe it. In this sense, what is seen represents a consensus that can claim to be real, even though individual viewers do not—initially—believe it (Luhmann 2000: 110).

Unlike public ceremonies, however, the attack on September 11 was an event that was not staged and that was also not a scheduled program component; rather, it struck suddenly, spontaneously, and informally, like all sorts of crises and catastrophes. Unlike royal weddings, catastrophes are neither expectable nor memorable (they have not happened yet), and they are thus excluded from any horizon of meaning. Mary Ann Doane has also shown how these moments depend not only on televisual liveness but also on overlapping temporal levels (Doane 1990: 222ff). A fundamental synchronization between the on-screen action and the external world ensures the first level of incessant, continuous, and uniform events, which emerge as images and announcements. These events arrive through a certain cycle of repetition, as each announcement is repeated multiple times. An event is shown through a number of sequential announcements from various perspectives or particularly through always new yet routine updates, which ensure its continuous presence until the cycle ends and becomes part of the past. While the individual temporal objects—that is, the events—are constantly developing and eventually being replaced, the present itself remains uniform and stable, or more precisely metastable, like the ripples on a stream. According to Doane, this is the basic level of "information."

There is also the level of the "crisis." When the number of repetitions and recursive variants exceeds a certain degree and the presence of the constantly updated event lasts longer than usual, then the events are compressed into an ongoing crisis. The "catastrophe" finally occurs when a current event intersects and overlaps with both of the other levels—the normal, clocklike temporal rhythm of regular sequential moments of information and their consolidation into the special dramaturgies of the crisis. The catastrophic event then replaces all other events and broadcasts, even entertainment. It is articulated through extremely dense and frequent repetitions and updates, which override the entire program schedule. It would not be catastrophic if it did not do this—that is, if there was no loose and dense carpeting of live coverage (Doane 1990: 228). In other words, the "flashy" present of the sudden and extensionless event would not be possible without the continuous and extended present of the live broadcast. Catastrophes come from a different, unimagined present—a different space of events—and that is what makes them so uncanny. Nevertheless, they need a negative body, so to speak, which they can penetrate, disrupt, divide, or destroy. Despite all their intermittence, they must be articulated in the extended and uniform stream of the present in order for them to occur at all.

Even more: examples such as the terrorist attack of September 11 or the opening of the wall on November 9 show that television has been working from the very beginning to transform the frightening, exhilarating, or at least incomprehensible event from the punctiform state to the extended state of the present (Engell 1996: 129–53). This conversion can happen once again through the repetition of the same, such as the famous images of airplanes crashing into the World Trade Center in the sky over New York or the people sitting on the wall late at night in Berlin, as well as through an escalation of live switching in time and space. In the case of catastrophes, this also includes the search for causes and explanations, which is actively promoted with live experts, edited animations, and archival material. In this way, the formless and extensionless nature of the catastrophe, which makes it inconceivable and unimaginable, is reintegrated as far as possible and acquires a form through television's pool of images, which is similar to Eco's findings. A key aspect of this process is that the event is shown as anticipatable ex post, and is made predictable retrospectively by the possibilities of television itself. It then becomes, if only in retrospect, part of the extended event stream. We will encounter this process again in connection with the historical and historiographical function of television.

Nevertheless, the live events of television can never entirely escape the logic of the instant or merge with the continuous duration of succession. Like the condition of "being-able-to-be-different" (Anders-Sein-Können), the participation in nonparticipation, the formation of a nonconsensual reality, and the ablation of the event through television, which are fundamental to live events, reveal another suspiciously paradoxical difference—namely, its serious and shocking relationship to the external world of sense is perhaps dimmed but by no means extinguished through its subsequent recontextualization and renormalization. The event always retains an unassailable strangeness, inexplicability, uncontextualizability, unexpectability, and unpredictability. Long after the images of a catastrophe have been archived, cited a thousand times, and continuously molded in all sorts of contexts, they still evoke their uncanny origin in another time horizon whenever they are rerun.

## Critique of Liveness: The Division of Time

While the live nature of (primarily early) television has always been identified as a central feature of the medium, as in the works of Bazin, Cavell, Eco, Scannell, and Zettl, there has also been a critique of the theoretical topos of "liveness"—particularly in the 1980s. In her sharp analysis of the concept of "live" television, for example, Jane Feuer rejected Herbert Zettl's apologia for "liveness" (Feuer 1983: 12–21). Zettl promoted the view that television was indebted to "liveness" due to its fundamental technical form, which is similar to the view that we have undertaken here with the concept of the switch image (Zettl 1978: 3–8). According to Feuer, however, this is pure ideology, as nothing on television is really "live" in a technical sense, and television merely wants to make us believe that it produces synchronicity and simultaneity. We will come back to this critique in two later chapters (those on flow and the "instant replay"). It should only be added here that Feuer's position at least with regard to the technological state of television makes perfect sense today. When I watch a soccer game on my television, for example, I can also hear the sound of the television in front of the Lebanese restaurant across the street through my open window. The sounds of cheering and shouting from the restaurant's television arrive roughly three or four seconds earlier than those from my own, as it receives its signal directly from satellites while mine receives its signal from the internet. It thus appears that there is no precise concurrence between television receivers or also presumably between the signals they receive and the event in the stadium itself.

Deborah Esch's "In the Event" also provides a critique of "liveness" (Esch 1999: 61–70), and she uses the exact example of a concurrent transmission of an event on radio and television that is precisely not concurrent or fully synchronous. Esch does not see this as a shortcoming, however, as she is influenced by the theoretical and philosophical concept of deconstruction to question phenomena like immediacy, presence, and simultaneity. This questioning leads her to suggest that television is not a medium of presence and liveness but rather, on the contrary, a medium that depends on the *impossibility* of presence and liveness.

Esch explains her basic argument—that television produces not concurrence but rather a belief in concurrence, which it then unsettles—using a paradox that we have already encountered—namely, the idea that other viewers believe what each individual viewer does not believe (i.e., a nonconsensual reality), which is a claim made by television itself. In this sense, the wording of Nipkow's definition of television, which precisely does not take presentness into account, would need to be taken seriously.

In contrast, Esch proposes to invoke and identify the difference of the medium to itself—an idea that clearly reflects her training in deconstruction, as developed by Paul de Man in literary theory and above all Jacques Derrida in philosophy (Esch 1999: 63). If it is true that television is deeply rooted in time, as we have also assumed here, then the process of self-differentiation must be questioned and explained, as time only exists when something does not fully coincide with itself—that is, when something succeeds or precedes itself. In this sense, it would be possible to conclude, like Gilles Deleuze, that time is nonidentical with itself, as it is associated with the phenomenon of becoming-other (Deleuze 2013: 37ff). There is no "actual" concurrence that is not accompanied by displacement or nonconcurrence, yet the time of the event only exists because of this displacement. The nonconcurrence of liveness thus establishes the space of the event or the temporal body that the event needs in order to occupy space. In terms of the difference between synchronicity and simultaneity, this means that there is no sharp distinction between a point in time and duration. Every point in time is already differentiated within itself and separated from itself, which opens up the space for the continuous and simultaneous present in which the event itself occurs. Time is due not to concurrence but rather to nonconcurrence, and we participate in this nonconcurrence precisely through television.

These ideas could also be applied to the switching of the switch image. In the case of analog tube television, for example, a closer examination shows that there are no precise, incorporeal cuts or switches between the images; rather, all of the odd-numbered lines of the pixel image are "written" first, followed by all of the even-numbered lines. During the transition from one image to the next, the newly emerging image is thereby inscribed into the still persisting image, and for a slight interval both images are operative on the tube (as well as on the human retina) at the same time. The switch thus initiates the overwriting of the old image but not its immediate replacement, which means that the switching process is by no means extensionless; rather, it is differentiated within itself into two images. If one assumes that the switching of the image scans, punctuates, and articulates the flow of continuous time, which makes simultaneity possible, then one must also assume that this is only made possible because of the inner differentiation of the synchronous moment. One could even talk of the *unfolding* of time from the present, which includes precisely what it is not. In this sense, the switching process would acquire its own body as an image, and it would no longer be limited to a pure, incorporeal difference or extensionless point in time.

From this approach Esch develops a sharp critique of Cavell's thoughts on the concurrence of television and the suspension of temporal flow in a continuous and overseen present through *monitoring*. According to Esch,

Cavell's theory of concurrence is precisely television's own theory of itself, insofar as it is the theory that television wants to make us believe (Esch 1999: 65). However, Cavell forgets the artificiality as well as the fragility, inner inconsistency, and differentiating tendency of this concurrence, as he does not discuss the "fact of television," which in practice embodies delays, interruptions, deferrals, and thus its fundamental nonconcurrence (Esch 1999: 67). We will also come back to this analysis again in the chapter on the "instant replay."

In light of these considerations and observations, it is possible to expand on the time-theoretical definition of the switch image. If it does not involve the tension between the extensionless moment and extended duration, then it apparently consists of microscopic and macroscopic simultaneities, which are of shorter and longer duration. (We are still talking about the technology of classical tube television here, although we have seen that nonconcurrence still persists after digitization.) In the case of television at least, there are thus no clear-cut synchronicities but rather only diverse simultaneities, which overlap and intersect with one another and which are only jointly possible in their abundance and fullness. They scan and articulate one another and furnish extensions or temporal bodies for one another. They use each other as synchronous points, whose extensions are relatively weak, or durations, whose extensions are relatively strong. In this respect, it is not wrong to refer to "live" television and synchronicity, as liveness still occupies a central position in and for television; however, live transmission and synchronization are both different than initially assumed. The opposition between experienced and experienceable liveness, such as the opposition between the sustained instant of the "killer pass" and the clear-cut synchronicity of the technical switch, also vanishes. In television, experience and switching are always already taken as temporal forms that are entangled with one another and only possible in relation to one another. Their differentiation would be retrospective and quantitative.

## Critique of Liveness: Pseudo-Events and Events on Strike

Another critique of the television event and of television presence questions not the time but rather the location of the event. So far we have assumed that events exist—that is, they take place in the external world and their visibility is transmitted to other locations while they are still taking place— and critics like Eco and especially Dayan and Katz have explicitly accepted the idea that broadcast are "faithful" to these events. However, there are also events that are specifically designed for television, that are staged through television, and that would not exist without television, even if they may take place in the external world (which then becomes part of the internal space of television itself). We will analyze the largest of these events, the 1969 flight to the moon, in a later chapter. Daniel Boorstin referred to this type of event as a "pseudo" or television-induced event, in which television is only synchronous with itself rather than with the world in the form of the (temporal) object at location A (Boorstin 1992). In other words, its presence is self-presence, and the society of television is then not the given society, in which television operates, but rather the internal space and product of television itself, which becomes, according to Guy Debord's famous critique, a society of the spectacle (Debord 1994). Jean Baudrillard expanded on this idea by questioning whether events were not only dependent on television but also did not actually exist at all (Baudrillard 2010: 1–42). The pseudo-event and the public spectacle, which is based on nothing, would then be replaced by the mere simulation of the event. Events went on strike long ago, says Baudrillard, as they refuse to happen (Baudrillard 1994: 21–7). As a result, nothing "real" can be "live" on television; rather, there is only a simulation of simultaneity. Baudrillard applied this idea in a highly provocative way to the Gulf War of 1990–1, which was widely criticized at the time as a "television war" that positioned viewers as "soldiers" through "live coverage." According to Baudrillard, the Gulf War did not take place (Baudrillard 1995: 23–8), and the ideological power of television was not that it could make the war take place but rather that it could make viewers believe in its existence (or, in this case, its consensual reality) and behave accordingly, even when they criticized it.

The cynicism of this argument is hard to surpass, though Baudrillard would say that it only counters the cynicism of television itself as an apparatus of global power. Television would then no longer be only concurrent with itself instead of the external world; rather, it would be concurrent with nothing except its own concurrence. It would be connected not with reality or society but rather only with itself. In light of the earlier discussion concerning the diversity of simultaneities and the nonsimultaneity of the presence of the switch image, it can be said that even this internal differentiation of the present—that is, the temporal nonidentity of the switch image with itself—opens up multiple simultaneities that are divergent rather than congruent with one another. In their interconnection, the medium and its simulation would also come apart. The society, power, and ideology of television could then only be established through its nonsynchronicity and nonidentity.

## From the Economy of Time to Boredom

Whether we conceive of time as a primal separation (like poststructuralism), whether we conceive of the horizontality of the instant as providing access to its temporality (like Heidegger), whether we limit ourselves to the technical functions and forms of timing and synchronization, or whether we see time as duration (like Bergson) and television as simultaneous time, it remains clear that television functions as a "live" form of simultaneity that produces presence, events, and processes. Time appears to be both the initial fact of television as well as its end product. "Live" television provides time with a body, thereby organizing it and making it experienceable and accessible. This also constitutes its economic function. Whether we pay fees, subscribe, or participate in the financing of television through advertising revenue, television always occupies our time, which is first produced by television itself. This time constitutes the economic raw material of television in the form of the duration of our observation or attention (Franck 1998), which is timed and formatted by television through the preparation of individual programs or broadcasts and well-defined standard time periods (breakfast time, day time, prime time, and late night). Moreover, it is sorted and differentiated according to target groups, such as age and gender groups or income levels. This formatted time—our time—thus acquires the form of a commodity, which is sold in two directions at the same time: on the one hand it is sold to the advertising industry, which can now specifically target our time, while on the other hand it is also sold back to us.

Television would not be television, however, if it did not at the same time undermine this process of formatting and economizing time. In terms of the production of the present and simultaneity in live television, this takes place through the *boredom* in which television is embedded, which conveys a sense of being present at and simultaneous with nothing.

## References

Aristotle. 2005. *The Physics: Books I-IV*, trans. by Philip H. Wicksteed, and Francis M. Cornford. Cambridge, MA: Harvard University Press.

Baudrillard, Jean. 1994. *The Illusion of the End*. Stanford: Stanford University Press.

Baudrillard, Jean. 1995. *The Gulf War Did Not Take Place*. Bloomington: Indiana University Press.

Baudrillard, Jean. 2010. *Simulacra and Simulation*. Ann Arbor: University of Michigan Press.

Bazin, André. 2014. *André Bazin's New Media*, ed. by Dudley Andrew. Oakland: University of California Press.
Bergson, Henri. 1889. *Essai sur les données immédiates de la conscience*. Paris: Felix Alcan.
Bergson, Henri. 1988. *Matter and Memory*. New York: Zone Books.
Boltanski, Luc. 1999. *Distance Suffering: Morality, Media and Politics*. Cambridge: Cambridge University Press.
Boorstin, Daniel. 1992. *The Image: A Guide to Pseudo-Events in America*. New York: Vintage.
Cassin, Barbara, ed. 2004. *Vocabulaire européen des philosophies: Dictionnaire des intraduisibles*. Paris: Seuil/Le Robert.
Cavell, Stanley. 1982. "The Fact of Television." *Daedalus* 111, no. 4: 75–96.
Dayan, Daniel, and Elihu Katz. 1987. "Performing Media Events." In: *Impacts and Influences: Essays on Media Power in the Twentieth Century*, ed. by James Curran, Anthony Smith, and Pauline Wingate, pp. 174–97. London: Methuen.
Debord, Guy. 1994. *The Society of the Spectacle*. New York: Zone Books.
Deleuze, Gilles. 2013. *Cinema II: The Time-Image*. London: Bloomsbury Academic.
Dewey, John. 2008. "Art as Experience." In: John Dewey. *The Collected Works of John Dewey, 1882–1953. The Later Works, 1925–1953, Vol. 10: 1934*, ed. by Jo Ann Boydston. Carbondale: Southern Illinois University Press.
Doane, Mary Ann. 1990. "Information, Crisis, Catastrophe." In: *Logics of Television: Essays in Cultural Criticism*, ed. by Patricia Mellencamp, pp. 222–39. Bloomington: Indiana University Press.
Eco, Umberto. 1989. *The Open Work*. Cambridge, MA: Harvard University Press.
Engell, Lorenz. 1996. "Das Amedium. Grundbegriffe des Fernsehens in Auflösung: Ereignis und Erwartung." *montage a/v* 5/1: 129–53.
Engell, Lorenz. 2013. "The Tactile and the Index: from the Remote Control to the Hand-Held Computer. Some Speculative Reflections on the Bodies of the Will." *NECSUS. European Journal of Media Studies*, 3.
Esch, Deborah. 1999. *In the Event: Reading Journalism, Reading Theory*. Stanford: Stanford University Press.
Feuer, Jane. 1983. "The Concept of Live Television." In: *Regarding Television*, ed. by E. Ann Kaplan, pp. 12–21. Frederick: University Publications of America.
Franck, Georg. 1998. *Eine Ökonomie der Aufmerksamkeit. Ein Entwurf*. München: Hanser.
Gell, Alfred. 1998. *Art and Agency: An Anthropological Theory*. Oxford: Clarendon.
Gumbrecht, Hans Ulrich. 2004. *Production of Presence: What Meaning Cannot Convey*. Stanford: Stanford University Press.
Heidegger, Martin. 1982. *The Basic Problems of Phenomenology*. Bloomington: Indiana University Press.

Heidegger, Martin. 1992. *History of the Concept of Time: Prolegomena.* Bloomington: Indiana University Press.
Heidegger, Martin. 2008. *Being and Time.* New York: Harper Collins.
Hickethier, Knut. 1998. *Geschichte des deutschen Fernsehens.* Stuttgart. Weimar: Metzler.
Husserl, Edmund. 1991. *On the Phenomenology of the Consciousness of Internal Time (1893–1917).* Dordrecht, Boston, London: Kluwer Academic Publishers.
Kierkegaard, Søren. 1980. *The Concept of Anxiety.* Princeton: Princeton University Press.
Latour, Bruno. 1986. "Visualization and Cognition: 'Drawing Thigns Together.'" In: *Knowledge and Society: Studies in the Sociology of Culture Past and Present*, vol. 6, ed. by H. Kucklick, pp. 1–40. Greenwich: Jai Press.
Leibniz, Gottfried Wilhelm. 1863. *Mathematische Schriften. Initia Mathematica. Mathesis universalis, vol VII: Die mathematischen Abhandlungen.* Halle: Gerhardt.
Luhmann, Niklas. 1995. *Social Systems.* Stanford: Stanford University Press.
Luhmann, Niklas. 2000. *The Reality of Mass Media.* Cambridge: Polity Press.
Marschall, Rick. 1987. *The Golden Age of Television.* London: Bison.
Scannell, Paddy. 2014. *Television and the Meaning of Live.* Cambridge: Polity Press.
Serres, Michel. 2008. *The Five Senses: A Philosophy of Mingled Bodies.* London, New York: Continuum.
Souriau, Etienne. 2015. *The Different Modes of Existence.* Minneapolis: Minnesota University Press.
Zettl, Herbert. 1978. "The Rare Case of Television Aesthetics." *The Journal of the University Film Association* 30, no. 2: 3–8.
Zola, Émile. 1893. *The Experimental Novel and Other Essays.* London: Cassell Publishing Company.

# 3

# The Series (1)

If time is the raw material of television, then this pertains not only to the synchronicity of the point in time during the switching process and the simultaneity of the event during the live broadcast but also to the consecutive *succession* of broadcasts in the program sequence. In the case of television, this succession is organized in a specific *serial* form. The *seriality* in the arrangement of broadcasts can also recur within the broadcasts themselves through the sequence of switching processes and camera changes. The fact that early television was and had to be serial was a consequence of its unconditional liveness, as this liveness required seriality. In addition to the principle of liveness, on which it was based, television is thus dominated by a second principle, which is derived from the first, and that is the principle of the *series* (Fahle and Engell 2005: 17f).

There were initially technical alternatives to live television (Abramson 1974: 58–62). Even in its experimental phase in the 1930s, television could have been used to broadcast feature films, as the necessary device for this (a film scanner) had been invented long before. There was even a peculiar technical television system, the so-called intermediate film system, in which images were recorded on celluloid film and then immediately developed, converted into electronic signals by means of the film scanner, and transmitted via radio. The broadcasts were slightly delayed instead of live, but the process was slower and more expensive than producing live images with the electronic tube, so the film scanner was actually only used to show feature films. In the early period of television, however, there was little need for an additional playback medium for feature films, and the film industry also resisted this practice. By the end of the 1940s, moreover, television caught on as the medium that could do something that no other medium could, including cinema—namely, as the electronic live medium that we described in the previous chapter. As such, it experienced its lasting impression as the medium that facilitates the synchronous and simultaneous dissemination of moving images.

## Seriality and Transmediality

Television could transmit, but it could not store. It could neither produce nor reproduce any copies of its broadcasts. Even fictional entertainment formats, like television plays, were broadcast live and therefore not recorded, which meant that they could never be rebroadcast (except in exceptional cases). Early television thus possessed an exclusively hetero-medial and fragmentary archive, as only scripts, plans, photographs, notices, and so forth could be preserved, but not the broadcasts themselves (there was no way to record electronic images). Everything was lost in time, and as a result television had no past for itself (Engell 2000: 97f). Whether as an extended present or an extensionless point in time, television was a medium that existed entirely in the present. That was also one of the differences between television and radio, as radio had integrated gramophone records into its production methods at least since the 1930s, and it especially used this durable sound storage medium to play recorded music (Kittler 1999: 94ff). Certain pieces could thus be reproduced identically and rebroadcast repeatedly over the radio using the same storage medium. Radio could also create its own medial archive, and it could even become integrated into the music industry and the commodity form (gramophone records were themselves serial products that were sold in stores).

Television could not do anything comparable, yet it could learn and adopt something from radio. Despite its link to the present, it could develop a form that extended its own time beyond the present, and this form was precisely the series. Unlike the live image, the series was not a characteristic achievement of television. Indeed, the series was always already transmedial, as it originated in literature and continued in the popular press, comics, and radio (Kelleter 2015; Jenkins 2006: 93–130). It has also been adopted by newer media. No matter where it arises, however, it is always exemplary of television, as seriality not only on television requires the basic operation of *switching*. This confirms, as we will see in detail, both of the theories of seriality consulted here. First, television as a switch image has a genuinely televisual approach to seriality, which reveals its foundation in switching and which it can also incorporate into its existing serial forms. Second, at no other point and in no other medium was there ever so much experimentation with the serial form, such an abundant development of serial forms, and such an extensive reflection on the serial itself. Television did not invent the *series*, but it appropriated it to such a degree that it can be said that simply everything on television is organized serially. And because of its origins, this applies precisely to the basic operation of the switch and the principle of liveness. In particular, as we will see in more detail, the series is the operative memory of television itself. It allows the view of the present to extend beyond its own limits into the past and the future. In order to do this, it needs not storage but rather only the distinction between the known and the unknown, which can be renewed in every present, and that is why it involves operative memory in contrast to storage memory. It is by no means an assault of the present on all other time, as Alexander Kluge said; rather, it is a temporal leap over the immediate present (Kluge 1985).

In addition to the live broadcast, therefore, the form of the *series* is television's second eminent and prominent contribution to the media and popular culture of the mid- to late twentieth century and even the early twenty-first century. As many people have said, the television series has long since moved beyond television into other media, where it has been tremendously successful (Maeder 2013). As with the live image, however, we will argue the opposite: wherever there are live images, there is television, and wherever there are serial narratives in images, there is also television. Even though live broadcasts and series were both developed in radio, they only evolved into formative cultural formats in television, and this is particularly true of the series, which has been differentiated into the vast range of subtypes and boundary phenomena that we know today. Currently, by means of the series, television can finally extend above and beyond television itself.

However, not everything that appears in a large number of sequential installments is already a *series*; rather, a sequence of objects or events only becomes a *series* when they originate from the *series* in a way that continues the *series*. The *series* precedes its component parts, yet it also emerges from them. Günther Anders wrote that the series is neither the general nor the individual but rather a third (Anders 1956: 180). It is once again ontographic, as it perpetually updates itself from episode to episode. This presupposes that it can refer to its own arrangement and operations, if it knows or is conscious that it is a sequence in whatever form. The *series* at least sets conditions on perception, as it only becomes observable when one assumes that it knows or is conscious of its own sequential form and seriality. This sounds complicated, but it is precisely what happens every day on television. Not only is the screen event sequenced, but it also develops an operative knowledge of seriality that is contained in the form of the *series* itself. The television *series* is television's knowledge of its own seriality or even the seriality of the external world, of which it is a part.

## Series of Identity and of Difference

This is precisely why television is a privileged site of reflection of modernity. Series production as a method of manufacturing goods and thus also seriality as a form of goods already prevailed with the rise of mechanization and industrialization in the modern era (Mumford 2010: 205ff; 269–73). However, it is dominated by a very particular kind of serialization that we will call *identical serialization* in analogy to Gilles Deleuze's concept of "identical repetition" (Deleuze 1994: 285ff). It is historically a technique of reproduction, and its characteristic feature is the production of a large number of identical copies or "tokens," which are manufactured from a single model or "type" (Peirce 1906). These copies may be numbered, but they are otherwise indistinguishable from one another. The printing press is an early and prominent example of this kind of serialization, and the industrial manufacturing of goods in the nineteenth and twentieth centuries is another. These manufactured goods are no longer distinct objects, like those produced by artists and artisans; instead, they are only numerically distinct, and they are only economically relevant as parts of a large set. According to Günther Anders' formulation of the economic ontology of industrialization (and of television), the merely singular does not exist (Anders 1956: 179f).

Because these objects are completely identical to one another, the point in time of their production was not important. Identical serialization is based on and dominates space, like the large hall where identical machines manufacture serially identical goods and where the operations of both the machines and their workers are repeated in an identical form. The goods are then distributed to the market, which is conceived as a large space or territory, which they are supposed to permeate and dominate as they compete with other serially manufactured goods. This space is also a system of simultaneity, as goods are supposed to be available everywhere at the same time (Leibniz 1863: 18). In the end, it is not possible to perceive the individual copy without referring to the mass of other copies, as they are ubiquitous (they can be found everywhere) and omnipresent (they can be found at all times). Serial products do not even register a temporal sequence through their deterioration, as they can always be replaced by a new identical copy; instead, they only mark the passing of time artificially when there is a mode or model change, such as the seasonal changes in fashion and the annual model changes in the American automobile industry, especially in the classical age of television from the 1950s to the 1970s.

The manufacturing of identical goods also requires absolute uniformity in the entire production process and in the physical actions and gestures through which they are produced by industrial workers. Individuals are thus molded and disciplined accordingly. Yet at the same modern subjects are also increasingly required to express themselves as individuals through goods and possessions, and to be exempt from the conditions of mass society (Bourdieu 1984: 42–55). This difficult and paradoxical undertaking is made possible through the targeting of individual consumers, which allows completely identical commodities to be charged with individually appropriable meanings. Mass-produced goods can then support the formation of identity, and this is precisely the function of advertising, which in turn constitutes the economic backbone of at least American television. This is the first connection between serial production and the seriality of television.

In addition to identical serialization, there is also a second form that can be called *different serialization*, again in analogy to Deleuze's concepts (Deleuze 1994: 285ff). It is a time-critical process, in which the sequence or succession of events (such as the production of objects) functions not as simple reproduction according to a pattern but rather as repetition in time. However, every repetition is slightly distinguished from its predecessor, if only through the time of its execution; in this case, doing the same thing is never precisely the same. There are usually also other small differences. This different, temporal serialization underlies certain modern artistic processes, such as when Monet continuously worked on the same composition in an entire series of pictures or when Kandinsky worked on his project of abstraction. The *different series* can assume many forms, depending on whether the serial sequence progresses in a certain direction or reaches a goal and whether this goal is contingent and imposed or inherent and compelled by its own developmental logic. In each of these cases, *different serialization* can be understood as a generative or even creative process that produces something new. It is both time-based and time-generating. It allocates every object or event in the series to a precise point in time as well as a precise position relative to the other points that pertain to each object or event. It thus thematizes both the now and the not-now, and it bypasses the mere present event in view of a more comprehensive time horizon.

It is very easy to differentiate between these two types of serialization using the example of film. Film functions technologically, microscopically, and aesthetically according to the principle of *different serialization*, as the individual frames of each shot (excluding the use of editing) look almost exactly the same as the frames that come immediately before and after, but only almost. They still maintain a minimal difference to one another, which ultimately accounts for the impression of movement when the images are projected. The differences between the individual frames of each shot thus embody the temporal quality of film itself. While these frames constitute a different or temporal series on the celluloid filmstrip, large quantities of absolutely identical copies of the entire film (tokens) are produced from a single negative (type) according to the macroscopic logic of the market, and the distributors attempt to deliver all of these copies to the screens of a defined market territory on the same day. The formation of cinematic genres can also be seen as a form of serialization, which can be categorized as identical or differential depending on one's point of view.

## Series as Cycle and Series as Medium

Stanley Cavell developed precisely this view of genre in film as a series, and he also applied it to the seriality of television in a significant way (Cavell 1982). He notes that everything on television is arranged according to the principle of serialization—including the live broadcasts, such as talk shows, and the feature films incorporated into the program flow (Cavell 1982: 86). Television constantly switches (and switches its viewers) back and forth between entirely different modes (reports, shows, television plays, etc.), yet these modes are all arranged serially, and this is precisely what ensures their switchability (Cavell 1982: 86f, 89). Switching is the basic operation of television, but Cavell says that collective seriality is the aesthetic medium that enables the switching process as a transition between the heterogeneous. He then compares the foundation of television in switching and seriality with the formatting of genre in Hollywood films, and he relies on his own prior distinction between two basic types of genre formation in film (Cavell 1982: 79). "Genre-as-cycle" involves a group of films that share one or more key features and that are based on a common formula. Such films are thus made according to a blueprint or ur-exemplar of the genre (examples would include Murnau's *Nosferatu* as the first extended vampire film and Josef von Sternberg's *The Docks of New York* as the first gangster film). All of the films in the cycle are variations of the same formula or type, and the genre is exhausted when all of the variations allowed by the formula have been run through without being surpassed or destroyed. Films can still be added, but the genre as a whole cannot develop any further (Cavell 1982: 80).

There is also the special case in which the blueprint or formula is not imposed at the start and does not already exist in an original film. The sequence of films then gradually determines the formula, such as by testing the essential characteristics of the films in a particular genre. The variants then precede the formula or type, but this does not change their basic relations. Once the formula has been established, the variants have already been produced and the genre cannot develop any further, even though it may persist for a long time.

According to Cavell, something entirely different applies to the "genre-as-medium" (Cavell 1982: 80–2). In this case, there is no blueprint, formula, or "type" but only "tokens." Every film can also add or subtract essential characteristics and elements or even redefine the borders of the genre itself.

There are also no privileged reference films that would serve as a model or an example; instead, the films in such a genre are constantly negotiating among themselves over what the genre actually is and how it is to be determined, and this negotiation is precisely the genre. Films belong to a genre (as medium) when they participate in this negotiation and thus relate to one another rather than when they adhere to a particular list of criteria and characteristics. This process also tends to be never-ending; it may gain or lose momentum, but it remains alive and productive because it always generates new forms.

Cavell immediately classifies the seriality of television as the first type, which is identical or identity-forming, as each television series can be reduced to a "formula" that is shaped into all sorts of variants (Cavell 1982: 82f). This model soon shines through all of the episodes of the series, even when it is only gradually developed or revealed. In the terms used here, it could be said that for Cavell the seriality of television follows the logic of identity, since it focuses on the relations between token and type. It is also characteristically space-based and space-forming, and television is therefore a spatial medium. Despite the fact that the individual episodes of a series are broadcast (and produced) consecutively, they always reproduce the same formulas, and they thereby staunch the successive flow that governs television itself, as the same thing always occurs regardless of the point in time.

Cavell thus distinguishes between the essential, which pertains to the formula of a television series, and the merely accidental, which pertains to the distinguishing features of each variant or episode. He also sees the series as a form of identical repetition or reproduction, as every episode contains the same content or structure, which completely negates or overrides the difference between the points in time when the preceding and succeeding episodes of a series or serial broadcast appear. He thus removes different seriality from the seriality of television and consequently concludes that television does nothing but suspend the linear progression of time. It brings the world to a halt and implies that everything is in order, while outside everything is actually becoming increasingly uninhabitable and disastrous, and it does this precisely through serialization. Cavell never seriously considers the possibility that a television series could behave like the "genre-as-medium."

## The *Emergence* of the Series

Let's make up for this. The development of the series from the basic seriality of television and thus from liveness occurred gradually through *emergence* (Luhmann 2012: 77). This began, as it did in radio, with the same thing always happening at the same time. Fixed programming slots were then established, such as for the news and certain entertainment formats. The continuing stream of time was thus punctuated by islands of recurrence—if not of the same, then of the similar. Television and the serial form of succession already amalgamate here with that of identity: something remains exactly identical, while something else exhibits difference. Similarity is initially based on the genre of the broadcast (such as news, sports, quiz shows, and television plays) and usually on a consistent studio setting and staff (such as the so-called anchorpeople, who were given this name for precisely this reason). Television thus conforms to a paradoxical form of time measurement and of everyday life—namely, the recurrence of the identical and the rhythmization of time. In everyday life, time is both cyclical and linear. Although time moves inexorably forward, all noontimes have something in common— namely, they are all noontimes (even though they are always on different days). Weekdays, months, and seasons also recur in the same way (even though they are each different). Television conforms precisely to this rhythm, like radio and the newspaper before it, only more closely and firmly; in the process, it also enables its creation, consolidation, and circulation in the first place. Television thus conforms to a time created by itself (Luhmann 1995: 89f). This *basic serialization* of television, which affects its program structure and which it has exhibited since the establishment of regular and somewhat extensive broadcasting operations, already has a clearly recognizable ontographic quality.

However, this must be distinguished from seriality in a narrower sense, which refers not to the serialization and rhythmization of the entire program schedule but rather to a particular form of series as a genre within this schedule. The television series in this sense emerged from the basic serialization of fictional television plays, which were actually theatrical performances held before cameras in a studio or radio plays performed for television. These plays were already fundamental program components when television was still experimental and there was not yet a program schedule, such as the famous broadcast of *The Queen's Messenger* in the United States in 1928 (Barnouw 1990: 61f). Similar experiments also took place in Germany (Hickethier 1998: 46f). In England, the transmission of stage performances was discussed as one of the possible applications of television in the 1930s, before the introduction of regular large-scale operations; imagine middle-class viewers sitting at home in front of the television wearing formal evening clothes and watching the performance as if they were in a theater box (Zielinski 1999: 108 et passim). The television series is therefore a *fictional* and *narrative* format, and the major advantage of fiction (as the etymological origin of the word shows) is that it can be produced in almost any way and also in a series. They can be made and to some extent controlled, and in principle they are independent of current events and whatever is happening in the external world (even though they may be linked to themes or events in the world, and they may refer to these events in many ways). Fiction is something beyond everyday life and reality, and it takes place in a fundamental "elsewhere" and even "elsewhen" (which makes fiction no less real than reality itself, however) (Luhmann 2000: 52–8; Koch and Voß 2009). Nevertheless, it is something that is really produced and that can even be produced in a series.

The first surge of serialized fictional television plays followed the consolidation of broadcasting and the establishment of fixed programming slots that specified the days and times when different programs would be broadcast. In the case of American television, these programming slots could then be sold to certain commercial firms, which could reserve and use them to advertise their products. Each programming slot could then be associated as closely as possible with each sponsor or advertiser, and the brand name of each firm could even be incorporated into the titles of the programs, such as *The Philco Television Playhouse*, *The Motorola Television Hour*, and *Kraft Television Theatre*. The serialization of television was thus tied to the serial production of goods (Marschall 1987: 66–87).

## Plurality and Seriality

As a next step, these series tried to acquire a specific characteristic that would set them apart from others in the selection of pieces, styles, genres, or casts. From early on, therefore, the production of the series in television was not distinguished from other, nonserial forms; rather, the various formats, which were still in the process of being developed, competed with each other through profiling. Viewers were then supposed to be committed and constrained to specific products, which were advertised during the breaks in the television play. You could say, for American television at least, that the raw materials of television discussed earlier—namely, electrical current, signal flow, visibility, and time—were joined at this point by another raw material—namely, money. This applies particularly to American television, which was always organized commercially. Money is especially connected to time through the seriality of television. From this perspective, television is a serialized form of the conversion of time into money.

The television plays performed and broadcast during these fixed programming slots now had something in common, and they exhibited a specific similarity with one another. This similarity could involve a common topic or genre, which emerged through a series of individual television plays with different casts and settings. This pre-serial format remained on television until the 1960s, so the series *Alfred Hitchcock Presents* as well as the science-fiction series *The Twilight Zone* can be placed in this tradition (Marschall 1987: 86f). However, this soon gave rise to the first stand-alone television series, in which not only the genre but also the setting, cast, and often the basic dramaturgy of each piece remained the same. This reduced production costs and at the same time ensured recognizability, and in the early period crime series were particularly successful, such as *Man against Crime*; *Martin Kane, Private Eye*; and *Mr. District Attorney* (Barnouw 1990: 130ff).

These series were still performed live, just like all other broadcasts (especially those that were nonfictional). This means that the time of the production was directly proportional to the time of the narrative, as the story had to be told precisely within the allotted airtime, from which it was impossible to deviate. Erik Barnouw sees this as a significant difference between the television series and the radio series, in which the number of spoken words clearly specified the length of the broadcast. This was not so easy on television due to the use of movements and gestures. Barnouw describes, for example, how the ending of each episode of *Man against Crime* incorporated a so-called Search Scene, in which the detective searches for a crucial piece of evidence in a suspect's apartment (Barnouw 1990: 131). This scene functioned as a temporal buffer, as the detective could take several minutes slowly and carefully searching through everything or he could head straight to the hiding place, depending on the amount of time remaining. In short: a television series was a fictional narrative that was performed live at a fixed time, that had a fixed topic and cast, and that advertised the same products. In keeping with its character as a television play, each broadcast had a clear beginning, middle, and end, and it thus represented a self-contained narrative.

In American television, the gradual emancipation of the television series from live television began in 1955. Until then, the film industry had successfully prevented broadcasters from using film cameras by means of patent law. This was one of the main reasons for the production of live television, as it was impossible at the time to record electronic images directly without celluloid. This position was softened, however, when ABC commissioned the Hollywood studio Warner Brothers to produce a Western series in their studios using their technology and personnel. In return, Warner would be allowed to advertise their films during the breaks. Thus began the era of the "filmed series" (Barnouw 1990: 193–8). The method of producing a series changed dramatically, as the production time of each episode could be extended, it became possible to repeat individual takes, and editing was no longer performed live through switching but rather afterwards at the editing table. Strictly speaking, the episodes were completely different from feature films, as they were short (a maximum of forty-five minutes), they were constantly interrupted by advertisements, they were broadcast weekly, the composition of the image was adapted to the small size and coarse grain of the screen, and they had ridiculously small budgets compared to feature films. Even though they were entirely different from feature films in terms of their structure, narrative technique, mode of reception, and appearance, however, they still largely replaced the performance mode of live television, and the character of television began to shift.

The differences between the various series formats gradually became more important for the definition of the serial than the differences between live and filmed series, and it was precisely through this internal differentiation that television was able to repeat and reflect its own basic seriality. This is yet another example of the process of consolidation and separation that already characterized the early days of television, as we have seen. This process can, in turn, also be described as a form of series, as the medial and transmedial development of televisual seriality itself constitutes a series of successive steps (Beil et al. 2016: 8ff).

## Soap!

The closed nature of the episodes, which ultimately reflect the daily and weekly rhythm of everyday life, was by no means mandatory. This brings us to a key distinction within the televisual series, which is no longer based merely on the topic, style, or characters. In addition to the episodic series, which is broadcast weekly in the evening, there is also the continuing series, which is broadcast daily in the morning. In order for a series with daily broadcasts during the day to have viewers, it must first establish and prepare an audience, which most likely consists of people who are home and can watch television at the same time each day. American television thus played a central role in producing the social type of the American housewife (Spigel 1992: 73–98), and it also affected and virtually defined the housewife's economic function. In the classic economic terms of production, consumption, and reproduction, the function of the housewife was always ideally on the side of reproduction, whether it be biological reproduction (through the bearing of and caring for children) or the restoration of the husband's labor power at the end of the working day (through the preparation of food and the providing of comfort). This reflected the central position of the sphere of production in industrial society, to which all other spheres were subordinated.

This changed in postwar capitalist society, however, due to overproduction. By the middle of the century, technical developments had made manufacturing so productive that in principle there could no longer be any shortages of industrially produced goods. On the contrary, far more commodities were being produced than were needed. The problem was how to sell, discard, and replace them with new ones, and it thus became necessary to accelerate the distribution and circulation of goods. The enormous expansion of the advertising industry in the 1950s and 1960s served precisely this purpose, and this expansion was due at least economically to the expansion of television. (This process, to which television owes its existence, is clearly depicted in the series *Mad Men*.) The expansion of the advertising industry was also connected to an expansion of the sphere of consumption, as consumption suddenly appeared to be the decisive force driving the economy and the spending of money became as important economically as the earning of money. The women who had been pushed out of production as housewives (following the wartime economy) were thus compensated with a new status as economically important subjects, who were supposed to be able to make decisions regarding a good portion of the family budget (Spigel 1992: 73–98). That is why the programs addressed to housewives, which were broadcast daily in the morning, particularly advertised products that were supposed to interest them, such as laundry detergents and cleaning products. The content of these programs, which became known as "soap operas," also addressed the interests required of model housewives, as they were almost exclusively about partnership, neighborhood, parenting, and household problems, and they were more concerned with emotional relationships than dramatic actions.

"Soap operas" were also produced live. The expense and complexity of these productions were very high, and there was a strong division of labor, such as script writing. Agnes Nixon's productions were particularly successful, as she ran a well-organized operation that virtually dominated the genre in the 1960s (Cantor and Pingree 1983). Due to the pressure of the daily schedule, it was only possible to hold rudimentary rehearsals. Generally speaking, three fixed stages were built in the corners of the studio, such as two apartments and a street corner, which allowed for two to three parallel storylines and which could hardly ever be changed (Morton 1997).

However, the housewife was not supposed to sit silently in front of the television and enjoy the program. Since the days of radio, it has been known that there are two fundamentally different modes of electronic mass media consumption: concentrated and casual. Concentrated reception is when viewers sit silently facing the television, as in the theater, the cinema, or the reading of a book or newspaper. Casual reception is when viewers turn away from the device or move around in the surrounding space. This mode of reception particularly applied to the housewife, who was supposed to be able to continue her housework while watching television. A series with self-contained or stand-alone episodes in the tradition of theater required concentrated reception, but casual reception required another broadcast aesthetic that functioned largely through the spoken text, which could be heard even when the viewer was unable to see the screen (Cantor and Pingree 1983). It also had to provide ample redundancies, so that the narrative threads did not immediately come apart when an image was missed. The need for slow progression meant that a self-contained narrative could no longer be told in a single episode; instead, the narrative continued from one episode to the next. This was possible precisely because of the daily broadcast rhythm, as viewers could remember the state of the narrative from the previous day, but it would have been more difficult for them to remember the state of the narrative from the previous week.

The production conditions of the soap opera also changed following the transition to the filmed series, even though they were still produced live for some time (Cantor and Pingree 1983). While some characteristics remained the same (such as the emphasis on close-ups and slow narrative progression), the new production logic resulted in an increase in the number of storylines, which made them more complex (Fröhlich 2015: 417ff). In the case of episodic prime-time series, the sudden increase in quality (from the perspective of established film aesthetics) was so extreme that Western series in particular became the most popular programs of the late 1950s, replacing the live shows that had previously dominated the program schedule. Television's first "golden age" had thus ended.

## Episodes in Continuing Series

If we want to come back to the opposition between the series as cycle and the series as medium, which we encountered earlier in Cavell's work, then the distinction between the episodic series and the continuing series is of the utmost importance. First, a family series with daily continuing episodes could obviously be described as a medium, in Cavell's sense, because it is endless. While even the most long-lasting soap operas eventually end, these endings are external to the narratives themselves, which are always oriented toward the future and the process of slow yet endless transformation: life always goes on. The slowness of soap operas also reveals their rootedness in difference, as the individual shots and sequences are connected to one another by minimal variations that to some extent lead nowhere and could easily be skipped according to the logic of the narrative.

The principle of the smallest difference also links the individual episodes of the series. The soap opera accomplishes this through its characteristic use of multiple storylines: each episode features (in the early days) three to (today) seven subplots (Fröhlich 2015: 417ff). This means that in a single episode one storyline can be introduced, another can be further developed, and another can be concluded. The storylines can also be interrelated in different ways, as they can split off from existing storylines (such as when someone moves out and starts their own family) or be added from an external space (such as when someone moves in next door). There could be contrasting or causal relationships between the storylines, or they could merge with one another. Even though narrative elements frequently recur (conflict, reconciliation, sickness, romance, etc.), the basic setting does not remain the same. The past is also available as a resource for alterations, as completely unknown characters or episodes from the characters' histories can appear at any time and transform the entire setting. In any case, the main subject matter of soap operas consists of genealogical questions as well as questions of reproduction, relatedness, and cohesion through unbroken chains of relations. According to Cantor and Pingree's famous phrase, soap operas consist of "one endless middle" with "no beginning or end" (Cantor and Pingree 1983: 65). They are the time of the present as it extends itself to the future and the past. Their present is that of duration in the Bergsonian sense as a temporal dimension that is constantly changing and becoming something else. They are designed not for stagnation but rather for the emulsion of time.

The theme of change also defines the microaesthetics of the soap opera, which tends to present faces on which a change in expression is looming but not yet realized (such as a reaction to something previously seen or the receiving of a communication). A twofold thematization of the serial connection then occurs, and it occurs precisely through this thematization. First, the quantity and variety of these expressions are naturally rather limited and are themselves schematized in the soap opera, and this involves the gradual emergence of facial movements or transitions from one affect to another; generally speaking, we can never know which reaction will occur. Gilles Deleuze assumes for film not only that affixations can be displayed in the close-ups of faces but also that the images themselves are mutually affixable, as they are accessible and tangible for one another even before they explicitly and concretely react to another (such as through editing) (Deleuze 2013a: 97–101). The same can be said of the close-ups in soap operas, which constitute a central tool of the form. They express not so much the emotions of the people represented as the fundamental tangibility of the images through other images—that is, their plasticity as a formational medium.

Second, the close-ups in soap operas also refer to other preceding or succeeding images, which not only affix and affect but also concretely activate or cause them (or which they activate or cause). Everything in a soap opera has a cause and effect, which can be seen at the macroscopic level (in the relationship between the past and the future) as well as the microscopic level (in the interlinking of shots). The entire series is actually not (yet) a causal chain but rather a continuation of impulses, which result from the past and have an effect in the future and which could be shown in reverse or be replenished or reinforced through new impulses from outside. The soap opera thus condenses an affective logic into a causal logic by initiating the reshaping of the former through the latter, although it does not see this process through to completion (Engell 2012).

## Cliffhangers

A frozen close-up of a (usually female) face is often used at the end of an episode, and these images are associated with a characteristic feature of the continuing series known as the cliffhanger (Fröhlich 2015: 445–50). In its classic format, a cliffhanger is the final image of an episode that stops in the middle of a gesture or an edited sequence, such as when a panning shot begins but is not completed, when there is a shot whose reverse shot is left out, or when the storyline is simply suspended. The continuation of the impulse does not occur and is postponed to the next episode, which promises to conclude what has already begun. In the cliffhanger, therefore, not only is the viewer unaware of what has affected the face shown on the screen (such as when a reverse shot is left out) but the final image of the episode that is coming to a close is also already affected by the next episode precisely because the subsequent image does not appear. The cliffhanger thus extends beyond itself through this affect-image (in Deleuze's sense), which enables the emulsion of time.

Psychologically, the cliffhanger is based on the "Zeigarnik Effect." In her Gestalt psychological studies in 1928, Bljuma Zeigarnik was able to demonstrate that ongoing or interrupted actions, which are in a sense incoherent yet capable of being coherent (such as the open orders a waiter must keep in mind), are remembered longer and more intensively than completed actions (such as the orders that have already been filled) (Zeigarnik 1927). The basic assumption of Gestalt psychology, which we also already encountered earlier in connection with Dewey's concept of experience, is that open and closed formation processes can be opposed to one another (Dewey 2008). Zeigarnik also accepts this assumption, although she does not accept the idea that perception tends to prefer closed forms; instead, she shows that interruption is a productive and generative principle in that it boosts memory. Contemporary continuing series make even more extensive use of this principle, as cliffhangers appear not only at the end of the episodes of the series as a whole but also at the end of sequences within the episodes, which are dedicated to one of the three (to seven) storylines—particularly those that neither begin nor end in the episode but rather continue indefinitely.

Lastly, there are also microscopic cliffhangers that provide a brief delay or pause within an ongoing sequence, charge its continuation with suspense, and thematize the dependence of the individual shots to the other shots (Fröhlich 2015). In the sense of the "Zeigarnik Effect," this means that the coherence and closure of the parts of the story are also increasingly interrupted. This interruption is still usually (though not always) schematic, yet every cliffhanger raises the question of how the storyline could continue, and the course of the series pursues the repeated repetition of this question, which is always answered in a different way. The subject of the soap opera is its own continuation as either the content-related negotiation over family, genealogy, and reproduction or the aesthetic/artistic process itself, and this thematization of temporal and generative coherence is—in the cliffhanger at least—linked to the interruption of coherence. In other words, the continuing series consists of the discontinuities through which new connections constantly emerge, and this endless process ensures its own continuation. It can thus be said that the continuing series is a form of different serialization, which functions not only as a cycle but also as a medium (in Cavell's sense).

## Episodes in Episodic Series

Something else seems to apply to episodic series, which consist of self-contained episodes that are broadcast weekly at fixed airtimes. Unlike the episodes of a continuing series, the episodes of an episodic series are not related to one another and do not create any conditions for one another. For viewers, this has the advantage that they can tune into the sequence of episodes at any time without missing anything that would be important for their understanding of the story. The most influential formats were the successful crime series from the era of live television mentioned earlier (*Man against Crime*; *Mr. District Attorney*; *Martin Kane, Private Eye*) and the Western series from the era of the "filmed series" (*Rawhide*, *Gunsmoke*, *Bonanza*, among many others) (Barnouw 1990: 195ff). It seems that the Western series of the 1950s likely provided the precise model on which Cavell based his evaluation of the series in general and of television as a whole.

In this case, changes do not continue from one episode to the next; rather, the storyline and structure are constrained by a strict formula and the need to provide closure, as the central conflict is always resolved by the end. The individual episodes also feature the same cast and settings, and in addition to close-ups the images are dominated by medium and long shots as well as establishing and panoramic shots, which are reasonably frequent despite the small size and limited resolution of the screen. Unlike the episodes of a continuing series, therefore, the episodes of an episodic series function as short and simple feature films.

Within the episodes, the passage of time is driven by the storyline (unlike in soap operas, where time is practically slowed down and feelings often take the place of actions); however, the individual episodes are not connected to one another through the continuous flow of time or separated from one another through temporal jumps. Indeed, the temporal relationships between them are not defined at all. Earlier episodes do not lay the groundwork for later episodes, and later episodes never refer back to earlier ones, which makes them completely inconsequential to one another. There are also no cliffhangers, as this would make no sense. In other words, the prime-time episodic series does not deal with its own seriality and even denies its existence. Due to the lack of change between episodes, it actually seems to function cyclically by converting the progression of time into a serial structure that is identical and spatial, which is precisely how Cavell interpreted television as a whole.

The fact that this involves Western series, however, makes it particularly interesting to look more closely at Cavell's concepts of genre, which he applied to the series itself. The Western series represents the combination of a film genre and televisual seriality. Several of these early "filmed series" were also based on Western films, such as *Broken Arrow* and *Colt .45*, and this was a kind of secondary use for the producing film studios. Cavell never specifically commented on Western films as a genre, but there seems little doubt that this genre functions as a medium in Cavell's sense, as it constantly debates the genre itself and this is precisely how the genre continues. However, the Western seems to lose this ability as a television series.

What is true of the series form is also true of their narrative content. David Buxton has convincingly shown that the Western series (like other prime-time episodic series of the 1950s and 1960s, such as crime or science-fiction series) negotiates the core of human nature and behavior (Buxton 1990). The central issues include our origin (we have spoken here of genealogy) and the standards of our behavior. Ideologically, according to Buxton, the episodic series of the 1950s and 1960s served to position a community that was either closed or open to the outside as the natural form of coexistence. It especially served to promote the economic doctrine of the "New Deal" and the new consumer society, which was also thought to be in accordance with human nature (Buxton 1990: 21–71). Many of the episodes of *Bonanza*, for example, actually deal with established and market-dominating businesses (ranches, stores, hotels, etc.) that are prevented from maintaining their position by illegitimate means and thereby defeating the emerging competition from within (and also often from outside) the community. It always goes against the tendency toward monopolization (such as the monopolization of water) and promotes pluralization and equal opportunity through competition.

In addition, however, it is surprising to what extent the Western series is dominated by an entirely different setting—namely, that of the family. The constellations of characters are defined entirely by familial relationships between brothers, fathers and sons, mothers and sons, as well as fathers and daughters. There are also distant relatives, who occasionally appear and then disappear again. Even the characters who are absent are connected by family ties. On *Bonanza*, for example, Ben Cartwright's three sons come from his three dead wives, and his last wife even lies buried on the "Ponderosa" ranch. The central location, where everything always converges, is also the family dinner table, just like in the family series. However, the protagonists are largely detached from their origins (even though they must always recover them and then become detached from them again), and they do not procreate.

The episodes only deal with change through the heroes' efforts to integrate whatever is new and strange, which usually comes from outside and is rejected by the rest of the community, so that nothing ever changes. In series in which the heroes are wandering adventurers who have no fixed location but instead come to a different place as outsiders in each episode (such as *Trackdown*, *Rawhide*, *Maverick*, as well as the outer space series *Star Trek*), the new often turns out to be something that was already previously known.

## Memory

We can now describe more precisely how both of these series function as the operative memory of television, which by itself cannot be recorded. This formulation is based on the theory that memory is not necessarily the storage of something from the past, such as in a repository, archive, or depot; rather, there is also another kind of memory, which is constantly in operation and in motion in the present. Heinz von Foerster refers to this as "memory without record," Aleida Aßmann refers to it as "functional memory," and Elena Esposito refers to it as "operative memory"—a term borrowed from

Niklas Luhmann (Foerster 1985: 133–75; Assmann 2011; Esposito 2002). The underlying operation is the distinction between two other operations—namely, remembering and forgetting. To remember is to treat something that occurs or that one comes across as if it had already occurred or been encountered—that is, as if it were already known—and to forget is to treat something as if it were entirely new (Esposito 2002: 24ff). Operative memory thus functions like a gatekeeper or switch. This distinction can be recognized through its effects. When I meet someone whom I have never seen before, for example, I behave differently than when I meet an old acquaintance. For operative memory, the actual facts are completely irrelevant and the true state of affairs may be unknown; the only thing that matters is the tentative choice between remembering (treating a person as if she were familiar) and forgetting (treating a person as if she were unfamiliar), which is based not on a memory of previous experiences but rather solely on present communication signals.

The basic operation of operative memory is thus a switching process, as it involves choosing between remembering or forgetting; it can also involve switching from one to the other. Elena Esposito argues that television has a tremendous impact on the social practice of memory in modern society because its news coverage, sports broadcasts, and weather reports constantly distinguish the already known (or redundant) from the new (or information), which ensures that news reports from the previous day become obsolete and can be assumed to be known. It simultaneously produces both the actuality of the unknown (the present) and the assumption of the known (the past) (Luhmann 2000: 20, 33, 37f).

The fictional episodic series provides a blatant example of how television not only performs this switching between remembering and forgetting but also recursively reminds us of this process while it is being performed. Remembering and forgetting are thus observed (and remembered or forgotten) in the episodic series, as every switch between remembering and forgetting in a *series* is an event that can itself be remembered or forgotten through the *series*. It is important that these distinctions are simultaneously operative at one and the same level (the latter, for example, is not performed from a higher vantage point). They merely take place in different temporal rhythms and scales—namely, first in the rhythm of the individual episodes and second in the rhythm of the series.

First, the episodic series goes along with the traditional assumption that memory—even operative memory—can only be attributed to human subjects, and it thus brings the characters into play as carriers of memory. Memory is clearly privileged within the self-contained storylines of the individual episodes, as the main characters already know one another and they are introduced neither to us nor to one another. They are also familiar with the setting of the story and at least a few of the secondary characters, and they know what they have to do, as they develop fixed behavioral patterns. Even when something new is added (such as a newly discovered planet, a new case, and a stranger), it is made familiar and thus committed to memory over the course of the episode. Even the elimination of an actor (such as Barbara Bel Geddes in *Dallas* or Diana Rigg in *The Avengers*) and also occasionally a character (such as Adam in *Bonanza* or Kookie in *77 Sunset Strip*) remains completely unnoticed and inconsequential for the other characters within the diegetic universe of the episode. This transformation of the unknown into the known and thus the incorporation of the present into the past constitutes the basic mode of the episodic series.

Something else applies, however, when we switch to the rhythm of the series and the sequence of episodes. The characters in an episodic series, such as *Bonanza* as well as *Star Trek*, *The FBI*, or *The Untouchables*, have no stored memory and accumulate no experience from one episode to the next. They thus experience the same adventure from week to week (at least structurally) without any reference to earlier adventures. They are also incapable of learning or remembering anything, as their memory capacity within the individual episodes is erased from one episode to the next. For each event they must decide once again whether something familiar or unfamiliar is happening, and by reading their behavior we are able to discern that they have decided to treat the already known and redundant—namely, the standardized characters and formulaic plots that they encounter—as always operatively new. In other words, they typically decide to treat the various characters and events that they encounter as new, even though these characters and events represent well-known types that they have already encountered dozens of times. The series consequently possesses its own memory, and the sequence of episodes can be rearranged in virtually any order (unlike the sequences within the episodes themselves). A typical example is the first episode of *Star Trek*, in which the hero, Captain Kirk, encounters a woman with whom he previously had an affair without initially recognizing her, as a foreign planet erases his memories (i.e., produces operative forgetting). Memory here transcends the individual brain or consciousness (in this case, Captain Kirk's) and is distributed over a broader configuration.

## Borrowed Memory

Through this configuration the series already provides reading instructions for its further continuation, as the same thing that happens to Captain Kirk upon arriving on the foreign planet also applies to viewers upon encountering television—namely, they must also forget that they are watching structurally similar and often virtually identical episodes every week. They do this for aesthetic reasons and for the sake of aesthetic pleasure; indeed, Kierkegaard already represented forgetting as a possible strategy of aestheticization in the face of a boring and monotonous lifeworld (Kierkegaard 1942; Engell 1987). A series is thus by no means simply the sum or sequence of its episodes; rather, it is a unique entity with its own memory. While the individual episodes conform to the operation of remembering, the basic element of the series is not its extension across episodes but rather the operation of forgetting. In other words, the memory operations of the episode and the series are directly opposed to one another, and they articulate and permeate one another through this opposition. The juxtaposition and interpenetration of these opposing memory operations, which must be performed simultaneously, reflect the function of serial memory.

Something else applies when we turn from the rhythm of the series to that of the program schedule as a whole, which is beyond the timeframe of the series characters. The operation of remembering is once again evoked through the allocation of a cyclically recurring airtime, such as Tuesdays at 8:15 p.m., as operative memory identifies each individual Tuesday evening as part of a longer series of similar evenings. In other words, viewers are prompted to switch from the operation of remembering within an episode to the operation of forgetting within the series and then back to the operation of remembering within the schedule. The operative memory of television is thus distributed across technology, fiction, aesthetics, temporal order, and biology, and it must to some extent use, borrow, control, and absorb the memories of viewers (Voß 2013). The switching from remembering to forgetting, and vice versa, is not up to the discretion of the viewers; rather, it arises from a complex constellation of images, characters, dates, and times, which generate this discretion through remembering and forgetting. This reveals the possibility that it is not necessarily the producers or viewers of television who switch the image; rather, the event on the screen also activates or constitutes a switching process—namely, between remembering and forgetting.

This switching, distributing, controlling, and using of memory also applies to the continuing series, although in this case the process is inverted. Here, the positions of the individual episodes in a continuing series are by no means arbitrarily interchangeable; rather, every episode has a definite position in relation to its predecessor and successor. The same also applies to the diegetic world. Just as the episodic series is about forgetting, the continuing series is initially about remembering—that is, treating something as already known or at least building on something that is already known. This is why the episodes often begin with a wrap-up of what happened in the preceding episodes. The characters in a soap opera also gain experience from one episode to the next, which allows them to learn and change, and they constantly refer to the past—that is, they react to new events as if they had already occurred or their origins in the past could be recalled. They greet new arrivals like old acquaintances, for example, so that viewers learn something about the past that has not yet been revealed; and they look back at the most tragic events in light of the endless chain of similar events that are all part of life.

Unlike an episodic series, the setting of a continuous series also changes. Families fall apart, companies go bankrupt, and characters leave (for narratively motivated reasons) or come back from the dead (even if an entire season must be retroactively dismissed as a dream, as in the case of Bobby Ewing). Conversely, however, the individual episodes are dominated by forgetting. The characters are never calm or indifferent, for example, as they are always newly affected by the same things. Every wedding and funeral seem like the first, every crisis arouses the same strong emotions, and every recurrence seems like the first time. The continuing series is thus also characterized by a switch between the operation of the individual episodes (forgetting) and that of the series as a whole (remembering), which precisely prefigures the operations of the viewers. Particularly in the soap opera and its derivatives, the operation of remembering in the rhythm of the series is essential, as it allows viewers to navigate the multitude of characters and events and it strengthens their attachment to the continuing narrative. The operation of forgetting in the rhythm of the episode is equally as important, however, as it allows the repeated events to have the same emotional weight for the viewers as they have for the characters, such as the various attacks on J. R. Ewing on *Dallas*.

## Secret Agent Series

The episodic series of the 1950s comes very close to Cavell's analysis of the television series in general, as it emphasizes the annihilation of time and the reduction of the new to the known. There may still be some fundamental doubts concerning his argument, however, such as his implicit assumption that whatever recurs is essential and that whatever varies is incidental. Why is this necessarily the case? It is interesting, in this regard, that another type of episodic series emerged in the mid-1960s—namely, the secret agent series.

Some successful examples include *The Avengers*, *Mission: Impossible*, *The Persuaders*, *I Spy*, *The Man from U.N.C.L.E.*, and *Department S*. The detective series *77 Sunset Strip* was also an important precursor, and *Miami Vice* is perhaps an even more important later representative. The secret agent series retained the basic principle of the episodic series, as self-contained and stand-alone episodes were broadcast every week, there was no definable temporal relationship between each episode and its predecessor and successor, and there were no multistrand storylines or cliffhangers. The basic form of the individual episode was nevertheless completely altered, as it acquired serial characteristics and was aligned with forgetting and the production of difference (Engell 2011: 115–33).

What all secret agent series have in common is that they are concerned not with the essential, which remains constant, but rather with the accidental, which varies (Buxton 1990: 140–60). More specifically, it becomes impossible to distinguish between them. This starts with the heroes of the secret agent series, who are constantly playing games. They are neither genuine nor honest; rather, they are always adapting, disguising themselves, and sneaking around. Their ability to equip themselves overrides all questions concerning their character, and the objective of their mission is always to deceive and outwit their opponents without becoming recognizable. On *Miami Vice*, for example, the heroes Crockett and Tubbs are at the same time the drug dealers Cooper and Burnett, and in several episodes neither we nor they can tell precisely who they are. The central objects of the secret agent series are therefore disguises and clothes, such as uniforms, ball gowns, sportswear, professional clothing of all kinds, as well as accessories like monocles and medals, jewelry, and glasses. The use of deceptively similar rubber masks is particularly striking, especially in *Mission: Impossible* and *Department S*, and the ultimate mask is the one that conceals the same face behind it. The focus is not on the people wearing the disguises but rather on the accessories themselves, which are always new.

Secret agents have this facility with disguises because they initially present themselves and make themselves appear; they only exist at all as something that has already been presented. Even when undisguised, they typically present themselves in extremely fashion-conscious outfits (such as the characters of Emma Peel and her partner John Steed in *The Avengers*). Crockett and Tubbs were similarly famous for their Armani suits and Ferrari sports cars in *Miami Vice*. Outside of her activities as a secret agent, the character of Cinnamon Carter in *Mission: Impossible* (played by Barbara Bain) was a famous fashion model (just like the actress herself), and she specialized in the making and wearing of completely changeable clothing. The identity of the character thus arises from her mutability, her processual identity, and her ability to change into any style. What especially distinguishes secret agents from their opponents is that the latter are badly dressed—that is, they have no taste or their taste has simply gone out of fashion (Buxton 1990: 74ff). Furthermore, the circumstances in which they receive their orders are entirely unclear, as they do not support a particular nation, ideology, or economic interest. Being a secret agent is, for them, a game in which the better player wins, and the better player is the one with the better-fitting clothing and the perfect way of wearing them.

The foundation of the secret agent series takes a special turn in the case of *Miami Vice*, as the relationship between stable subject and external appearance is extended to the relationship between narrative content and visual aesthetics. That is, a fixed story is no longer converted into and clothed in suitable images, which then recount the story; rather, attractive images are arranged in a sequence according to aesthetic criteria, such as color, background music or rhythmic acceleration, and delay effects, as well as internal and external relations. The images thus do not illustrate but rather generate the plot. This can also be observed in early secret agent series, as they do not present but rather produce an exciting plot.

## Serial Secret Agents

A second and closely related ability is technical performance—that is, the ability to direct and advance an operation using technical tools (Beil et al. 2016: 44–9). In addition to their mutability and representational competence, secret agents are also skilled in the handling of technical and to some extent fictional devices. New components are used in each episode, such as ingenious rope hoists, miniature bombs, tracking devices, rare poisons, fantastic burglary tools, concealed harpoons, zero gravity boots, listening and photographing devices, communications technologies, and bizarre cars and planes. We will come back to the fictional nature of these devices. *Miami Vice* particularly focuses on cars, guns, and surveillance equipment, and the secret agents are always linked to, dependent on, and in control of their apparatuses, which demand all of their attention.

Thirdly, coordination techniques and abilities are also particularly important (Engell 2013: 50f), as secret agents always have an elaborate plan, according to which everyone must perform specific and coordinated actions at specific points in time. Clocks and clocklike tools are therefore particularly important, and the development of the secret agent series parallels the development of communications technologies. The actions of each team member are directly related to those of the other members, although the connections between them may only be apparent from their effects. Over the course of the episode, these disconnected individual actions give rise to a functional sequence. We are thus faced with a plan, which we do not know, and tendentially a blind algorithm, which the secret agents also cannot know as long as they are following their instructions. In *Miami Vice* this principle extends to the entire narrative. Shots and sequences are sometimes incorporated without any reference to narrative logic. Chase sequences, for example, might not move the storyline of an episode forward but instead be incorporated for purely aesthetic reasons, such as to accelerate the flow of images. Something similar also applies to the alternation between day and night sequences, which is not rooted in anything other than the process of switching itself. Switching from day to night thus aesthetically foregrounds the very nature of television as a switch image.

Fourthly and finally, however, secret agents also possess the ability to improvise in case something unplanned or unforeseen occurs, which is always the case (Engell 2013: 56). No matter how much they may otherwise act as mere instruments in the hands of someone else, they immediately develop surprising and creative solutions that deviate from the script. The production of an illusion (it is always about deceiving their opponents) through transformation, adaptation, and improvisation thus unfolds thematically on four levels: representational competence, technical skill, coordination ability, and creativity. A script or blueprint of how everything is supposed to go only exists for each individual episode; it arises from the specific context of the case, and it only works in the end because it counts on deviations. Secret agents in general are characterized by the fact that they are not simply passive instruments in the hands of their employers; nor do they possess the classical agency of the strong Western subject. We will come back to this elsewhere (Gell 1998).

In short, the secret agent series negotiates the relationships between constancy and change, formula and variation, essence and accident, and substance and appearance from the reverse perspective by emphasizing exteriority and mutability. This negotiation may be conducted in a similar way in the weekly self-contained episodes, yet each time it subverts the expected formula once again. The difference between identical and different serialization—or between identity and difference, which is negotiated in relation to these serial types—is thus absorbed into the episodes and even into the main characters, as the episodes and characters also function like a series. In other words, seriality becomes recursive in the secret agent series, and it even gives rise to serial secret agents. The episodes of *Miami Vice* also incorporate this treading-in-place (Auf-der-Stelle-Treten) as the recursion of the episodic principle. In many cases, for example, the arrested perpetrators (particularly when they are big bosses) are released in the end at the behest of higher powers, or they escape due to intentional negligence, or others have already taken their place. The entire investigation and mission were pointless, and everything starts over again.

## The Third Series

The secret agent series is thus a variant of the episodic series that undermines the identification of the recursive with the essential, which challenges the distinction between identical serialization, which functions as a "series as cycle," and different serialization, which we could call a "series as medium" in Cavell's sense. Equally as paradoxical with regard to the idea of the series as the operative memory of television becomes the distinction between remembering, which is related to the formation of the identical and redundant in the episodes, and forgetting, which is related to the formation of difference and information in the series. Television is not only subject to both of these forms of serialization, but it also reflects them in the *series* in that it connects, weaves, contours them to each other and has them refract each other. This discovery once again offers a new way of seeing the relationship between the identical and the different, which in television can apparently only exist in close connection to one another.

Gilles Deleuze takes a different approach than Cavell, as his philosophy of seriality is based on literary forms in which consecutive events constitute a serial sequence (Deleuze 2004: 44–50). He primarily focuses on Lewis Carroll's *Alice in Wonderland* and Edgar Allan Poe's *The Purloined Letter*—the latter particularly with regard to Jacques Lacan's famous interpretation of the story (Lacan 2006: 6–48). In each case, Deleuze hypothesizes that the basic form of the series is an infinite regress, which is logically inconsistent (he speaks here of a paradox), as each word is defined by another word that explains or duplicates the first, and this word is then defined once again by another word, and so on. It is not possible to refer to a television series as an infinite regress, as the episodes usually move forward and progress. Nevertheless, a series is infinite in and of itself, even though it actually stops at some point. In the case of soap operas, as we have seen, it is even possible to add new pasts (such as origins or backgrounds) that expand in both directions. This endless chain is a series, and Deleuze assumes that it can be divided into two different series or subseries. On the one hand, there is the succession of terms that each serve to define the preceding terms. Each episode of a television series, for example, spells out or varies another aspect of the formula. Deleuze refers to this as the subseries of signifiers. On the other hand, there is the succession of terms that are each about their definition or variation, and Deleuze refers to this as the subseries of signifieds. The signifiers constantly change from one term to the next, while the signifieds remain (at first) relatively stable. This obviously involves the same terms, which function in both subseries at the same time depending on the perspective from which they are viewed—that is, in complete heterogeneity and simultaneity—and which thus constitute the series as a whole (Deleuze 2004: 44).

Deleuze's series cannot even be defined as a form of different serialization due to the lack of even the slightest comparability between the subseries of which it is composed. It also cannot be compared to *catastrophes* in news coverage, which are associated with the background noise of continuous *information* through the mediated layer of the *crisis*, as we saw above with Mary Ann Doane (Doane 1990). Unlike catastrophes, which arise from the same event space as information, the events of the second subseries come from an entirely different space and never occur in regular, identically serial sequences. Rather, both subseries are accompanied by a constant deferral, and they transform one another in that "[t]here is thus a double sliding of one series over or under the other, which constitutes both, in a perpetual disequilibrium vis-à-vis each other" (Deleuze 2004: 47). An obvious example of this can be seen in *The Invaders*, in which new characters constantly appear (besides the main character, architect David Vincent) and turn out to be invaders who literally come from another space (i.e., they are extraterrestrials). Their appearance is indistinguishably similar to that of humans, yet they can nevertheless be recognized by two specific characteristics: their little fingers cannot touch their other fingers and their wounds produce red dust instead of blood. There is thus a series of humans and a series of extraterrestrials, and each human is a signifier that embodies or represents an extraterrestrial as its signified.

The key feature of this concept of the series in comparison to others is that there is a distinction between the (relatively) constant and the (comparatively) mutable. However, it is impossible to determine in advance whether something will come into play as a constant or a variant. One can practically switch between them. What can be done with a series of words, concepts, things, or identities can also be done with a series of sentences and their meanings and even with a series of "events" (Deleuze) and things or thing-states (Dingzuständen) in the physical world. The series of words or concepts takes place on the surface of language, the series of sentences or meanings takes place within language, and the series of events or things takes place outside of language (Deleuze 2004: 45).

In order to think further about the transferability of this philosophical concept of the series to television, it is possible to say that it involves a series of images as optical surfaces, a series of shots and sequences as narrative units, and finally a series of (fictional) events and characters (Fahle 2011). All three of these levels are serialized, as they can each be divided into two subseries. What is astonishing about this model of serialization is that the same elements (images, narrative segments, diegesis) function on both levels and belong to both subseries depending on the perspective from which they are viewed. Both of these subseries are thus formed at the same time from the same events or statements, and the simultaneity of these two successions ensures the cohesion of the series as a whole. In order to express this in terms of the switch image, it could be said that the series (as a whole) constantly switches back and forth between the subseries (of which it is composed) or that viewers are constantly prompted to shift from one of these subseries to the other and thus from the series itself. Every episode of a television series is at the same time a repetition and a variation of a formula.

## The Series as Discontinuum

Besides switching, there are two different operations that ensure the cohesion of these subseries—that is, the subseries of signifiers and the subseries of signifieds. The first is the operation of sameness or similarity, in which events or objects are connected to one another or even have the same function on both sides. This operation can also take different forms, such as that of successive continuation (in which both subseries together form a sequence of events, like in the continuing series where every episode functions at the same time in the series of predecessors as well as the series of successors). However, individual episodes can also form such a series. *The Invaders*, for example, consists of a series of attempts on the part of the hero to escape from extraterrestrials and seek shelter with authorities, supervisors, or protectors, whose unmasking as extraterrestrials leads to another escape. Cohesion is also ensured by the identity of the people acting in both subseries. For example, an episodic series always has a fixed cast (such as Kirk, Uhura, and Spock in *Star Trek*; Ben, Adam, Hoss, and Little Joe in *Bonanza*, or again David Vincent in *The Invaders*), but each character in the cast is at the same time both a stereotype and a variation. Serial cohesion is also ensured by the similarity of situations (such as the unmasking of extraterrestrials in *The Invaders* or the evening meal in *Bonanza*) and settings (such as the repeated and standardized shots of the "Ponderosa" ranch and Virginia City in *Bonanza*, which establish serial continuity).

Surprisingly (and in contrast to Cavell), the constants or similarities that ensure cohesion are precisely not essential to the series. As Deleuze emphasized, the essence of the series only comes to light when the (small or large) differences between the elements outbalance their similarities—that is, when serial cohesion is formed by the operation of differentiation (Deleuze 2004: 46f). This is precisely why it is potentially fruitful to think about the series in this way. Unlike almost everywhere else, the serial is seen here not as formulaic and repetitive but rather as discontinuous. As an example, Deleuze refers to the case in which two completely different stories (about the same elements) make it possible for the characters to develop undefined and unstable identities. This narrative diversity and character instability are not only the case but also the subject of the soap opera, and the same applies to episodic secret agent series like *The Avengers, Department S*, and later *Miami Vice*, whose investigators also have unstable identities. The decisive factor is that the parts of both subseries shift in relation to one another, which Deleuze refers to as "double sliding" (Deleuze 2004: 47).

A rudimentary form of this can already occur in the classical episodic series. The two main settings in *Bonanza*, for example, do not constitute a single recurring identity; rather, they complement, correlate, and define one another as the other of the other. What they mean for one another (threat or help, competition or partnership, mistake or correction, etc.) only becomes apparent over the course of the episode. Both subseries define one another in a similar way, as they complement one another yet nevertheless vary. There is therefore no constant formula in the series that could stabilize the relationship between both subseries. In addition to a number of other standard recurring settings in *Dallas*, for example, there is also the "Cattlemen's Club" and the "Oil Baron's Club." Both of these settings define and refer to one another (ex negativo, but that makes no difference); however, they also each refer to one of the Ewing family's spaces—namely, Southfork Ranch and the office building in which Ewing Oil resides. Whenever it appears, the "Cattlemen's Club" can always be read as either the opposite of the Southfork Ranch or as the counterpart to the "Oil Baron's Club." In addition, the differences between these spaces also refer to the differences between the two brothers, Bobby and J. R., even though both of these characters can otherwise be found in both of these spaces. The series of views of all these spaces thus constitutes a double series, in which each space functions as both the shown space and the opposite or equivalent of another shown space—that is, as a space that defines another space either ex negativo or through continuation.

The disguises in *Mission: Impossible* do something similar, as every disguise either conceals (defines by its opposite) or represents (defines by its equivalent) another disguise. A disguise is always something visible that is superimposed over something invisible, but in the next moment what was previously invisible can be made visible only to conceal or represent another invisibility. In *Miami Vice* this would be the series constituted by the colors (white, pink, apricot, turquoise, black), each of which shows something (such as the colored objects) and means something (such as a style). These colors thus function in both the purely differential subseries of signifiers and the subseries of intended meanings, but they function in these subseries by means of the same images.

## The Series of Reflections

It is also important that the subseries of signifiers always produces a surplus with regard to the subseries of signifieds. This is easy to verify in television, particularly when one thinks of the previously mentioned example of *Miami Vice* and its visual excess. At the level of signifiers, this surplus simply consists in the present (and always temporary) visibility of the images or rather the places, people, events, and objects that they depict. When a character hides beneath or behind tricks and deceptions, for example, then all that can be seen is the current disguise. Another disguise may have been seen earlier or will soon be seen again, but right now it is only virtually and invisibly present. Deleuze also assumes that this surplus is expressed through an asymmetrical presence. The signifiers are actually supplements wherever they appear, while the signifieds are precisely not to be found in their place. This is obvious for secret agents, as they do not belong in the place where they are found— namely, the world of their opponents, where they must be disguised—and they can thus be understood as an excess or surplus. They also constitute a series in Deleuze's sense:

> It has the property of being always displaced in relation to itself. If the terms of each series are relatively displaced, *in relation to one* another, it is primarily because they have in themselves an *absolute* place; but this absolute place is always determined by the terms' distance from this element which is always displaced, in the two series, *in relation to itself.* (Deleuze 2004: 48)

They are not there, where they are, and they are never found at their own place, if they have such a place at all. They are thus "paradoxical instances," which once again mirror both the subseries of which the series itself is composed—once as a surplus and once as a lack. In the subseries of signifiers they are "mobile empty places," as they have shells or disguises but not bodies, and in the subseries of signifieds they are "occupants without a place," as they occupy bodies but not specific locations (Deleuze 2004: 47).

The starship "Enterprise" can be understood as such a mobile empty place, as it has no place of its own, yet it can nevertheless be found everywhere and is in this sense excessive. Something similar can be said about the characters in *Rawhide* or *The Fugitive*. The same even applies to this world—that is, the world of television reception or the "real" world of the viewers. Characters always belong not only to the diegesis but also to this world, as Horton and Wohl famously pointed out and Ien Ang confirmed using the example of *Dallas* (Horton and Wohl 1956; Ang 1993). They never appear or become visible in this world, yet they nevertheless have a presence, which can exceed that of real family members and in relation to which their appearance on the screen can only be an explanation or illustration. Both subseries are successive within themselves and synchronous between each other. They can thus be conceived as "coalescent"—a concept that Deleuze uses elsewhere and that we will later take up once again to describe the switch image (Deleuze 2013b: 82f).

If we claimed at the beginning in a perhaps somewhat unmotivated way that a series is a serial assemblage or sequence only when it is aware of its own seriality, refers to it, and thereby advances itself, then "paradoxical instances," characters who are not self-identical with themselves, and mobile empty places are moments when the series reflects on itself in that both of the subseries of which it is composed mirror one another: continuation follows.

# References

Abramson, Albert. 1974. *Electronic Motion Pictures*. New York: Arno Press.

Anders, Günter. 1956. *Die Antiquiertheit des Menschen, vol. 1: Über die Seele im Zeitalter der zweiten industriellen Revolution*. München: Beck.

Ang, Ien. 1993. *Watching Dallas: Soap Opera and the Melodramatic Imagination*. London: Routledge.

Assmann, Aleida. 2011. *Cultural Memory and Western Civilization: Functions, Media, Archives*. Cambridge: Cambridge University Press.

Barnouw, Erik. 1990. *Tube of Plenty: The Evolution of American Television*. Oxford: Oxford University Press.

Beil, Benjamin, Lorenz Engell, Dominik Mader, Jens Schröter, Herbert Schwaab, and Daniela Wentz. 2016. *Die Fernsehserie als Agent des Wandels*. Münster: Lit.

Bourdieu, Pierre. 1984. *Distinction: A Social Critique of the Judgement of Taste*. London: Routledge.

Buxton, David. 1990. *From "The Avengers" to "Miami Vice": Form and Ideology in Television Series*. Manchester: University Manchester Press.

Cantor, Muriel, and Suzanne Pingree. 1983. *The Soap Opera*. New York: Sage.

Cavell, Stanley. 1982. "The Fact of Television." *Daedalus* 111, no. 4: 75–96.
Deleuze, Gilles. 1994. *Difference and Repetition*. New York: Columbia University Press.
Deleuze, Gilles. 2004. *The Logic of Sense*. New York: Continuum.
Deleuze, Gilles. 2013a. *Cinema I: The Movement-Image*. London: Bloomsbury Academic.
Deleuze, Gilles. 2013b. *Cinema II: The Time-Image*. London: Bloomsbury Academic.
Dewey, John. 2008. "Art as Experience." In: John Dewey. *The Collected Works of John Dewey, 1882–1953. The Later Works, 1925–1953, Vol. 10: 1934*, ed. by Jo Ann Boydston. Carbondale: Southern Illinois University Press.
Doane, Mary Ann. 1990. "Information, Crisis, Catastrophe." In: *Logics of Television: Essays in Cultural Criticism*, ed. by Patricia Mellencamp, pp. 222–39. Bloomington: Indiana University Press.
Engell, Lorenz. 1987. "Wechselwirtschaft und vertauschte Ansprachen." *Tumult Zeitschrift für Verkehrswissenschaft* 11: 102–15.
Engell, Lorenz. 2000. *Ausfahrt nach Babylon. Essais und Vorträge zur Kritik der Medienkultur*. Weimar: VDG.
Engell, Lorenz. 2011. "Erinnern/Vergessen. Serien als operatives Gedächtnis des Fernsehens." In: *Serielle Formen. Von den frühen Film-Serials zu aktuellen Quality-TV-und Online-Serien*, ed. by Robert Blanchet, Kristina Köhler, Tereza Smid, and Julia Zutavern (Zürcher Filmstudien, Bd. 25), pp. 115–33. Marburg: Schüren.
Engell, Lorenz. 2012. "Folgen und Ursachen. Über Serialität und Kausalität." In: *Populäre Serialität: Narration—Evolution—Distinktion. Zum seriellen Erzählen seit dem 19. Jahrhundert*, ed. by Frank Kelleter, pp. 241–58. Bielefeld: transcript.
Engell, Lorenz. 2013. "Über den Agenten. Bemerkungen zu einer populären Figur der Dia-Medialität." In: *Paradoxalität des Medialen*, ed. by Jan-Henrik Möller, Jörg Sternagel, and Lenore Hipper, pp. 41–58. München: Fink.
Esposito, Elena. 2002. *Soziales Vergessen. Formen und Medien des Gedächtnisses der Gesellschaft*. Frankfurt/M.: Suhrkamp.
Fahle, Oliver. 2011. "Das Bild und das Sichtbare und das Serielle. Eine Bildtheorie des Fernsehens angesichts des Digitalen." In: *Blickregime und Dispositive audiovisueller Medien*, ed. by Nadja Elia-Borer, Samuel Sieber, and Georg Chgristoph Tholen, pp. 111–33. Bielefeld: Transcript.
Fahle, Oliver, and Lorenz Engell. 2005. "Einführung." In: *Philosophie des Fernsehens*, ed. by Oliver Fahle, and Lorenz Engell, pp. 7–19. München: Fink.
Foerster, Heinz von. 1985. *Sicht und Einsicht*. Braunschweig: Vieweg.
Fröhlich, Vincent. 2015. *Der Cliffhanger und die serielle Narration*. Bielefeld: Transcript.
Gell, Alfred. 1998. *Art and Agency: An Anthropological Theory*. Oxford: Clarendon.

Hickethier, Knut. 1998. *Geschichte des deutschen Fernsehens*. Stuttgart, Weimar: Metzler.
Horton, Donald, and Richard R. Wohl. 1956. "Mass Communication and Para-Social Interaction: Observations On Intimacy at a Distance." *Psychiatry* 19: 215–29.
Jenkins, Henry. 2006. *Convergence Culture: Where Old and New Media Collide*. New York: University of New York Press.
Kelleter, Frank, ed. 2015. *Populäre Serialität. Narration, Evolution, Distinktion. Zum seriellen Erzählen seit dem 19. Jahrhundert*. Bielefeld: Transcript.
Kierkegaard, Søren. 1942. *Repetition: An Essay in Experimental Psychology*. London: Oxford University Press.
Kittler, Friedrich. 1999. *Gramophone, Film, Typewriter*. Stanford: Stanford University Press.
Kluge, Alexander. 1985. *Der Angriff der Gegenwart auf die übrige Zeit*. Frankfurt/M.: Syndikat/EVA.
Koch, Gertrud, and Christiane Voß, eds. 2009. *Es ist, als ob . . . Fiktionalität in Philosophie, Film-und Medienwissenschaft*. München: Fink.
Lacan, Jacques. 2006. *Écrits. The First Complete Edition in English*. New York, London: W. W. Norton & Company.
Leibniz, Gottfried Wilhelm. 1863. *Mathematische Schriften. Initia Mathematica. Mathesis universalis, vol VII: Die mathematischen Abhandlungen*. Halle: Gerhardt.
Luhmann, Niklas. 1995. *Social Systems*. Stanford: Stanford University Press.
Luhmann, Niklas. 2000. *The Reality of Mass Media*. Cambridge: Polity Press.
Luhmann, Niklas. 2012. *Theory of Society. Volume I*. Stanford: Stanford University Press.
Maeder, Dominik. 2013. "Transmodalität transmedialer Expansion. Die TV Serie zwischen Fernsehen und Online-Medien." In: *Der Medienwandel der Serie*, ed. by Dominik Maeder, and Daniela Wentz (=Navigationen, 1/2013), pp. 105–26. Siegen: Universi.
Marschall, Rick. 1987. *The Golden Age of Television*. London: Bison.
Morton, Robert. 1997. *Worlds Without End: The Art and History of the Soap Opera*. New York: Abrams.
Mumford, Lewis. 2010. *Technics and Civilization*. Chicago: University of Chicago Press.
Peirce, Charles S. 1906. "Prolegomena to an Apology for Pragmaticism." *The Monist* 16: 492–546; auch in: (CP 4.537).
Spigel, Lynn. 1992. *Make Room for TV: Television and the Family Ideal in Postwar America*. Chicago: University of Chicago Press.
Voß, Christiane. 2013. *Der Leihkörper. Erkenntnis und Ästhetik der Illusion*. München: Fink.
Zeigarnik, Bljuma. 1927. "Das Behalten erledigter und unerledigter Handlungen." *Psychologische Forschung* 9: 1–85.
Zielinski, Siegfried. 1999. *Audiovisions: Cinema and Television as Entr'actes in History*. Amsterdam: Amsterdam University Press.

# 4

# Flow

As we have established, every switching process interrupts the signal and image flow of television and continues it in a different or similar way. It makes what came before distinguishable from what came after, and it thus distinguishes succession from copresence, and within the latter simultaneity from synchronicity. At a microscopic, technical level, switching processes articulate time in a way that is similar to Aristotle's concept of time as the calculation of movement. At a macroscopic, perceptible level, however, switching processes also make television programs distinguishable from one another, which results in program blocks. Switching also separates the individual sequences and shots from one another as units of meaning within programs, and it makes the episodes of a series distinguishable from one another, from the series as a whole (as viewed from outside the series), and from those of other series as well as other kinds of broadcasts, such as advertising, news, and sports. The switching of the invisible signal flow thus gives structure and meaning to the visible programs of television.

But what happens when the signal flow of television is not a flow at all but rather a chain of switching processes or operations that are constantly being interrupted? When the so-called flow of television already consists of discontinuity rather than continuity? When switching is unable to interrupt something because it is always already interrupted? When this discontinuous chain is designed such that the appearance of a signal or image does *not* predetermine the subsequent signal or image? When something on television is followed not by something specific or at least conditionally probable but rather by something more or less arbitrary? In this case the relationship between continuity and discontinuity is reversed, as the switching processes are no longer interventions that give structure and contour to a structureless flow. In fact, the exact opposite occurs, as the countless disconnected switching processes form a noncoherent, arhythmically structured chain of events, and a structureless continuity emerges as an effect of these incoherent switching processes. However, this continuity cannot be explained according to the principle of "order from noise," as it actually forms a coherent whole that has no order, structure, or meaning in a conventional sense (Holland 1998; Mersch 2013; von Foerster 1993: 269–81; 1949). This is precisely what happens in television at the level of the program sequence as a whole. To use Marshall McLuhan's famous phrase, one can say that television does not transmit a "message" as a structured unit of meaning but rather only a "massage" of the senses: the medium is the massage (McLuhan and Fiore 1967).

## Beyond Meaning

This overwriting of meaning through sensation or aisthesis was described by cultural theorist Raymond Williams using the concept of *flow*. This concept has since been much discussed, and his description has become a famous legend of television theory. After crossing the Atlantic by ship, still slightly woozy from the trip, he switched on the television in his hotel room in Miami (Williams 1992: 85f.). What he saw had very little in common with what he knew as television in Great Britain, as he was faced with a completely confusing, incomprehensible, and incoherent mess. Inconsistent fragments of different programs and genres from the repertoire of television appeared in rapid succession on his screen. They should have required a structured form of attention or reception that would allow the individual fragments to be distinguished from one another, just as viewers are normally able to distinguish between fictional and nonfictional formats on television. Here, however, the different program genres were condensed in such a quick succession that it was impossible for the (woozy) viewer to make these distinctions. Meaningful reception was entirely impossible.

We are familiar with this televisual practice, which has certainly accelerated since Williams' arrival in Miami in 1973: parts of feature films are interrupted by commercial breaks, which are in turn interrupted by breaking news reports, which are themselves distributed over several blocks; short previews are interspersed among these items, and fragmentary flashbacks or "recaps" remind viewers of what has already been seen; the beginning of a series episode is interrupted by the answers to questions from a quiz show and the announcement of the winners. Live broadcasts, recordings, and intermediate forms like "live on tape" jump wildly from one to the other. A return to any kind of main text is not recognizable. Every image is interrupted by other images, which are interrupted again by others. We already encountered something similar to this in our discussion of the beginnings of television programs, but Williams describes his experience in terms of a visual and above all semantic excess. All of the visual styles and markings of the different program genres as well as all of the meanings and references were completely scrambled. In the search for discursive consistency and stability, he thought that he saw characters from one film appear in another or characters from the advertisements appear in the films (Williams 1992: 85). This led to an "induction of meanings between programs" through contiguity and complexity, as they were closely juxtaposed and even interwoven (Wulff 1995: 22).

After some time, however, Williams began to grasp an entirely different effect, as the excess assumed a uniquely new form by creating the impression of a single, large, flowing continuity across all of the discontinuities between objects, contents, and genres. This new rhythm, to which Williams gradually adjusted, was like dancing or surfing on the *flow* of images. This surfing seemed to emerge from the chaos of switching and supplant it by following its own movement. Unlike Dewey's aesthetic experience, which Eco enacted in his television analysis, Williams' experience also apparently gave the impression that this rhythm was fundamentally infinite and incomplete (Eco 1989: 105–20; see also Chapter 2 in this volume). More particularly, it was not semantizable, as it was impossible to know what the entirety of the sequence was supposed to be about. Even though it was supposed to move toward its own still unknown meaning, such a meaning would obviously have nothing to do with the contents and meanings of the individual fragments. The operative, coherent totality, which is conveyed in every moment of the sequence, is no longer due to the individual elements, the programs, the links of the chain, or their interactions.

What is paramount with *flow* is a new interrelated activity that must simply be accepted as "television." It replaces the discrete transmission and reception of information or meaning, which is basically everything that Williams, like many other television theorists, had researched until then. In other words, the observation, pursuit, and understanding of something gives way to an objectless activity without intention or theme—a new form of coherence, which is pleasurable and to some extent intoxicating (Williams 1992: 88). This eventually gave Williams the idea that programs on American television are not programs at all in the sense of a meaningful arrangement of constituent elements. They also do not consist of elements that consist of other elements. The most important unit in American television is not the program, the scene, or the shot, but rather the *flow* of the continuous television evening as a whole, which emerges from the interruptions as well as from the interruptions of the interruptions yet is at the same time present as a whole in each of its individual moments. It arises from its divisions yet remains present as something undivided.

## Emergence and Immersion

In the *flow*, television stops functioning as discourse. For Williams, this does not mean that it is no longer capable of forming structures of meaning. This more far-reaching assumption was only later incorporated into television theory (Engell 1989). A clearly structured and meaningful arrangement is possible, and for Williams this was undoubtedly the rule (Williams 1992: 82f.). At the same time, however, the *flow* develops a second mode that diverges from the discursive. *Flow* happens, as it emerges from the basic noise of discontinuity and the destruction of discursivity, which it assumes and requires but does not actually cause. The term "emergence" refers to this kind of noncausal shift—an effect without an actual cause. We already used the concept of emergence in the previous chapter to describe the gradual formation of the series from live broadcasting, but it is actually a concept in systems theory that refers to the formation of a whole from separate parts, to which it nevertheless cannot be traced back—a phenomenon that is well known in physics, biology, and sociology (Iser 2013; Davidson 1980, 1984; Clayton 2006; Greve and Schnabel 2011). This applies, for example, to the emergence of a society, which is more and different than a large collection of individuals (Luhmann 1995: 22f.; Elias 2007; Durkheim 1966, 1953: 1–34). An organism is also emergent, as it cannot exist without its organs but is also not their sum; it produces them just as they produce it. The concept of emergence is also used, even by Williams, to describe the cultural and creative production of the new from the familiar (Williams 1977).

However, the sciences are mostly interested in the emergence of order, meaning, and cohesion at a "higher" level, such as the social order. Williams was also concerned with the phenomenon of emergence in popular culture, and he believed that it had a creative function. In this sense, the formation of a critical or minority interpretation of a product of popular culture that differs from a conventional, established interpretation is an emergent process. This is not the case with *flow*, however, as it does not interpret or mean anything, and it does not represent or produce any kind of order. *Flow* is not an ordering factor; rather, it is a sensory phenomenon that is free of any semantic meaning and does not operate at a "higher" level. The structured schedule of events is supposed to denote a higher level of complexity with respect to the individual programs, but *flow* does not function "above" the schedule; rather, the schedule transforms into *flow*.

If the *flow* emerges, however, then a complementary process involving the relationship between the image streams and the viewers occurs at the same time, and this process is *immersion*. Particularly in connection with aesthetics, immersion refers to the experience of an observing or participating subject sinking or being absorbed into an image world, from which the outside world is no longer perceptible. This immersion into a fictional environment can happen when watching a film, attending a play, or reading a book, but today the term is mostly used in connection with digital media of illusion and simulation (Voß 2008a,b: 69–86, 2009: 127–39; Grau 2003). It is easy to trace the experience of this immersive sinking using Williams' description of his own experience, as it involves tuning out other perceptions (outside of the darkened hotel room), experiencing excess (in relation to the usual units of meaning), and then being spellbound (by the *flow*).

According to Williams, what is crucial for the change between the traditional, discursively structured program sequence and *flow* is the disappearance or refunctioning of the intervals. In the structured program sequence, the intervals, pauses, and switches visibly and prominently separate the different programs or their internal elements from one another. They thus enable a transition from one closed semantic area to the next. The nature and degree of difference can vary, as the boundary between two episodes of the same series is very different from that between two episodes of different series. In the sequence of *flow*, however, intervals occur at any point within the program and its units of meaning. The same thing or something entirely incommensurable can be found on both sides of the transition, which does not reveal a third—the specific difference (*differentia specifica*) that could connect them as a unit of difference—and is thus no longer a kind of connection. Both of these divisions—those within units and those between units—are handled in the same way, so it is no longer possible to distinguish between switches within a program (such as between camera positions) and switches between programs. Separations between two episodes of the same series, two episodes of different series, two news reports, or a news report and an intervening advertisement effectively become the same. If the same intervals separate the episodes, series, reports, and programs, however, then it is no longer possible to distinguish between different levels of complexity. "Higher" and "lower" levels, such as episodes and series, reports and programs, or programs and schedules, become entangled with one another. This would also be a form of immersion between the image streams, although it would be unclear which stream was being absorbed and it would be impossible to describe them as merging, as we will see.

There is only one remaining level, on and in which emergent resonances form between the various interval rhythms. These resonances only exist as long as the image stream continues to feed them, which was already true of the television image and the signal stream. In this respect, *flow* is also an ontographic phenomenon of television. The intervals no longer separate or join anything, and they are thus actually no longer intervals; "the notion of interruption," Williams writes, "has become inadequate" (Williams 1992: 84; see also Engell 2000: 183–205). It would not be inadequate, however, to describe the interruption in a technical rather than semantic sense as a pure switching process, which is effective not in the sense of a meaning-generating articulation but rather as an audiovisual sensory stimulus, innervation, rhythm, and resonance. *Flow* is then not a cognitive phenomenon but rather an interaction between the technical apparatus and neurobiological aesthetics.

Williams always describes the emergence of *flow* as a deviation from the (for him) "normal" discursive television schedule, but it would be just as easy to approach it from the opposite direction by observing how it becomes the regular way of perceiving the schedule. Nevertheless, as Williams convincingly argues, *flow* begins to arise at the moment when there is no longer a single structured sequence of programs but rather multiple sequences. This idea is surprisingly familiar, as Gilles Deleuze also conceived of the organization of a paradoxical sensory effect of the serial as a deferral that extends between two or more incommensurable time periods, as we have seen (Deleuze 2004). Moreover, Deleuze's series is also an emergence phenomenon. On closer inspection, according to Williams, the linear and unidirectional program sequence disintegrates into two or more strands that intersect with but are not connected to one another, although he conceives of these strands in a very different way than Deleuze. For Deleuze, the basic model of the duality of the series was the sequence of signs, which breaks down into a chain of signifiers and a chain of signifieds. For Williams, however, it involves two sequences with different contents and genres—namely, the strand of the "actual" programs and that of the advertisements. The advertising is then not clearly relegated to the empty spaces provided for it, such as those between and within the programs; rather, it is integrated into the programs or program elements in a way that is largely transverse to their internal structure or rhythm and that follows its own formally measured time span. A further thing to bear in mind is that this second time series, unlike the first, does not progress, as the same commercial spots appear (within the chain of signifieds for Deleuze) again and again over the course of a programming day. A third series is then added, which is again completely transverse to both of the others—namely, the program previews and announcements. "And with the eventual unification of these two or three sequences, a new communication phenomenon has to be recognized" (Williams 1992: 84). That is precisely *flow*, which, according to Williams, can but does not need to occur against this background.

## Flow in Space

Williams can only read *flow* as a phenomenon of "unification" and thus of fusion. He conflates totality with unity rather than with diversity and heterogeneity. This is a conventional presupposition, which has also been read as an ideological bias. According to Jane Feuer, for example, there are *flow* effects that constitute only a part of the television experience, and it is a part that has historically been very limited (Feuer 1983: 12–21). This experience thus cannot be entirely subsumed under the concept of *flow*. A structured experience—Williams' "sequence as program"—remains at the same time completely possible. Williams himself also refutes the alleged indivisibility and unsegmentability of *flow*, as his analyses ultimately segment the televisual flow and thereby come to some relevant realizations. (Feuer's argument, though, overlooks Williams' serious doubts concerning his own method.) Moreover, Feuer assumes that *flow* has nothing to do with the "essence" of television itself, which is presumed to be technically contingent; rather, it is merely one of its historical manifestations. Flow is contingent on the aesthetics of television, and it is by no means necessary. Flow does not necessarily arise from the nature of television as a switch image, but the switchability of the television image is the precondition for flow, as it emerges from the sequence of switching processes. According to Feuer, however, it is possible to have television without switching, which would then only consist of long, uninterrupted shots (such as surveillance and weather cameras or the images sent from aquariums, intersections, and outer space) (Engell 2008: 299–322). A switchless form of "Bazinian" television (in the sense of the prohibition on montage in Bazin's film theory) would be entirely feasible and appropriate for the technology of television, such as the unedited, continuous, and uninterrupted coverage of sporting events, but it is never produced (this is of course a completely false conjecture, as the important details that television adds to sports would never be perceived in a continuous shot) (Bazin 2004: 75–82; see also Chapter 6 in this volume). According to Feuer, the reason for this is to be found not in an essential quality of television or a characteristic feature like *flow* but rather in ideological preferences.

She pursues these preferences in a sample analysis that examines the *flow* of the news program *Good Morning America* (Feuer 1983: 17–21). The program consists of an apparently uncontrolled flow-like mixture of the most varied themes, incorporates the most diverse types of images and image media, and connects countless places to one another through switching. According to Feuer, however, everything is held together not through a mysterious *flow* but rather through a deliberate strategy of integration, which is by no means related to format, content, or technologies but rather only to the form of address. The presence effect is due to a refined gaze strategy and a shot-reverse shot dramaturgy. Its focus is the anchorperson in the studio, over whose shoulders we see the faces of interview partners and foreign correspondents before the camera switches *directly* to their images and locations. What occurs here is therefore an entirely conventional (though intricate and expertly managed) form of *suture*—a "stitching" together of the real place where the viewer is located with imaginary places and external places that are also dependent on them—a visual strategy that is already familiar from film. This is supported by self-reflexive passages, such as when the members of a prominent family, dispersed across many residences, are interconnected to form a retrospectively "pseudo-live" simultaneity.

The *flow* arranged here thus takes place not in time but rather in space. In fact, Feuer eliminates the time factor completely, so *flow* is only a misunderstanding, as television is really based on space rather than time. The viewers are by no means led to heterogeneity, degrees of freedom, and temporal supertexts; rather, they merge with a large family in a vast, spatially dispersed, and reassembled home. According to Feuer, all of the contradictions and distortions are thereby lost. This again does not seem to be a very surprising insight; the earliest studies in the field of Cultural Studies already reached similar conclusions. On the other hand, it is extremely surprising that Feuer seems to sense this in the conclusion of the essay, as she assumes that if the public is preformatted through their integration into a spatial pseudo-flow, then any distinction in the hegemonic, minoritarian, and oppositional discourse, which is so valuable to Cultural Studies, loses its meaning. The formerly critical, enlightened observation that televisual discourse blurs any distinctions of race, class, and gender also becomes redundant and merely reinforces this criticized medial integration. Perhaps however, as Feuer says in an inimitable phrase, "this manner of articulating the problem is itself the problem" (Feuer 1983: 21).

According to this critique, Williams' *flow* constitutes an enormous unity or "unification," in which everything fuses together. This is very different from Deleuze, whose theory of seriality emphasizes the "incommensurability" from which the series as a whole heterogeneously arises. They thus maintain completely different views of the totality constituted by the flow as well as the series. On the basis of his understanding of totality, Williams must accept that one cannot actually say anything about the flow, as all (theoretical) language is itself discursive. The major methodological problem that accompanies the concept of *flow*, for Williams, is that he himself considers his own analytical tools and every known theoretical language as completely unsuitable for such an unfixed, flowing object, which manages without any discrete units or closed blocks of meaning (Williams 1992: 89). According to Williams, television criticism, analysis, and theory do not have any language capable of this at their disposal, as their concepts and assertions are themselves discrete units of meaning and everything they produce is organized as sequences of fixed components that adhere to a structured, meaning-generating syntax: "it is indeed very difficult to say anything about this" (Williams 1992).

## The Semantics of Flow

Williams has no other choice but to row bravely back behind his own observations again. Despite his assumption that *flow* is emergent (not caused) and that it is a category of reception, for example, he still maintains that *flow* is dependent on the intentions of the program providers—that is, on predictability and planning (Williams 1992: 86ff.). In particular, flow makes it easy to *add* something to the program sequence at any time, but it simultaneously makes it harder to *remove* something during the predetermined breaks between the programs. This is obviously in the interests of the program providers, as it is their strategy. In actuality, however, and according to its very definition, flow can at best be enabled, but it cannot be planned. Williams has to assume, therefore, that the planning of the flow remains hidden and unacknowledged, while the structure of the program sequence and its discrete units of meaning are visible and instrumental. For Williams, the structured program sequence also serves to make *flow* possible, even though it does not appear to share the manifest nonmeaning of *flow* itself. This at least reveals the possibility that the program mode has no priority or precedence over the flow mode.

As Hans Jürgen Wulff has shown, *flow* is based not on a higher or deeper, secret or hidden intended meaning, regardless as to whether this intention is direct or indirect, but rather on arbitrariness and accidental proximity (Wulff 1995: 23). *Flow* does not contain any stabile, fixed ideological discourse structure that would be retrieved, actualized, and in that sense represented by *flow*; rather, it is a phenomenon of excess that arises from its emergent and supervenient nature.

Williams acknowledges that it is impossible to model *flow* precisely, but this does not prevent him from analyzing it with precise means and concepts. He thus to a large extent renounces what he achieves. If we established earlier that flow leads to the collapse of the assumed levels of complexity (shots and episodes or episodes and series), then Williams' analysis overrides this insight again, as he attempts to understand the effects of *flow* on three different levels with the help of a written transcript of a news broadcast: first, in the interaction between the independent parts of the program, which can also be read as units of meaning; second, in the sequence of individual reports within the news broadcast, which he breaks down into thematic blocks, weather reports, and so on; and finally, in a shot-by-shot analysis, which tracks the flow from one shot to another and from one statement to another (Williams 1992: 90–112). Although it remains impossible to reconstruct the *flow* through this process, as it is made invisible and is practically inverted, it is still possible to examine the special properties of the articulated sequence, which makes *flow* possible and from which it arises. For example, Williams interestingly diagnoses virtually consistent switching and cutting frequencies across the entire surface of the *flow*, and all of the individual shots and news blocks have this fundamental meter or oscillation in common.

However, Williams mainly turns to the field of semantics and poetology, which is removed from the flow, and he discovers that metaphors and metonyms of flow, stream, and television in general appear periodically, regardless of the different program genres and levels of complexity (Williams 1992: 99). A semantics of temporality—or more precisely of actuality, which is at the same time transitory—is also established in the commentaries in the news broadcast that he analyzes. Phrases like "we now have more news about . . ." imply that the broadcast is constantly being interrupted by newly received reports, which motivate the abrupt switches from one theme to another. The passage of time itself thus appears to produce the *flow* (Williams 1992: 110ff.).

As something nondiscursive and inexpressible, the flow has at least some of the qualities that correspond to Jacques Lacan's notion of the "real" (in contrast to the symbolic and the imaginary) (Lacan 2013: 1–52, 2006: 197–268). It could at least be said that the relationship between Lacan's wordless and formless real and his discursive and structured symbolic is similar to that between Williams' concept of the flow and the schedule (as well as his own analysis). And just as Walter Benjamin's "Work of Art" essay formulated the concept of the "optical unconscious," so too would it perhaps be possible to conceive of the flow as the latent medial unconscious of television, which becomes manifest when expressed through the commonly found metaphors of time and stream (Benjamin 2006: 265). However, it is important to note that the flow is an emerging or superveniening event that is also technically induced. In other words, it does not simply exist and is by no means unconditionally or even primordially above all order.

A semantics of presence also corresponds to the flow in the explicit texts that it reshapes. The commentaries that Williams analyzes include constant references to time information, such as "today, fast, at this moment, while," and so on (Williams 1992: 111). This is also supported by stylistic moments like movement speed and fuzzy operations, which can be observed across all of the individual thematic blocks. Moreover, according to Williams, television itself is reflected in the commercial breaks that disrupt the news broadcast, as they present stereotypes, motifs, and stylistic elements that are characteristic of certain program types and genres, such as educational programs with their elaborate infographics, soap operas, crime series, and children's programs (Williams 1992: 112). Television is thus incorporated into television itself, and this is precisely what conveys the impression that even a brief passage of *flow* simultaneously contains the larger *flow* of the entire undivided television evening.

But this is not all: Hans Jürgen Wulff assumes that all of the unspoken knowledge of popular culture is negotiated in the flow (Wulff 1995: 34). The categories and elements in general cultural circulation, which underlie individual understandings as well as the understanding of individuals—such as individual television programs—are being tested on completely arbitrary texts and sense objects. The individual programs thus become merely allusions or references—loose indices of a cultural and apparently collective unconscious general context, which is not registered in each individual program and also cannot be controlled by them; rather, it is only rendered visible at all in the *flow*. Because for Wulff the *flow* thematizes the relationship between the general context and the individual programs, it simultaneously negotiates the relationship between the unspoken foundations and conditions of meaning in general and those of individually produced meaning. The techno-aesthetic timing event thus becomes a highly reflexive cultural process, a bit of self-assurance, and a test of the functional ability of cultural discourses and forms of knowledge. The goal of the *flow* is, says Wulff, to make an always already available but distributed and diffuse knowledge productive for the individual case and to format the always already unavailable knowledge in new kaleidoscopic constellations with many variants.

## Heterography

According to Wulff, as an agent of social self-reproduction, television also regulates the circulation of cultural knowledge and reinforces power relations in and through the *flow*. This is true and practically self-evident, but it can also be broken up by means of concepts developed by Williams and others. According to these theorists, the texts (and streams) of popular culture do not have one single meaning (Hall 1996: 128–38). In addition to the dominant or hegemonic meaning and function, they also permit other ways of reading—minoritarian and critical strategies of reception and interpretation—that run counter to the dominant or hegemonic meaning. We could assume, like Williams, that the ontographic writing of the *flow* is also by no means unambiguous or uniform but rather comprised of multiple writings, yet these cases still maintain the assumption of a closed, structured, and discursive horizon of meaning.

Unlike Williams, Wulff, and others, however, I would argue that the totality of the flow is by no means a homogenizing or merging operation; rather, it is deeply heterogeneous, as we already saw earlier in reference to Deleuze. This also applies to individual sections or passages of the flow. The self-similarity of television, whose image types and program genres are all invoked and can be found in each other and in their exclusive instructions for reception, would then mirror this heterogeneity in its own components. We must assume the same for the flow as an ontographic event, as it involves a superlinear *heterographic* ontography. It consists of multiple writings at the same time, which intersect with one another, run parallel to one another, overwrite and erase one another, and are once again separated from one another in every conceivable way, so that the overall structure of the flow extends continually and simultaneously in every direction and all of its strands, which are experienced precisely not as parts of a whole, are copresent. That is why the effect of the flow is initially confusing and unsettling, but this confusion dissolves once the linear, discursively structured mode of reading and its need for explanation, which produces forced meanings, is abandoned in favor of an aesthetic, somatic, and sensorial mode of reception, which is neurologically committed to rhythm and resonance (Wulff 1995: 35). The understanding of meaning, discourse, and decoding found in textual studies and cultural theory must constantly subsume the flow phenomenon as deficient or completely reinterpret it. An entirely unsemantic approach to the flow, as seen in media studies and the concept of "cultural techniques," is thus more appropriate (Siegert 2010: 95–118; see also Engell and Siegert 2010).

## Flow and Bodies

As a cultural technique, *flow* is the interaction of the perceptual apparatus, bodily state, and television's techno-aesthetic operating principle. When examining this more closely, one is confronted with another older concept, which the social psychologist Mihály Csíkszentmihályi developed and made familiar as *flow* in countless popular works since the 1960s (Csíkszentmihályi 1985).

Csíkszentmihályi's *flow* involves an individual experience that occupies an optimal position right in the middle between anxiety and boredom. This terminology seems remarkably close to the basic concepts of Martin Heidegger's existential philosophy, but it is configured here in a completely different way—namely, as bodily experience and perception (Heidegger 1995: 78–167; see also Engell 1989). According to Csíkszentmihályi, experience in a state of *flow* is completely autotelic—that is, it is released from external goals and objectives, including rewards or achievements. Simultaneously and paradoxically, however, the person in a state of *flow* is completely unconscious, automated, and absorbed by the external world in an extreme way. *Flow* is accompanied by a complete absorption in one's own action and thus especially in the tools and instruments of this action. According to Csíkszentmihályi, action, perception, observation, feedback, repetition, and variation all merge here into an autonomous chain of operations. In a state of *flow*, one operation follows another according to an internal logic that is completely embedded in the biological and technical bodies involved. It does not demand any additional perception or reflection, and it does not seem to require any conscious intervention (Csíkszentmihályi 1985: 38f.). To turn to media philosophy, this concept of the *flow* recalls Vilém Flusser's idea of the "gesture" as something that connects a used device or *dispositif* with the body and action of a person to form an operative dynamic unity (Flusser 2014).

However, Csíkszentmihályi is concerned not only with a spatial coupling but also above all with the temporal unity of a chain of operations. A person in the *flow* is entirely absorbed in an action—due to its dependence on tools and instruments, there can no longer be any action of one's own doing—and experiences the process as a consistent flowing from one moment to the next. She thereby experiences herself as being in control of her actions, yet at the same time she does not sense any separation between herself and the environment, between stimulus and reaction, between *res extensa* and *res cogitans*, or between past, present, and future (Csíkszentmihályi 1985: 36). Action thus merges with consciousness, as there is no external perspective from which the actor can observe herself and thus no self-reflexivity (and no subjectivity), which leads to self-forgetfulness (Csíkszentmihályi 1985: 42f.). The mental construct of the body is abandoned, and the acting person enters into a more intensive relationship with the physical body itself. In the terms of philosophical anthropology, one could presumably say that "having a body" largely withdraws behind "being a body" (Plessner 2019). With regard to phenomenology, one could also say that the living body (*Leib*)—a central category of many phenomenological approaches—disappears in favor of the body-object (*Körper*); in this respect, the *flow* would then be an anti-phenomenology.

In the light of these findings, television as *flow* is framed completely differently as a cultural technique—namely, it is a form of negative self-experience (i.e., self-forgetting) rather than a form a meaning production that has gone astray. Television as flow belongs no longer to articulation and thus to discursivity and the origin of meaning but rather to a specific experience of the body or at least of perception. However, it involves a self-experience that is constantly extended to an outside or opposite, on which it remains inescapably dependent; otherwise, it could not develop its specific characteristic of self-forgetting. Like Flusser's gesture, the *flow* is also only possible when connected or coupled with the image stream (and later, as we will see, with the remote control and with the entire *dispositif* of television). *Flow* is thus by no means self-sufficient or proprioceptive in the sense of a closed circuit. Television would then move away even more from the traditional process of generating meaning, and it would move even closer to other similar body and sensory techniques, such as sports, sex, and games as well as music or juggling.

Csíkszentmihályi also looked for *flow* experiences in other areas of life, and he often found them in the workplace through his interviews with surgeons, drivers, and domestic workers (Csíkszentmihályi 1985: 123ff.). The last example leads us directly back to television, as the rhythm of its programs and images—at least in the case of "daytime" television, according to Tania Modleski's famous and convincing theory—is closely and practically coupled with the rhythm of housework (Modleski 1983: 67–76). This involves not only the timing of daytime programs, which conformed to the routines f housework (and vice versa) that arose during the classical era of American television. We have already seen in connection with the soap opera that this also semantically and narratively supports occasional viewing while performing other tasks. Housework consists of the cyclical repetition of the same tasks, such as cleaning, washing, and cooking, which arise each day anew as if they had never been completed. The redundancy of housework and the redundancy of serial television also form resonances (and complementarities). Moreover, this once again invokes television as an acoustic image. Like radio, the sound of television also penetrates the ear, even when the gaze is directed at something else, and spreads through all of the rooms of an apartment as an acoustic massage. Two different flows—that of housework and that of television—thus flow into one another, and immersion occurs twice—once in the work and once in the (acoustic, optical) image stream.

However, this entanglement of the flow of housework and that of television sound must not be misunderstood as a merging, as both of these chains also represent a *heterography* in which two different wave patterns—

each presumably heterogeneous in itself—are inscribed in the same body and thus write this body at first. The *heterographic immersion* of the body into one stream is at the same time doubled and contained by its immersion into the other stream. This in turn sheds new light on one of the basic characteristics of *flow*, according to Csíkszentmihályi—namely, the centering of bodily functions on a very narrow range of activities. In sports, for example, this is accomplished through the rules of play, the spatial and temporal limitations of a game, and the special space to which it is relegated (Csíkszentmihályi 1985: 40f.). This also focuses consciousness on the present and allows the past and the future to fade away. When casually viewing television while performing housework, however, it seems as if the opposite could also be the case, as the flow occurs *heterographically* by surpassing one range of activities (i.e., housework) and pursuing another (i.e., television viewing) in a double immersion.

## Heterochrony and Presence

The overlapping of both rhythm chains generates the body's own resonant oscillation, and this obviously involves a process of pure desynchronization. In the case of television, what is "counted in movement" consists of the technically and aesthetically determined, clearly readable, and linearly structured or even chronological sequence of individual moments in terms of date, time, meter, or program. A non-chronocentric, nondiscursive, and body-related concept of time can emerge from this sequence, however, and this concept is precisely that of the *flow*. Television with the *flow* would be non-chronocentric because it would have little to do with precision timing, textual form and content, or the negotiation of meaning. Instead, it would involve a physically and materially based sensory and body technique. *Flow* would be a nonsynchronous or heterochronous simultaneity.

This quality of the *flow* as heterochronous and simultaneous at the same time also provides a new perspective on a serious objection that was raised against the view of television as a live or continuously updating medium. In her critique of the concept of *flow*, namely, Feuer asserts, that its presence effect (it always and only occurs in the here and now) is purely an ideological construct, as if there were no such thing as "presence" (Feuer 1983: 12). Furthermore, the operating principle of television does not provide any technological justification for this effect. The technology, and with it the aesthetics of television, could by no means determine its so-called essence, as it is extremely adaptable and can only be described historically, not essentially, in terms of the current state of technological development. According to Feuer, Herbert Zettl's "influential" book about television aesthetics is an example of such an essentialist argument, as he defines television as a medium of presence on the basis of the technical parameters of the cathode ray tube (Zettl 1978: 3–8). In this respect, Feuer's objections could aim at our own leading hypothesis here. Like the claims made earlier in this book, Zettl also stipulates that the television image is never truly present, as it is technically always in the process of becoming. As a result, it cannot define or determine anything. In contrast, film is a medium of definition, because it is capable of recording events, while television is at the mercy of external events that it cannot record.

Feuer describes this view in detail only to reject it sharply. First, assuming that Zettl's argument is essentially true with regard to the stream of events, Feuer points out that these events seem to be already preformatted for television as soon as they occur such that they can very well be seen as determined by television (Feuer 1983: 13ff.). We can confirm this argument with reference to Boorstin, Baudrillard, and many others (see Chapter 2 in this volume). Second, she argues that Zettl's basic premise with regard to the cathode ray and the status of the television image as something in the process of becoming is an ideological assumption, as it personifies the apparatus and humanizes the physical process. It is also based on a prior understanding, which merely utilizes the technical condition. In reality, however—and here Feuer sounds exactly like Esch and even draws from the same sources—the presence effect also functions with recorded programs, such as those recorded "live on tape," and it thus reveals nothing at all about programs that are actually "live." Rather, the belief in television as a medium of reality, as "live," as "the real thing" is the self-propaganda of the apparatus. The electronic intermediate storage and processing of the image is actually used everywhere, such as sports coverage and magazine formats. Television as a whole is a mixture of recorded, pseudo-live, and truly live broadcasts, yet it generally pretends to be a medium of presence. We will return to these technically induced mixed and extended forms of televisual presence when we discuss the transformations of television (see Chapter 6 in this volume).

Feuer's critique could apply just as well to the approach followed here, which also began with cathode ray tube television. What is most important, however, is that the *flow* always involves a heterographic and heterochronic simultaneity, particularly when it is entangled and intertwined with different types or phenomena of presence, as Feuer assumes. This simultaneity does not extinguish and dissolve the incommensurable diversity out of which it emerges, and it also does not transcend this diversity to reach a higher level of complexity and unity. On the contrary, it is an experiential form of heterogeneity.

## The Dionysian Switch

In addition, the *flow* as a whole only appears to be one side of a further heterogeneity. We have already encountered this earlier, as according to Williams it separates the flow mode from the program mode, the sensory from the meaningful, the sensitive and the cacophonous from the discursively structured perception of television. The fundamental ambiguity that is inherent in the sequence of screen events—namely, that they can be read as a program as well as experienced as *flow*—and that constitutes the specific appeal of the medium, as observed by Williams, still persists. A reduction of television to the *flow* would certainly be as inadequate as the reduction of the *flow* to the articulated timing that makes it possible, as is practiced in Cultural Studies. It thus obviously remains to be considered whether the *flow* actually always emerges from a structured, program-like discursive temporal experience, from which it can depart and to which it always remains tied, as we would assume, or whether the reverse is true, as the program mode also arises as a condensation from the previous flow mode. As we formulated earlier, both of these modes can revert or switch into one another. For Williams and especially for all further developments of the concept, however, it remains unclear how and when viewers switch from one mode of reception to another.

The switch between two temporal structures that are connected through television—one that is timed and generates meaning and another that floats and is beyond such timing—can also be viewed in a different way. To pursue one of Christiane Voss' ideas, program structure and *flow* could function in the sense of Nietzsche's concept of the *Apollonian* and the *Dionysian* (Voß 2013b: 119–32; Engell and Voß 2011). In his book *The Birth of Tragedy from the Spirit of Music*, Nietzsche identifies these two polar forces as the basic principles of ancient Greek culture and aesthetics (Nietzsche 2000: 1–144; Heidegger 1995: 72–4). According to Nietzsche, Apollonian culture pursues the ideal of harmony, proportionality, symmetry, measuredness, and moderateness and thus also the ideal of the logos and self-restraint. In contrast, Dionysian culture pursues the ideal of excess, ecstasy, loss of control, and self-transcendence. It is based on affect rather than cognition, and it prevails in its own established festival, the Dionysia, as well as in rapturous music and Greek tragedy, which do not provide insights but instead arouse fear and compassion.

The recourse to Nietzsche of all people is, by the way, not as remote and random as it might at first appear. The polarity between the meaningful and the sensual is Nietzsche's fundamental theme, and it is precisely for this reason that he is one of the key figures of media philosophy (Kittler 2013: 54f.).

His essay "On Truth and Lies in a Nonmoral Sense," for example, develops a theory of language that begins with the sound rather than the meaning of speech (Nietzsche 2012). For him, speech appears to be an innervation phenomenon—a complement to dance and music—and meaning emerges as its opposite. McLuhan's view that media are not about the "message"—not even the message that the medium itself is—but rather about the "massage" of the senses (which also has effects) is precisely in line with this materialistic assumption.

It is not difficult to correlate this polarity between sound and meaning, Dionysus and Apollo, to that between *flow* and program structure, although only as an analogy of course, as no one would claim that the scale and severity of ancient Greek culture has anything in common with television. On the Apollonian side is the well-structured and perhaps even balanced program, which focuses on discursivity, structure, and regularity and thus appeals to the sense of cognition. It involves mastery and self-restraint, and it produces the effects of subjectification and is even subject to the countability of movement. In contrast, the *flow* would be found on the Dionysian side, as it involves sensuality, transgression, and the loss of self. According to Csíkszentmihályi, the ecstatic can also be found in the *flow*.

As heterogeneous as they may be, Apollonian and Dionysian aesthetics are not simply juxtaposed; rather, they are mutually dependent in their polarity and, what is more important, they can change into one another. The Dionysian can suddenly break out, supplant the Apollonian, and then sink back into it again. It could even be said that ancient Greek culture was less a polarity than a switch between the Apollonian and the Dionysian. This is precisely what Voß expresses in the concept of the *Dionysian switch*, which puts this switching into operation (Voß 2013b: 120). If we relate this to television, it seems as if the activity of television involves something that corresponds to the function of the Dionysian switch. Television can thus be read as the interaction between program control and the experience of *flow*— that is, between an Apollonian practice driven by reality (and meaning) and a Dionysian practice driven by pleasure (and adventure).

There would thus appear to be two interconnected reasons for Williams' bafflement, as well as the bafflement of his critics, with respect to his discovery of the *flow*. First, it would be a result of the difficulty of conceiving of television as a dense sequence of non-semantic switching processes (instead of a machine for producing discourse and meaning) and of its reception as the mere processing and innervation of stimulus configurations and in any case as an event on a single level. In this regard, the theory of the *flow* is in good company. Second and more specifically, however, television theory cannot really understand television in general as a Dionysian practice and thus, like Voß, as a conditioned pleasure (even though it is always already contained). And so it also cannot conceive of a connection between them in the *flow*, which is made possible by the concept of a switch that toggles back and forth between both of these domains.

## Humor

Voß develops the idea of the Dionysian switch, incidentally, in the context of her philosophy of humor. According to Voß, Sigmund Freud conceives of humor as an effect of the interaction between the two basic drives of the human psyche—namely, the reality principle and the pleasure principle (Freud 1961). Voß, in turn, assigns the Nietzschean categories of the Apollonian and the Dionysian to this polarity by analogizing them to the reality principle and the pleasure principle, respectively. According to Voß, with reference to Nietzsche and Freud, humor constantly switches back and forth between these domains, and their interaction is central to it (Voß 2013b:124). However, the humorous effect of switching back and forth between the Apollonian and Dionysian is based on the fact that the switching itself is not intentional, predictable, or calculable; rather, the Dionysian switch (to stay with the metaphor) has a loose connection that unexpectedly and by itself transforms the one into the other. Humor occurs as a dysfunctional deviation from the controlled back and forth between the Apollonian and the Dionysian (Voß 2013b:129).

If it is somewhat simplified, this idea seems ideally suited to describe the practice of switching from the program mode, which conceives of television as the discursive production of knowledge and meaning, to the flow mode, which conceives of television as a technology of bliss that, as we have seen, is comparable to dance. For this purpose, it is sufficient to understand the allegedly timed event of the televisual text not as an articulation that generates meaning and signification but rather as the simple non-semantic switching and interswitching of images. In addition to its ontography and heterography, the switchability of the image ultimately constitutes the basic characteristic of television. Even if it is not equivalent to humor, the two-faced nature of television timing as the production of knowledge and meaning, on the one side, and a pleasurable bodily experience, on the other side, can still be seen as an oscillation—or, more precisely, as the heterography of an Apollonian and a Dionysian practice involving one and the same timing event. This includes the possibility of switching between them constantly and imprecisely, as if there is a loose connection. The containment of the Dionysian within the Apollonian would also be possible, of course, just as the theories of the *flow* propose. It is important to note, however, that unlike humor, which for Voß is based on the unreliability of the Dionysian switch, viewers can practice this switching—eventually even as a technical switching process. The remote control, which is perhaps the dominant Dionysian switch of television, gives them the possibility to intervene in the countless structured program texts that are typically juxtaposed on television. By creating a different timing sequence than the one already prescribed by television's image stream—namely, that of their own button presses—they can also produce an emergent *flow* in Williams and Csíkszentmihályi's sense. They then switch from the production of knowledge to the production of pleasure, thus alternating at will from an Apollonian to a (relatively) Dionysian practice and back again. We will continue to examine the reliability of this switch and the humor it provides later when we focus on the remote control.

# References

Bazin, André. 2004. *Was Ist Film?*. Berlin: Alexander.
Benjamin, Walter. 2006. "The Work of Art in the Age of Its Technological Reproducibility." In: *Selected Writings. Volume 4. 1938-1940*, ed. by Howard Eiland, and Michael W. Jennings, pp. 251–83. Cambridge, MA, London: Harvard University Press.
Clayton, Philip. 2006. *Mind and Emergence: From Quantum to Consciousness*. Oxford: Oxford University Press.
Csíkszentmihályi, Mihály. 1985. *Beyond Boredom and Anxiety: The Experience of Play in Work and Games*. San Francisco, London: Jossey-Bass.
Davidson, Donald. 1980. *Essays on Actions and Events*. Oxford: Oxford University Press.
Davidson, Donald. 1984. *Inquiries into Truth and Interpretation*. Oxford, New York: Oxford University Press.
Deleuze, Gilles. 2004. *The Logic of Sense*. London, New York: Continuum.
Durkheim, Émile. 1953. *Sociology and Philosophy*. Glencoe: Free Press.
Durkheim, Émile. 1966. *The Rules of Sociological Method*. New York: Free Press.
Eco, Umberto. 1989. "Chance and Plot: Television and Aesthetics." In: Umerbto Eco. *The Open Work*, pp. 105–22. Cambridge, MA: Harvard University Press.
Elias, Norbert. 2007. *Involvement and Detachment: The Collected Works of Norbert Elias, Vol. 8*. Dublin: University College Dublin Press
Engell, Lorenz. 1989. *Vom Widerspruch zur Langeweile. Logische und temporale Begründungen des Fernsehens*. Frankfurt/M., New York: Peter Lang.
Engell, Lorenz. 2000. "Die Liquidation des Intervalls. Zur Entstehung des digitalen Bildes aus Zwischenraum und Zwischenzeit." In: Lorenz Engell. *Ausfahrt nach Babylon. Essais und Vorträge zur Kritik der Medienkultur*, pp. 183–205. Weimar: VDG.

Engell, Lorenz. 2008. "Drei kleine Theorien des Testbilds." In: *Modernisierung des Sehens. Sehweisen zwischen Künsten und Medien*, ed. by Mattias Bruhn, and Kai Uwe Hemken, pp. 299-322. Bielefeld: transcript.
Engell, Lorenz, and Bernhard Siegert, eds. 2010. *Zeitschrift für Medien- und Kulturforschung (ZMK)* 1: 1, Topic "Kulturtechnik."
Engell, Lorenz, and Christiane Voß. 2011. *Aufhören/Weitermachen: Zur Polarität des Humors*. Accessed June 12, 2019. https://www.uni-weimar.de/fileadmin/user/fak/medien/professuren/Philosophie_Audiovisueller_Medien/Downloads/ Ringvorlesung-Engell-Voss_compr.mp3.
Feuer, Jane. 1983. "The Concept of Live Television: Ontology as Ideology." In: *Regarding Television*, ed. by E. Ann Kaplan, pp. 12-21. Frederick: University Publications of America.
Flusser, Vilém. 2014. *Gestures*. Minneapolis, London: University of Minnesota Press.
Freud, Sigmund. 1961. "Homour." In: Sigmund Freud. *The Standard Edition of the Complete Psychological Works of Sigmund Freud. Volume XXI*, ed. by James Strachey, pp. 159-66. London: The Hogarth Press.
Foerster, Heinz von. 1949. *Circular Causal, and Feedback Mechanisms in Biological and Social Systems*. New York: LLC.
Foerster, Heinz von. 1993. "Epistomologie der Kommunikation." In: Heinz von Foerster. *Wissen und Gewissen. Versuch einer Brücke*, pp. 269-81. Frankfurt/M.: Suhrkamp.
Grau, Oliver. 2003. *Virtual Art: From Illusion to Immersion*. Cambridge, MA: MIT Press.
Greve, Jens, and Annette Schnabel, eds. 2011. *Emergenz. Zur Analyse und Erklärung komplexer Strukturen*. Berlin: Suhrkamp.
Hall, Stuart. 1996. "Encoding/Decoding." In: *Culture, Media, Language: Working Papers in Cultural Studies, 1972-79*, ed. by Stuart Hall, Doothy Hobson, Andrew Lowe, and Paul Willis, pp. 128-38. London, New York: Routledge, Centre for Contemporary Cultural Studies University of Birmingham.
Heidegger, Martin. 1995. *The Fundamental Concepts of Metaphysics: World, Finitude, Solitude*. Bloomington, Indianapolis: Indiana University Press.
Holland, John H. 1998. *Emergence: From Chaos to Order*. Oxford, New York: Oxford University Press.
Iser, Wolfgang. 2013. *Emergenz. Nachgelassene und verstreut publizierte Essays*. Konstanz: KUP.
Kittler, Friedrich. 2013. *The Truth of the Technological World: Essays on the Genealogy of Presence*. Stanford: Stanford University Press.
Lacan, Jacques. 2006. "The Function and Field of Speech and Language in Psychoanalysis." In: Jacques Lacan. *Écrits: The First Complete Edition in English*, pp. 197-268. New York, London: W. W. Norton & Company.
Lacan, Jacques. 2013. "The Symbolic, the Imaginary, and the Real." In: Jacques Lacan. *On the Names-of-the-Father*, pp. 1-52. Cambridge, Malden, MA: Polity Press.

Luhmann, Niklas. 1995. *Social Systems*. Stanford: Stanford University Press.

McLuhan, Marshall, and Quentin Fiore. 1967. *The Medium Is the Massage: An Inventory of Effects*. New York: Bantam.

Mersch, Dieter. 2013. *Ordo ab chao – Order from Noise*. Berlin, Zürich: Diaphanes.

Modleski, Tania. 1983. "The Rhythms of Reception: Daytime Television and Women's Work." In: *Regarding Television: Critical Approaches – An Anthology*, ed. by Ann Kaplan, pp. 67–76. Frederick: University Publication of America.

Nietzsche, Friedrich. 2000. "The Birth of Tragedy." In: Friedrich Nietzsche. *Basic Writings of Nietzsche*, ed. by Walter Kaufmann, pp. 1–144. New York: The Modern Library.

Nietzsche, Friedrich. 2012. *On Truth and Lies in a Nonmoral Sense*. N. p.: Aristeus Books.

Plessner, Helmuth. 2019. *Levels of Organic Life and the Human: An Introduction to Philosophical Anthropology*. New York: Fordham University Press.

Siegert, Bernhard. 2010. "Kulturtechnik." In: *Einführung in die Kulturwissenschaft*, ed. by Harun Maye, and Leander Scholz, pp. 95–118. München: Fink.

Voß, Christiane. 2008a. "Fiktionale Immersion zwischen Ästhetik und Anästhesierung." In: *IMAGE—Zeitschrift für interdisziplinäre Bildwissenschaft*. Accessed June 6, 2019. http://www.bildwissenschaft.org/image?function=fnArticle&showArticle=126.

Voß, Christiane. 2008b. "Kinästhetische und semantische Dimensionen immersiver Erfahrung." In: *Immersion, Montage/av 17/2*, ed. by Robin Curtis, and Christiane Voß, pp. 69–86. Marburg: Schüren.

Voß, Christiane. 2009. "Fiktionale Immersion." In: *Es ist, als ob. Fiktionalität in Philosophie, Film- und Medienwissenschaft*, ed. by Gertrud Koch, and Christiane Voß, pp. 127–39. München: Fink.

Voß, Christiane. 2013b. "Der dionysische Schalter. Zur generischen Anthropomedialität des Humors." *Zeitschrift für Medien- und Kulturforschung (ZMK)* 1: 119–32.

Williams, Raymond. 1977. *Marxism and Literature*. Oxford: Oxford University Press.

Williams, Raymond. 1992. *Television as Cultural Form (1973)*. Middletown: Wesleyan University Press.

Wulff, Hans Jürgen. 1995. "Flow. Kaleidoskopische Formen des Fern-Sehens." *montage a/v* 4, no. 2: 21–42.

Zettl, Herbert. 1978. "The Rare Case of Television Aesthetics." *The Journal of the University Film Association* 30, no. 2: 3–8.

# 5

# Interconnecting

Who switches the switch image? This question raises the expectation that the actors of television will now be discussed, but who are the actors of television (in the sense of actor-network theory), and is this model even appropriate? The answer to this question is by no means self-evident. Niklas Luhmann assumes, for example, that only communication can communicate and not human subjects or actors (Luhmann 1996: 31). Human subjects are thus used by communication and then held responsible for it by means of (subsequent) attribution, but it is communication itself that communicates through subjects and by them. Is it then possible to say that switching itself switches the image, and what exactly would that mean? Maybe whoever switches the image becomes a switch and is used, operated, and activated by someone or something, such as other switches or their interaction in the switch?

## Direction

In Umberto Eco's analysis of live broadcasts, in which switching processes are performed with running cameras, the situation is very clear: the one who switches is the director (Eco 1989: 105–18). According to Eco, the director should be conceived as a classical authorial subject, as he makes responsible decisions calculatingly and passionately based on his experience and intuition. He then implements these decisions through the press of a button (or orders someone else to do so). If one looks more closely at this process, however, then the situation becomes more complicated. What exactly makes the director choose one switch over another? Is it the events themselves, which take place in front of the cameras and are supposed to be transmitted? Is it the intended effects? Who places the range of possibilities at the director's disposal and sets the conditions for switching? Apart from the director, there are countless other instances that are directly and indirectly involved in the switching processes of the switch image, and they can be both personal and impersonal, as they include people, devices (with their requirements and allowances), money (which is always at stake), and audience ratings (the form into which money is converted for television). There are also immaterial factors, such as habits and expectations, or the expectations of expectations. Finally, direction is subordinate to the assumptions about what the assumed viewers want and value. To borrow a term from Jo Reichertz and Carina Englert, one could talk here of a "corporate actor" and thus a heterogeneous, composite unity, to which the action can and must still be attributed (Reichertz 2006: 231–46, 2016: 149–68; Reichertz et al. 2014: 145–64). As the control center of the television broadcast, the "director" would then be only an address or a black box that conceals a complicated network of instances that produce and perform actions. This black box can also be opened and then understood as a collective or an "actor-network" in Bruno Latour's sense (Latour 1993; see also Engell and Siegert 2012). The corporate actor or actor-network is then also addressed as the bearer of actions and as the distributed intention behind deliberate acts, which can be attributed to it as a composite yet nevertheless responsible subject.

## Operations and Their Agents

However, switching is precisely not an action in the traditional and literal sense but rather an operation. Operations are neither actions nor simple ongoing processes. Like switching, they first appear as interventions in something extant, present, and ongoing (such as a surgical operation). This implies by no means that operations are a lower or diminished level of actions. On the contrary, in an entirely compatible sense Martin Heidegger undermines the concept of action in his distinction between "switching" and "ruling": technology switches, but the "physis" (and thus nature) rules (Heidegger 1995: 30f.). Heidegger's fundamental ontological argument cannot simply be broken down in terms of television of course (Scannel 2014; Dienst 1995; Engell 1989), but it could be the starting point for another approach to the question of the switch image; this can only be a preliminary suggestion here. It is not a (personal or corporate) acting subject but rather "the technology" that operatively intervenes in the merely "ruling" and simply present, existing nature through switching. The ruling nature is thus characterized by its processes and processuality; it is neither operative nor active. Technology thus consists in the operative intervention into the merely ruling and self-contained nature.

On closer inspection however, this intervention proves to be an ontological event for the later Heidegger (Heidegger 1993b). In particular, this kind of "switching" technology presents itself to existence (*Dasein*)—that is, to the basic executions of human existence—as the overall totality of all possibilities of fabrication (*Verfertigung*). To fabricate oneself and the world through technology (i.e., to switch) instead of just finding it is the inherent calling of existence. Being (*Sein*) addresses existence (*Dasein*) through technology as a "technical existence" (Bense 1949). Technology—or, for Heidegger, "enframing" (*Gestell*)—confronts existence with being, and existence must then position itself to it. For Heidegger, therefore, the technicity of operations—that is, of switching—gives rise to something that is far more fundamental than the mere subjectivity and intentionality of a purposeful action.

Operations are therefore not only interventions but also, secondly, fundamentally connected with technology and techniques. This concept always also implies the more or less skillful use of technical devices and complex instruments. Operations are then, thirdly, also applications (such as military or intelligence operations) with countless participants, and over the course of these operations precise manipulations and sub-calculations are performed. They are thereby controlled and conducted without any knowledge of the overall context which they produce and without any need to participate consciously in an overall intention. Hence, operations occur mechanically and are therefore also mechanizable. They proceed or are planned, prompted, produced, and performed, yet, and fourthly, they do not necessarily require acting subjects that think freely and independently and that are autonomously aware of what they are doing. And because operations do not require subjects, unlike actions, those that perform they are not actors but rather agents. The agents of television are thus very similar to the agents depicted in television series, as discussed earlier, as they receive orders from a third and possibly even unknown party, they operate instead of act, they must be proficient in the use of advanced technology, and they must cooperate (see Chapter 3 in this volume). In addition, operations do not necessarily have any goals (consider, for example, mathematical operations), and the concept of operation resonates with that of work (in Latin, *opera*).

In this respect, the question "who switches the switch image?" is not entirely correct, as it insinuates that there would be a more or less classical subject of the switching process as well as an object (i.e., the switch image). As an operation, however, switching does not have such a subject. Whoever switches is also always an agent. However, the question of the agents of television arises not only in relation to the direction and production of television programs but also already earlier. It arises even before the television is switched on but at the very latest when it is switched on. It also pertains to the viewers of television, as switching on is a form of physical contact between the viewers and television. This seems to be the way things stand, as it is the viewers who switch the television on, but how can the relationship between viewers and switch images be understood more precisely? In the course of television as an activity, the switch contact is ultimately repeated dozens and hundreds of times by viewers—namely, through the remote control. Who is switching here, how does this switching process proceed, and what is being switched? A special chapter will be concerned with the remote control as a transformation stage of the switch image, which then becomes a switch-over-image.

For the time being, we stay with early television which was already a switch image, but did not yet have the remote control. Even in early television, we have already made some observations on the operative relationship between television and viewers. For example, we noted that the television series uses (and must use) the memory of the viewer. The cohesion and correlation of the image sequences in a closed episode as well as a continuation requires the cohesion and correlation of viewer memory and image events. This correlation of images and episodes, on the one hand, and images and observers, on the other hand, can be addressed as a *double affixation*, whose visual and dramaturgical transformation is the *cliffhanger*. Viewer memory thus becomes an agent of the series, which can switch from forgetting (in the case of the episodic series) to remembering (in the case of the continuing series) and back again (in hybrid forms). The *flow* of television is also a phenomenon that emerges through the interplay between the neurological apparatus of the viewer's body and the switched signal and image flow, as we have seen. Like the device in general, the *flow* of television is also switchable, as viewers are able to switch from the flow mode to the program mode— that is, the viewing of the discursively structured program—through the Dionysian switch (Voß 2013: 119–32). The *flow* is also seen as a way to prevent viewers from switching the television off. And here, at the latest, in the case of non-switching (-off), the question of the actor and the switch has to be taken even deeper. First, the viewing of television is also already connected to (non-)switching before and after the viewer operates technical switches. Second, the relations and shifts between *active* and *passive* must be reconstructed more precisely for the operation of the switch and the viewing of television, which is based on switching.

## Sender and Receiver

For communication theory, it is clear that the relationship between the image stream and its observers is fundamentally asymmetrical (Lasswell 1948: 32–51). The model of communication used until today was originally based on the technical functionality of radio in the 1930s, in which the sender is not a receiver and the signal flow is directional and therefore irreversible. This is what distinguishes the one-to-many model of mass communication from the one-to-one model of interpersonal communication. Like television viewers, therefore, radio listeners must remain passive; they can watch and listen, but they are not equal and cannot reply directly. This resulted in the earliest and still most influential theory of media effects, known as the "hypodermic needle" thesis (Davis and Baran 1981: 19–52), according to which mass media manipulate audiences by injecting messages and ideologies into them. According to this theory, therefore, audiences are always inactive. As Bertolt Brecht already recognized in his theory of radio, this can only be changed by producing symmetrical relations—that is, by allowing listeners to become radio broadcasters and thus placing the means of production in the hands of the public, such as on a rotating basis (Brecht 2003: 29–31). Jean Baudrillard famously challenged this idea by arguing that it would not alter the nature of technical communication, as sending would remain separate from receiving and the signal flow would remain irreversible (Baudrillard 2007: 70–93). This would only change through the deactivation of technical communication and the (impossible) return to the immediacy of interpersonal communication.

This model was based on radio, and it made the sender an actor—that is, a corporate actor who was perhaps personified by the program directors—and the receivers passive bearers. In contrast, media philosophy and cultural theory have drawn a different picture of viewing in the age of television, which may be related to the European tradition of understanding the ear as a passive organ and the eye as an active organ. In 1956, for example, Günter Anders described the television viewer as an active homeworker, who is engaged in producing himself as a viewer through the act of viewing (Anders 1956a: 102ff). In order to do so, the television viewer has, first, to individualize, and, second, unlike a film viewer, to isolate himself in his home. He must also, thirdly, transform himself into a consumer by developing the precise needs that television and the advertising industry can satisfy (according to Anders, television does not sell Coca-Cola but rather thirst) (Anders 1956a: 176). Television viewers are thus actively involved, as they are working on themselves in order to become the counterpart with which television can work. They are made to be submissive, but they must produce and perform this transformation themselves under the direction and guidance of television. In addition to his intense critique of consumer culture, it is interesting that Anders conceives of viewers not as fixed quantities but rather as the products of a process and of the relation between their still emerging selves and the screen event. The relation—viewing—precedes the relatum—the viewer. He also conceives of viewing as a form of action, although it is a guided action that is only possible by following instructions. It is thus an activity that leads to passivation or submissiveness, even though this process is never complete and the viewer never stops working to become a viewer. For Anders, therefore, the viewer is again not an actor in the classical sense but rather an agent, and their actions are not actions but rather operations (the concept of the operation also echoes that of work).

Instead of radio or newspapers, television is also the model for popular culture and mass communication in the field of Cultural Studies. Viewing is also understood here as an active form of work rather than a one-sided passivation, although in this case the work of viewing involves "decoding" (Hall 1996: 128–38). According to Stuart Hall, John Hartley, and Raymond Williams, mass cultural texts do not possess a single unambiguous message that can be injected into viewers; rather, they have at least three levels of meaning at their disposal, which are called *dominant* (or *hegemonic*, to use Antonio Gramsci's concept), *negotiated*, and *oppositional*. Viewers must actively produce the meaning of a mass media product or text on one of these three levels by either projecting it onto or deducing it from the text. A dominant interpretation involves the least work because it is already aligned with socially dominant and therefore easily learnable patterns, such as the educational and entertainment formulas of the ruling class. A negotiated interpretation involves the insertion or interpolation of one's own concrete life experience and cultural conditioning. An oppositional interpretation is characterized by the observation and comparison of the differences between these interpretations and the formulation of alternative possibilities. It thus reflexively intervenes in mass media discourse through analysis and commentary, and it accordingly requires the most work and professionalism.

## Extensions of the Body

All of this takes place at the level of meaning and semantics, ideological effects, cultural appropriations, and thus messages. This is not the case, however, when we speak about television as a medium rather than a message. Everything that passes through or is embodied by the medium (as a "message") is subject to conditions that constitute the medium itself, since it is still true that media (and thus the switch image) set the world under conditions that they themselves are (Engell and Vogel 1999: 10). As a consequence, according to McLuhan, the message lies in the medium itself rather than in its transmissions; in order to use his flippant formulation once again, this means that the message lies in the massage or, more generally, in the touch and involvement between the medium and the human organism (McLuhan 1964: 7–24; McLuhan and Fiore 1967). McLuhan's still highly influential media theory was characterized by this media-anthropological principle from the very beginning, which means that his understanding of media (which he defined very broadly, as he considered all technologies to be media) was based on his ideas concerning the relationship between media and the human organism. However, McLuhan developed these ideas under the influence and particularly in his analysis of television, as we will see. For McLuhan, therefore, the question of the relationship between the screen event and the viewers serves a fundamental and theoretically formative function.

McLuhan assumes that media and tools in general are extensions of the human body. A human being is thus a surplus phenomenon. He surpasses himself and extends his effects beyond his own body into his environment. This is done with the help of prosthetic additions and enhancements of the body, such as hammers, levers, spears, wheels, telescopes, and so on. Mechanical apparatuses are thus externalizations and extensions of bodily apparatuses,[1] which have a double effect. The first effect is that the capabilities of the affected organ are increased enormously as soon as it is technically extended. The human adjusts his way of life according to the enhanced performance of the organ, yet this disrupts and decenters the balance and harmony of his other organs (McLuhan 1964: 45–52). At the same time, he increasingly encounters technical apparatuses in his environment that are nothing more than extensions of himself. Without recognizing this, the human falls in love with his own apparatuses, just as Narcissus fell in love with his mirror image. For McLuhan, this particularly applies to the modern period, when humans extended their memories and argumentative capabilities enormously through the printing press and became inhabitants of the "Gutenberg Galaxy"; as a result, the eye became the privileged organ of information gathering and the metaphorical embodiment of knowledge in general. The balance of the sensory organs, which McLuhan assumed was the natural and ideal state, was destabilized through such hypertropy—in this case, as ocularcentrism (McLuhan 1964: 88ff.).

The second effect of these extensions is the famous self-amputation (McLuhan 1964: 47ff). In order to reestablish a balance between the organs, according to McLuhan, the human body, notwithstanding the hypertrophy, simultaneously separates itself from the limb or organ of perception affected by an extension. The corresponding capabilities and functions of the unequipped body atrophy, and the human allows them to be assumed by his machinery. As a result, he effectively becomes an apparatus of his apparatuses—he even becomes their sexual organs. One could adduce, for example, that humans allow their legs to atrophy after the development of the automobile or that they allow the protein-based memory of the body to weaken following the development of more efficient inscription systems. And as soon as there is a new extension of another organ and the reestablished balance once again gets into difficulties, there is another hypertrophy and another self-amputation. Self-amputation is an extremely painful process, however, which the human can only endure through permanent narcotization. This would include the "contents" of television programs, which numb viewers and make them incapable of recognizing the "actual" message of television, which is the medium itself. This narcotization is precisely what prevents people from understanding the overall context of the "extensions of man." According to McLuhan, self-amputation precludes self-knowledge (Maye and Scholz 2015: XV).

The human, though, must remain networked and connected to all of these extensions, as they must be directed and controlled, and he does this by means of his central nervous system. However, he can externally displace, reify, technologize, and finally amputate all of its individual capabilities, such as the perceptual capacity of the sensory organs, the transmission functions of the neurological apparatus, and at least some of the cognitive abilities of the brain; this is precisely what leads to the emergence of technical media in a narrower sense, such as telegraphy, telephony, radio, television, and finally electronic data processing. According to McLuhan, media in this sense were thus externalizations of the central nervous system, which then affect the central nervous system. Media and humans are related, as they mutually produce and functionalize each other; indeed, they are effectively (double) agents. This also applies to the human entangled with television as a being with the capacity for consciousness, perception, communication, and ratiocination. Even with respect to these, the human is an agent.

## Organ Projection

Before looking more closely at the specifics of television, it is worth looking at another, older anthropology of technology (and media), within which McLuhan's concepts are often contextualized—namely, Ernst Kapp's organ projection thesis, which he developed a hundred years earlier in his *Elements of a Philosophy of Technology*. The similarity between Kapp's "organ projection" approach and McLuhan's "extensions of man" approach is obvious, as McLuhan also assumes that tools, techniques, and technologies are externalizations of the human body and especially extensions of individual organs, which then affect this very body. As a result, this parallel is frequently noted, debated, and evaluated in media theory, although these discussions are almost exclusively limited to German media theory, as Kapp (unlike McLuhan) does not play a significant role in media theory outside of Germany (Grampp 2011: 79f.; Hartmann 2006: 79f.). To summarize this debate briefly, their comparative evaluation is usually in Kapp's favor, as McLuhan's concept lags behind Kapp's much older position in terms of his theoretical and philosophical consistency or for various other reasons; while Kapp uses Hegel to make a metaphysical argument, McLuhan lapses into the esoteric (Derrida 1982: 329).

The central idea in Kapp's philosophy of technology is the concept of organ projection. Put very succinctly, it says that humans completely unconsciously project the qualities of the human organism onto their technological inventions and creations, including simple tools and later complex machines (Kapp 2018: 27–35). Humans can only recognize their own functioning in them later, when they encounter it in the form of fixed and functional devices and machines externally standing in front of them. For example, lifting equipment can suggest the mechanics of bone structures, power engines induce an understanding of metabolic processes, and perceptual organs can be conceived as optical devices. Kapp's treatment of the postal system is particularly impressive and can be compared favorably to the groundbreaking work of Harold A. Innis, who was also one of McLuhan's teachers (Kapp 2018: 2236ff.). Writing is already related to memory for Kapp, just as McLuhan conceives of writing as an outstandingly important externalization—namely, that of memory (Kapp 2018: 202f., 210f.; McLuhan 1964: 199). The concept of organ projection can also perhaps be extended today to neuronal processes, which could be interpreted as switches in light of the electronic brain. According to Kapp, however, organ projection reveals the structures and qualities of nature or even the cosmos, which is microcosmically condensed and present in the human body, whose form is perfect and by no means an agglomeration of scarcities or surpluses (Kapp 2018: 31f.). Humanity and nature are harmoniously unified in the body, even if they differ in scale, and this unity is revealed through manmade technology, in which it comes into its own. Kapp's idea of harmony also resonates with McLuhan, although he does not appeal to Hegel's idealism, which is mandatory for Kapp.

## From the Axe to the Screen

Like Kapp, McLuhan assumes that technological externalizations are not conscious or intentional imitations. There are thus valid parallels between their concepts, which also constitute a conceptual tradition, even if Florian Sprenger is correct in pointing out that there is no evidence and it is highly unlikely that McLuhan read Kapp's work (Sprenger 2013: 279–88; Sprenger 2012). There could still be similarities between their approaches even if McLuhan could not have known Kapp's text, which was not translated into

English. As Henning Schmidgen explains, the organ projection thesis was widely discussed outside of Kapp's philosophy of technology, such as by Claude Bernard and McLuhan's teacher Teilhard de Chardin (Schmidgen 2017: 33f.). From an anthropological perspective, McLuhan can at most be criticized for reinventing the wheel or lagging behind the earlier approach. However, McLuhan's assumption that people are ignorant of their technologies and thus of themselves is considerably more detailed. For Kapp, the inconscience of organ projection is simply given; in his chapter on the unconscious he essentially describes it as something unknown and does not explain it any further (Kapp 2018: 22; 115–20). However, this condition is cured in the second phase of organ projection—backward projection—in which humans learn to understand their organs and thus their own nature in light of their devices. This is very different from McLuhan, for whom unconsciousness or narcotization necessarily emerges from the process of externalization itself and for whom this condition cannot be readily cured or even recognized.

For Kapp, the process of organ projection can thus be distinguished from the conscious and intentional technical imitation of the body, as in protheses and Homunculi, which lead to mechanical simulation rather than organ projection. More complex technical apparatuses and machines, which are developed from simple tools, are thus especially relevant and productive epistemological instruments, as they go beyond simple representationality, such as between an arm and an axe, and enable more complex forms of self-knowledge, which is at the same time also knowledge of nature.

All technical activity and knowledge come from and go back to the human; instead of distinguishing the human from nature, however, they integrate it into nature. In terms of technical culture, the human is the absolute center but not the observer, describer, or even technical master of nature. In Dieter Mersch's sense (Mersch 2018: 102–31), technology is not metanature and the human in general is not a metabeing but rather a diatechnical, performative quality. Technology is not situated between human and nature, governing them both, and it does not transcend them, which would be the case if it were a "meta" medium; rather, it is the means by and through which the human is "diamedially" connected to itself. Humanity and technology produce one another by using one another "diamedially" (Mersch 2018: 117–19; 124f.). According to Kapp, however, this occurs through a clear reflexive privilege of the human, which ultimately recognizes its own nature by means of technology, while the reverse never happens. McLuhan replaces the idea of self-knowledge and knowledge of nature at a higher level with the idea of universal entanglement on one and the same level, and reflection is thus replaced by recursion and feedback.

In terms of media philosophy, the organ projection thesis gives rise to the question of whether all instruments of knowledge (and thus all technologies) are commensurate with one another by proceeding in a single common epistemological direction or whether they could also release contradictory knowledges of the human and nature. Kapp takes the axe, the steam engine, and the telegraph as the starting point of his thoughts, whereas McLuhan keeps his mind on the most advanced medium of his time—namely, television. This makes an enormous difference when looking back at older media and machines or just considering the anthropological foundations themselves. The underlying assumption of the organ projection thesis is that our own externalized nature can be read in our technical devices, yet they each allow something different to be read because they each focus on a different aspect of our nature. For example, the human and the world of the axe—or recognized from the axe—could be entirely different from the human and the world of cinema or television. McLuhan provides countless short chapters on different media that create different views of the world that exist alongside others, yet he also presents his fundamental understanding of what a medium is, which is based explicitly on the model of television.

What is the special relationship between television and the viewer or agent of television, from which they first arise, beyond mere extension? McLuhan offers an implicit answer to this question, which represents a second, divergent variant of media anthropology. It conceives of television in terms of its interplay with its viewers, and hence avoids the accusation of anthropocentrism. It consists of defining television as a product of its interaction with viewers, who nonetheless are not presupposed as already given but rather only brought into existence through this interaction itself, which is certainly less logically consistent. There are thus three elements that primarily characterize television as a medium: its "coldness," its tactility, and its physical intervention in the human body.

## Hot and Cold Media

The qualities that make television the paradigmatic "cold" medium involve a particularly unusual figure of thought for McLuhan. Cold media are distinguished from hot media in that they compare and present themselves to the human perceptual apparatus in different ways. Hot media address a single sensory organ, just as print and—*cum grano salis*—cinema address the eye and telephone and radio address the ear. In contrast, cold media and particularly television simultaneously address multiple sensory channels and thus produce the famous "interplay of senses" (McLuhan 1964: 24–35; 344–6).

Secondly, hot media are sensorially rich, however, and they provide more sensory information than the human central nervous system can process at one time. The perceptual apparatus thus focuses on selection. In contrast, cold media are sensorially poor and provide less sensory information than human organs can perceive. In order for it to be configurable at all, this information must be supplemented by unconscious and preconscious interpolation and configuration efforts. As a result, the activation of the perceiving central nervous system and its integration into the data flow is heightened in the case of cold media and particularly television (McLuhan 1964: 270–1). The development of this fundamental differentiating feature could have been based on contemporary media debates, in which television was accused of being sensorially poor due to its small image, low resolution (North American television had only 525 lines), and weak sound. McLuhan's preference for cold media accepted this diagnosis but reversed its evaluation. It is perhaps interesting for us that this is actually a scarcity thesis that originates from the medium rather than humans: television is characterized by its deficiency, and it thus methodologically retains the relative deficiency of a medium in general as a characteristic feature (it is relative because the classification of hot and cold can only be determined by comparing media, and it is also dynamic because cold media can heat up and hot media can cool down). The cold medium increases the entanglement of the data shown on the screen and the perceiving central nervous system, as they are both imperceptibly and inseparably coupled together, whereas the hot medium separates them from one another. Classical tube television, with its small screen, coarse pixel patterns, shaky images, program structure and variety, and even its casualness and ubiquity, always requires and receives special neurological attention, as it involves and immerses its users and their neurological apparatuses. What we perceive on television does not simply exist; rather, we must exert effort to help bring it into existence.

Such a rigid categorization of human-medium relations soon raises doubts, which McLuhan addresses through three complications. First, the two essential elements—that is, the focus on one sense and the abundance of sensory information—do not necessarily apply at the same time and to the same extent in order to qualify a medium as hot or cold. Second, media are always only defined as hot or cold in relation to one another, so there is no absolute difference between these categories. This precautionary measure indicates once again that McLuhan's thinking, in contrast to many allegations, is not media-ontological but rather fundamentally relational, which also makes his anthropology a media-relational approach. And third, McLuhan explains the difference between hot and cold as historically or at least evolutionarily variable, as hot media can cool down and cool media can heat up (McLuhan 1964: 36–44). This allows him to explain the various macroscopic, media-cultural effects of television on different media societies, such as Europe, Asia, and North America, although his grasp of these effects is completely intuitive if at times surprisingly instructive.

Cold media and particularly television thus develop strong entanglements, which we already identified earlier as anthropo-mediatic (see Chapter 1 in this volume). Cold media interweave human perception and the offered perceptual material in such a way that they drive, propel, or even produce one another. Perception and its object both emerge at the same time only from their prior entanglement—that is, from the anthropo-mediatic relation of television itself. Beyond that, however, we can also notice this entanglement in the case of cold media, while hot media tend to disconnect us and confront us like the object confronts the subject. In other words, cold and hot are qualifications not only of media but also of the relations in which they are involved. McLuhan's idea that media in general can be read from the degree of their entanglement with the human organism and nervous system was thus based on television, which he considered the exemplary cold medium.

## Touch

Something similar applies to the qualification of television as a tactile medium—a characterization that is clearly recognizable as deriving above all from anthropological and initially even anthropocentric sources. In determining which medium addresses which sensory organ, McLuhan establishes a special position for the sense of touch by claiming that it encompasses all of the other senses. These other senses are nothing else than specializations of the sense of touch—that is, of the skin—as they developed through its folding and forming. For example, the sense of taste developed with the tongue, the sense of hearing developed with the eardrum, and the sense of sight developed with the retina (McLuhan 1964: 308). The sense of touch thus encompasses all of the other senses, and a medium that addresses the sense of touch is nonspecialized (and generally relatively cold) and can thus macroscopically transcend all other specializations and even, according to McLuhan's utopian turn, differentiations and detachments in society and the world (McLuhan 1964: 118 et passim; see also 342; 345; 364).

It might seem surprising that out of all media McLuhan considered television, which clearly addresses the sense of sight, as a tactile medium. He could have easily referred to its maximal entanglement of image and sound, which had already been frequently observed, or even its primary function as (ambient) sound. Instead, he assumes that the sense of touch is a "close-up" sense, whereas the sense of sight is a "distant" sense (McLuhan 1964: 132–3; 344; 354–5). Television is undeniably a "close-up" medium both physically, as the screen is as close to the viewer as the camera is to the people and things on which it focuses (which the small format of the image also requires), and metaphorically, as the gaze scans the image in the same way that the cathode ray scans the inner surface of the tube. In an illuminating and often neglected passage, McLuhan expressed his appreciation for how television takes an interest in the textures and surfaces of simple things, such as the blankets and saddles in Western series (McLuhan 1964: 349).

McLuhan's idea of the tactility of television and its all-encompassing, anti-specializing, and globalizing function has two consequences. First, as already mentioned, television can only be understood and sensibly modeled from its relation to the possibilities of human perception and action. Second, and more importantly, his privileging of tactility shows that he ideally sees this relation as a form in which the human and the medium merge or have always already been merged, even before the separation or separability of one from the other. The thesis of the specialization of the senses points to this.

Television makes the prior involvement of the human and the medium, which could only be separated gradually and thus subsequently, conscious and perceptible, and it thereby revises this development at the same time (McLuhan 1964: 207; 308; 340). The sense of touch is also phenomenologically the sense in which it is the most difficult to separate the subject and the object. Feeling something always means at the same time feeling oneself, and vice versa, whereas we do not necessarily hear ourselves while listening and we only see ourselves while looking with the help of external media. A medium of touch is thus not detached but rather anthropo-mediatically entangled with the central nervous system that uses it. Maurice Merleau-Ponty's consideration of the blind man's cane is well known: is the cane an extension of the arm and the sense of touch or is it part of the material environment, through which it registers and shows itself to him (Merleau-Ponty 2002: 165f.; Dreyfus 1997: 252)? In this example, the question of who is touching or affecting whom cannot be conclusively determined. Consequently, McLuhan thus associates the culture of touch with the enveloping quality of the skin. He repeatedly emphasizes the connection between the sense of touch and the kinetic or kinesthetic sense, which strictly speaking does not facilitate the perception of objects or the outside world but is instead proprioceptive (McLuhan 1964: 207; 308). He also explicitly points to the connection between the sense of touch and involvement with another body— namely, to sex and sexual involvement (McLuhan 1964: 132–3; 354).

## Internalizations

McLuhan's idea of the non-containedness and incompleteness of television pertains not only to the image, which requires a supplement, but also to the neurological apparatus of the involved viewer. In an often-overlooked passage, McLuhan explains that the viewer is the (actual) screen and the images are transmitted not just to the tube surface but to the viewer's retina. Just as the cathode ray reaches the inner surface of the screen, so too do the optical signals from the outer surface of the screen constitute a "light brigade" (a metaphor borrowed from James Joyce) that simultaneously reaches through the surface of the eye to the photosensitive interior of the organism (McLuhan 1964: 341; 357). In other words, the viewer does not look into the tube but rather becomes the tube. This metaphor ultimately reverses the entire media anthropology of externalization with which McLuhan began, as it is not about the extension of the human but rather the internalization of the medium. The image would then be the result of a dual operation, as the supplemental intervention of the viewing brain into the cold medium is accompanied and even preceded by the intervention of screen technology into the brain. Something is added to the neurological apparatus before it does anything, as it switches from acting to undergoing or from *pragma* to *paskein*. The image is then literally due to an affect—namely, a contact between the organism and the medium—and it is no longer possible to determine which one is the agent of the other. In this respect, McLuhan cannot be criticized by arguing that media anthropology should no longer consider the extension and amputation of the body and must instead start from the invasive infiltration of media technology into the body, as he already established precisely this reversal (Jörisson 2007: 200f.).

However, McLuhan's metaphor can also be read in terms of Kapp's organ projection thesis by conceiving of the picture tube as an unconscious projection of the eye. The human as screen, like the image that emerges in it, would then be an internal projection process that is inherent in the neurological extension of the cathode ray and would not be due to an external (rear) projection of the one onto the other and vice versa. Because the human as a metaphorical screen is always already an image or image carrier, it no longer requires a technological mirror as a self-image or self-projection that would not already be an introjection. If we take this metaphorical concept seriously, then television no longer requires any anthropology (run by humans) in order to shape humans. It is sufficient that at the same time and to the same extent that the screen image is ontographically written, the neurological image also *anthropographically* arises not only in the organism of the viewer but also practically *as the viewer*. Television is an anthropography not only because it describes, depicts, and denotes humans (even though it obviously does all of these things extensively) but also because it operates on the same level as the biological organism and is entangled with it (to take McLuhan's metaphor further).

Television thus produces, that is, writes, the viewers it needs so that they will produce the images that constitute television itself. If the viewer is the screen, then there is no longer anyone who watches, scans, or reads this screen from outside or from above. It would be an image without an external viewer, who would not be part of the process of image production and circulation. In this view of television, however, there would also not be any televisual human-images or anthropography that would not be operatively involved in the ontographic production of the image. The viewer is also now no longer a strong agent, who manipulates, switches, controls, perceives, and ascribes meaning to images. The viewer is now no longer a product of her own operativity but rather an operative result of the anthropographic interconnection of the "human" and the "medium." Whenever this switching plays an active and activating role, it is at the same time already affected and passivated due to the "traffic of affect" (Voß 2015: 63–116).

McLuhan's description of the viewer as the screen is incidentally almost identical to Gilles Deleuze's often-discussed phrase "the brain is the screen" (Deleuze 1986: 26). The equation of these expressions is justified, as McLuhan essentially focuses on the central nervous system of the television viewer and thus his brain and its neurological embeddedness. Unlike McLuhan's description, however, Deleuze's formulation has given rise to extensive debates in contemporary media philosophy. For example, it has been heavily used by the friends of brain research, who believe that films take place not (only) on the screen but (also) in the brain of the subject, where they can be localized and studied with the help of image-generating processes—that, in turn, clearly descended from the screen and transmission technologies of television (Pisters 2012). If this were true, then it would mean that these visualized thoughts or "neuroimages," which are only accessible as image streams or moving screen images, arise from the interaction between images and can only exist in pictures as its habitat and *conditio essendi*. We will come back to this.

As McLuhan observed, television does not stop at the boundaries of the body, as the cathode ray (or its optical extension as a light signal) reaches the retina. Switching on the television is therefore a strange operation. Just as it allows the electrical current to penetrate the components of the television set, so too does it allow the optically extended cathode ray to penetrate the eye and the central nervous system of the human organism. It thus shifts the people in front of the screen from an at least agential condition, in which they perform operations, to a passive condition, in which they are affected by operations. Even though it is still unclear who is actually doing the switching, the viewer who switches on the television set is also always at the same time switching on herself—that is, she is switching herself from an agential to an affected condition.

## Couch Potato

All of this takes place once again as a metaphor at the microscopic, technical, and neurobiological level of pixels and rays. As a form of behavior, however, it also has perceptible and observable consequences that are not only metaphorical but also empirical. Perhaps the strongest macroscopic manifestation of this affection—that is, passivation through television—is the frequent description of the viewer as a submissive, immobilized, and insubstantialized "couch potato." Hartmut Winkler analyzed the "couch potato" in a wonderful short text, which begins (without referring to Williams) with a description of his own experience of *flow*, which he calls "sliding" (Winkler 2006: 93–101). He finds himself in a state of inactivity, indifference, and waiting, in which he sees everything and nothing. While in this state, the relationship he maintains with the images is inseparably interconnected with the relationship between the images themselves. Because these images affect and in particular overwrite one another (like the cathode ray), they also affect and overwrite the viewing subject: "I want the images to pull other images out of me" (Winkler 2006: 94). The television has always been accused of deactivating the viewer in precisely this way. Winkler also describes his students' enthusiasm for computer games, which—unlike boring television—activate users and allow them to control the narrative of the game through their own actions. Indeed, the moment of "interactivity" was always emphasized in the early decades of gaming culture.

Winkler questions precisely this idea of a subjectivity that asserts itself through activity and resists passivity. He considers Horkheimer and Adorno's assumption that the subject is imposed on us so that the work-oriented society is able to function, and he cites Lacan's concept of the subject as an imaginary construct that can be traced back to the mirror stage (when the infant observes itself in a mirror, recognizes his image, and sees himself for the first time as a well-formed physical unity, which it could never have experienced before). In contrast, Winkler insists that the interconnection between subjectivity and action in late and postindustrial society (and especially, it could be added, in neoliberalism) has transformed the subject from an imaginary, visual, and discursive construction, as with Lacan, into one that is practical and active. Using Foucault's concept of *governmentality*, he assumes instead that the subject now governs itself yet nevertheless submits through and in activity.

We already encountered a similar concept with Günter Anders, who described viewers as homeworkers who were occupied above all with their own self-production and self-preparation as obedient consumers. Winkler assumes, however, that this form of work is performed not in front of the television but rather in daily social practice, in which the form of work penetrates all forms of life. In other words, the process of subjectification involves not discourses (i.e., the symbolic) and images (i.e., the imaginary) but rather practices. According to Winkler, who cites Foucault, power no longer wants passive subordination but rather active participation. The assertive subject, who is capable of acting, is no longer the antithesis of power, domination, and exploitation but rather their collaborator and accomplice. In the terminology chosen here, we would once again refer to this figure as an "agent." However, this still makes a difference. As we have seen, all agents are double agents and assert their own self-interest, yet this self-interest can only be "theirs" to the extent that they are subordinate to and allow themselves to be used by their employers. Winkler adds that the vast area of free time is always shaped more profoundly by work-like structures of discipline and imposed action. Intellectuals are particularly proud of how they have learned to adhere to a self-imposed work discipline for any length of time. Computer games, which are experienced as emancipatory when compared with mass media, also consist of highly efficient and obedient activities that closely resemble the structures of work.

Markus Stauff reaches a similar conclusion in his thorough study of the digitalization of television, which also refers to Foucault's concept of *governmentality*: compared with "old" analog television (which we are discussing here), "new" digital television is an activation machine that assists in the production of self-managing and self-exploiting neoliberal subjects, who are ready and willing to act (Stauff 2005). If their action serves to prepare them to be the active subjects that the action itself requires (not only as work), however, then imaginary and symbolic processes are free for something else. According to Winkler, this is precisely what happens in the mode of "sliding" in (classical) television, as the relationships and operations between the images and their interconnection with the subject lead to desubjectification. Like Stauff, Winkler also assumes that there is the potential for insubordination, even though it is only available as a retrograde caricature: "The couch potato seems almost subversive in this context, as it is a relic of an obsolete phase in the imaginary constitution of the subject that still holds its position in front of the screen" (Winkler 2006: 100).

One could speculate here as to whether the viewer changes into the state of being merely present-at-hand (*Vorhandensein*) or "ruling" invoked earlier, which is before or beyond all subjectification, as if one could also switch over from "switching" into "ruling" or interconnect them both; television would then be precisely this merging of "switching" and "ruling" or "techné" and "physis." However, Winkler sees this process as analogous to Siegfried Kracauer's characterization of "those who wait." According to Kracauer, they maintain an attitude of openness and a commitment to the "non-enforceable" and "transformational," as it is impossible to say when and if it will occur at all (Kracauer 1995: 138–40, quoted after Winkler 2006: 101). We will discuss this position of simultaneously activated and deactivated waiting in more detail (and very differently) in a later section on boredom as an anthropographic constellation of transformed television (see Chapter 12 in this volume).

Winkler ultimately points out that subjectivity and action are already connected to one another in language, as the structure of the sentence inevitably requires a subject, a predicate, and an object. The figure of the active subject is thus already inscribed into discursive rationality based on the medium of language. This applies to declarative as well as interrogative sentences, but it does not apply to an operating, switching, agential, and affective rationality based on the medium of television, which knows warmth and coldness, tactility and entanglement, the emergence of flow and sliding, ruling and waiting, and so on. In this respect, as already noted, the form of the question posed at the beginning of this chapter—"Who switches the switch image?"—cannot be answered appropriately with the criteria and operations of the switch image as interconnected image. Within the meaning of the question, one must then actually answer that it is the switch itself.

## Note

1 Peter Sloterdijk agrees with McLuhan here, yet the surplus thesis stands in stark opposition to the popular scarcity thesis in the succession of Arnold Gehlen (Sloterdijk 2001; Gehlen 1988: 13; 28–30; see also Maye and Scholz 2015: XIVf.).

## References

Anders, Günther. 1956a. "Die Welt als Phantom und Matritze." In: Günther Anders. *Die Antiquiertheit des Menschen, vol. 1: Über die Seele im Zeitalter der zweiten industriellen Revolution*, pp. 97–211. München: Beck.

Baudrillard, Jean. 2007. "Requiem for Media." In: Jean Baudrillard. *Utopia Deferred*, pp. 70–93. New York: Semiotext(e).
Bense, Max. 1949. *Technische Existenz*. Stuttgart: DVA.
Brecht, Berthold. 2003. "The Radio as an Apparatus of Communication." In: *New Media. Theories and Practices of Digitextuality*, ed. by Anna Everett, and John T. Caldwell, pp. 29–31. New York, London: Routledge.
Davis, Dennis K., and Stanley J. Baran. 1981. "A History of Our Understanding of Mass Communication and Everyday Life." In: *Mass Communcation and Everyday Life: A Perspective on Theory and Effects*, ed. by D. K. Davis, and S. J. Baran, pp. 19–52. Belmont: Wardworth.
Deleuze, Gilles. 1986. "Le cerveau, c'est l'écran. Entretien avec Gilles Deleuze." *Cahiers du cinéma* 380, no. 2: 25–32.
Derrida, Jacques. 1982. "Signature Event Context." In: Jacques Derrida. *Margins of Philosophy*, pp. 307–30. Chicago: The University of Chicago Press.
Dienst, Richard. 1995. *Still Life in Real Time: Theory after Television*. Durham: Duke University Press.
Dreyfus, Hubert L. 1997. *What Computers Still Can't Do: A Critique of Artificial Reason*. Cambridge, MA, London: The MIT Press.
Eco, Umberto. 1989. "Chance and Plot: Television and Aesthetics." In: Umerbto Eco. *The Open Work*, pp. 105–22. Cambridge, MA: Harvard University Press.
Engell, Lorenz. 1989. *Vom Widerspruch zur Langeweile. Logische und temporale Begründungen des Fernsehens*. Frankfurt/M., New York: Peter Lang.
Engell, Lorenz, and Bernhard Siegert, eds. 2012. *Zeitschrift für Medien-und Kulturforschung (ZMK)*, 2, Topic "Kollektiv."
Engell, Lorenz, and Joseph Vogl. 1999. "Vorwort." In: *Kursbuch Medienkultur: die maßgeblichen Theorien von Brecht bis Baudrillard*, ed. by Claus Pias, Joseph Vogl, Lorenz Engell, Oliver Fahle, and Britta Neitzel, pp. 8–11. Stuttgart: Deutsche Verlags-Anstalt.
Gehlen, Arnold. 1988. *Man: His Nature and Place in the World*. New York: Columbia University Press.
Grampp, Sven. 2011. *Marshall McLuhan. Eine Einführung*. Konstanz, München: UVK.
Hall, Stuart. 1996. "Encoding/Decoding." In: *Culture, Media, Language: Working Papers in Cultural Studies, 1972-79*, ed. by Stuart Hall, Doothy Hobson, Andrew Lowe, and Paul Willis, pp. 128–38. London, New York: Routledge, Centre for Contemporary Cultural Studies University of Birmingham.
Hartmann, Frank. 2006. *Globale Medienkultur. Technik, Geschichte, Theorien*. Wien: facultas wuv.
Heidegger, Martin. 1993. "The Question Concerning Technology." In: Martin Heidegger. *Basic Writings*, ed. by David Farrell Krell, pp. 307–41. New York: HarperCollins.
Heidegger, Martin. 1995 (1929). *Fundamental Concepts of Metaphysics: World, Finitude, Solitude*. Bloomington, Indianapolis: Indiana University Press.
Jörisson, Benjamin. 2007. *Beobachtungen der Realität. Die Frage nach der Wirklichkeit im Zeitalter der Neuen Medien*. Bielefeld: transcript.

Kapp, Ernst. 2018. *Elements of a Philosophy of Technology: On the Evolutionary History of Culture*. Minneapolis: University of Minnesota Press.
Kracauer, Siegfried. 1995. "Those Who Wait." In: Siegfried Kracauer. *The Mass Ornament. Weimar Essays*, ed. by Thomas Y. Levin, pp. 129–40. Cambridge, MA, London: Harvard University Press.
Lasswell, Harold D. 1948. "The Structure and Function of Communication in Society." In: *The Communication of Ideas: A Series of Addresses*, ed. by Lyman Bryson, pp. 32–51. New York: Harper & Brs.
Latour, Bruno. 1993. *We Have Never Been Modern*. Cambridge, MA: Harvard University Press.
Luhmann, Niklas. 1996. *Die Wissenschaft der Gesellschaft*. Frankfurt/M.: Suhrkamp.
Maye, Harun, and Leander Scholz. 2015. "Einleitung." In: Ernst Kapp. *Grundlinien einer Philosophie der Technik: zur Entstehungsgeschichte der Kultur aus neuen Gesichtspunkten*, ed. by Harun Maye, and Leander Scholz, pp. VII–L. Hamburg: Felix Meiner Verlag.
McLuhan, Marshall. 1964. *Understanding Media: The Extensions of Man*. London, New York: Routledge.
McLuhan, Marshall, and Quentin Fiore. 1967. *The Medium Is the Massage: An Inventory of Effects*. New York: Bantam.
Merleau-Ponty, Maurice. 2002. *Phenomenology of Perception*. London, New York: Routledge.
Mersch, Dieter. 2018. "Meta/dia Two Different Approaches to the Medial." In: *Thinking Media and Beyond: Perspectives from German Media Theory*, ed. by Briankle G. Chang, and Florian Sprengler, pp. 102–31. Abingdon, Oxon, New York: Routledge.
Pisters, Patricia. 2012. *The Neuro-Image: A Deleuzian Filmphilosophy of Digital Screen Culture*. Standford: Stanford University Press.
Reichertz, Jo. 2006. "Das Fernsehen als Akteur." In: *Medien der Gesellschaft— Gesellschaft der Medien*, ed. by Andreas Ziemann, pp. 231–46. Konstanz: UVK.
Reichertz, Jo. 2016. "Weshalb und wozu braucht man einen 'korporierten Akteur.'" In: *CSI. Rechtsmedizin. Mitternachtsforensik*, ed. by Carina J. Englert et al., pp. 149–68. Wiesbaden: Springer.
Reichertz, Jo, Lorenz Engell, Carina Jasmin Englert, Natascha Kempken, Dominik Maeder, Jens Schröter, and Daniela Wentz. 2014. "Das Fernsehen als Akteur und Agent." In: *Die Mediatisierung sozialer Welten*, ed. by Friedrich Krotz Cathrin Despotovic, and Merle Marie Kruse, pp. 145–64.Wiesbaden: Springer.
Scannell, Paddy. 2014. *Television and the Meaning of Live*. Cambridge: Polity Press.
Schmidgen, Henning. 2017. *Horn oder die Gegenseite der Medien*. Berlin: Matthes und Seitz.
Sloterdijk, Peter. 2001. *Das Menschentreibhaus. Stichworte zur historischen und prophetischen Anthropologie. Vier große Vorlesungen*. Weimar: vdg.

Sprenger, Florian. 2012. "Die Einführung als Medium. Sven Grampp liest McLuhan in seiner Einführung vierfach." *literaturkritik.de*, Nr. 2, Februar 2012. Accessed February 2, 2018. http://literaturkritik.de/id/16298.

Sprenger, Florian. 2013. "Extension Extended—Ernst Kapp, Marshall McLuhan and their affiliated correspondence." In: *McLuhan's Philosophy of Media—Cenbtzennial Conference*, ed. by Yoni van den Eede, Joke Bauwens, Joke Beyl, Marc van den Bossche, and Karl Verstrynge, pp. 279–88. Brussels: Koninklijke Vlaamse Academie van Belgie voor Wetenschappen en Kunsten.

Stauff, Markus. 2005. *Das neue Fernsehen. Machtanalyse, Gouvernementalität und digitale Meiden*. Münster: Lit.

Voß, Christiane. 2013. "Der dionysische Schalter. Zur generischen Anthropomedialität des Humors." *Zeitschrift für Medien- und Kulturforschung (ZMK)* 1: 119–32.

Voß, Christiane. 2015. "Affekt. Affektverkehr des Filmischen aus medienphilosophischer Sicht." In: *Essays zur Filmphilosophie*, ed. by Christiane Voß, Lorenz Engell, Oliver Fahle, and Vinzenz Hediger, pp. 63–116. München: Fink.

Winkler, Hartmut. 2006. "Nicht handeln. Versuch einer Wiederaufwertung des couch potatoe angesichts der Provokation des interaktiv Digitalen." In: *Philosophie des Fernsehens*, ed. by Oliver Fahle, and Lorenz Engell, pp. 93–101. München: Fink.

Part II

# Trajectories, Expansions, Intensifications

We have observed the beginnings and the operative foundations of television, including the operation of switching on; the central formats of live broadcasts, series, and flow; and lastly the entanglements of viewing. We have thereby more closely analyzed the basic operation of switching in terms of its ontographic and anthropographic effects and have taken a look at its semantics, particularly through several selected television series. We have become acquainted with some of the functions and modalities of the switch image, such as emergence and immersion, remembering and forgetting, tactility and visuality, suffering and effecting, affectivity and agentiality. We have addressed the interrelations that give rise to distinctions and overlaps and that are put into operation through the switching of the image, such as the distinctions between the Apollonian and the Dionysian, the latent and the manifest, simultaneity and synchronicity, and activity and passivity.

However, television is not stable. This means not only that television, like many media, is subject to development and ultimately cannot be defined by the assumption of an authentic, stable, and invariant essence; rather, it is inherently unstable and constantly evolving. It is not subject to change; rather, it *is* change. This is due to the basic condition of ontographic switchability. As a switch image, it is built around various switching operations and proceeds through countless further operations resulting from them. However, operations are interventions that constantly produce differences between what comes before and what comes after, which is also true of television. Moreover, television is fundamentally ontographic, which means that these differences are always registered and recorded in the switch image itself. The switch image thus constitutes television itself as a particular and distinctive type of technical image that *flows*. It is not only the images produced by or shown on television or by television that change; rather, it is the television image itself. But this is not all: while the development of other media is often described in terms of a before and after or a series of epochal ruptures,[1] this is difficult in the case of television, as its foundations are constantly being revised. However, these revisions occur alongside various progressive forms, which can be described, and it thus appears that television can best be described in terms of the different lines, types, or modes of its own continuous development since the 1960s. Its continuous development can even be condensed into certain thrusts, through which phases of the evolution or transformation of the medium can still be observed. Three of these progressive forms will be examined more closely in the second part of this study (there are certainly more). These phenomena and their consequences lead to a (more or less) complete revision of the technical and aesthetic foundations of the television industry and thus of switching (with the latent and the manifest), the tube image (with the continuously ontographic image signal of live broadcasts), series (with remembering and forgetting), flow (with the Dionysian switch), and anthropographic viewing.

These three progressive forms are, firstly, the shift of the switch image into another state along certain *trajectories*, which add new and modified basic operations to the switch image. Our example of this will be the gradual conversion of television through the possibilities of image recording and replay in the 1960s, which particularly transformed the live quality of television. Secondly, television was also extended into increasingly vast spaces, which it reshaped into image spaces along the lines of *expansion*. The paradigmatic example of this is the reshaping of space travel as a television event or of the space program as a television program, which first culminated in the 1969 moon landing—an event that shifted the planetary order of the image and the gaze as well as the position of humans in the cosmos of images. Television was thirdly also *intensified* or condensed through the implementation and effects of the remote control as the standard instrument of television, which became observable in the late 1970s and early 1980s. The remote control transformed the basic operation of television—that is, switching—and converted the television image into a recursive switch image that was applied to itself. These three progressive forms of televisual evolution also interact with one another, which can be observed in the digitalization phases from the 1990s to the present. Digitalization entails the end of the tube image and the continuous signal flow, which we have assumed so far, and it thus represents a further revision of the primary foundations of television. It also leads to the fanning out, self-transgression, and redistribution of the switch image across countless screens and operational formats, which we are observing today. The switch image ontographically engages its world and anthropographically engages its viewers through its digitalization.

## Note

1 This has been repeatedly attempted in the case of film, such as silent and sound film; the studio system and auteur cinema; classical, modern, and postmodern cinema; or the movement-image and the time-image.

# 6

# Instant Replay

All television was live television. The mark of liveness is still and will presumably always be associated with television, yet it is no longer true. The possibility to record images and to switch back and forth between live and recorded images was gradually and increasingly incorporated into television, and this process began early on. In fact, image recording even preceded live television, as even before tube television was developed the principle of image scanning allowed a previously recorded celluloid film to be transmitted and received through the ether as an electromagnetic signal. And after it was already apparent that liveness would be the over-arching characteristic of the new medium of television, the so-called "intermediate film system" was also tested, which simulated liveness and produced a kind of delayed present through the immediate recording, developing, and scanning of recordings on celluloid (Abramson 1974: 58–62). This experiment was short-lived, however, and television never became an additional channel for the distribution of feature films. While the playback of films remained an integral part of television, it gradually became something entirely different—namely, a medium characterized by liveness, as discussed earlier. This was due to various reasons, and for American television there were mainly two (Barnouw 1990: 193–5; Winston 1986: 81–3). First, there was still no technically feasible way of electromagnetically recording image signals during the "golden age of television" (i.e., before 1956). There were records and tapes, but it was impossible to store the much larger amounts of data necessary for image recording. Television images could thus not be recorded as such in their technical modality. It is also important to note that magnetic image recording involves the recording not of images but rather of instructions, according to which the picture tube writes the images.

In the absence of a separate recording process for electronic images, the only option left was to use film and film scanning for image storage. This required the installation of film cameras next to television cameras, which would independently register the scenes to be recorded. In addition to the production of television images, therefore, everything had to be produced once again on film. This process was used to some extent in the context of news and sports coverage, for which cumbersome television cameras were replaced by light and flexible 16 mm film cameras outside of the studio. However, this process was not suited to be a basic principle of television production in general. This is related to the second reason for the lack of recording in early television: the American film industry, which was economically highly concentrated and integrated, recognized television as a fierce competitor and initially sought to boycott the medium by refusing to allow television companies to use its patented means and methods of production. Even if they would not have shied away from the enormous expense, television broadcasters were only allowed to work with film recording techniques on a very limited scale.

This period of the so-called freeze lasted from 1948 to 1953, but the politics changed when Warner Bros. decided to work with television instead of boycotting it. Warner agreed to produce a fixed number of television episodes on celluloid in the Warner studios, which would then be broadcast on ABC using the scanning process. This began the so-called filmed series. In exchange, Warner was allowed to promote newly released films during the commercial breaks. This agreement served as a model, and the first series produced and broadcast in this way were Westerns, which were already informed by feature films and even used the same sets, crews, and casts. Series production thus migrated from the television studio to the film studio, and the characteristics of live television plays were replaced by those of feature films, which was particularly true of episodic series. This not only changed the narrative style, which was now oriented toward the conventions of film and had less redundancy, but also replaced time-variable sequences like the "search scene," which could be fast or slow as needed, with a designed rhythm and more rapid cutting. The operation of switching from one camera to another during the live broadcast was thus replaced by the traditional process of montage, which was only subsequently performed on previously filmed material. Unlike a live broadcast, in which viewers are able to see the operation and its result as it develops, a filmed episode is fixed long before it is broadcast.

The transition to film was accompanied above all by an increase in the rationalization and efficiency of series production, as it permitted postproduction as well as a more highly organized division of labor. Television series, and particularly Western series, subsequently replaced live shows, and particularly quiz shows, as the highest-rated prime-time programs (Barnouw 1990: 193–8). In the following decades, television developed from a purely live medium into a medium that could switch back and forth between the transmission of (film) recordings and live components. This had several consequences, including the emergence of the magazine format, which is still well-represented today. In this format, live elements (such as moderation and conversation) alternate with recorded contributions that are preproduced on film and then incorporated into the live broadcast. While the live passages mostly come from the studio, the filmed contributions mostly come from an external space, such as the everyday world or the world of politics. This format is also the basic form of television news. For decades, therefore, the main mode of nonfiction television programming remained the live broadcast, which constituted—and still constitutes—the unique quality of television and all its hybrid forms.

## Videography

Something entirely different applies to electromagnetic image recording. It does not move intermedially between film and television, like film recording, but is instead embedded directly into the switch image. This primarily applies to the macroscopic level—that is, the level of the program and its structure. The more electronic image recording intrudes into the process of production and distribution, the more space is claimed by reruns (i.e., identical reproductions), which was not possible when television was dominated by live broadcasts. These reruns allow the broadcasting event to be temporally extended, which results in an expansion of television itself, as cost-neutral reproductions can fill time slots that could not be filled or would be expensive to fill with new productions. In this respect, we are already dealing here with an expansion of television. The possibility of viewing a missed program or reviewing a program that was already broadcast did not immediately change viewing habitats, but it did change them profoundly. Video artist Les Levine was thus able to write in the 1980s that everything on television is a repetition of everything on television (Les Levine, quoted after Gruber and Vedder 1983: 164). The nonexistence of the merely singular, which Günter Anders saw as characteristic of the ontology of the serial both within and beyond television, is thus exacerbated and becomes recursive (Anders 1956a: 179f.). The way in which television uses the viewer's memory, as we have already observed in the series form, assumes entirely new forms and processes when it occurs in collaboration with image storage instead of a live broadcast. This gives rise to new relations of temporalization and new forms of production— particularly the production of the past as a rerun embedded in the present. We will therefore observe these macroscopic changes again in connection with the disposition of the past and the history of and on television.

This chapter, however, will initially examine how electronic videographic image recording operates and functions at the microscopic level. Unlike recording on celluloid, namely, it does not just diminish, contradict, or replace live transmission; rather, it helps to reduce, override, and relativize liveness in favor of a reproductive temporal mode by supplementing the typical methods of television production with those of film. It also leads to the development of hybrid forms like the magazine format, which expands and generally transforms the canon of televisual forms by including both live and recorded blocks. But it also far more deeply affects the foundations of the television image, as electronic image recording penetrates and intervenes in the live itself, thereby transforming the nature of the live image without causing it to stop being live. It produces an entirely new and technically induced type of simultaneity and presence, which does not exist outside of television. Electronic image recording does not negate or oppose the live nature of television; rather, it intensifies and changes it by converting the live into something new. This also changes our understanding of the ontographic operations of television, as they become vague and complex, reversible and retroactive. The flow of the live is detached from that of the events and begins to flow back into itself. Televisual ontography stops being a purely linear process and instead forms reversals and loops, thereby becoming flat in the manner of a time plane.

This applies, for example, to the possibility of flagging a program as "live" even though it is actually recorded, which did not exist prior to the development of videography. This was accomplished simply by producing a program live and recording it on tape instead of actually broadcasting it live; the program can then be broadcast in its original form at a later date as "live on tape," but it can also be modified prior to the broadcast through postproduction. In this case, the image retains its live quality as a "pseudo-live" simulation as long as the cutting and splicing is performed through switching instead of montage. This kind of production technique is thus able to exploit the advantages that accompany recording. Lastly, there is the process of "near to live," in which the program is initially produced on tape, like the intermediate film system discussed earlier, and then broadcast with a short temporal delay of a few seconds or a few minutes. This makes it possible to eliminate mistakes and malfunctions as well as to intervene for the purpose of censorship. All of these processes mediate between the live and the prerecorded, which makes the distinction between the continuous present and the concluded past seem fluid and unclear. They thus give rise to a vague, indefinable, and extended present, in which the live and the prerecorded are able to masquerade and seamlessly transform into one another. Jane Feuer concluded from this that there is no such thing as simultaneity; rather, there are only different ways of simulating simultaneity. In other words, the present and thus the live are not the basic modes of television due to technical constraints; rather, this is a purely ideological construct (Feuer 1983: 12–21). This obviously depends on which concept of the present is supported and identified as the one asserted by television, but it is certainly worth noting that television becomes detached from the linear flow of time and that it becomes an instrument of navigation on a temporal plane that it itself first unfolds.

However, television already began to operationalize a unique form of image recording even before these processes of extended and simulated liveness were developed and videography was established as an archival technique (with the goal of rerunning programs from the production archive). In contrast to all of the variants named earlier, its effect was—and still is—not to extend the live outward, dissolve its boundaries, and make it interchangeable or simulatable but rather to turn it inwards, intensify it, extend it into itself and make it complex. This process turns the televisual present into an entirely new temporal event, which transforms the ontographic structure of television, and the introduction of this new image technology thus constitutes a trajectory of television as a whole. Through this process the switch image exposes itself to a change that it first produces as an intervention. I am referring here to the "instant replay"—that is, the immediate repetition of the image in the context of a live broadcast, which is often performed in slow motion. It is impossible to overestimate the slow-motion replay's contribution to image culture and its impact on television as a live medium, as the temporal ontography of the instant replay, which writes time bidirectionally by operating simultaneously backward and forward, established television's own highly remarkable form of the present. It is strange, therefore, that there has never been any concise theoretical consideration of the instant replay until now. As a result, we will begin with a series of case studies.

The recording of electromagnetic signals had long been a concern of the development departments of various device manufacturers, particularly in Germany, and magnetic tape recorders were already in wide circulation in the 1940s (Abramson 1974: 133–4; 172–7). The problem of video recording was largely electromechanical, as it was necessary to increase tape speed in order to process the enormous amounts of information in images. The first functional video recorder was the AMPEX Quadruplex, which was a gigantic apparatus with five-centimeter-wide magnetic tapes that came on the market in 1956 (Abramson 1974: 62–7). This device enabled the recording of television image signals, but it was financially costly not only to purchase but also to operate, as the tapes were expensive and the device required two to three workers. It thus took considerable time before magnetic tape recording became the norm (Daniel, Mee and Clark 1999: 153–69). In the 1960s, for example, the use of AMPEX machines was still more often an exception— particularly in news coverage, which required a certain degree of flexibility. The introduction of this new technology initially went more or less unnoticed by viewers. Due to its high costs, AMPEX technology was also not suitable for archival purposes. As a result, there was no comprehensive recording and archiving of television images and programs prior to the mid-1970s, which had serious consequences for the historiography of early television (see Chapter 10 in this volume). In the beginning, therefore, the time allocation of television remained virtually unchanged.

## Replay

The first spectacular use of early AMPEX technology, in which viewers could clearly notice the blending of recorded and live coverage, occurred precisely on November 24, 1963. Following Doane's model of the catastrophe, the assassination of John F. Kennedy captivated the attention of television coverage in countless live special broadcasts (Doane 1990: 222–39). A small regional television station subsequently transmitted live footage of the transfer of Kennedy's assassin, Lee Harvey Oswald, from police headquarters to prison in Dallas, Texas. While this story was actually more of local interest, it was nevertheless broadcast live across the country by NBC (JFK1963NEWSVIDEOS 2013). The television reporter waited for Oswald's arrival with an unidentifiable group of people in an underground garage, where he was supposed to be picked up by a prison transport. As soon as he appeared, however, nightclub owner Jack Ruby suddenly stepped out of the row of bystanders and shot Oswald directly in front of the live cameras, which continued to broadcast this (at least as a television image) visually and acoustically confusing situation. NBC recorded the broadcast on AMPEX, and after this spectacular and unexpected course of events it was able to repeatedly show the decisive seconds when Ruby stepped up to Oswald and shot him at close range.

The repetition of this spectacular report in the dense sequence of news broadcasts that followed was driven in part by the fact that the event was only vaguely perceptible in the images and their repetition thus promised to provide a better understanding of what happened at this deadly moment. It was supposed to enable the visualization of the decisive moment when the shot was fired, when Oswald collapsed, or even when Ruby first moved and the entire course of events began to emerge as an unexpected deviation that was foreseeable but could no longer be stopped. This repetition did not occur in the mode of the "instant replay"—that is, it did not take place in direct connection with and in the immediate context of the continuing live broadcast—but rather only after at least thirty minutes. It was also impossible to decelerate the tape recording so that the event could be observed more closely in slow motion. However, the recording was made available to countless other stations and was shown hundreds of times over the next twenty-four hours. This shocking event, which was the first murder ever committed before a live television camera, is still present in the collective media memory of America; for example, it was fictionally reconstructed once again in the recent series *Mad Men* using the original material, which is still available.

A real instant replay, which follows immediately after the live broadcast of the event itself, took place exactly one week later. The traditional football game between the army and the navy was originally supposed to take place on November 24, but it was postponed one week due to Kennedy's assassination. Shortly before the end of the game, Carl "Rollie" Stichweh, the quarterback of the army team, which was lagging behind, caught up to the navy team with a spectacular six-point play. Less than a minute later, apparently in the most unlikely way, the same Stichweh made another touchdown with exactly the same play, or at least that was how it appeared to viewers following the game on CBS. What they had actually seen, however, was the first instant replay immediately following an event—a new technique developed by television director Tony Verna (Verna 2009: 2f.; 10ff.; Malinowski 2010). According to Verna's own proud recount, this had only been possible by means of a technical trick. When mechanically rewinding a videotape, it was normally very difficult and time-consuming to go back to a specific point. However, Verna came up with the idea of playing a beeping sound on the audio track of the tape at the beginning of each play (which are clearly distinct in football due to countless time-outs). The sound marked the beginning of the passage to be replayed, and it could be easily heard while rewinding. Replays could thus be shown immediately following the plays.

## Slow Motion, Freeze Frame, and Reversal

Then, in 1967, the AMPEX HS 100 came onto the market, and it was specially designed for slow-motion replays. Interestingly, it originally used not a magnetic tape, but rather a video disc that could progressively slow down the images to a standstill or "freeze frame." This expansion of the instant replay soon permeated sports coverage, where it triggered a surge of aesthetic creativity (Barnouw 1990: 348–52). With the help of television, it became possible to see things that had never before been seen in the stadium or anywhere else: "Brutal collisions became ballets, and end runs and forward passes became miracles of human coordination" (Barnouw 1990: 348). Within a very short time the instant replay became a standard operation of football broadcasts on television. Stadium camera systems were also changed. Instead of only using one camera to follow the game in long shots, as before, three additional cameras, each connected to its own recording device, took close-up shots of plays and followed individual players. As Marshall McLuhan noted, football on television became something entirely different from football in the real world, as a strange new reality or counter-reality emerged (Comstock 1991: 65–6; McLuhan 1964: 355–6). As a televised event, football made a career jump, which also had an effect on sports in general—particularly from an economic perspective (Ibid.; Comstock 1991: 71–3; Barnouw 1990: 348). The same was soon true for baseball as well. It was helpful that American sports (football, baseball, and generally speaking also hockey and basketball) consist of calculated plays and countless time-outs (unlike soccer, which ideally proceeds with few interruptions). This provided time for instant replays, which could fill the breaks in a way that was suitable for television. In 1964 CBS even bought its own baseball team, the New York Yankees. Shortly afterwards the California cable television company Subscription TV acquired the New York Giants and the Brooklyn Dodgers and relocated both teams to its own service area, where they continue to play today as the San Francisco Giants and the Los Angeles Dodgers.

In 1976 instant replay systems were also included in the game itself, as they were supposed to allow plays to be reviewed during time-outs and they thus served to support either the referee or the coach. Goal-line technology (or the goal decision system) is still debated in soccer today, although now under digital and thus considerably expanded conditions, such as the number and positions of the cameras and the additional operations on and in the image. However, it is significant that live television images are now shown in the stadiums themselves on enormous screens that magnify the plays occurring on the field. It is even possible to see a slow-motion replay while the game is still being played. We will specifically discuss the production of this circular interaction between screen images and the stadium audience elsewhere (see Chapter 9 in this volume).

Another spectacular use of the slow-motion replay took place on May 1, 1994, during the live broadcast of the Formula One auto race in Imola, San Marino ([Formula 1 San Marino 1994]; see also France Automobile 2017). While driving into a long curve, known as the Tamburello curve, the Brazilian race car driver Ayrton Senna, multiple world champion, went off the track live on television (in Germany, the race was broadcast on RTL). Instead of following the curve, he drove straight ahead and crashed into a wall. He was then flown to a hospital, where he died shortly afterwards.

As the race continued, recordings of the accident taken from different perspectives (including the cockpit camera of Michael Schumacher, who was driving behind Senna) were inserted again and again like instant replays. Increasingly slowed-down versions were also broadcast during the ongoing race. However, they focused not on the crash itself but rather on the moment before the crash, when something must have happened to Senna's car that forced him to drive straight ahead instead of following the slight curve to the left. Lengthy investigations conducted by the relevant authorities determined that this must have actually been the crucial moment when the car's steering column broke, although there are other ways of interpreting the material that suggest Senna might have made a driving error. More specifically, he might have driven too fast over the bumps before the curve, which disrupted the airflow under the car. As a result, he might have lost traction and his car might have become unsteerable, in which case the broken steering column would have been caused by the accident rather than vice versa.

My final example is a legendary incident that occurred during the extra time of the final match of the 2006 FIFA World Cup in Berlin when the French soccer player Zinedine Zidane, who was of paramount importance for his team, knocked down his opponent Marco Materazzi with a head butt to the chest (dcmdcmdcm 2006). Zidane's attack came out of nowhere and seemed not only grossly irregular but also entirely unmotivated. Materazzi and Zidane had each scored one goal by that point. Zidane immediately received the red card in what was advertised as the final game of his career, and Italy became the world champions. The actual scene had escaped the live transmission and could only be seen in a slow-motion replay from a camera that had been exclusively directed at Zidane throughout the game. This replay was then inserted into the coverage, and it revealed that a fierce and excited Materazzi had actually yelled at Zidane, which made Zidane's claim that Materazzi had vulgarly insulted him seem more plausible. In the following days, viewers began to sympathize with Zidane, who was furnished from that point on with the image of a tragic hero who was maliciously provoked and subsequently lost control.

## Ontography of the Instant Replay

In this last example, as well as the case of the accidental death of Ayrton Senna, the instant replay accesses a timeless mythogene. Through its possibilities of production, distribution, and above all repetition, it plays an important role in the creation of popular culture heroes and iconic images, which become detached from the mere course of events. Slow-motion replays can also play an important role in the making of history, which was particularly evident in the example of Oswald's assassination and the images of September 11. We will examine the historiographic dimensions of the instant replay separately (see Chapter 10 in this volume). What is most relevant here is that slow-motion replays are characterized by time fields that operate on either side of perceptible and experienceable time. Slow-motion images are not only embedded in meaning-giving processes of a trans-dimensional and trans-historical scale, like mythologization, but also at the same time engaged in detailed analysis, which leads to the virtually microscopic physical causalities that are below the thresholds of perception or sensation. The slow-motion replay apparently involves a technically induced and explosive expansion of a present that is microscopically contracted, infinitely repeatable, and at the same time distributed culturally through mythology.

However, time functions between both physical microtemporality and cultural timelessness, as it is accessible to human organisms and societies through perception and experience, remembering and expectation. The instant replay is also highly effective within rather than only in the exceeding of these thresholds. The moment of the present and its ontography are thus extremely important for television as a live medium.

In order to obtain information on the instant replay's specific ontology of the present it is helpful to consult Niklas Luhmann's theory of time. Luhmann understands the present as the time period in which an event or an action can still change or be changed (Luhmann 1995: 42f.; 78f.). Luhmann thus conceives of the present as an extended period and not (only) as a specific point in time; he also conceives of it as the juxtaposition of these presents—that is, the specific point in time and its constant reversibility. This understanding of the present can also be understood as the interaction of simultaneity and synchronicity, which is experienced and perceived as the release of tension. In other words, a sequence is perceived at a certain moment, and the tension lies in whether the predictable consequence will actually occur. This is particularly apparent in sports, such as at the beginning of a play. By choosing the intervention in an ongoing event or process as his guiding principle, Luhmann also calls for a fundamentally operative understanding of time that—no matter how complex reciprocal causalities may be—links time and intervention together. Time is necessary for the performance of interventions because they themselves always already require time; on the other hand, time also always emerges from interventions, such as the distinction between earlier and later.

We can take this up: The instant replay reverses this process, as it questions the precise moment when an event could be expected or could no longer be changed—that is, the point in time when its emergence was already past. The search for this moment requires time, and during this time the event continues as a present that can still change. The instant replay thus simultaneously generates past, present, and future—namely, expectation—and embeds them in the continuous present. By intervening in this process—that is, the sequence of live images—the instant replay interrupts it without really interrupting it; rather, the processes are combined and carried along together. This occurs either through switching between the continuing image and the slow-motion replay or through the split-screen process, in which a second (preferably smaller) image appears on the screen and both the live images and the instant replay images are seen at the same time. The slow-motion images remain stagnant, and they thus represent the past of the ongoing event, which progresses further and further ahead in time; nevertheless, they are closely connected through the uninterrupted flow of events and even through the assumption of causality. The instant replay shows why things have taken a particular course, whose further consequences can now be seen. Causes and effects are thus integrated through this intervention, which operatively produces a form of the present that recursively confirms and verifies itself as a continuous present. It seeks and marks the starting point of what is now seen—that is, the moment that paved the way for everything that followed. It identifies itself as the result of an operation—namely, as an interruption of the synchronous image flow, as a technical delay and replay from the tape, and lastly as its reinscription back into the image flow. It carries within itself a second or counter-present, which is different yet indistinguishable from the first and which functions on the same level and in the same flow (Deleuze 2013b: 82–6).

On the other hand, the instant replay also conceives of the present as a specific point in time—particularly in terms of its analytical power. In the case of the car accident, for example, it is the moment when the steering column breaks and the event becomes irrevocably tragic (or, in other cases, triumphant) according to purely physical laws. According to Luhmann, this is the precise moment when the present stops being the present. However, this moment is always only definable as such retrospectively through the complex technical procedure of its uncovering. In other words, it only comes into existence after it is removed from the course of events. Moreover, the instant replay does not detach the moment from this process, like the photographic snapshot, as it is never isolated (that would be an ontological process) but rather remains part of the process itself. It is also possible to dodge around this moment by moving the image forward and backward in slow motion. The ontography of the instant replay thus operates through the manipulation of the present, whether in the form of the future past (i.e., the point after which it is no longer possible to change what is yet to come) or the timelessness of a mythical presence (i.e., it will always have been this way ever since) (Engell 2019).

Three different timing techniques thus characteristically run parallel to and into one another. The first is the live broadcast, which continues in the background of the instant replay and claims to synchronize the events taking place with their appearance on the screen. The second is the initially instantaneous and subsequently loop-like repetition of the event, which constantly renews the passing present moment on the screen—if not by extending the length of its duration then through the potentially infinite return of its presence. However, this duration is actually foreign to the characteristic feature of the event, which in a strict sense already expires again at the moment it occurs (Deleuze 2004: 186–93). The third is the slowing down of the image until it is brought to a standstill, "freeze frame," or "arrêt sur image," which is followed once again by its reacceleration back to normal speed. The "freeze frame" takes the moment out of the ongoing event and makes it temporarily endless (Engell 2010: 172–91). It is important to note, however, that the standstill of the image in the instant replay is by no means an immobile still image. The image signal is not halted but rather reproduced up to twenty-five times per second. Further temporal relationships arise between and in these synchronizations. While the slow motion is still running, however, other things occur on the screen that are necessarily concealed from it. The live stream keeps on going relentlessly in the background, although it is typically invisible and often only audible in the form of commentary; it has recently also been kept present as a small image within the image, which constitutes a blended mode of lesser presence. This gives rise to a tension between the continuing live image and the loop-like circuit of a past moment, which suspends the linear flow of time in favor of a moving standstill that is like "treading water." The idea of the present as a continuous, ongoing process and the idea of the present as an extensionless elementary point in time thus overlap in two ways. At the macroscopic level, this occurs through the tension between the replaying of the recording and the ongoing live broadcast. At the microscopic level, this coupling of the moment and its extension is brought about by the fluid transition from normal speed to slow motion to the still image. More specifically, this multiple overlapping precedes the event in terms of its temporal logic, as it is a necessary condition for anything to be able to occur, and it is explicitly extracted and exposed as a screen event through this instantaneous technical intervention, which makes it available to human perception.

## Twofold Ontography

The ontography of the instant replay has two special features that correspond to the characteristics we have observed until now. The instant replay initially records being (*das Seiende*) once again as a performance through its own performance, as in the course of a play in sports or an accident in racing. The first special feature of the instant replay, however, is that it is differentiated from the image that continues in real time, yet it still remains on the horizon of this image. It is recognized as a technical intervention, as time axis manipulation, as back flow, as the artificial deceleration of an image that has already been seen, and as a second and recursive ontographic operation on the already ontographic material. The repetition identifies the events that have occurred (and nonetheless are still continuing) as written and recorded, yet at the same time it also brings these events back into the present—that is, the ongoing live broadcast. Unlike the continuing image, therefore, the instant replay records the ontographic process itself, as it broadcasts something live that is also at the same time a recording. What is broadcast, then, is not a complete recording but rather a continuing recording of the present itself, including the repeated performance of rewinding and switching back, which is simultaneously both a transmission and a recording. The instant replay thus adds a form of temporal recursivity to the already-known characteristics of ontography, which, unlike all other forms of reflexivity and self-reflexivity, operates at the same level, without an outpost or second level, and is in this sense immanent.

The second special feature is that two ontographic processes, which we initially analyzed separately, overlap in the instant replay. More specifically, ontography appears in the instant replay as a videographic imaging process that enables the visualization of an operation or condition that is normally concealed or closed off. It does this through the process of deceleration, as we are unable to see fast enough or keep a record of what we see. We are normally unable to perceive or relate to the breaking of a steering column during a race or the vaulting of a ball during a free kick in soccer. The ontographic process thus reveals a particular way of being, which is not perceptible or representable for us except through a purely technical process. This process allows us to see not only the necessarily elusive moment but also at the same time how it necessarily eludes us. We are dealing here with an operative separation (and linking) of that which exists *for* the technical process and us, the viewers of the event, and that which exists *without* us, before it is made accessible through technical operations. However, this separation and linking are not detached from us or the videographic and ontographic operations. In this sense, the distinction between that which exists for itself and that which exists through and for the technical process is only visible and operative when it remains part of and emerges from the continuing present of the running images.

This is important because two dominant notions of ontography differ from each other at this point. In the phenomenological tradition, as represented by Sebastien Blanc and Michael Stadler, ontography occurs precisely through the unavoidable integration of description and recording (and what phenomenology calls consciousness) in what is described and recorded and thus in the fullness and diversity of being itself (Blanc 2000: 289–310; Stadler 2014). In contrast, the school of speculative realism and object-oriented ontology, particularly Graham Harman and to a certain degree Ian Bogost, sees ontography as a diagrammatic and graphic process that can override and undermine this correlationism (Harman 2010: 124–35; Bogost 2012). Ontography is thus a technique that transcends representation, as it allows material being to be recorded without us—that is, without the intervention of a consciousness that is understood as immaterial. In terms of media history, incidentally, this assumption can be traced back to photography, which was already seen as enabling the self-recording of light or nature as a whole and which Bogost thus identifies as a prominent ontographic process. In terms of media theory, the concept of self-recording is obviously highly problematic—in this form at least—as it does not take the operative performance of the apparatus into account. In other words, it ignores the contribution of the apparatus—that is, the recording equipment—to ontography.

The instant replay actually presents the ontography of television not only as a process for revealing and paradoxically participating in a way of being—namely, without us—but also as a way of being itself—namely, the way of being of the television image, which only occurs at all as the performance of its drawing or writing. In the instant replay, this performance is reversible, repeatable, and even stoppable as a specially generated counter-present. The stopability of the video image is thereby precisely not the freezing of the signal flow but rather the tenacious repetition and constantly renewed recording of the same signal sequence, which is also an uninterrupted but loop-like process. Technical reproduction also does not give the recorded image an ontic stability as a durable thing; rather, the image remains existentially dependent on its continuing operationalization. And these two moments of ontography—as the way of being of the recording process and as revealing a way of being from its performance—are ultimately connected and amalgamated in the instant replay. The decisive moment, which the instant replay reveals, only exists in and through the repeated reproduction of the recording process (on the magnetic tape), to which it owes its existence.

## Chronography

This observation of the temporal ontography of the instant replay starts from human and social timing processes, as it refers to perception, experience, and expectation. Another far less anthropocentric interpretation can be developed again from Deleuze's *The Logic of Sense*, which presents a highly idiosyncratic interpretation of the philosophy of time of the ancient Stoa (Deleuze 2004: 186–93; Sellars 2007: 177–205). According to Deleuze, time was understood within the school of Stoa not in terms of different temporal stages, such as the past, present, and future; rather, it consists of two completely different physical states or organizational forms, whose relationship to one another is initially unclear. In other words, it was understood as the initially unmediated difference between two completely different concepts of time. According to Deleuze, the two concepts that constitute the Stoic understanding of time are *Chronos* and *Aion*. Both Chronos and Aion conceive of time as the relationship between the past, present, and future, but they do this in entirely incommensurable ways (Mengue 2003: 41–7).

Chronos apprehends time above all as the extended present of that which exists and endures—that is, the material, physical, and spatially extended body, which is at the same time the origin of movement, action, and blending (Deleuze 2004: 186). For our purposes, this would apply to the stream of live images on television or the sequence of episodes in a television series. What is detached from this extended and real present is that which no longer exists (such as the past of the series or the previous episode) and that which does not yet exist (such as the future of the series or the next episode). The present is thus circumscribed by the past and the future. On the other hand, however, the past and the future always refer to the continuing present as its other and its effect. They are only past and future in relation to the continuing present, and they are thus aspects of the present itself. This is confirmed by the instant replay: the decisive movement that it reveals is only decisive because of what happens next (and what has already happened in the course of the broadcast). When seen from a higher ontological perspective beyond the performance of the present, they thus appear to be the past and the future of what is currently happening. This means that they are just as present as the present itself, into which they can contract (such as the series as a whole or the sequence of an entire soccer game). This newly extended present is then immediately circumscribed by a new past and future, and so on (Deleuze 2004: 186f.).

From the highest divine perspective, time ultimately forms a single present, in which everything is simultaneous (in terms of television, it is like a dimensionless flow). As Chronos, then, time is always narrowly circumscribed yet at the same time infinite. It thus involves two movements: the (relative) extension of the present toward and in relation to its constantly shifting boundaries—that is, its new pasts and futures—and the (absolute) movement of contracting the past and the future into a single present that enfolds, envelopes, "complicates," and cyclically traverses everything (Deleuze 1969: 190). Even without a divine perspective, both of these movements can be seen as technically produced paradigmatically in the instant replay, as it extends the present in both directions at the same time (by rewinding into the past while the broadcast is still ongoing) and it condenses entire processes through a repeated cyclical traversal of the same signal to the decisive or (to borrow Lessing's phrase) "fruitful" moment, in which the entire sequence contracts and the present transforms into the past (Lessing 1967: 14f.).

This concept of time is not only evident in the Stoa but also supported prominently by Augustine (Aug. conf. XI 18-26; see also Flasch 1993). It also reappears in modern philosophy in Husserl's phenomenology of internal time-consciousness, such as the idea of an extended and sustained present beyond the mere moment. It extends into the past through retention, which returns to the past by remembering, and it extends into the future through protention, which runs ahead by anticipating. This double movement thus enables a contracting, simultaneous continuation, such as a melody heard in a succession of tones (Husserl 1991: 21–75, here: 27–36; 54f.). Another example would be the constant tension during a play in sports, as mentioned earlier, which viewers experience as an ineluctable presence and as "being present" (*Dabeisein*). Henri Bergson's philosophy of time is also indebted to the concept of Chronos, including his central concept of "duration" (*durée*), which Deleuze discusses extensively elsewhere and from which he later derives his entire philosophy of film (Bergson 1988; Deleuze 1988, 2013a,b).

## Change and Measurelessness

According to Deleuze, surprisingly, moments of becoming and of gradual development pose a problem for Chronos. While Bergson renounces the measurable and only measurable time of positivism (and of Aristotle) (phys. IV 10-14) by focusing precisely on moments of emergence, change, and creativity, these moments represent an unceasing paradox for Chronos. (This would of course also affect the time of television as a live medium as well as the time of the instant replay.) In particular, as Plato already assumed and the Stoa maintained, that which is in the process of becoming must be distinguished from that which already is and continues to be as it now is. In other words, that which is (still) changing is part of another way of being than that which simply is, and that which is (still) developing has not yet occurred. In direct opposition to Luhmann's view, then, becoming does not mean being present in the sense of a relevant and stable "being-as-it-is" (*So-Sein*); rather, it is merely provisional. In other words, that which is conceived as constantly becoming and changing will never fully arise or be present. According to Deleuze's formulation, becoming is thus a "sidestepping of the present" (Deleuze 2004: 188). If this were true, then it would obviously also affect the time of television as a live medium, as the live image would not be a performance but rather a sidestepping of the present, as it does not record anything. On the other hand, however, becoming (like the running image) must go through the "now" of the present in order for it to occur (in the relative movement of the extension). The stable being of bodies and substances can actually account for the extended present of Chronos but not for the changing of its qualities, such as its growth or aging (Deleuze 2004: 187f.). This recalls Stanley Cavell's view of television as including everything that it shows in a single extended present through "monitoring" and excluding any change in its serial formats through stereotypes (Cavell 1982: 75–96). For Cavell, therefore, television as a whole is precisely a "sidestepping of the present"—that is, the increasing uninhabitability of the world. We dismissed this view earlier in terms of the seriality of television, yet the instant replay seems to be an unconventional articulation of precisely this paradox of frozen change, as it represents the abyss of Chronos. The instant replay seeks out the one decisive "now-moment" within a process or development, but it cannot permanently detach this moment from the process, like a snapshot or (according to Lessing) a sculpture. In other words, the instant replay cannot freeze this moment once and for all and give it a permanent presence as something that is (or was) exactly as it is; rather, it must constantly amalgamate this moment with the ongoing extended present.

Deleuze identifies a second problem of Chronos using the concept of the "measure" or "measurelessness" (Deleuze 2004: 187). Chronos explicitly includes time as a measure (and a number, like Aristotle). The extended bodies of the present are always circumscribed and measured, like the present itself, and the contraction of temporal levels in a divine simultaneity also lends them a measurement and a proportionality. For the purpose of this study, the switching processes in the running image can be understood as boundaries in this sense, as they mark beginnings and endings and they set limits to a shot within a sequence of shots, to a sequence within a program, to a program within the program sequence, and to the program sequence as a whole. In doing so, they adhere to the criteria of proportionality and conformity. However, the changeable and insubstantial qualities of the bodies that are inherent in these processes, which are not provided for in Chronos, evade this proportionality and conformity. They transcend the proportional present through their finitude as well as their infinitude, which results in measurelessness. Like the flow of television or the rejection of clear beginning and end points in individual programs, they can get out of control, degenerate, proliferate, and "become mad." According to Deleuze, this can not only happen locally to a single well-defined body, which then loses its form; rather, it can also spread and eventually even include the integration of all temporal levels in a cycle of the present. The entire extended present then "becomes mad," and it renounces a measured circulation in favor of an unfathomable vortex, much like the transition from the program mode to the flow mode of television. This subversion is the other constant danger of Chronos, and the instant replay can also be seen here as a version of this danger. The well-measured duration of a shot that shows a movement from beginning to end is undermined in the instant replay by a completely plastic time (and obviously also by time axis manipulation), which arbitrarily extends and interrupts the processes. If something transforms a football game into an absurd ballet, a reproduction of an always identical microsequence, or a constant back and forth, as in the example cited earlier, then the abyss of measurelessness opens and threatens to dissolve the time of Chronos.

## Aionography

According to Deleuze, the time of Aion is opposed to that of Chronos (Deleuze 2004: 187–9). Instead of circumscribing the present through the past and the future, it involves the constant division of time into the past and the future through the present. In this respect, the time of Aion is no longer ontological in the sense mentioned earlier—that is, its aim is not to determine what is and it no longer refers to "being-as-it-is" (*So-Sein*) in the form of continuing, existing, or becoming; rather, it behaves operatively, as it is based on the operation of division and differentiation. Only the past and the future are extended and exist (though absent), while the present is their extensionless and incorporeal yet constant division and differentiation. Their division through the "instant" of the present is also constantly updated in the past and the future, as that which comes earlier and that which comes later can always be further differentiated from one another (Deleuze 1969: 193). As a result, time is completely unbounded by the past and the future; in the present of their (relative) differentiation, conversely, it is maximally provisional and therefore finite. Whereas the time of Chronos cyclically merges, the time of Aion is also completely linear, as the past and the future are not bordered (by a constantly expanding present) but instead infinitely divisible (Büttner and Ries 1997: 355; Sellars 2007: 18–24). Tony Verna's improvisation of the beeping sound on the videotape, which marked the decisive point where the instant replay should begin, is in this sense not a chronological or *chronographic* operation but rather a paradigmatically aionical or *aionographic* operation. The beep differentiates between the section that comes before it, which is not reproduced, and the section that follows it, which is shown once again as a replay. The beep itself is thus reproducible, as every piece of videotape can be divided into a before and after in this way. Finally, a second point in time is also already implied in every beep, such as the decisive moment in each play that is the primary focus in the center of the replay and that keeps dividing the replay in different ways. This second point in time even becomes the actual subject of the replay, as it is encircled, manipulated, and repeated in forward and reverse slow motion during the ongoing broadcast and thus before the viewers' eyes (as in the example of Ayrton Senna's accident or countless sports broadcasts today). This also involves the division of time into a before and after, which is shown to viewers as a technical, operative process.

The behavior of the instant replay as an aionographic process is thus the opposite of its behavior as a chronographic process. As we have seen, the instant replay as a chronographic process performs time in the form of a generally continuous and cyclical present, which is bounded and infinite at the same time. In the aionography of the instant replay, conversely, the present functions in the form of an incorporeal point in time (whether it be that of the beginning of the replay, which is marked by the beep, or that of the decisive turning point, the "fruitful" moment, or the singularity of the process). Instead of being represented as an extension, it is marked as an operation. According to Deleuze, the "pure event" of the division of time itself is also always both in the past (the beep) and in the future (it is being looked for). Aion can thus be conceived as the "*pure empty form of time*, which has freed itself of its present corporeal content" (Deleuze 2004: 189). This means that events, for Deleuze, are singular—that is, they are independent of persons and individuals. Becoming (i.e., the decisive turning point of an event) also arises in the non-extended event as a singularity that separates two extended conditions from one another in the sense of a before and after and thus always operates in both directions at the same time (i.e., the past and the future). If the event (the beep) supersedes the extended body, then the time of Aion also refers not to qualities but rather to (superficial) attributes, which can be present as well as absent (Deleuze 2004). In principle, the beep can be placed anywhere. The placement of beeps on the magnetic tape is the non-extended, event-forming operation of dividing time, from which time emerges as a series of points that contract and expand into a line.

Two different series or lines thus develop in the instant replay, which are actually two different kinds of time that are both aionically formed by the operation of dividing. The first is the purely formal and now completely revisable (unlike in Verna's time) determination of the beginning of the replay (its end coincides with a re-entry into the ongoing present and thus with a transition to chronographic time). The second involves the singularly important turning point of the event, which the instant replay exposes and after which everything is different than it was before. However, this also divides two completely different horizons—namely, the completely non-semantic and formally operational world of the beeps on the tape and the world of dramatic and corporeal events, which culminate and contract in the decisive moment. The twofold linear time of the replay thus separates the world of formal and functional yet meaningless (formal) events and articulations from the semantic and meaningful world of bodies and (formed) substances, such as those of the football game and its players.

## Meaning

Deleuze draws the far-reaching and surprising conclusion that Aion enables language through this separation (Deleuze 2004: 189f.). "Language" here refers not only to human verbal language but to all language-forming structures, including images, films, and cultures in general. However, language is only possible when the merely material sounds are separated from the meanings that they express, which are incorporeal, immaterial, and even metaphysical. This separation removes language from the simple condition of bodily actions and passions, which prevents it from mixing with the disruptions of the body. According to Deleuze, meaning is also an incorporeal event that "insists" (Deleuze 2004: 188–90) and thus always precedes its articulation in language. In other words, it is an event that awaits its expression in language and thus ultimately awaits us. Deleuze's eventualistic concept of meaning is obviously unconventional, and it is directly opposed to an entire series of established concepts of meaning, such again as Luhmann's (to name only one). Luhmann sees meaning as the "and so forth . . ." of experience and action, which is precisely what is separated from meaning for Deleuze. Deleuze's concept of the event must, in turn, remain unworkable for Luhmann's concept of meaning production. Deleuze's assertion of an incorporeal, event-forming meaning also appears to have no relevance at all for the instant replay, as there is no immaterial or metaphysical meaning that precedes Verna's signals, and these signals are just as material as the events happening on the field.

Deleuze's idea is helpful, however, if it is subjected to a double reversal, and both of these reversals stem from the ontographic nature of the instant replay—namely, from its recursivity and its immanence (in contrast to ontology, which needs an outpost). First, we can complicate Deleuze by assuming that the division of two equally operative time series (formal and semantic) recursively reacts to itself and recurs within the semantic chain of singularities. Their separation into a meaningful and singular event (the decisive turning point, the "fruitful" moment) and a purely functional, arbitrary, and repeatable event (the beep) then entails further separations. In particular, the instant replay reveals precisely that the decisive turning point ultimately cannot be revealed and thus suspended. It does not actually belong to the images themselves. As we have seen, the image decelerated to a standstill or "freeze frame" (a sustained repetition) reveals nothing whatsoever as an image. The significance of the decisive moment lies not in the moment itself but only in the sequence of images that come before and after it—that is, in the lead-up to the moment and its consequences. And while it is looked for there, it once again remains absent. That which is decisive in the decisive moment is always outside the image. The second reversal is related to this "outside." For Deleuze, meaning is outside language. As a media-philosophical assumption, this is highly problematic due to Deleuze's late-structuralist privileging of language. If one includes the technical operativity of the imaging process (and thus the switchability of the switch image), however, then another picture emerges. It would then be logical to assume that the singular moment does not already exist in a metaphysical realm beyond the chain of images but is instead emergent—that is, it first emerges from these images and their operations, though without originating from them. The emergence of the moment does not change its non-belonging to the images of the replay. Under these conditions, the singular moment does not belong to the decelerated and reproduced flow of images, but it also cannot exist without them. If Deleuze is right that the moment (and thus meaning) is waiting for its articulation, then it is waiting to emerge from the instant replay.

Chronos and its relationship to Aion then come back into the picture. They are not only complementary but also completely external and inaccessible to one another. Nevertheless, they need and are inscribed in one another, as the incorporeal, featureless, purely functional, and singular present of Aion requires a "representation" in the present of Chronos. Conversely, Chronos requires a "third present" that encloses, separates, and protects the measured present of the extended and sustained body and the subversive "becoming-mad" of mutable qualities (Deleuze 2004: 191). This representation and protection are performed by a "present of the pure operation" (Deleuze 2004: 192).

Deleuze cites actors, dancers, and mimes as examples. In the realm of technical images, however, the pure operation and the interaction of Chronos and Aion can detach from human bodies and activities. The pure operation is ontographically and thus ontotechnologically reproducible as an emergent effect in the instant replay. In the instant replay, the aionographic way for images (rather than bodies) to be present in their own movements occurs between the catastrophic poles of the chronographic present. One of the dangers of Chronos, as we have seen, is an explosive proliferation of transformations, which sweeps away all duration and ontic stability. The other danger is a total frozen standstill. The technical inscription of the aionographic present in the chronography of the instant replay thus actualizes and materializes the meaning that emerges from it. At the same time, it prevents the chronographic subversion from disrupting duration and assimilating transformation. The aionographic present in the instant replay thus involves a "counter-actualization, [. . .] which comes to duplicate the [duplication]" once again through the deceleration and reversal of the replay itself (Deleuze 2004: 192).

## The Counter-Present of the Instant Replay

The *counter-actualization* of the events, which is technically performed in the instant replay by the switch image, is thus not their reproduction but rather their duplicated duplication and complement. It is the other of the present in the present. The present of the live broadcast and its counter-actualization in the instant replay differ from and compete with one another, yet they also belong and work together. The simultaneity of the "real" present and the counter-actualization also affects additional and large parts of television. Their interaction can be observed, for example, from the separation between the real sports event and the television event since the introduction of the instant replay. It can also be traced to the transformations of the "live on tape," the "pseudo-live," and the "near to live" invoked earlier, which sets free different presents. It also includes the macroscopic realm of the rerun and the repeat. Even recorded and repeated programs are then not simply reproductions but rather (their own) counter-actualizations. However, television constantly differentiates and connects both the present and the counter-actualization by constantly switching back and forth between these different forms of replay. As we will see, the forms of so-called reality television, which have become widespread since the late 1990s, also began ontographically as a switch image in the counter-present and the counter-simultaneity. Electronic image recording thus transformed television. It now no longer simply represents sequences of real and fictional events and reproduces their present but also provides them with counter-actualizations while they are still happening. The switch image furnishes the televisually present world with a complement by its ontography. It needs this complement in order to avoid becoming rigid and (according to Cavell) uninhabitable or being dissolved in the excess of measurelessness. The counter-present opposes the present and blends with it to form a reality that looks (almost) the same but that owes its existence solely to television.

## References

Abramson, Albert. 1974. *Electronic Motion Pictures*. New York: Arno Press.
Anders, Günther. 1956a. "Die Welt als Phantom und Matritze." In: Günther Anders. *Die Antiquiertheit des Menschen, vol. 1: Über die Seele im Zeitalter der zweiten industriellen Revolution*, pp. 97–211. München: Beck.
Aristotle. 2005. *The Physics. Books I-IV*, with an English Translation by Philip H. Wicksteed and Francis M. Cornford, Cambridge, MA, London: Harvard University Press.
Augustine. 2016. *Confessions II. Books 9–13*, ed. and trans. by Carolyn J.-B. Hammond. Cambridge, MA, London: Harvard University Press.
Barnouw, Erik. 1990. *Tube of Plenty: The Evolution of American Television*. Oxford, New York: Oxford University Press.
Bergson, Henri. 1988. *Matter and Memory*. New York: Zone Books.
Blanc, Sébastien. 2000. "L'ontographie ou l'écriture de l'être chez Merleau-Ponty." *Les Etudes philosophiques* 3: 289–310.
Bogost, Ian. 2012. *Alien Phenomenology, or What It's Like to Be a Thing*. Minneapolis, London: University of Minnesota Press.
Büttner, Elisabeth, and Marc Ries. 1997. "Deleuze und die Natur des Ereignisses im Kino." In: *Der Film bei Deleuze/Le cinéma selon Deleuze*, ed. by Oliver Fahle, and Lorenz Engell, pp. 350–60. Weimar, Paris: Verlag der Bauhaus-Universität Weimar.
Cavell, Stanley. 1982. "The Fact of Television." *Daedalus* 111, no. 4: 75–96.
Comstock, George. 1991. *Television in America*. London: Sage.
Daniel, Eric D., Dennis C. Mee, and Mark H. Clark. 1999. *Recording: The First Hundred Years*. London: Wiley-IEEE Pr.
dcmdcmdcm. 2006. *Zidane knockt Materazzi aus - und bekommt ROT*. Accessed September 2, 2018. https://www.youtube.com/watch?v=K9owfWFzdnQ.
Deleuze, Gilles. 1969. *Logique du sens*. Paris: Les Editions de Minuit.
Deleuze, Gilles. 1988. *Bergsonism*. New York: Zone Books.
Deleuze, Gilles. 2004. *The Logic of Sense*. London, New York: Continuum.
Deleuze, Gilles. 2013a. *Cinema I: The Movement-Image*. London, New York: Bloomsbury Academic.

Deleuze, Gilles. 2013b. *Cinema II: The Time-Image*. London, New York: Bloomsbury Academic.

Doane, Mary Ann. 1990. "Information, Crisis, Catastrophe." In: *Logics of Television: Essays in Cultural Criticism*, ed. by Patricia Mellencamp, pp. 222–39. Bloomington, Indianapolis: Indiana University Press.

Engell, Lorenz. 2010. "'Are You in Pictures?' - Ruhende Bilder am Ende bewegter Bilder, besonders in Ethan und Joel Coens 'Barton Fink'." In: *Freeze frames. Zum Verhältnis von Fotografie und Film*, ed. by Stefanie Diekmann, and Winfried Gerling, pp. 172–91. Bielefeld: Transcript.

Engell, Lorenz. 2019 (expected). "'Seither' und 'Immer Schon'. Zwei Zeitfiguren bei Friedrich Kittler." In: *Kittler 1985/1986*, ed. by Till A. Heilmann, and Jens Schröter. n. p.: Springer.

Feuer, Jane. 1983. "The Concept of Live Television: Ontology as Ideology." In: *Regarding Television*, ed. by E. Ann Kaplan, pp. 12–21. Frederick: University Publications of America.

Flasch, Kurt. 1993. *Was ist Zeit? Augustinus von Hippo: Das XI. Buch der Confessiones*. Frankfurt/M: Klostermann.

[Formula 1 San Marino 1994]. N. d. Accessed September 14, 2018. https://www.youtube.com/watch?v=fCrUdyPY02k.

France Automobile. 2017. *GP de Saint-Marin 1994*. Accessed November 17, 2019. https://www.youtube.com/watch?v=z7Mam-wRbZk&t=2329s.

Gruber, Bettina, and Maria Vedder. 1983. "Les Levine." In: *Kunst und Video. Internationale Entwicklung und Künstler*, ed. by Bettina Gruber, and Maria Vedder, pp. 164–6. Köln: DuMont.

Harman, Graham. 2010. *The Quadruple Object*. Winchester, Washington, DC: Zero Books.

Husserl, Edmund. 1991. *On the Phenomenology of the Consciousness of Internal Time (1893–1917)*. Dordrecht, Boston, London: Kluwer Academic Publishers.

JFK1963NEWSVIDEOS. 2013. *KRLD-TV Footage of The Oswald Shooting*. Accessed July 16, 2019. https://www.youtube.com/watch?v=m5khMFFKslw.

Lessing, Gotthold Ephraim. 1967. "Laocoön or the Limits of Painting and Poetry." In: Gotthold Ephraim Lessing. *Laocön. Nathan the Wise. Minna von Barnhelm*, ed. by William A. Steel, pp. 1–110. London: Dent.

Luhmann, Niklas. 1995. *Social Systems*. Stanford: Stanford University Press.

Malinowski, Eric. 2010. "Dec 7, 1963: Video Instant Replay Comes To TV." In: *Wired*, 20/12/1207. Accessed September 2, 2018. https://www.wired.com/2010/12/1207army-navy.game.first-instant-replay/.

McLuhan, Marshall. 1964. *Understanding Media: The Extensions of Man*. London, New York: Routledge.

Mengue, Philippe. 2003. "Aiôn/Chronos." In: *Le Vocabulaire de Gilles Deleuze*, ed. by Robert Sasso, and Arnaud Villani, pp. 41–7. Nice: Les Cahiers de Noesis, 3.

Sellars, John. 2007. "Aion and Chronos: Deleuze and the Stoic Theory of Time." *Collapse* 3: 177–205. Also published in: *Academia*. Accessed June 26, 2018.

http://www.academia.edu/9816442/Ai%C3%B4n_and_Chronos_Deleuze_and_the_Stoic_Theory_of_Time.
Stadler, Michael. 2014. *Was heißt Ontographie? Vorarbeit zu einer visuellen Ontologie*. Würzburg: Königshausen & Neumann.
Verna, Tony. 2009. *Instant Replay: The Day that Changed Sports Forever*. New York: Creative Publishers.
Winston, Brian. 1986. *Misunderstanding Media*. Cambridge, MA: Harvard University Press.

# 7

# The Space Image

July 21, 1969, is the most important day in the history of television, and the moon landing is the greatest television event of all time. This is first of all due to the overlap of three different movements or trajectories of television. The first movement is the *expansion line* of television. Television is spreading. This line reached a culmination point or singularity (although not its end) in the flight to the moon, as television never again achieved such coverage. This includes the actual coverage of space, as television signals have never again been transmitted across such a distance and television cameras have never again been placed so far from viewers. However, the coverage of television on July 21, 1969, was also determined to be the highest ever according to the criteria of empirical communication research, as the flight to the moon achieved the highest relative audience rating—that is, the highest number of actual viewers in relation to the number of possible viewers. The roughly 600 million viewers who watched the landing on the moon comprised a seventh of the world's population at that time and a half of all people who had access to a television.[1] Eric Barnouw thus rightly titled his section on the Apollo program "Cosmic Nielsen" after the Nielsen Institute, which dominates the measurement of television ratings in the United States (Barnouw 1990: 423–5). Lastly, the coverage of the flight to the moon was also the highest in terms of its duration—at least in a few countries—as it was the most extensive live broadcast of all time and thus the largest temporal object of live television according to chronographically measured time. It is best to add that the spatially largest object ever shown on television was also made visible with the flight to the moon—namely, the planet Earth. The expansion line, which takes effect in these temporal and spatial extensions, is one of the driving forces behind the constant transformations of television.

At the same time, however, the moon landing condenses the entire development and (self-) transformation of television into a single event. Changes in the basic situation of the switch image, its ontographic modes, and its operations of liveness, seriality, flow, and anthropomediality are combined and concentrated into one point in the moon project. Furthermore, the flight to the moon not only incorporates the past but also embodies the vanishing lines of the future of television, as this event not only prepares but also concentrates its further development. The expansion into space and across the surface of the Earth is thus contrasted and complemented by an extreme *contraction* of television in the moon program. And third, it also involves a movement of reversal, return, and *recursion*. Television sent its images back to the Earth (and not, say, out into space), and its gaze was also turned back to the Earth in a spectacular way. Even though the camera they carried with them was left behind on the lunar soil (for weight reasons), television still ultimately returned to the Earth. Maximal expansion, a high degree of concentration, and a completed recursion, operating collectively yet inconsistently in the flight to the moon, effectively transformed the television of 1969 into something else—a first "New Television" (Stauff 2005).

## Cosmos Live

With all of this, we can assume that the flight to the moon was an event organized and produced by television itself. It transformed outer space into the inner space of television by making it the largest possible studio. It could at least involve a pseudo-event in Boorstin's sense, or possibly even a Baudrillardian simulation (Boorstin 1992; Baudrillard 2010: 1–42). That is why there are endless speculations and conspiracy theories concerning the simulated nature of the moon landing, which was allegedly only staged in a studio or in the Nevada desert; according to these theories, there was never anyone on the moon. These theories are misleading, however, as they assume that the flight to the moon was lacking reality. The reality of the flight to the moon was supposedly only brought about for the purpose of deception—that is, it is the reality of a fictional yet impenetrable illusion, like a pseudo-event. Or it could no longer be marked due to its indistinguishability from non-reality, and it was thus weak or entirely dissolved, like a simulation. But the idea of a deficient, weak, or evanescent reality must meet certain ontological conditions, as it draws a line between image (such as the image of television) and reality even when it deplores its loss. If we assume that television is fundamentally ontographic, though, then the images do not oppose, reference, or reflect an external reality. First, the reality of moving images, which is only available as and in the process of its production, is not weaker as an ontography than that of other images. Second, the ontological status (*Seinsstatus*) of the reality written through the images of television (or other ontographic media) is also not reduced in comparison to that of another or an external reality; rather, it is important that the specific properties and operations of the medium—in the case of television, its switchability—confer their special nature or mode of being to the ontic reality that they produce.

The flight to the moon thus ideally represents the expansion of the ontographic process far beyond the switch image, the studio, and the living room into a planetary and extra-planetary dimension. The ontographic image of reality becomes an image of ontographic reality (Fahle 2005: 77–91), as its worldwide dissemination through television and the production of evidence in the live image was at the same time the purpose of the enterprise as well as its precondition. Television was involved in the space project from the very beginning, and the flight to the moon was already planned as a gigantic, live television event. This applies, first and foremost, to the technical equipment. Technologies originally developed for television were also employed for the space mission, such as for the steering of the spacecraft. Conversely, television cameras developed specifically for transmitting from space and from the moon were mounted on and in the space capsule (Barnouw 1990: 423; Marschall 1987: 66–81). The very first operation that preceded the astronauts' exit from the capsule onto the lunar soil was to uncover the camera mounted on the landing module using a wire rope hoist. In order to save space, by the way, this camera was mounted upside down and thus showed the lunar soil above and the spacecraft and the astronauts below. After arriving on Earth, these confusingly weightless images were rotated 180 degrees and only then broadcast.

Besides the technical equipment, the Apollo mission was also one of the most important undertakings of the cold war and to a certain extent its culmination. Like a war, it was a continuation of politics by other, high-tech means. At the same time, however, it was propagated in the name of a vague but universally addressed collective humanity, which the United States merely operatively represented. Something similar was provided by the science-fiction series *Star Trek*, in which the "U.S.S. Enterprise" explored the galaxy on behalf of a confederation of states that included the entire Earth but that could also be recognized as an expanded United States. The Apollo mission was thus supposed to win and transcend the cold war at the same time. In order to succeed, it was necessary to operate directly and simultaneously before the eyes of a newly established collective subject—an integrated global public—and to appear clear and transparent at all times. Television was the only medium capable of this. In addition, there was also pressure to justify the enormous financial resources that had to be directed into the project. In particular, the American public had to be convinced of the meaningfulness and feasibility of the flight to the moon, and this is something that television had to accomplish. In fact, of course, not everything from the current Apollo program was on display, and not everything was shown live at the exact time it happened. There was no way that every mistake would actually occur in front of running cameras. The alleged transparency and the evidence of preparing and performing the flight to the moon were obviously aesthetic constructs (like every live broadcast). As with the direction of live television, according to Eco, the program instead switched back and forth between various settings, a number of which were explicitly not part of the ongoing events but rather in television studios; some of the material was also prerecorded and played as "near to live." These possibilities constituted precisely the expanded potential of the switch image.

Television not only provided the technical and ideological conditions of the flight to the moon but also dominated the entire enterprise by implementing its own formal requirements and demanding its maximum benefits (Engell 2008: 150–71). For example, the flight to the moon was not incorporated into the program without any preparation; rather, live broadcasts of space flights had already been produced and transmitted worldwide by countless stations since the Apollo 7 mission in October 1968. These broadcasts included the rocket launches, the return of the capsules (which descended spectacularly into the Pacific Ocean with three parachutes), and above all live broadcasts from space. During these flights NASA itself thus operated in the live mode of television, and there remained plenty of opportunities for accidents and catastrophes that could have occurred in the middle of the live broadcast.

The flight to the moon thus generated an enormous amount of tension and excitement, which encouraged participation. This was not its only regime of affect, however, as it also incorporated the aesthetics of the sublime. The flight of Apollo 8 in December 1968, during which a manned capsule circled the moon for the first time, was particularly spectacular. On Christmas Eve 1968, American television transmitted an unbelievably emotional special broadcast from inside the capsule (Hiebel et al. 1999: 638). Through the small window the planet Earth could be dimly recognized over the horizon of the moon. This was accompanied by the sound of the three astronauts reading aloud from the Bible—not the Christmas story but rather the story of creation. In light of the phenomenal size and impact of the planet, the cosmos, and the meaninglessness of humanity, the broadcast demonstrated the phenomenal ability of the human subject to endure, give meaning, and conquer the cosmos through (technical) reason. The motif of the sublime was already politically superimposed here. The moment of global participation was not only semantically declaimed and reclaimed but also physically implemented through the live broadcast and its synchronization and simultaneity effects with the course of the space flight and with the planetary regime of broadcast times. Moreover, to follow McLuhan's thesis, the level of viewer involvement was especially high because of the degree of "coldness" of the television image, as the very poorly defined black-and-white images from space made their anthropo-mediatic entanglement particularly tangible.

## The Apollo Series

Television, however, integrated these highly charged live highlights into a complex structure of different serializations, which lent extension and endurance to the moon program. First, there was the sequence of the flights themselves, which were numbered consecutively and held together by an incremental logic, as they each involved an increasing distance from the Earth, a longer duration, and more complex processes (Barnouw 1990: 425). The flight to the moon was thus subject to the serial logic of the television series, which culminated in Eric Barnouw's assumption that Neil Armstrong's name played a significant role in his selection as the first man on the moon, as it seemed plausible to most Americans that this hero was supposed to be the namesake of a famous series hero, Jack Armstrong, who was known as the "All-American Boy." In light of Armstrong's first erratic sentence from the moon, which must have been determined in advance, Barnouw also noted that "everything went by the script" (Barnouw 1990).

However, this incremental movement could not continue after the first landing on the moon. Although the subsequent missions until 1972 were longer and more complex, as seen by the deployment of the lunar rover, public interest rapidly declined, which led to the cancellation of the series and the discontinuation of manned flights to the moon after Apollo 17. Only the dramatic rescue of the astronauts after the explosion of a fuel cell on the way to the moon during Apollo 13 managed to capture the interest of the public once again.

Second, in addition to the broadly defined seriality of the moon program and its numbered episodes (at least starting with Apollo 7), each flight had its own dramaturgy, which proceeded from the beginning preparations and the live broadcast of the launch to the accompanying news coverage and the live images from space to the return and the follow-up reports. Third and lastly, there were also numerous independently produced accompanying broadcasts from the studios of national broadcasters in different parts of the world. Their task was to explain again and again the technical sequence of the flight to the moon and its various phases, including acceleration, gliding, deceleration, turns, couplings, transfers, and so on. The most complex technical operation of its time was explained through the technically as well as sociologically most complex medium of its time. In their annual reports, broadcasters in Germany later proudly referred to their enormous expenses in connection with the Apollo mission (Zweites Deutsches Fernsehen 1970: 216). In the phase of Apollo 11, for example, Zweites Deutsches Fernsehen (ZDF) had its own studio for the flight to the moon, which contained a replica of the lunar module that was true to scale. Specialized journalists were also employed and flagged as experts on space travel.

Günther Siefarth was the space travel expert for the then leading German public TV station ARD. This personnel decision was particularly interesting because Siefarth was also an expert on projections, which at the time was a brand new and experimental method that he first brought to television precisely in 1969 in the context of news coverage of the parliamentary elections. His sensational election night coverage was, at least in Germany, the beginning of election nights and later of the entire election as a television format. The dramaturgy of the live broadcast of the election night was also similar to that of the moon night in its use of actualized projections that constantly advance toward the presumed outcome, which we will examine more closely. The counting of votes was first mathematized through the projection, which transformed counting into calculating, and a televisual serial narrative was then constructed from the sequence of calculations. As a result of the suspenseful dramaturgy of the election night coverage, which paradoxically combined the expectation of a surprise and the calculation of the probable outcome, the simultaneity of unpredictability and predictability, and the sensationalism and reliability of television itself, at least in this part of the political life of the country, also became part of the inner space of television. In this context, however, it is perhaps significant that the calculation of projections and ratings rely on the same mathematical and informatic instruments. The quantitative statistical method extends from here into other social areas. It becomes an instrument that determines political and administrative acts as much as the market and the media, through which it returns back to itself. The quantified and mathematically modeled society, which only exists at all through and as calculation, can of course also be seen as an ontography or even sociography—a type of operation through which society writes itself—but this is something that sociology must explore.

The expert broadcasts were complemented by reports of the training, preparations, biographies, and everyday lives of the astronauts as well as discussions of the political and moral dimensions of the enterprise. For roughly one and a half years, until the return of Apollo 13 in April 1970, the flight to the moon thus became a sustained and finely interwoven program component in many parts of the world. The topic also engaged the entire media network of television. This does not mean that print media also extensively addressed the topic of the moon landing; rather, it means that the television coverage and its modalities became a recurring theme. A kind of astronautical-televisual complex spread out across the catalyst of program guides. Even during the moon night, the attention of writing observers was focused on the appearance (and creation) of the event in and through television as much as on the event itself (Kühnert 1969: 7; Hickethier 1998: 274f.).

The flight to the moon was thus a perfect vehicle for the expansion of television, and this also applies to the results of manned space travel. While its scientific uses are highly controversial, its economic value lies above all in the telecommunications industry. This includes but is not limited to the defense industry, as the surveillance and observation of the planet from space also pertains to its climate and weather, the control and direction of movement and navigation on the surface, but above all (in economically profitable terms) the mobile transmission of images, sounds, and texts from every point to every other point on Earth. In the system of planetary ontographies, which operate from space, the televisual switch image and its derivatives waveringly maintain a high degree of economic relevance. In short, the main beneficiary of the flight to the moon was television itself and its expansion. Television thus used the space flight for its own purposes and benefits as much as vice versa (see also Barnouw 1990: 308–13).

## Boredom

The fiftieth anniversary of the flight to the moon recently provided the occasion to rewatch some of the live special broadcasts from the night of July 20 and 21, 1969 (CBS News 2019; Ems-Dollart Media 2016a,b; Bootdiskerror 2019), which led to a series of interesting observations. The first is the astonishing time regime of the evening—particularly the second part, which involved waiting for the live images from the moon (and the exit of the astronauts). The lunar landing vehicle had touched down on the moon on schedule, and it was only revealed much later that this landing had just narrowly succeeded. The first subsequently published video recordings of the lunar soil taken from the landing vehicle during its approach are actually still semantically and aesthetically spectacular. After they landed, the astronauts were scheduled to remain in the vehicle for a few hours and to begin with the exit only after this period of rest.

For the live broadcast this would have meant the termination of the transmission and its resumption the following morning or midday (American time). The largest mass public of all time would have been dismissed without an image of triumphant success, and they would have had to be painstakingly reassembled once again on another day. According to official sources, the astronauts were reportedly unable to rest because they were too excited and burning for action. After some uncertainty it was thus decided to move up the exit so that it would take place during the ongoing broadcast, which as a result had to be drastically extended in terms of time. It would be worth waiting, even though the exit was not immediately possible, as it still required a few technical preparations. In a brilliant directorial idea, an early arrival produced the effect of a delay. Everything was delayed, yet at the same time the broadcast not only satisfied but even exceeded the schedule. The present extended itself again in a looping movement, and the perceptible effect of this extension primarily consisted in making the worldwide viewership wait. A planetary and almost cosmic waiting period was thus inserted into the middle of the most suspenseful and meaningful live broadcast in history—a gigantic intermission observed collectively by 600 million viewers at the same time.

It is worth looking more closely at this intermission, and it will help to consider the connection between this (long) wait and the phenomenon of boredom (Engell 1989). For Martin Heidegger waiting for something is the basic form of boredom (Heidegger 1995: 86f.), and we already encountered something similar in our discussion of Hartmut Winkler's notion of waiting as an attitude of openness with respect to what is still pending (see also Chapter 5 in this volume; Winkler 2006: 101; Kracauer 1995: 138–40). Boredom was thus the defining feature of the live broadcast of the most important event in television history (or even human history, if one follows the sound of time). However, it is not simply an uncomfortable feeling, which is due to bad dramaturgy or direction and could also arise differently or not at all; rather, according to Heidegger, it is one of the two paradigmatic "moods" in which existence (*Dasein*) is confronted with nothingness in an existential way (the other is fear) (Heidegger 1993: 99; see also Revers 1949). The events that normally scan and articulate time disappear in boredom. Something either does not occur at all (Jean Baudrillard speaks of a "strike of events" in the world of mass media coverage) (Baudrillard 1994: 21–3) or proves to be as hollow, empty, and irrelevant as the attractions of hedonism.

Heidegger refers to boredom as "*that which holds us in limbo and yet leaves us empty*" (Heidegger 1995: 87, my emphasis), and his example is the experience of waiting at a rural train station for a train that is long overdue. Even more relevant would be the case of waiting for a train when one doesn't know when or whether it will arrive at all. Heidegger calls this form of boredom, which involves waiting for something that has been promised, "becoming-bored by something"—namely, by the absence of an event. He identifies a second form of boredom as "being bored with something," which occurs not when an event is absent but rather, conversely, when it occurs repeatedly yet remains irrelevant, such as because it has no consequences. This is paradigmatically the case with pastimes (Heidegger 1995: 90f).

And lastly Heidegger refers to a third form as "profound boredom," which has no reference point and is not provoked by any occasion. This form represents another increase with respect to the "held-back and left-empty," and according to Heidegger it involves "entrancement" and "failure" (the latter in the sense of a deprivation or denial): it denies not only the relevant event (such as the exit of the astronauts or the arrival of a new report, which disappears in the gap of the switch), and thus synchronizes with nothing, but also the event form as such. It places existence (*Dasein*) before nothingness (Heidegger 1995: 138–40).

Nevertheless, boredom captivates the bored existence and prevents it from turning away. As Heidegger writes:

> What is entrancing in this attunement is not the determinate time-point at which the specific boredom arises; for this determinate "now" sinks at a stroke (as we have seen with the operation of switching, L.E.) [...]. Nor is that which entrances, however, a more stretched "now," such as the span of time during which boredom persists. [...] Neither merely the present nor merely the past nor merely the future, nor indeed all these reckoned together—but rather their *unarticulated unity* in the simplicity of this unity of their horizon all at once. (Heidegger 1995: 147f.)

The production and perceptibility of this unity on a dramatic scale (in every respect) was an epoch-defining achievement of the television coverage of the 1969 flight to the moon (Zec 1985: 17–23).

## Chronic Boredom

However, the images of waiting and boredom from the moon night can also be related to the concepts of time used in Chapter 6—that is, Chronos and Aion—which Gilles Deleuze developed and attributed to Stoic philosophy (Deleuze 2004: 186–93). The chronographic and aionographic features of television appear once again in these images, only this time at a planetary and extra-planetary scale. Chronos infinitely expands in boredom and becomes achronological. Time thus becomes definitionless; as no events occur, it can no longer be defined as a relation between events and subsequently also no longer as a division between the past and the future. Linear time orientations thereby disappear; time is experienced no longer as the counting of movement but rather as an extended simultaneity that expands in its three dimensions (past, present, and future) at the same time.

Meaning also subsequently disappears insofar as it is understood not as an "indefinite proliferation" (Deleuze 2004: 35) or even as "nonsense" (Deleuze 2004: 78f.) but rather as the "'and so forth' of experience and action" (Luhmann 1995: 60). What occurs instead is the contraction of the temporal horizons and dimensions of Chronos, which we already observed with the help of the instant replay. Every future and every past is also only another present. The problems of Chronos also appear, such as the problem of measurelessness and the lack of proportionality (see Chapter 3 in this volume). The overflowing duration of the live broadcast with its open ending, its poor organization, and the lack of events during the period of waiting indicate this measurelessness. And it spreads from here to all of the other aspects of the flight to the moon, such as the boundless number of viewers, the inconceivability of the distances, and possibly even the measurelessness of the entire enterprise.

Boredom can then even turn into its complement—fear—which places existence before nothingness, here in the form of the mere emptiness of space. This is thematized in the chronography of waiting time as live boredom. The boredom of the moon night even gives rise to delays within the delays, which are due to the technically conditioned duration of the transmission and which undermine the absolute synchronicity of the live broadcast. While they are normally irrelevant, these gaps in the switching operations between the individual locations of the absent event now become noticeable and thematic in the interval in time. The broadcast always switches to the control center in Houston whenever there is a new report, but the image and the sound do not arrive at the same time, as they hurry ahead or lag behind the report. Within the already arrested period of waiting, time appears as a chain of gaps and intervals, and any point in time, even one yet to come, appears to be already over. This includes the present moment, which is marked by switching as just another gap or interval in the coherence of time. The time of switching is structured not by events but rather precisely by their absence—that is, their sinking into the intervals between the events (those that have already occurred or those that have yet to occur). This creates an unfathomably deep effect of simultaneity with nonsimultaneity.

The second problem of Chronos, as we have already seen, lies in the moment of becoming—namely, in the peculiar mode of being of the approaching and upcoming event (see Chapter 3 in this volume). We are waiting for it, but it has still not occurred, and it is not coming any closer, as chronologically counted time has been suspended or become meaningless. It has been promised, yet it fails to materialize over the hours of waiting. Waiting and boredom (as perpetual waiting) actually appear as the "evasion of the present" of the event mentioned by Deleuze. Boredom settles in this evasion.

## Univocity

Due to the massive scale of the experience of the televisual moon night, however, this evasion of the present was not individual, incommunicable, or, in Heidegger's diction, "mine" (*jemeinige*). On the contrary, it was deeply embedded in what Heidegger refers to as "the They" (*das Man*) and what others would call the public (Heidegger 2008: 127–30). Around 600 million people across the globe simultaneously waited for three hours, held-back and left-empty, for something whose occurrence was not ultimately denied but still uncertain, like a late train. The global public of boredom and waiting was also repeatedly addressed in the ongoing broadcast, such as by switching to various distant locations where viewers were waiting and by estimating the total number of viewers worldwide. Through the simultaneity of waiting, the boredom of the moon night could be entirely removed from psychology and individual experience. Whereas boredom, for Heidegger, refers to a fundamental temporality as the form of being of existence (*Dasein*), it emerged in the moon night as the operational result of the switch image and at the same time as its ineluctable operational basis.

Boredom does not affect the individual subject of temporal perception as much as it affects Chronos itself. Gilles Deleuze describes the unstructured and simple unity of time that emerges from this as "unanimity" or univocity (Deleuze 2004: 203–7). The phonetic and semantic closeness of the concepts of the voice and univocity is surprising. If the televisual moon night is conceived as univocal, then this would presumably first evoke a sonic phenomenon—namely, the specific nebulous sound of radio communication, which could be heard during large portions of the broadcast and which provided the guiding tone of the evening. However, Deleuze's univocity refers not to boredom but rather again to the concept of Aion—that is, time as an operation of division that is incorporeal yet performed by bodies, that lends reality to chronological time, and that prevents its collapse into boundlessness and stagnation. Univocity means that the articulation of time—in the sense of structure and expression, division and communication—allows different things to occur simultaneously and collectively without somehow diminishing their differences.

This is related, on the one hand, to the irreducible multiplicity and diversity of beings (*das Seiende*) and, on the other hand, to the traditional ontological assumption of the unity of being (*Sein*). Deleuze's idea of univocity affirms both sides, but he starts from the unity of being, which is no longer (ontologically) above everything and connecting it together but instead (ontographically) in everything and separating (or articulating—or even writing) it (Deleuze 2004: 205f.). Without expanding on this in more detail, it is striking that, like boredom, univocity also blurs distinctions, such as those between active and passive or nonsense and meaning. The extensionlessness, incompleteness, or, as Deleuze says, emptiness of all events expresses itself univocally in each individual event. The switchings of the moon night, which occur but lead nowhere and in that sense fail, thus express the emptiness of the event, which always remains possible (or even impossible) yet still pending. The possible (such as the still pending event of the astronauts' exit), the real, and the impossible all exist to the same degree and in the same way. In univocity, every event ultimately coincides with the event of its representation. This last point leads us back to the ontography of television because, as we have seen, the unanimity of the event and of the televisual description is precisely the distinguishing mark of the entire operation.

## The Switch Image in the Age of Its Experimentation

Today, fifty years later, much more is known about the risks and perils of the flight to the moon than was visible in 1969. The flight to the moon was an experiment, and experiments can fail. Because it was a television event, however, the experiment also applies to television. This is due not only to the ontographic nature of television, which describes, underwrites, and records its own operational sequence and simultaneously inscribes this description into the sequence; rather, it is also due to the nature of the experiment itself. In his famous essay on painting and philosophy in the age of their experimentation, for instance, Jean-François Lyotard gave a description of experimental art and thought that reveals the ontographic aspect of the experiment (Lyotard 2012: 147–75). In particular, the experiment involves finding out the rules that artistic work follows in and through the course of this work. In other words, experimental art wants to find out what it is doing by doing it. It doesn't already know what it is; rather, its search for what it is constitutes its way of being or acting. According to Lyotard, the same is true of experimental thought in philosophy (Lyotard 2012: 173). The scientific experiment produces a phenomenon as an effect that can then be observed and recorded. As the trace of an invisible event, it is supposed to prove a hypothesis concerning the function of the experimental setup and procedure. If the desired phenomenon occurs, then the hypothesis was correct. The scientific experiment is thus a "phenomenotechnique" or a method of producing traces or images (Bachelard 1984: 171ff.).

This coincides, at the other end of the spectrum of cultural and epistemic prestige, with television. Like television, experiments are serially organized. They are never alone but instead form series. The series types identified earlier can thus also be found in the experimental world of science as well as art, as all (scientific) experiments must be exactly reproducible in order to be considered valid. The same result must always appear under the same conditions. In this sense, experiments form identical series. At the same time, however, experimental work in the laboratory as well as the studio proceeds in countless incremental steps, which each differ slightly from one other, as minor changes are made to the experimental setup and procedure. This is supposed to produce a particular result (or another one), which would make the experimental setup and procedure understandable. A series of consecutive experiments with slightly altered conditions, like a differential television series, thus reveals what is actually going on in the experiment itself.

However, this ontographic recursion applies not only to artistic and philosophical experimentation. Science historian Michael Lynch used electron microscopy to show how the recording or inscription of an experimental process—which is essential for any experiment—can also intervene in the process while the experiment is still proceeding (Lynch 2013: 444–62, 2019: 148ff.; Mody and Lynch 2009: 1–36). Moreover, according to Lynch, the microelectronic epistemic object first emerges in and through the feedback coupling of the experiment with its own recording while it is in progress (live, so to speak). In the case of electronic microscopy, the epistemic object exists only insofar and for as long as it is written, which here means altered or shifted. The similarity between this process and television is striking. Lynch also calls this process "ontographic"—a term derived from his own concept of "epistemography."

## Three Phases of Experimental Television

As an experiment, the flight to the moon was one in a dense chain of television experiments. Not everything on television is experimental in Lyotard's sense, but television has always attempted to determine what it is actually doing, how it functions and operates, and what it therefore is in doing what it does—namely, producing and circulating switch images. The switch image does not need theory in order to understand itself; rather, it has operatively given itself its own concepts and activated them through its own activity. It is also possible to distinguish between three phases of televisual experimentation, which each call something different into question (Engell 2009: 15–46). The first phase extended from the 1910s to roughly 1936, when television emerged from technical-scientific laboratory experiments. In particular, the picture tube was used as an instrument for detecting electromagnetic vibrations, as it first generated them—systematically and under controlled conditions—and then made them visible. The image thus provided information about the functioning of the apparatus that produced the image (Pias 2002: 69–89; Abramson 1974: 20–4). Additional experiments gradually showed that the apparatus could be manipulated in order to visualize something entirely different from itself and its effects (in which the process of visualization itself is always inscribed, as we have seen). The light effects on the surface of the tube are thus no longer traces of processes occurring within the device but rather systematically created images, which can now also represent something other than the conditions of their own production (Rheinberger 1997: 103f.).

When it left the technical-scientific laboratory, television was addressed no longer just to specialists (i.e., video engineers) but also to the public, which was not interested in the functioning of the tube and the transmission, as they saw the device as a black box that should be looked at rather than into. The second experimental phase of television thus used the device to determine something about its functioning not as a technical apparatus but rather as a communicative structure, *dispositif*, and social institution—namely, something about its audience, its possible economics, and its legal regulation. In traditional terms, it can be said that in the second phase television experimented with the public in public. This can already be seen in the Nazi Summer Olympics of 1936, which featured two competing technical systems—a tube apparatus and an electromechanical system based on the Nipkow disk—as well as the broadcasting of the sports events in publicly accessible "television rooms," which was the first experiment with television in public space (Hickethier 1998: 33–48; Zielinski 1999: 139; 144–6). This search for the place of television continued until a room was created for it—namely, the living room of the nuclear family. Countless studies have examined how the familiar family room in the home—particularly in the suburbs—first formed around the television. For example, John Hartley has shown that there had never before been such a room, and Lynn Spigel has traced in detail how television gradually structured this private room (Hartley 1999: 92–111; Spigel 1992). However, the second phase also involves an experiment on the production side of television. Between 1948 and 1951, the American television industry as a whole was subjected to precise observation by its own specially established agency—that is, the Federal Communications Commission. During this "laboratory period of television," it was not possible to alter the market and other working conditioning of television; in other words, the boundary conditions were controlled, as is the case in an experiment (Barnouw 1990: 113). The goal was to clarify the need for regulation and the competitive conditions of the new medium.

Viewing was also subject to experimental conditions, as it was observed and recorded. However, this did not occur through television itself but was instead delegated to a separate agency and apparatus, which was then coupled with television. We are speaking here about quantitative audience research and audience measurement and calculation. The rating was an entirely new separate object, which was first generated by technical and mathematical processes. For this purpose, a separate device—the telemeter—was installed in selected households. The data it generated (i.e., ratings) became decisive factors in the production and programming decisions of television broadcasters (Abelman and Atkin 2002: 156–69; Nielsen 1950: 24–34).

This brings us back to the flight to the moon. As already mentioned earlier, the closeness of the projection process to the technology of the flight to the moon on television initially appeared to be contingent; however, the mathematics and technical instruments of projection are the same as those used to determine ratings. It is therefore no surprise that at roughly the same time as the flight to the moon broadcasters were testing an increasing number of formats that experimented with a direct link between ratings and broadcasts. These formats made ratings and their changes in relation to broadcast content into the content of the broadcasts themselves. In German television in 1969, the program *Wünsch Dir was* (*Make a Wish*), which was already spectacular at the time, was particularly well known for this. Due to the lack of an appropriate telemetry process, though, it occurred indirectly: at the end of this quiz show, viewers within a particular geographical region of the broadcast area (such as a large city) could vote for the winner by switching on all of the electrical appliances in their apartments. The image would then switch over to a television crew positioned in the power station responsible for that particular region, whose camera would be directed at a measuring instrument that would register the increase in power consumption (Kubitz 1997: 89). The relationship between the public and the broadcast was thus researched within the broadcast itself, and it even became a control parameter of the further progress of the broadcast. In other words, the outcome of the experiment determined the further progress of the experiment. In addition, the electrical image also registered the condition of its own possibility—namely, the electrical current. These processes were later refined and digitized, of course, but similar kinds of voting processes are still part of various broadcasting formats.

## Space as Television Laboratory

In the flight to the moon, the experimental structure of television was extended to an almost limitless degree and distributed across countless laboratories that were networked with one another: the launching and landing sites, the space capsule and lunar module, the control centers and decentralized studios. They were all connected to one another during the live broadcast through constant switching, and part of the attention of the experiment was applied to the functionality of this networking. The complexly distributed experimental setup was used to test itself through its operation. Its success was a condition and component of the success of the flight to the moon, as the astronauts would have been lost without a communication link and the entire effort would have been in vain without images from the moon. As in early television, the first dimension of the moon experiment—that is, the first uncertainty that had to be eliminated—was the question of the functionality of the apparatus itself. The second dimension of the experiment—that is, the second uncertainty that had to be eliminated—was if and how a globally synchronized viewership of unimaginable proportions could be created. In this sense, the frequent supply of information and reports about the worldwide dissemination of the moon broadcast during the broadcast itself was a decisive part of the experiment. The culmination of this moment was undoubtedly the collective (or collectively communicated and identified) worldwide waiting for the exit of the astronauts. At that moment, merely "being-able-to-be-there" (*Dabeiseinkönnen*) was considered "being-there" (*Dabeisein*). By doing what it does, television itself here actually revealed the principle of its own functioning.

This also addresses the third dimension of experimental television, which applies not to the structure and operativity of the device or the media-specific public but rather to the feedback between observation and the process of the experiment (Engell 2009: 34–8). This feedback introduces a third form of uncertainty. When the process of the moon night is examined once again, for example, what stands out is the question of how the possibility of an early exit to the lunar surface was decided during the ongoing broadcast. There was the claim that the astronauts were too excited to rest, but the expectations of the largest mass audience of all time were also communicated. The 600 million viewers were supposed to be held together for as long as possible, and their sheer number was communicated for the purpose of increasing the pressure of expectation. Half of the world could not be waiting in vain. The pressure of expectation that television itself had created thus informed the decision to extend the broadcast and exit early. The question posed by the waiting period was precisely whether this would succeed.

A comparison between this television event and another significant event that came twenty years later shows that this was a risk (for television) (Ludes 1991: 79–86; Hanke 1990: 79–86; Engell 1996: 129–53). Television also built up an enormous pressure of expectation during the opening of the Berlin Wall in November 1989. From the beginning of the month, all of the border crossings were densely and literally surrounded on the western side by the vans of countless television broadcasters, whose correspondents reported hourly about the imminent or soon to be expected opening of the border. Like the moon night, the billions of television viewers were also supposed to produce the live event for which they were waiting merely through their expectation. This experiment failed, though, as the government of the German Democratic Republic ignored the television and the broadcast vans withdrew. When the wall was actually opened on November 9, contrary to all expectation, the surprise was produced once again. The programmed event could then interrupt the program through special switching operations, which in that sense especially restored television, if of another order. The improvised nightly hazy and blurry images created the impression of an unexpected and surprising turn of events. Either way, the switch image was the winner.

## The Visible Planet

The basic property of experiments is not only that they can succeed or fail but also that they can produce phenomena that are entirely different from those they are supposed to produce. The apparatus then accomplishes something that is entirely different from what it is supposed to achieve. This often remains annoying or unnoticed at first. The experiment itself creates a new uncertainty and a new unknown—an uncontrolled effect that must be investigated through new experiments (Rheinberger 1997: 24–37). This also applies to the moon experiment. Apart from its massive contribution to the history of waiting, the space flight also involved a fundamental transformation in the history of images. In particular, the most spectacular and successful image from space showed not the moon or the men on it but rather the Earth. The look back at the planet had already been shown on television during the reading of the creation story from the space capsule of Apollo 8 at Christmas 1968, but now the Earth could be seen above the horizon of the moon. However, this image was also rotated before it was transmitted in order to conform more closely to our habits of perception, as the Earth appeared not above the lunar soil but rather to the side of the horizon of the moon, which was vertical in the image. This must have made its impact all the more powerful and virtually epochal. Günter Anders describes it in his log-style text about the flight to the moon (Anders 1970). The image of the Earth as seen from the moon shows the planet in its Copernican position in the infinite expanse of space. In doing so, it appears in two ways at the same time. On the one hand, it appears monumental, dominant, and beautiful, especially in the color photographs distributed later, which have a much higher resolution. On the other hand, it also seems alone and insignificant against the empty black background. The images thus document the Copernican-Galilean order of the cosmos, in which the planet Earth is not only a rotating ball but also a marginal location in space.

However, the look back at the Earth from space not only confirms but also massively disrupts the Copernican order. According to Anders, its first disruption is precisely its confirmation (Anders 1970: 96). It had previously only been possible to calculate and extrapolate the position of the Earth in the cosmos—that is, the position of our human habitat and thus our human position in the cosmos in a physical sense. Copernicus made the movements of the stars calculable on the basis of the heliocentric model, which explained these movements better than the geocentric model. Galileo's telescope observations of the moons of Jupiter did not make the Earth's orbit around the sun visible; rather, it only showed that there were celestial bodies that orbited not the Earth but precisely Jupiter. Everything else was deduced from this, as conditions in space were assumed to be analogous to those on Earth (Vogl 2007: 14–25; Stengers 1995: 290ff.). These deductions were all abstractions based on logic and mathematics, but now there was an image that furnished evidence of what for centuries could only be assumed, believed, or at best calculated and deduced. According to Anders, the relieving function of this image was also disconcerting, as it had wide-ranging anthropological dimensions (Anders 1970: 97). As an experimental setup became an apparatus or technical object, it relieved us of the need to draw conclusions based on analogy and mathematics. Counting and writing, logic and discourse, withdrew behind the image that they themselves produced, leaving us alone. An extremely complex apparatus was nevertheless required to provide the evidence that would yield immediate and clear insight, and this apparatus functioned as a third that mediated between the exterior position in space and our own gaze on Earth. In fact, it was actually the most complex setup that had ever been constructed, and television functioned as its center. The anthropological shift was thus media-anthropological.

But that is not enough. As a special televisual *dispositif* not only for the image but also for its instantaneous and worldwide distribution, the technical apparatus potentially, asymptotically, or at least allegedly catered to all of the inhabitants of the Earth at the same time. This was a complete reversal compared to the telescope, as viewers must go to the telescope whereas television comes to them. It could also be said metonymically that viewers must lean toward the telescope and away from the television and that they never look at television individually but rather only as a collective. Anders notes, interestingly, that this collective also includes the astronauts, who could potentially receive the television program broadcast on Earth in their spaceship. According to Anders, they would thus see themselves through the eyes of others and adopt the attitude of non-involvement that characterizes television viewers in general (Anders 1970: 98). Even if, like McLuhan, we continue to assume here that television is a cold medium precisely because of its anthropo-mediatic involvement, it is nonetheless true that the flight to the moon involved an unconventional dual entanglement of internal and external perspectives. While viewers looked out into space from inside their living rooms and found the camera looking back at them on Earth, this entire image simultaneously reached through space to the astronauts inside the space capsule, who in turn looked back at the Earth looking at them. Television thus viewed the planet not only as a visual object but also as an image-forming and image-viewing object. It did not show the Earth in the sense of an illustration; rather, it put the Earth into the image and thus made it an image. In other words, the flight to the moon made the Earth perceptible as a visual picture but not merely as an image of the Earth; rather, the Earth was newly defined as a visible planet.

## The Planet Opens Its Eyes

As we have seen, the massive message of the image of the moon was precisely its own instantaneous global distribution. It was as if not the viewers but rather the entire viewership, which represented the global population with which it tended to coincide, was able to look at its own habitat. If we see this population as part of its habitat or as part of the entire ecosphere of the planet, then we can continue to follow Anders, who claims that the planet opened its eyes during the moon night and saw itself (Anders 1970: 90; 96). The instrumental structure of television is actually a huge *dispositif*, which spans the entire planet with cameras and screens that are interconnected over broadcasting systems of all kinds. It has grown together with the planet, using its resources and altering its conditions, and now it even reaches out into space. At the same time, it also moves more closely toward its users and incorporates them into itself, just as its cold images are conversely only realized as neurological effects inside its users. Television entangles its human viewers with itself—and the entire planet along with them—and it does this from the very moment when it makes the planet visible before and for the eyes of its inhabitants.

Hence, it is only logical that in the period following the flight to the moon Earth as an image recorded from space gained an incredibly wide distribution as popular photography. Despite their brilliance, however, these images no longer had the fragmented, shaky, and over-lit silvery magic of the television images of the moon night. Unlike television images, the pull of which consisted not least in their ephemerality, these images were readily available and retrievable at any time. These photographic images, which were often edited, also manifest a deeply anti-Copernican feature: unlike the ephemeral and blurry light phenomena shown in the televised coverage of the flight to the moon, they show a heroic planet that even if it is no longer the center of the cosmos is nonetheless still the center of pictorial attention. It could be seen everywhere—on book and magazine covers, posters, advertisements, and so on—and it stood precisely for "our blue planet"—that is, for the view of the Earth as a whole, as the isolated center of the universe, and yet still (as Copernicus determined) as a cosmologically marginal and fragile entity. Since the time of the flight to the moon, therefore, this image has become an iconic statement for every concept of a global ecology that views the planet as a complex but powerful whole. This obviously includes the "Gaia" hypothesis, such as Erich Jantsch's work, as well as the "Whole Earth" approach of the late hippie culture and the model of "System Earth" (Jantsch 1980; Brand 1970). The image of the Earth recorded from space was to be found, for example, on the cover of the German edition of the groundbreaking book *The Limits to Growth*, which was the first systems-theoretical study to view the planet as a connected and closed system with limited resources and with feedback systems that turn effects into causes. This extends to contemporary models of the planet, such as models of global climate that have switched from photographs of the "Blue Marble" recorded during the flight to the moon to computer images of an overheated "Red Marble," as well as to contemporary debates on the Anthropocene (Schneider 2014: 183–93).

But that is not enough, as we have not yet reached the turning point constituted by these images. In order to show this, we must go back a little and switch from the temporal structure of the flight to the moon, which we initially observed in our discussion of boredom, to its spatial and visual structure. The Copernican turn actually brought a general uncertainty and a narcissistic humiliation to the European modern era by displacing the planet Earth from the center of the universe and sending it into orbit. But something else developed in parallel to this—namely, (central) perspective. With the implementation of perspective as a pictorial form and a mode of perception, the anchor points and vanishing points of perception were established. This separated the subject from the object of perception and made it independent, sovereign, and even superior, as it was the reflexive form capable of confronting and subjugating the irreflexive (Günther 1963: 22; 30–6). In this sense, the classical modern observing subject moves to a location from which it focuses on something at another location that presents itself to the observer. Both of these locations are simultaneously separated from and connected to one another through the gaze and its structure, such as the "visual pyramid" of central perspective. Perspective thus takes on an important function in the formation of the Western subject.

Television was also originally part of this tradition. This was identified at the beginning of our study with Nipkow's definition, which stated that the purpose of the apparatus is "to make an object at location A visible at any location B" (while the object is still at location A) (see Chapter 2 in this volume; Hickethier 1998: 15). The moon images also initially follow this scheme as long as they appear on the moon. However, something entirely different occurs when these images are transmitted back to the Earth, which is their purpose, as television was then able to visualize an object that was none other than the entirety of all possible locations—that is, the planet Earth—and to transmit an image of this entirety to all possible locations on the planet. If the resolution of the image were scalable enough, then the location where I am—that is, location B—would in principle be visible in the image itself, and it would thus be (part of) the object at location A. In other words, the object that is made visible—the planet Earth—would itself be the location where the object appears, and the object made visible at the location where it appears would *be* this location. Nipkow's definition of television and television itself, as we have known it ever since, collaborates in these multiple short circuits between locations, between objects and locations, and between objects and their visibility (such as the transformation of the planet into an image, as already mentioned).

In order to achieve this effect, however, it must simultaneously go beyond and outside itself. The projection from A to A and the nesting of A and B only function when the image of location A returns again from A to A (the same could be shown, of course, from the location of the observing subject, B). The image of location A is not visible at location A of its own accord; rather, a complex technical apparatus is needed to produce this image (at another location) and then bring it back. This requires an additional location C—that is, an outpost beyond the configuration of A and B. In the case of Apollo 8, this was initially a technical artifact—namely, the space capsule—and later the moon. Today there are countless artificial satellites that serve the same function. The images of the Earth seen from space and from the moon also bring all of these locations into the picture, as the images are always framed by the lunar soil, the window of the capsule, or some other part of the technical vehicle. The famous photograph of the Earth mirrored in the bronze-colored visor of the helmet of an astronaut on the moon is almost iconic. In order to be an image, the Earth appears here as an image within an image—that is, as an image seen from a location that itself becomes another image.

## Eye and Gaze

In order to see that this reversal is of fundamental relevance, it is useful to draw on Maurice Merleau-Ponty's distinction between the eye and the gaze, which was further developed by Jacques Lacan (Lacan 1998; Merleau-Ponty 1964: 159–90; see also Bernet 1999: 105–20; Zupančič 1996: 32–58). The eye is understood as the geometrical anchor point of the subjective observation of the world. It constitutes the starting point of the construction of central perspective as a "visual pyramid," and it introduces the concept of the classical observing subject, which separates and subjugates the object by producing an image of it. Lacan provides a diagram of this configuration that features a horizontal pyramid whose apex corresponds to the position of the eye on the right and that is bordered on the left by the object (Lacan 1998: 69). In this configuration, the image is a plane or cross-section of the pyramid between its apex and its (open) base. The image is thus a linear projection of the object onto a surface that lies between the position of the eye and the object, and the object is at the disposal of the subject precisely through the image. This configuration is exemplified in Dürer's famous drawing of perspectival construction, in which a framed piece of glass with grid lines is positioned between the painter and the object and the projection of the object is clearly visible on the glass. The object visible to the eye thus emerges in the image as its linear and perspectival projection.

The gaze, though, is something entirely different, as it is the instance in which the subject sees itself as being exposed. The subject looks at itself as being observed by the gaze (Lacan 1998: 91). Lacan is not necessarily referring here to a concrete human observer. Any type of surveillance of the subject comes into consideration, including everything the subject sees as an "other"—namely, all objects of desire. For Lacan, the structure of the gaze is also part of an optical pyramid (Lacan 1998: 105f.). This time, however, the gaze occupies the apex, from which a bundle of rays emanates. The subject is not the master of the gaze but rather its object, and it thus constitutes the base at which these rays are directed (in Lacan's famous diagram it is a vertical line because the pyramid is horizontal). The subject paradoxically wishes to show itself without being seen, and in order to avoid being completely subjected it presents an image of itself to the gaze. As in the first pyramid, this image is a plane or a cross-section of the pyramid between the apex (which now represents the gaze) and the base (which now represents the subject). According to Lacan, this image functions as a screen with which the subject shields itself, as it presents something other than itself to the gaze and hides behind this (false) image. This attempt is never entirely successful, however, as the gaze still recognizes the subject at the edges of the image (Lacan 1998: 108). For the subject, however, it is the gaze of the other (which does not have to be another subject) that leads to the emergence of this image.

The subject sees itself exposed to, observed, and hence subjugated by this gaze which it locates in its environment. The gaze also originates from what the subject sees, which is the gaze itself. The gaze is thus located as a place and a point on the plane that the subject understood as the base of its visual pyramid. This allows Lacan to superimpose these symmetrically identical pyramid diagrams by laying the apex of one pyramid onto the base of the other (Lacan 1998: 106). Both of the vertical cross-sections coincide in the middle of this superimposition—that is, the image as the "perspective grid" of the eye and the screen as the subject's mask and shield from the gaze. Lacan derives further psychoanalytic complexes from this, such as scopophilia, exhibitionism, narcissism, and desire (Lacan 1998: 193ff.). In the context of television and the image of the Earth, however, two other things are important. First, following Lacan, we must assume that everything we see also sees us, and we must allow its gaze to rest on us in order for us to be produced as subjects—that is, as the other of the other. Second, our images have a double function: they show something that they represent, and they simultaneously shield us from the gaze to which we are subjected by serving something to it.

Let's look at this dual structure of the eye and the gaze and the dual function of the image with regard to television. For the eye of the viewer, to begin with, the world outside of television appears on the screen of the television image in the same way that the object appears on the drawing grid of the painter in the perspectival configuration. In this case, television would correspond to the first visual pyramid, as the position of the eye would be location B in Nipkow's definition, location A would lie on the plane of the object, and the television image would be the grid between them. Based purely on the form or diagram, though, it is surprising how closely Lacan's second visual pyramid resembles the technical configuration of the picture tube of television. Lacan also identifies the gaze as a "point of light," which would lie at the source of the cathode ray. The screen would then actually be the screen or shield in Lacan's configuration, and the viewing subject would be the plane of the pyramid's base. This also recalls McLuhan's description of how the images of television are transmitted to the retina of the viewer. If Lacan's second pyramid were correlated with Nipkow's definition of television, then the gaze would be at location A—the location of the object—and the screen image would be the shield that prevents the gaze from seeing through to location B—the location of the viewer. The television image thus prevents reality from directly seeing and addressing us. It protects us from it (an idea that recalls Cavell) (Cavell 1982: 75–96; see Chapter 1 in this volume), and we still gladly offer ourselves to it. We will return later to the idea that it is the world that sees us through the television, and not vice versa, when we discuss digital television.

## The Total Image

However, the flight to the moon does not involve a perspective that originates from an individual, psychological, or human subject; rather, it literally involves an all-seeing perspective. In other words, it is not a matter of individual locations A and B but rather of all eyes and of all of their preceding gazes. As Richard Dienst points out, television was always already provided with the vision to make the entire world visible all over the world (Dienst 1995: X; 5f.). Dziga Vertov already dreamed in the 1920s of connecting "any given point in the universe with any other given point" through a combination of film and radio (Vertov 1984: 20). The flight to the moon and the image of the Earth have come closest to fulfilling this promise. If one follows Lacan, though, then the Earth can only be seen as a whole and as the totality of all locations A and B when it itself sees. Lacan himself points out, however, that a whole can never be spoken, never become discourse, or, at least for Dienst, never be seen. Significantly, Lacan introduces a television conversation, which was later published under the title "Television," with precisely this idea: he will always say the truth but never the entire truth, as the entirety can never be spoken (or shown) (Lacan 1990: 3–46). In other words, it remains shielded. Dienst identifies this with the impossible desire for an all-seeing and totalizing gaze, which was particularly promised by the earliest television utopias. He also uses the invisibility of the whole to explain countless paradoxes of television, such as the paradox of *flow* as the emergence of a boundless and structureless coherence from small fragmented individual pieces (Dienst 1995: 26–33). With the flight to the moon, however, television goes in the reverse direction, as it does not pursue fusion but rather dissection. If the image of the planet returns to the planet, and the gaze of the planet looks at the planet, then the all-seeing becomes an image and a screen that blocks and prevents it. The image of the planet is then surrounded by other images that shield it, and the gaze at these images in turn requires new shields. The images want to be seen but can never actually be seen. Every television image is thus identified as the gaze of another image, which must be prevented through the construction of another protective screen image. The entirety of all points A and B in Nipkow's scheme cannot be defined (in the sense of high-definition television), as it dissolves into an unmanageable mass of images of all individual points A and B, which reciprocally see one another as eyes and gazes and which thus represent one another as images and block one another as screens.

One of the widely circulated photographs from the flight to the moon featuring the reflection of the Earth on an astronaut's helmet was already mentioned earlier in connection with the pre-Copernican tendency to heroize moon travel. The basic dual configuration of eye and gaze is already doubly inscribed here, as the image of the Earth appears within the image on the visor, which is curved like a gigantic cyclopean eye and which, in turn, shields the eye of the astronaut from the light. At the same time, it also shields us from the (direct) gaze of the Earth, just as Perseus' mirror shields him from Medusa's petrifying gaze. Eye, gaze, image, and screen are thus superimposed over one another. Due to the impossibility of seeing the whole on television, however, they are not superimposed but rather juxtaposed as images within the image and gazes cast from images. This can also already be found in the live broadcast of the flight to the moon. Two images from this broadcast are particularly significant in this regard and are even more important for the televisual logic of the flight to the moon than the images of the lunar module and the astronauts on the lunar surface. The first is President Nixon's famous telephone call to the astronauts, during which he appeared on one half of the screen using an advanced split-screen process. This half of the image was captioned "Live From White House," while the other half of the image featured the astronauts on the moon with the caption "Live From Moon."

Like the reception of television in the space capsule, which Anders discusses, this construction turns all of the actors in the image into spectators who are first seen by what they see or, in terms of the switch image, are switched to that which is switched to them (today one could undoubtedly say that they click onto that which clicks onto them, and that is precisely what is beginning here). Regardless of what Nixon actually saw, he appeared to be able to see the connected astronauts and they appeared to be able to see him with the help of precisely the same television pictures that the viewers themselves also had at their disposal. Each half of the image thus represented the image object to which the other half was connected, and from this perspective they were perceived as connected to one another and to the live broadcast, which allowed both of them to be seen by viewers. Both halves thus served as the location A for one another, and they also served as a collective location A because of their combination. The president (as an image) saw the astronauts just as they saw him, and vice versa. Each half of the divided and doubled image was thus marked as an image that was connected to the other half. This peculiar composition, which was expressly synthesized through technical processes carried out at a third location (thus another location C, such as a broadcast van or television studio), could be seen from a different location where the viewers themselves were situated. These multiple locations, image objects, and gazes looked at each other and looked back again.

## The Big Switch Image

The other image was even more impressive, and it was the most frequently shown image of the entire broadcast—namely, the image of the NASA Mission Control Center in Houston, Texas. Men (and a few women) in white shirts sat (or stood) and looked at monitors and papers on the numerous rows of white tables, and a huge projection screen bordered by American and NASA flags could be seen on the far wall. It was impossible to identify what was on the countless screens in the room, but they included radar and monitoring images, weather charts, measurement diagrams, oscillator images, and later, after the moon landing, also live images from the lunar surface. They also included the images of the ongoing television program, which frequently appeared on the big screen, as well as images that reported and documented the sympathetic response of the worldwide audience during the broadcast. The control center with its countless screen images was thus nothing else than a television control room, through which all of the images of the live broadcast ran successively and in parallel. It was the image in which all location A's came together and became visible—and it itself also became visible on nearly all of the screens on the planet.

When the image of the control center was transmitted to the viewers' screens at home, it allowed all of these images and locations to be accessed from the viewers' locations (Engell 2019: 15–30). In this way, the control center itself was brought into circulation as an image. The control room thus did not remain hidden but instead became an image; however, it was not the master or central image of the broadcast, as it was also subject to the switches that were performed there. In other words, the switching of the image of the control center was performed in another control center that remained invisible but that was just another one of the many networked control centers distributed across the globe. The switch image ultimately reaches the viewers' screens and all screens in this way, and the nature of television as a switch image thus becomes the subject of the broadcast itself. For every image there was always at least one other image that showed the location from which the first image was seen and switched. Every image thus bore the mark of other images, even when their location was not included or visible within the image itself, like the spacecraft or the lunar surface, and every image was an image only to the extent that it was seen and switched from these other images, around which it orbited like a satellite (and vice versa, of course).

This has two implications. First, it means that the images (like Lacan's objects) look back, and they look back not only at the subjects looking at them but also at one another. The human viewers are involved in this interaction in that they see these images from the locations where they are situated, and these locations—and thus the viewers—are already implied in the images themselves. Every subjective anchor point is also only the vanishing point of another image and another gaze. This, in turn, means that the subject of the gaze is by no means the source or the target of the gaze relation. It is at best a temporary effect of the interaction between the images, which mutually observe and orbit one another. The relations and operations between the images thus precede the images and their viewing subjects, and the modern certainty of the viewer's perspective is gone. What was conceptually developed in advanced theories of the gaze and subjectification in the mid-twentieth century—above all by Lacan—was operationalized and implemented in the television coverage of the flight to the moon in 1969 and in principle in all television ever since.

Second, however, this must all be conceived no longer in terms of sight, eye, and gaze but rather in terms of the switch image and the "click." Generally speaking, television replaces Lacan's gaze with the "click," as it is a primarily tactile rather than visual medium, as McLuhan points out, and its characteristic feature is that it provided the first switchable image by making every point available to every other point. The processes of subjectification, shielding, and representation no longer operate (only) through seeing, looking, and watching but are also implemented as switching processes and relations. For example, the reduction and aesthetic poverty of technical images (such as those of mobile phone screens as compared to those of cinema screens), their massive reproduction, and their accelerated circulation are precisely related to the fact that the visual nature of these images is less important than their switchability. There is always less to see and more to switch. This transformation is of fundamental importance for the further development of television and the entire circulation of images today. The consequences were unforeseeable in 1969, but they will continue to occupy us in the future. As images, fixed locations and subjects became circulating addresses from which all other addresses could be observed, and these addresses marked the locations to which and from which images could exist and circulate. Ever since the flight to the moon, the planetary habitat has merged not only with that of images but also with the entirety of their locations and paths of circulation. Through television, images can be switched from every location on the planet to every other location, and every location can count on being switched from an image at another location at any time. As a result, every location can in principle appear at every other location in that it can be switched from there. Images are switches between images, and they not only look at one another but also switch one another. We have now actually arrived at a point where every location can become the subject of a picture and thus switched to not only one but all other locations through global coverage, which has been made possible by television, news reports, surveillance cameras, digitally uploaded images, and all other kinds of media. This development first began with the flight to the moon. Television made it possible, and more advanced media have completed and implemented it.

It is therefore only logical and practically imperative to update the relationship between viewers and television images and the involvement of viewers in the television image as a switch image—that is, to shift from the gaze relation to the operation of the switch. This began with the flight to the moon, but it was complex, it took years, and it completely transformed television once again.

## Note

1 Lady Diana's funeral in 1997 actually had far more viewers—an estimated 2.5 billion, which was almost half of the world's population at that time—but a smaller portion of the total number of possible viewers. The number of television households worldwide has steadily increased since 1969, and it is still growing. In this respect, the expansion movement of television is by no means finished.

## References

Abelman, Robert, and David J. Atkin. 2002. *The Television Audience: The Art and Science of Watching TV*. Cresskill: Hampton Press.

Abramson, Albert. 1974. *Electronic Motion Pictures*. New York: Arno Press.

Anders, Günther. 1970. *Der Blick vom Mond. Reflexionen über Weltraumflüge.* München: C. H. Beck.

Bachelard, Gaston. 1984. *The New Scientific Spirit.* Boston: Beacon Press.

Barnouw, Erik. 1990. *Tube of Plenty: The Evolution of American Television.* Oxford, New York: Oxford University Press.

Baudrillard, Jean. 1994. *The Illusion of the End.* Stanford: Stanford University Press.

Baudrillard, Jean. 2010. "The Precession of Simulacra." In: Jean Baudrillard. *Simulacra and Simuluation*, pp. 1–42. Ann Arbor: The University of Michigan Press.

Bernet, Rudolf. 1999. "The Phenomenon of the Gaze in Merleau-Ponty and Lacan." *Chiasmi International* 1: 105–20. Topic "Merleau-Ponty: L'Heritage Contemporain. The Contemporary Heritage. L'Eredità Contemparanea."

Boorstin, Daniel. 1992. *The Image: A Guide to Pseudo-Events in America.* New York: Vintage.

Bootdiskerror. 2019. *Mondlandung - ARD-Übertragung vom 20./21.07.1969.*

Brand, Stuart, ed. 1970. *Whole Earth Catalog.* New York: Portola. Accessed July 31, 2019. https://www.youtube.com/watch?v=q6i6MTUYjjM.

Cavell, Stanley. 1982. "The Fact of Television." *Daedalus* 111, no. 4: 75–96.

CBS News. 2019. *Apollo 11 Moon Landing 50th Anniversary, Live Stream.* Accessed July 31, 2019. https://www.youtube.com/watch?v=QBdyzTvA3oA.

Deleuze, Gilles. 2004. *The Logic of Sense.* London, New York: Continuum.

Dienst, Richard. 1995. *Still Life in Real Time: Theory after Television.* Durham: Duke University Press.

Ems-Dollart Media. 2016a. *MONDLANDUNG- Livesendung, WDR 20./21Juli 1969 Teil 1.* Accessed July 31, 2019. https://www.youtube.com/watch?v=30QA1xwEiZg.

Ems-Dollart Media. 2016b. *MONDLANDUNG- Livesendung, WDR 20/21.JULI 1969 Teil 2.* Accessed July 31, 2019). https://www.youtube.com/watch?v=tfZLFZoQ6Bg.

Engell, Lorenz. 1989. *Vom Widerspruch zur Langeweile. Logische und temporale Begründungen des Fernsehens.* Frankfurt/M., New York: Peter Lang.

Engell, Lorenz. 1996. "Das Amedium. Grundbegriffe des Fernsehens in Auflösung: Ereignis und Erwartung." *montage a/v*, 5, no. 1: 129–53.

Engell, Lorenz. 2008. "Das Mondprogramm. Wie das Fernsehen das größte Ereignis aller Zeiten erzeugte und wieder auflöste, um zu seiner Geschichte zu finden." In: *Medienereignisse der Moderne*, ed. by Friedrich Lenger, and Ansgar Nünning, pp. 150–71. Darmstadt: Wiss. Buchges.

Engell, Lorenz. 2009. "Fernsehen mit Unbekannten. Überlegungen zur experimentellen Television." In: *Fernsehexperimente. Stationen eines Mediums*, ed. by Michael Grisko, and Stefan Münker, pp. 15–46. Berlin: Kadmos.

Engell, Lorenz. 2019. "Bilder aus dem All. Das 'Anthropische Prinzip' und der Planet Erde als medienanthropologische Inszenierung." In:

*Medienanthropologische Szenen. Die Conditio Humana im Zeitalter der Medien*, ed. by Christiane Voß, Katerina Krtilova, and Lorenz Engell, pp. 15–30. München: Fink.

Fahle, Oliver. 2005. "Das Bild und das Sichtbare. Eine Bildtheorie des Fernsehens." In: *Philosophie des Fernsehens*, ed. by Oliver Fahle, and Lorenz Engell, pp. 77–91. Paderborn: Fink.

Günther, Gotthard. 1963. *Das Bewusstsein der Maschinen. Eine Metaphysik der Kybernetik*. Baden-Baden: Agis.

Hanke, Helmut. 1990. "Umbruch im Fernsehen der DDR." *Ästhetik und Kommunikation* 19, no. 73/74: 79–86.

Hartley, John. 1999. *Uses of Television*. London, New York: Routledge.

Heidegger, Martin. 1993. "What Is Metaphysics." In: Martin Heidegger. *Basic Writings*, ed. by. David Farrell Krell, pp. 89–110. New York: HarperCollins.

Heidegger, Martin. 1995. *The Fundamental Concepts of Metaphysics: World, Finitude, Solitude*. Bloomington, Indianapolis: Indiana University Press.

Heidegger, Martin. 2008. *Being and Time*. New York et al.: Harper Collins.

Hickethier, Knut. 1998. *Geschichte des deutschen Fernsehens*. Stuttgart, Weimar: Metzler.

Hiebel, Hanns H., Heinz Hiebler, Karl Koger, and Herwig Walitsch. 1999. *Große Medienchronik*. München: Fink.

Jantsch, Erich. 1980. *The Self-Organizing Universe: Scientific and Human Implications of the Emerging Paradigm of Evolution*. Oxford: Pergamon Press.

Kracauer, Siegfried. 1995. "Those Who Wait." In: Siegfried Kracauer. *The Mass Ornament: Weimar Essays*, ed. by Thomas Y. Levin, pp. 129–40. Cambridge, MA, London: Harvard University Press.

Kubitz, Peter Paul. 1997. *Der Traum vom Sehen*. Dresden: Verlag der Kunst.

Kühnert, Hanno. 1969. "Die Mondnacht." In: *Frankfurter Allgemeine Zeitung*, July 7, 1969, p. 7.

Lacan, Jacques. 1990. *Television: A Challenge to the Psychoanalytic Establishment*. New York, London: W. W. Norton & Company.

Lacan, Jacques. 1998. *The Seminar of Jacques Lacan. Book XI: The Four Fundamental Concepts of Psychoanalysis*. New York, London: W. W. Norton & company.

Ludes, Peter. 1991. "Die Rolle des Fernsehens bei der revolutionären Wende in der DDR." *Publizistik* 36, no. 2: 201–16.

Luhmann, Niklas. 1995. *Social Systems*. Stanford: Stanford University Press.

Lynch, Michael. 2013. "Ontography: Investigating the Production of Things, Deflating Ontology." *Social Studies of Science* 43, no. 3: 444–62.

Lynch, Michael. 2019. "Ontography as the Study of Locally Organized Ontologies." *Zeitschrift für Medien- und Kulturforschung (ZMK)* 10, no. 1: 147–60.

Lyotard, Jean-François. 2012. "Philosophy and Painting in the Age of Their Experiment." In: Jean-François Lyotard. *Textes dispersés I: esthétique et théorie de l'art. Miscellaneous Texts I: Aesthetics and Theory of Art*, pp. 147–75. Leuven: Leuven University Press.

Marschall, Rick. 1987. *The Golden Age of Television*. London: Bison.
Merleau-Ponty, Maurice. 1964. "Eye and Mind." In: Maurice Merleau-Ponty. *The Primacy of Perception: And other Essays on Phenomenological Psychology, the Philosophy of Art, History and Politics*, ed. by James M. Edie, pp. 159–90. n. p.: Northwestern University Press.
Mody, Cyrus C. M., and Michael Lynch. 2009. "Test Objects and Other Epistemic Things: A History of the Nanoscale Object." *British Journal for the History of Science (BJHS)* 1–36. Accessed May 28, 2019. https://depts.washington.edu/ssnet/archive/ModyandLynch_Test_objects.pdf.
Nielsen, Arthur C. 1950. *Television Audience Research for Great Britain*. Chicago: Nielsen Corp.
Pias, Claus. 2002. *Computer-Spiel-Welten*. München: Sequenzia.
Revers, Wilhelm Josef. 1949. *Philosophie der Stimmungen*. Meisenheim: Hain.
Rheinberger, Hans-Jörg. 1997. *Toward a History of Epistemic Things*. Stanford: Stanford University Press.
Schneider, Birgit. 2014. "Red Futures. The Colour Red in Scientific Imagery of Climate Change." In: *Disaster as Image: Iconographies and Media Strategies across Europe and Asia*, ed. by Monica Juneja, and Gerrit Jasper Schenk, pp. 183–93. Regensburg: Schnell + Steiner.
Spigel, Lynn. 1992. *Make Room for TV, Television and the Family Ideal in Postwar America*. Chicago, London: University of Chicago Press.
Stauff, Markus. 2005. *Das neue Fernsehen. Machtanalyse, Gouvernementalität und digitale Meiden*. Münster: Lit.
Stengers, Isabelle. 1995. "The Galileo Affair." In: *A History of Scientific Thought: Elements of a History of Science*, ed. by Michel Serres, pp. 280–314. Oxford, Cambridge, MA: Blackwell.
Vertov, Dziga. 1984. "Kinoks: A Revolution." In: Dziga Vertov. *Kino-Eye: The Writings of Dziga Vertov*, ed. by Annette Michelson, pp. 11–21. London: University of California Press.
Vogl, Joseph. 2007. "Becoming Media: Galileo's Telescope." *Grey Room* 29: 14–25.
Winkler, Hartmut. 2006. "Nicht handeln. Versuch einer Wiederaufwertung des couch potatoe angesichts der Provokation des interaktiv Digitalen." In: *Philosophie des Fernsehens*, ed. by Oliver Fahle, and Lorenz Engell, pp. 93–101. München: Fink.
Zec, Peter. 1985. "Mana oder die 0_Funktion der Television." In: *Unser Fernsehen! Vom Pantoffelkino zum Terminal*, ed. by Norbert Nowotsch, and Rainer Weißenborn, pp. 17–23. Drensteinfurt: Huba.
Zielinski, Siegfried. 1999. *Audiovisions: Cinema and Television as Entr'actes in History*. Amsterdam: Amsterdam University Press.
Zupančič, Alenka. 1996. "Philosophers' Blind Man's Buff." In: *Gaze and Voice as Love Objects*, ed. by Renata Salecl, and Slavoj Žižek, pp. 32–58. Durham, London: Duke University Press.
Zweites Deutsches Fernsehen. 1970. *Jahrbuch 1969*. Mainz: Informations- und Presseabteilung ZDF.

# 8

# Switching

## Remote Control

As we have seen, the return of the switch image from the moon to the Earth established the conditions for an enormous concentration and intensification of television. Television began to display images within images, and the paradigmatic model for this was the image of the control center in Houston, Texas. In addition, television began to circulate images of the entirety of everything visible and their locations, and the paradigmatic model for this was the image of the planet Earth as seen from space. Television thus positioned itself in the image space of total visibility, which Richard Dienst refers to as *transvisibility* (Dienst 1995: 26–33). Third, the images then literally began to look back at one another (and to their viewers). And finally, the images stopped functioning as "ensembles of opto-phonetic data," as they were normally understood, and began to act instead as switching points between countless other switchable images.

All of this established the necessity and the conditions of possibility for an auxiliary device that was detached from the television and was later even supposed to be autonomous. This device was the *remote control*, which made it possible to operationalize and (as the name says) control the concentration and intensification of television. The increased complexity of the switch image after its return from space was reduced through the remote control. This occurred paradoxically through a drastic increase in the number of possible switching operations, as the remote control allowed not only the director but also each individual viewer to select, watch, and deselect one image to the benefit of another one from a huge number of possible images. In other words, it allowed the selection to be revised and repeated at any time and for any number of times. This, in turn, paved the way for another dramatic increase in complexity and a further intensification. However, it involved not only an increase but also a structural change, as new and improved possibilities of image switching were literally placed in the hands of the viewers. The new switching operations were performed no longer centrally for the convenience of all viewers but rather by the viewers themselves and through their fingers with the press of a button. The remote control is another ontographic tool, as it activates a specific and not predetermined chain of switching processes that only exists in the course of its production through the keystrokes. The creation of a unique sequence of images also transforms the television evening into an ontographic event, which already changes the basic nature of television in a highly significant way.

## Between Magic and Command

The cultural and technical history of the remote control and remote effects goes back a long time. It can obviously be traced back to magical practices and media, as magic wands and voodoo rituals are tools and practices with remote effects. It was also incorporated into modern illusionism and stage magic through newly engineered optical, acoustic, or electrical effects. The ethnologist Alfred Gell even argues that the artworks of the European tradition belong to the same category as magical objects in animism and totemism. Flagged as being themselves generated, they produce effects in viewers across space and time—or these effects are at least attributed to them (Gell 1998: 25–48). We will come back to this interesting dimension of the remote control later. In any case, even the widespread "hypodermic needle" theory of empirical media research cannot function without the construction of a remote effect; all mass media were accordingly nothing else than remote controls in the hands of the few who controlled the many (Davis and Baran 1981:19–52). And lastly it can obviously be said that the television image, as a *transmission-image*, is itself always already a remote effect of what it makes visible; the switching from one camera to another by the director, such as during a live broadcast, results in a change of the image on every remote screen. However, the remote control represses the nature of the television image as a transmission image in favor of its nature as a switch image. We will also come back to this later.

The first remote control, through which a viewer could operate the television without directly touching the buttons on the set, was significantly called "Lazy Bones" and was introduced by the manufacturer Zenith in 1950 (Zenith: Remote Background n. d.; Bellis 2018). It was connected to the television with an extremely heavy cable that ran through the living room. Unlike later visions of viewers who supposedly became active and empowered through the remote control, this early device was designed precisely to reduce unnecessary activity or at least superfluous movement. It was initially a tool for the sluggish "couch potato" we already encountered earlier rather than the active neoliberal "prosumer" that would later be propagated. Legend has it that the director of the company, a certain Eugene F. McDonald, commissioned the development of "Lazy Bones" because he was tired of watching commercials, and he assumed that his customers were tired of watching them as well (Zenith: Remote Background n. d.). Viewers were thus supposed to be able to follow programs without interruptions and without standing up. This was the beginning of the use of the remote control to switch away from commercials, which became known as "zapping." However, the electromechanical device was cumbersome, as it controlled electromotors that mechanically operated the frequency regulator in the television set, which was slow. The thick cable was also ugly and dangerous, and the batteries were quickly depleted due to its relatively high energy consumption. The remote control did not initially catch on in this form, so in 1955 Eugene Polley developed a remarkable device for Zenith called the "Flash-Matic" (Early Television Museum n. d.). This device was wireless, and it thus joined the remote control to the tradition of wireless remote controls that had already been experimentally developed and tested since the late nineteenth century. For example, in 1895 Jagadish Chandra Bose fired a gun using radio waves, in 1896 Guglielmo Marconi and William Preece wirelessly produced a ringing sound in another room during a public demonstration, in 1898 Nikola Tesla received a patent for his wirelessly operated boat, the "Teleautomaton," and in 1903 Leonardo Torres Quevedo built a remote-controlled robot, the "Telekino," which could even steer a boat (Yuste and Palma 2005: 1379–82; Gupta, Engineer and Shepherd 2009: 106; O'Neill 1944: 167).

In 1939 the manufacturer Philco also used radio-based technology to develop a remote-controlled radio called the "Mystery Control" (Radiomuseum n. d.). This device was interesting because it used *impulse modulation* to differentiate between the various commands (volume control, channel switching, etc.). Instead of being coded through varying frequencies, the commands were thus conveyed as a varying number of signal impulses transmitted in quick succession, and the number of impulses determined the function that would be performed. From the perspective of the history of technology, the "Mystery Control" was thus the first digital device in radio electronics, and the digitization of radio (and later of television) began exactly with the remote control. This was also why so much importance was attached to it in the continuing transformation processes of television. However, Polley's "Flash-Matic" initially functioned differently, as it used light as a transmission medium. Light sensors were mounted on the four corners of the television set, and the remote control consisted of a kind of light pistol that could aim a beam at one of the sensors. An electrical current was then released in the television set, and it could switch the channel forward or back, turn the sound on or off, and switch the entire device on or off.

This device also did not catch on, as it was difficult to aim the light pistol at the sensors and it was easy for other light sources, such as the sun or overhead lights, to activate the sensors and trigger unwanted channel changes or switch the device off. Hence, in 1956 Zenith introduced another new device, developed by Robert Adler, which was called the "Zenith Space Command" (Wired 2007). This name made the connection between the remote control and space travel explicit; it was the time of the Sputnik shock and the incipient "space race," which led to the flight to the moon. The "Space Command" functioned on a mechano-acoustic basis: by pressing one of the four large buttons, air was forced through a pipe that generated an inaudible ultrasonic sound. There were four such sounds, which an acoustic sensor in the television was able to distinguish and convert into electrical signals. This device was enormously successful, and subsequent apparatuses after 1961 were able to generate sounds electronically, which was far less cumbersome and also less costly. The remote control finally caught on in this form in the 1960s, and millions were also initially distributed by other manufacturers. In Germany the devices were called "Telepilot" and "Teledirector" (*Teledirigent*). They also had undesired side effects, as dogs could hear the ultrasonic sounds and were often highly irritated. The ultrasonic sounds that accompanied everyday events, such as dropping keys on glass surfaces, could also activate unwanted channel changes or switch the device off.

## Digital and Universal

In the 1970s, the further development of the remote control was largely driven by Siemens (Berkner 2013). The number of functions that could be coded in sufficiently differentiable ultrasonic frequencies had since become too limited for the growing demands. After the number of available channels had increased dramatically through new broadcasting technologies (like cable reception and satellite technology) and the elimination of broadcasting monopolies (starting in Italy in 1977 and subsequently also in almost all other countries), for example, the function of shifting up and down the list of channels was no longer sufficient. In addition to changing the channel, the remote control was also supposed to provide more effective and rapid random access, and other image functions were supposed to be controllable as well, like brightness and contrast. A new complementary medium called *Teletext* was also introduced in 1977 (in Germany it was known as Videotext). It was a very primitive precursor to the internet, as it similarly called up written information that could be read on the screen (Faatz 2001). These images (which were already called "pages") were transmitted in the fractions of a second between the consecutive images on tube screens, which were known as "blanking intervals." Three-digit numbers activated the selected pages, and the remote control was supposed to enable this selection from hundreds of pages.

Siemens solved this problem by once again converting the remote control to a new underlying technology—namely, infrared waves (Berkner 2013: 3f.). Siemens was particularly engaged in the area of optoelectronics at this time. They chose to use infrared waves because they could be produced electronically and then converted back into electrical signals using sensors, and they also allowed for extremely short impulse sequences. The new remote control, which came onto the market in 1976 and functioned as the "Telepilot" for Grundig receivers, produced a wide variety of signals that could be distinguished by the number of impulses. It thus enabled numerical (i.e., digital) coding, which means, once again, that the digitization of television first began with the remote control. In addition, switching between channels was made easier through the development of the "capacity diode," as it became possible to switch directly from one frequency to another without tedious channel scanning. Thanks to these innovations, the infrared remote control was established worldwide in relevant quantities, and since 1980 it has been included as standard equipment for televisions (instead of a costly extension). In principle, the remote control still functions today on the basis of this development. Remote controls also soon migrated from the immediate periphery of the television to other parts of the household, such as DVD players, slide projectors, stereos, garage doors, air conditioners, kitchen appliances, personal computers, and much more. As the number of remote controls in the home increased, it became necessary to introduce the universal remote control (which can operate many or all devices), remote control finding devices, and eventually dual remote controls. Indeed, many devices now have two remote controls: one that has an enormous number of buttons (sometimes more than sixty) due to its multitude of functions and another that only controls the old basic functions of the device. The functions of the remote control are now increasingly migrating to the mobile phone, which has also become a ubiquitous and universal medium.

## The Cultural Technique of Selection

However, the remote control is not just a device that produces effects from a distance. In fact, it only produces effects from a very short distance—that is, the distance between the viewer's seat and the television set. Rather, its main function is to support a very specific cultural technique—namely, selecting from an expanded range or repertoire of offerings. It allows the viewer to *navigate* this range of offerings and particularly to revise and repeat the process of selection. Its implementation is obviously related to the development of a capitalist consumer society, which is of tremendous importance for television in general, as we have already seen in connection with the soap opera genre and television advertising (see Chapter 3 in this volume). The remote control follows this in various ways. Randomly selecting from an open range of offerings is a *consumption technique* that is important for everyday life under surplus conditions due to market competition, as in a supermarket (Brauns 2004: 117–27; Certeau 1988). It is significant that television shopping already existed in the 1950s in the United States, such as the program *Television Department Store*, which presented products that viewers could order by mail (Spigel 1992: 79). It was even promoted as a program that allowed mothers to teach their daughters at home about the cultural technique of selecting from a wide range of products. As a universal selection machine with reverse and repeat functions, the remote control was a further development of this technique, and it fit into an environment that increasingly offers a selection of not only commodities but also lifestyles, life plans, career choices, visual appearances, and interpersonal relations—a selection that could also be revised and repeated. This has increased ever since, although the gesture has now changed, as switching has been replaced by *swiping*. During the selection process, therefore, the persons making the selections are addressed as allegedly autonomous and as subjects who articulate themselves precisely through the operation of selection. It is obviously not hard to recognize that the freedoms of the selection process are strongly conditioned. We have already seen earlier that the subjects of image switching are precisely not subjects in the strongest sense of the term; rather, they are *agents*, who are integrated in a complex network of material and immaterial conditions. Their main characteristic is not that they are simply actors but rather that passivation and activation are entangled together in them in a striking way. We will follow up on this in relation to television when we pursue these considerations regarding the anthropomediality of the switch image (see also Chapter 12 in this volume).

One of these conditions is particularly apparent in relation to the classical remote control—namely, the switching subject is visibly woven into *power relations*. The person holding the remote control or command device is in a different position than those who are not. As a gesture of addressing, pointing, and producing an effect, the remote control is part of a tradition of gestures of power and privilege. It thus initially articulated and reinforced existing inequalities. This is clearly shown in the advertising for televisions in the era of the remote control, in which a male, mostly a father surrounded by his wife and children, usually holds the device and determines what is on. However, the remote control can obviously also be passed from hand to hand within a group whose members are equal partners, not least because the ongoing process of selection can be exhausting.

As a cultural, social, and physical technique as well as a technology of selection, revision, and repetition, the remote control is also incidentally part of the genealogy of the *computer mouse*. This is true not only technologically, as the wireless computer mouse similarly sends commands to the computer using infrared technology; rather, the computer mouse—or, more specifically, the mouse button—also extends the selection process far beyond the offerings of television to include everything that can be shown on computer screens and in clickable windows. The mouse continues what the remote control began, and it does so on a much wider scale by representing the experiencability of the world as the broadest possible repertoire of possible selection decisions, as a horizon of selection possibilities, and as itself selectable. Since the development of the remote control, the world has offered itself to be selected and as a selection, and the mouse has put this program into operation on an unimaginable scale.

## Communication Theory

The first field in which this change was visible was that of communication and its theory. Until then, communication through television was largely understood in the context of Claude Shannon's extremely popular and instructive model of communication, which still represents the epistemic core of communication studies today—*cum grano salis*—in the form of Lasswell's model of communication (Shannon 1948: 379–423; 623–56; Lasswell 1948: 32–51) or, in other contexts, the Bühler-Jakobson scheme. It assumes that communication consists of a *sender* (which refers to a technical aggregate rather than a person) that sends a *message* composed of signals to a *receiver* (which is also a device). In order to do this, the sender needs a *channel*, through which it can reach the receiver, and a *code*, which stipulates how the signals should be recomposed. In addition, the signal flow must be protected from *interference*, and the receiver must be able to provide *feedback* to confirm that the message has been received. This model does not require any semantics or pragmatics (the meaning and effects of signals are entirely irrelevant). It is a purely technical model of communication that was created to describe technical signal transmission processes, and it was actually oriented toward the functionality of radio. Applying this model to radio or television is therefore always redundant.

Bühler und Jakobson's model of communication is slightly different, as it is oriented toward language (Bühler 1990: 30–9; Jakobson 1960: 350–77). They also assume that senders and receivers are speakers and listeners (and thus human beings), that the message has a content that is supposed to be communicated, and that this content refers to the real world that the senders and receivers inhabit and share, which is called the *horizon of reference*. Moreover, the communicative act has an *intention* and produces an *effect* (which does not necessarily coincide with the intention). This is summarized in Lasswell's famous phrase: "Who said what, in which channel, to whom, with what effect?" And even in this study, we have understood television as a transmission medium in accordance with Nipkow's definition—namely, as a medium that transmits the visibility of an object from one location A to another location B (see Chapter 2 in this volume). Our approach is thus based neither on technical devices alone nor on classical human actors but rather on agents as their amalgam and their entanglement in anthropomediality.

After the flight to the moon, however, everything situated at each location A, as well as the totality of all location A's, potentially became visible at every location B, and they were even always already there as possibilities. Every location and everything visible could be an image, and every image could be connected to every other image. But whatever is already present or already there no longer needs to be transmitted. We actually already anticipated this condition when we discussed the light-emitting diode that indicates the presence and availability of electrical current and signal flow in the switched-off device. Everything is already there, and it is available at any time. It no longer needs to be transported or transmitted to where it is; rather it is all around us, and it only needs to be activated and selected. The question is no longer how the image gets from location A to location B, as it is possibly always already there; rather, the question is which of the countless possible images should be visible at location B and which ones should not be visible. In other words, the problem is no longer transmission but *selection*: which images should emerge from the sea of possibilities at which time, and which images should sink below the surface and remain latent? The remote control instrumentalizes the operation of selecting from a range of possibilities, as it is the medium that performs this selection. And because it involves not just any selection but rather a selection from a mass of switch images, this also occurs through the operation of switching. The remote control allows viewers to effectively access a switching process that was previously reserved exclusively for the director—namely, the operation of switching from one image to another image in a vast and constantly mutating mass of images (Engell 2003: 53–77).

Niklas Luhmann has already formulated a theory of communication that returns to the foundations established by Shannon and Bühler but completely abandons the emphasis on transmission in favor of the *operation of selection* (Luhmann 1995: 141f.), and a glance at his theory will thus be useful for developing a theory of the remote control. According to Luhmann, every communication that is actually made was first selected from a range of possible communications. In the case of linguistic communication, it could be said that a speaker (Luhmann calls this the *ego*) says something specific and nothing else, that the communication can be formulated in this way or another way, and that both what is said and the chosen formulation are based on decisions that could have turned out differently. Luhmann refers to the content of what is said as the *information*, and he refers to the chosen formulation as the *communication*. In the case of television, the chain of visible images is also a result of selection. The images in a live broadcast, for example, are selected by the director, as Umberto Eco described (Eco 1989: 105–22). What is unique about live television is that what is communicated is not only the result but also the ongoing process of selection itself, and this is precisely what constitutes the ontographic nature of live television. If one begins with Shannon's mathematical concept of information, unlike Luhmann's model, then the information of a signal sequence (such as images, sounds, or words) is based on the degree and *level* of its selectivity (Shannon 1948; see also Bense 1969, 1979). The more improbable a communication is, the more information it contains, and its *improbability* is thus directly proportional to the number of other possible communications. If I select a channel from three possible channels with the help of the remote control, then the information content of this selection (i.e., its statistical improbability or originality) is lower than if I selected a channel from three hundred possible channels.

For Luhmann, in contrast, the selection of a communication follows a second selection—namely, the operation of *understanding* (Luhmann 1995: 143f.). According to Luhmann, understanding involves a distinction between information and communication or between that which is said and the way in which it is communicated. Understanding thus distinguishes between two different selections that interact in the communication. The information that someone (Luhmann calls this instance the *alter ego*) infers from or ascribes to a message is thus also a product of the communication itself, as it is a product of understanding—that is, of the distinction between information and communication—and by no means a predetermined state or fact of the world or *reality* external to the communication. However, understanding is also selective, as every message can be understood in different ways. The distinction between communication and information can turn out differently, and the information can also be different depending on the alter ego. Information, communication, and understanding are thus three selections that form an operative unity, and for Luhmann this is precisely what constitutes communication (Luhmann 1995: 147).

## Remote Control as Communication Technology

This can also be easily found in television communication: while watching a program, the alter ego distinguishes between information (what the program is about and the facts that are communicated or could have been communicated instead) and communication (how the facts are communicated and the alternative ways in which they could have been communicated). And this distinction—that is, understanding—can be made in many different ways. It is selective, so the information itself is also, in turn, dependent on the way in which the alter ego makes this distinction. What is special about mass media communication, like television, is that there is obviously no specific individual addressee, as it is directed at a more or less undefined audience. The selectivity of understanding is thus particularly emphasized, as the viewer's understanding is always related to how they assume other viewers understand the same communication. Unlike individual communication, therefore, the possible understandings from which the viewer selects are just as important as the viewer's assumptions about how other viewers understand the program.

The remote control completely changes the process of television communication. It can also be described in terms of information, communication, and understanding, but these selections are made on a completely different basis. More specifically, these selections are no longer purely immaterial *acts of consciousness*; rather, they are due to the *operation* of a technical device—a specific *gesture*—and they are performed precisely as switching operations—that is, as the pressing of buttons (Flusser 2014: 162–4). From the perspective of the remote control, the program also no longer functions as a communication containing information that can be distinguished from it through the operation of understanding; rather, the program itself is now (part of) the information, and the communication is the sequence of programs that are actualized on the screen. The message that can be differentiated into information and communication is now no longer the program but rather the television evening as a whole, which is a collage of numerous fragments (Winkler 1991). The viewers, who ultimately compose the television evening through their selections, thus assume no longer the function of the alter ego but rather that of the ego. With the help of the remote control, they constantly select from a wide range of programs that are available at the same time. In addition to the choices made by viewers and the chains of switching and selection operations that these choices make operative, other choices and chains are also possible. If communication is understood as selection, then the sequence of programs represents the assembled information and the sequence of selection operations represents the communication, which is also selective because it could have turned out differently. The consecutive pressing of buttons thus produces a sequence of selections, through which the television evening is written. It is also written precisely while it happens, and it lasts as long as the chain of commands from the remote control continues. The function fulfilled by the director in live television is thus transferred once again to the viewer, which again reveals the fundamentally ontographic *mode of being* of the television evening (rather than that of only the image or the program).

In this case, however, it would seem as if television communication has not a multitude of unspecified addressees, as is typical of mass communication, but rather no addressees at all, as the communication is communicated to no one other than the viewer herself, who writes and watches it at the same time. In other words, the selection of programs and program fragments that constitutes the television evening is initially addressed to no one other than the viewer herself. As a form of communication, it would thus be a monologue—provided that the selection operations of the viewer with the remote control can be distinguished from those of the selected programs. The viewer would then be the ego and the alter ego at the same time. This would obviously only be true if the viewer were sitting alone in front of the television and not in a group, such as a family, which is often the case. Besides the power factor, which was already mentioned earlier, a group would be an audience for the selection decisions—that is, for the communication of what the remote control performs. The communication would then have consequences, as it could provoke satisfaction, dissatisfaction, rejection, discussion, or even, as is typical of television, collaboration and participation in this second level of direction, whose product is not the live broadcast but rather the course of the ontographic television evening.

## Television with an Implicit Remote Control: MTV and News Channels

Staying with a single viewer, one could argue that television broadcasters are very well able to observe and understand her television evening by means of the simplest form of empirical and quantitative audience research—that is, the measurement of viewer ratings. Broadcasters have long been able to calculate the selection as well as the retention time of programs (Zubayr and Gerhard 2017: 130–44). This is admittedly only done using statistics, which only calculate the viewing habits of roughly a thousand television households; the rest are extrapolated. The television broadcaster thus identifies the viewer not as an individual person, consciousness, or psychic system but rather only as a statistical quantity, and the informational content of her entirely personal television evening is derived precisely from the fact that it is distinguished from the communication itself; it could even be described as a pure construct of the broadcaster. However, it can hardly be said that the viewer addresses the broadcaster with her switching behavior. He might observe her, but she does not communicate anything to him. The collaged message of the television evening spent alone is only addressed to the viewer herself; if anything, she conducts a conversation with herself by switching back and forth between programs.

The switch image nevertheless *knows* that it can be selected, and it reacts to this. The condition for this is its switchability, and it refers to this switchability as an essential feature in that it constantly interrupts itself until there is no longer anything uninterrupted and the phenomenon of interruption in the flow ceases to exist. The remote control is thus accompanied by the interruption of the uninterruptable or even discontinuation as a second-order category. In addition to the flow that already takes place in individual linear television programs, a second flow that cuts across all channels and flow can now also be created, and what we already determined about the first flow similarly applies to the second. Even more than the first, the second flow is linked to a physical action of the viewer, no matter how minimal it may be as a mere chain of button presses. It articulates the already articulated flow once again and nevertheless also flows with it. In this respect, it does not involve an observation or a reflection; in other words, it is not a "second-order" flow in the strict sense of a higher level. Instead, it involves a lateral relationship with reciprocal crossing and crisscrossing, deviating and converging, sliding up and down stream. The remote control uses the first flow and feeds back to it.

This can be seen very clearly in the individual program components and broadcasting formats that arose with the diversification of channels and the implementation of the remote control as a selection machine in the 1980s. The first example of this was the format of *music television,* which was highly innovative in its time (Engell 1989: 243ff.). Music television is television with an already built-in remote control. The basic mode of music television was therefore not semanticity but rather asemanticity, like the music itself, as music videos do not mean anything at all. They can obviously assume meanings and form narrative connections, but these meanings and connections only arise from a repertoire of images that is different for every video. Meanings and narratives accrue to the images, but they are not presupposed by them or assumed to be always already available and only expressed afterwards. The music video begins with pure communication rather than information. The information is not transmitted but rather produced through its differentiation from communication by means of selection, and this production is the "content" of the video. The selection processes of the remote control thus retroactively become a model for the images that the remote control manipulates.

Something similar also applies to news channels—another entirely new program genre of the 1980s, for which CNN in particular serves as a model. While news television seems to be highly semanticized, as it features events in the outside world, it develops an entirely new image culture of multiple switching. This includes the practice of allowing reports from other locations that are not shown in the image to run along the lower edge of the screen; sometimes there are even two continuously scrolling news tickers that are placed one above the other. The image does not linger on these preselected events and places, but it could switch over to them (and back again) at any time. News channels also use split-screen images, in which a primary image stands out from a secondary image, but the secondary image does not fade or cut out, so it is always possible to switch back and forth between the two images. This makes it possible to follow several different chains of events at the same time, just as the viewer is able to follow two or more channels by switching back and forth between them with the remote control. Like the viewer in front of the television, the anchorperson in the studio seems to be able to switch between places, events, and event types and thus navigate back and forth over the surface of events.

## Series and Casting Shows

The incorporation of the logic of the remote control into the very broadcasts is also visible in the *series formats* of television programs. The prime example remains the series *Miami Vice*, which we already examined more closely earlier (Engell 1989: 242f.; see also Engell 2003; see also Chapter 3 in this volume). As an almost purely episodic series, *Miami Vice* seems unremarkable at first: the basic plot has a series of variants, but it still remains stable, as there is no development from week to week. Within this narrative, semantic, or logical specifications, however, the individual episodes constantly switch back and forth between genres, styles, colors, speeds, and settings, as we have already seen. For example, the inventory of colors, locations, or types of movement (walking, dancing, driving, jumping, etc.) constitutes the range—or repertoire—of offerings from which each episode is freely and arbitrarily created. It is particularly relevant that luxury consumer objects and consumerism in general play a prominent role—from clothing and accessories to vehicles and other status symbols to drinks, drugs, prostitution, and even advertising (which *Miami Vice* itself also is). The connection between the remote control as a selection machine, the television that incorporates the remote control, and the pressure to consume is thus made explicit but no less imperative. *Moonlighting* has similar features, as the arbitrary arrangement of the sequences is a response to the arbitrary way in which the viewer handles these sequences using the remote control. Arbitrariness here means the freedom of choice that is actually communicated and that constitutes the communication from which the information or "content" of each sequence is generated, as it can be this way or another. If every communication can also turn out differently, and this is precisely what enables communication, then the contingency of television that incorporates the remote control reflexively becomes the "content" of the communication, which is itself also contingent. Not only can everything also be different, as everything is a product of consecutive and mutually interacting processes of selection (like all communication), but this is also explicitly referred to. In this sense, television in the era of the remote control is conscious of contingency and selectivity. The format of *Moonlighting* also incorporates the remote control by thematizing the feedback from the second level to the first level, to which television with an implicit remote control owes its existence. This occurs through a displacement, such as when viewers are directly addressed, the protagonists break character and discuss the dialog, or the plot (such as a wild chase) spills over onto the set and the studio.

Later series thematize the other side of selectability, which turns into a forced choice. In the world of the remote control, like that of universal commodity consumption, in which self-actualization is based on self-selection, it is impossible not to choose, as the pressure to choose always prevails. The remote control also instrumentalizes an imperative. In this situation, avoiding this pressure and not choosing can be a possible strategy. Life and relationship decisions, which are not easy to revise, can then (at least narratively) be delayed. This happens, for example, in a series like *Ally McBeal*, in which the protagonist appears to be trapped in a childlike woman's body as she simply persists contemplating the decision whether or not to enter adult life. Her otherwise rational career and love life is also permeated with the highly amusing and childlike perception of omnipotence and animism, which actually seems to grant her power within her surroundings, and it is striking how often she even produces remote effects. *Sex and the City* can also be read in this sense as a large-scale yet abandoned attempt to avoid mate selection; like *Miami Vice*, the connection between the system of consumption and the pressure to select is also presented here in a particularly opulent and affirmative way.

Television with this kind of *implicit remote control* has also produced entire television genres. The content of an entire group of tremendously successful formats is devoted to nothing more than selecting and deselecting—particularly with regard to people. These formats include *casting shows*, such as the internationally distributed *Next Top Model* format or programs like *The Bachelorette* or *Survivor*, in which a winner is chosen from a group of candidates through the successive elimination of contestants. This choice is staged with enormous dramaturgical effort, and it generates a chain of climaxes that sustain the format for weeks and sometimes even months. It provides space for prediction as well as subsequent reappraisal, which occupies the accompanying media of television during the broadcast periods of these shows. The deselection functions as an extended illustration of the principle of the switch image that underlies television and is decoupled and intensified in the remote control. Switching here applies not only to an image but also to a series of images and an entire format. Insofar as it involves the "real" livelihoods of the candidates, television here extends its ontography beyond its borders by ontographically generating a reality—namely, as a form of existence (such as that of celebrities) that disappears when television disappears (Ziemann 2011: 39–114; 65).

In doing so, it is entirely irrelevant whether the deselection is performed by a jury or a lone participant or whether elements of audience participation are integrated, as in the globally successful format of *Big Brother*. This choice is always characteristically staged as a deselection, as with zapping, and the deselected are then eliminated from the program. In this sense, the implicit remote control is clearly distinguished from the explicit remote control, as the consecutive and convergent chain of choices leads to a conclusion that cannot be revised or repeated. However, casting shows could only develop and catch on after the principle of selection—and particularly deselection—was transferred from images to people. Every person involved in the selection process reacts to the candidates in the same way that viewers react to television images. The motif of mate selection particularly points to cultural practices that are part of everyday digital culture in the form of online dating services and platforms. The gesture of *swiping* is here applied to human faces and figures, which becomes casual, whereas on television the selection process involves a great deal of aesthetic, dramaturgical, and technical effort.

## Choosing, Dreaming, and the Entire World

One of the very few theories of the remote control was developed by Hartmut Winkler, who argues that the remote control simultaneously offers relief from and an alternative to the pressures of everyday life (for this and the following see Winkler 1991: 59ff.). The television viewer counters the aesthetic and semantic arbitrariness to which she is exposed by exercising her own arbitrariness. For example, she can emancipate herself from the temporal parameters of the program sequence by asserting her own internal clock. She thus produces a form of resistance and orientation in (at least) three ways, which Winkler develops with reference to Siegfried Kracauer, Walter Benjamin, and Sigmund Freud. First, Kracauer already assumed that fragmentarity and incoherence were essential features of the modern world, which is no longer resigned to a closed horizon of meaning (Winkler 1991; see also Kracauer 1960: 297f.). This is all too often concealed, however, by the offering of closed meanings. The practice of introducing more incoherence into the already incoherent structure of television by dispersing what has already been dispersed, which is made possible by the remote control, is therefore a reasonable exercise of affirmation and appropriation. Winkler is thus opposed to the idea of reconstructing an integrated flow through television.

Winkler develops the second level of simultaneous insubordination and affirmation using Benjamin's concept of *shock* (Winkler 1991: 96–101). It is assumed that the modern world is dominated by a massive sensory overload—an enormous density of events—and modern humans are thus fundamentally irritated. They must defend themselves from this irritation by protecting themselves from their own latencies, which enables them to immunize themselves against external stimuli so that they remain unnoticed and ineffective. In order to ensure the effectiveness of this protection, however, it is sometimes necessary to put it to the test, like a fire drill. This means that they must intentionally expose themselves to certain selected events and endure the resulting irritations. This is what happens in the case of shock, such as in the voluntary observation of shocking images or the recognition of shocking information. Winkler transfers this idea to television. Unlike film, however, in which shocking close-ups are common (such as the excess of violence), television does not simply expose the viewer to shock; rather, she produces it herself (it could at least initially be assumed). In other words, the viewer does not use the running television images to immunize herself; rather, she deliberately immunizes herself against these images through "latency protection" (*Latenzschutz*) (and thus, to go beyond Winkler's assumption, against external reality, as Cavell's idea of *monitoring* also serves as a form of immunization against the catastrophic situation of the world). In order for this latency protection to remain operational, however, it must be constantly tested, and this testing occurs precisely through switching. Every switching process with the remote control is accompanied by an interruption of coherence, and each interruption gives the viewer a new shock. Like Benjamin, Winkler speaks of a "reeling" (*Taumeln*) that arises and exposes an entirely new view of reality (Winkler 1991: 106). If this radical destabilization normally remains a selective experience, however, then it is condensed and stabilized by the multitude of switching processes on television. What is pervasive in this is neither the intentions of television providers and producers nor the conscious attitudes, opinions, and intentions of the viewer but rather the images themselves and their configurations, which obey their own logic and offer their own access (Benjamin calls this the *optical unconscious*) (Winkler 1991: 104; Benjamin 1999: 512). The optical-acoustic material becomes operative through its own will.

Third and lastly, Winkler compares this condition of expanded and altered experience through switching to the condition of *dreaming* (Winkler 1991: 138–47). The relationship between the viewer and the screen event is much more intimate when the viewer uses a remote control. In the sense traced here, this relationship can be formulated as a strong or close anthropomediatic entanglement. The viewer thereby navigates not only the surface of the images but especially between the program's predetermined and preproduced series of images and the whims of her own imagination. The unconscious takes effect here, as in dreaming, and it articulates itself through switching processes. Even though its articulation makes use of the available, preformulated, and stereotypical image sequences, it reveals not only what has been individually repressed but also what has been socially marginalized. The visible images on the screen are thus related to the unconscious in the same way that, according to Freud, manifest dream content (i.e., what is seen and experienced in a dream) is related to latent dream content (i.e., what a dream "means") (Winkler 1991: 149f.). And this dream then applies to the possibility of a coherent world and a closed horizon of meaning, or at least this is always Winkler's subtext. If Winkler is right, then this would articulate the wish for and the possibility of not only a whole but a complete world— that is, an all-encompassing and healed world.

## Double Contingency

We have already encountered this moment of allness or the idea that television not only makes everything visible but also allows this allness either to be captured in an image or to emerge from images. It appeared in at least a few interpretations of the model of flow, and it also appeared in the previous chapter as the total image of the entire planet. Richard Dienst speaks of the omniscience or "transvisibility" of television in this sense (Dienst 1995: 5). From the perspective of the remote control, however, the image does not make the world visible; rather, it makes the visibility (of the world) switchable. Television in the era of the remote control is not about allness and totality but rather about selectability. Everything that exists can be selected and controlled, so the world is the entirety of everything selectable and the ultimate repertoire of all selections—including their inexhaustibility, as the remote control suggests that every selection can be endlessly revised and repeated.

However, the world of selectability and *contingency* that television maintains with the remote control (and with programs that integrate the effects of the remote control) must not be understood as a completely random, stagnant, and unstable world. In fact, it generates important practical and ethical problems regarding the irreversibility of time and the finitude of the world, as selections cannot be endlessly revised and reproduced simply due to the passing of time (as well as the transience and finitude of human existence). Despite this fact, or precisely because of it, the world is in an improbable yet stable condition as the product of continuous and arbitrary operations of selection. The reason for this is the relationship between the ego and the alter ego (Luhmann 1995: 105f.). The alter ego is as little defined in the understanding of a message as the ego is in its formulation; rather, the alter ego chooses a particular understanding from a range of possibilities (and thus creates, as we have seen, one particular piece of information instead of another one). However, the ego can never know which of the countless possible ways of understanding the message the alter ego has chosen. The ego and alter ego are opaque to one another, like black boxes. But the alter ego can answer or in any case send a message that is connected to or builds on that of the ego (in this sense, it can slip into the role of the ego). Of course, the alter ego can also refuse to answer and thus reject the inherent range of possible choices—namely, the offer to select a communication—or answer in a way that the ego cannot relate to its own utterance even with the best of intentions. However, such a refusal, query, or objection is also an acceptance of the range of possible understandings, and it shifts the selection back to the ego (Luhmann 1995: 51ff.; 143ff.). In any case, the ego will probably understand this message as an answer—that is, as a reaction to the ego's message and as an expression of how the alter ego selectively understood it.

This is obviously a pure hypothesis or assumption, but the ego will understand the alter ego's message on the basis of this assumption, and it will select another communication from the range of possible reactions. Every message offers a range of possible choices and is understood on the basis of these assumed choices. Neither the ego nor the alter ego has the faintest idea whether the other has understood something or even anything at all, but they hypothetically assume this understanding through their selections, and they respond with additional selections, communications, information, and understanding. What is more: they each assume not only that the other is communicating on the basis of understanding and selectivity but also that the other is doing precisely the same and is thus assuming a selective, informing, and understanding behavior toward the other. According to Luhmann, the essence of communication is that I allow your behavior to set conditions on my behavior, and I assume that you do the same in reverse and that you also assume the same of me. This conditionality consists of the fact that a behavior or a message offers a range of possible replies through connected behaviors or subsequent messages. A message does not specify a certain reaction, but it is also not open to any arbitrary reaction; rather, it presents a horizon of possibility from which the reaction will arise—through selection—or at least that is what the participants in the communication assume of each other. In this respect, every subsequent behavior is conditioned by the previous one, as it is at least assumed to be selected from the range of possibilities made available by the previous behavior or message. Communication thus becomes the hypothetical entanglement of stabilizing, iterative, but baseless assumptions (Luhmann 1995: 365ff.).

Every communication, understanding, and information is selective and could also turn out differently. Everything that could be different than it is and is therefore not fixed, causally determined, or without alternatives, is contingent. Contingency is the way of being of that which could just as well be different. Contingency is a product of selectivity, for what is selected could have also turned out differently (otherwise it would not involve a selection). The behavior of the participants in a communication is contingent, and messages can only be linked to one another because they are contingent and can also be different. The ego and the alter ego both assume contingency, and they even assume that the other assumes this assumption. The famous *double contingency*, in Luhmann's sense, is thus actually a double double contingency, as the assumption is doubled on both sides (i.e., each one assumes the contingency as well as the assumption of contingency of the other) (Luhmann 1995: 107f.).

The switch image, which always emerges from selection processes, becomes contingent once again through the remote control, and this contingency is always articulated through switching operations. Apart from its early beginnings, it was obviously always possible to choose or switch between two or more programs, yet this choice could be explained—that was the purpose of program guides and previews. A revision of this choice was also highly unlikely so long as each channel change meant getting up from one's seat and approaching the television set. It was also always possible not to watch television at all. The program was thus constantly contingent, but this contingency was a negligible variable that could be ignored. The evening and the program did not have to coincide, but they largely did. Contingency only became significant in its doubling through the remote control.

## Paleotelevision, Neotelevision, and Televisuality

The switch image, which emerges from the process of selection through switching back and forth, affirms, doubles, and emphasizes its contingency. It is aware of it, and it is thus linked to a transition that is considered canonical in the historiography of television—namely, the transition from paleotelevision to *neotelevision*, which occurred around 1980. It was first observed by Umberto Eco and later described in more detail by Roger Odin and Francesco Casetti (Eco 1985: 190-9; Casetti and Odin 1990: 9-26). What is most important in Eco's brief sketch is that television images can no longer be characterized by their mediating function. Television is no longer a window to the world, it is no longer subordinate to the world, and its images are no longer transparent in the sense that they make the world visible; instead, television images now make themselves visible, and they are based no longer on the world and reality but rather on other images (Eco 1985: 196f.). *Representation* enters a state of crisis, and this transition is not caused by something occurring elsewhere, such as an aesthetic or political movement; rather, it is caused by television itself (Eco 1985: 198), as it is attributed to the increase in the number of channels and the opening of the market (beginning in Italy in 1977). The implementation of the remote control can also be added to the top of this list. The now doubly switchable and doubly contingent image is no longer necessarily what it is, as it is always something else at the same time. It no longer describes what it is but rather always announces the possibility that it could be something else. It thus emphasizes its dependence on selection and its own manufactured nature.

Odin and Casetti expanded on these ideas (Casetti and Odin 1990: 10f.) by observing that in neotelevision the old, didactic, and all-knowing arrangement of paleotelevision, in which there is always a communication and knowledge divide, is replaced by cooperative and open forms. Instead of informing viewers about issues or providing one-sided commentary, issues are discussed, especially in the burgeoning talk show format, which Cavell also sees as becoming a principal part of television. Feedback processes—we already discussed the absurd "light test"—became an increasingly important part of program planning, which eroded the one-way orientation and authority of television. Odin and Casetti also described several phenomena from the early period of television as typical features of neotelevision, such as the interruption of coherence and image flow (Casetti and Odin 1990: 15–18). As we have seen, however, this operation has always been part of television, and it is also the basis of televisual flow. It merely operates differently in commercial and American television than in state-owned or public European television. Nevertheless, something changes here: the interruption is now doubled through the intervention of the remote control and the second operationalizability of images, and this occurs to such an extent that the concept of interruption loses its meaning.

Another characterization of neotelevision, which is important for this argument, is that it marks the emergence of a new type of image—namely, *transitional images* (Casetti and Odin 1990: 19). This involves visual intermediate images that are mostly already digitally generated and that are activated by the transition from one image to another. For example, the previous image is wiped away, folded, turned, compressed, formed into spirals, subjected to lighting effects, and so on, and newly selected images arise from these patterns and movements. These kinds of "fancy transitions" make explicit not only the transition from one image to another but also the operation of switching itself, as this operation is granted its own image that does not describe anything or have any semantic meaning. This development is vitally important for the switch image, as the images that emerge are exclusively images of switching, which they themselves ontographically implement. In certain broadcast forms, such as commercials, music television, and the newly emerging news channels, these images can accumulate to such an extent that they perform more than just a hinge function; when the image text contains such a large proportion of transitional images, then the images between which the transition is produced also seem to consist of transitional images.

This development is closely related to the introduction of digital tools for image processing, which began with the digitization of television through the infrared remote control, as we have already seen. Digitization essentially allows for the precise control of individual pixels, and it thus redirects and changes the writing flow of the cathode ray, which becomes discontinuous. For example, all of the pixels (or areas) of a certain color can be removed from an image and replaced by other information, such as parts of another image. This would be the famous *blue* (or *green*) *screen* process of television. *Video feedback*, *motion control*, and *nonlinear editing* are further examples of such processes. In video feedback (or video assist), the viewfinder of the camera is made accessible to everyone participating in the recording using video monitors, which allows for other forms of interaction and feedback effects. Motion control enables previously impossible movements of studio cameras using hydraulic tools. Nonlinear editing makes it possible no longer simply to add one video image to another (as in assembly editing) but also to insert images into an already existing image sequence. The expanded and simplified tools of image manipulation and processing also entailed a completely new visual style for television as a whole. More precisely, they caught on because they laid the groundwork for a new stylistic orientation, which was economically and communicatively necessary and which was again connected to the remote control. John Caldwell referred to this new style as *televisuality* (Caldwell 1995), which foregrounds purely visual image or exhibition values. The individual channels must differentiate themselves from each other in order to be identified in the flood of offerings, and they thus develop their own unique visual style, which is characterized above all by the use of visual and technical effects. Televisualization is especially driven by the new competitors on the television market, such as CNN and MTV. Insofar as style is a medium through which images refer to, emerge from, and give rise to other images, televisuality intensifies the already inherently self-referential and *non-representational* aspect of neotelevision (Luhmann 1990b: 191–214). Caldwell even assumed that television establishes a self-reflexive and self-aware relationship, as the images of television contain and conduct an implicit discussion of what television is and how it looks (Caldwell 1995: 331; Luhmann 2000b: 239f.). The images thus already have an implicit remote control at their disposal before they are switched back and forth on the viewer's screen. Every channel and every image knows that it can easily be replaced and that this is something it must prevent.

## Selection Styles

Televisuality makes television aware of its own contingency at precisely the moment when this contingency is doubled by the remote control. Every image that appears on the viewer's screen can be switched away and replaced by another image at any time with the touch of a button. Any image can thus follow any other image, and there is probably not any possible connection between them that is not actually performed on any screen. Even though these images are completely independent of one another (the feature film on one channel has nothing to do with the quiz show on another, the commercial on a third, or the news coverage on a fourth, etc.), they still set conditions for each other insofar as they are made selectable. Whatever I choose is chosen in relation to all other offerings. Every image competes with every other image and articulates itself as one of many possible images. What I want to watch depends on what else there is to watch, as watching an image always involves a consideration of the other images that could be watched instead. And because the images that could be watched are constantly changing (through the program sequences on all of the countless channels, which are not really or only very crudely synchronized), the available conditions of contingency are also constantly changing. In this respect, what the television images of the flight to the moon prefigured, as an experimental forerunner, also applies to the remote control, as every television image is seen from the perspective of another television image. With every image that I select, I am deselecting all of the other images.

In this way, however, the different ways of using the remote control are recognizable as *selection styles* and thus different figurations of contingency. For example, I can use the remote control in such a way that it selects something specific and not anything else. Luhmann would call this an *indeterminate negation* (Luhmann 1990a: 21–79). On television, however, I can also have an albeit brief look at what I do not want to watch before deciding what to watch and what to stay with. This would be the selection style of *grazing* or looking at the range of available programs so that there is an adequate impression of the field before a decision is made. In this case, nothing is excluded; rather, the movement is additive and involves saturation, overview, or the impression of comprehensive allness (at least of the current range of programs). What I do not want to watch is thus still watched in an incomplete, dimmed, or reduced way, as it is considered and incorporated into the selection of what I do want to watch. It does not simply disappear; rather, it remains available as a kind of copresence that lends a special selective and (as we have seen) informative value to what is actually watched.

However, it is also possible that there is something specific and defined that I do not want to watch, and I am willing to watch anything else. According to Luhmann, this would be a *determinate negation* (Luhmann 1981: 35–49). As a selection style of the remote control, this would be *zapping* or the elimination of the unwanted, which we encountered earlier and which often serves to avoid advertising. Zapping does not make advertising completely disappear, as it remains effective and real insofar as it triggers the switching process and thereby sets it under conditions. We also often switch back to the original channel in order to see if the advertising is still continuing. Zapping can also be connected to grazing in that we use the commercial breaks to see what is being offered on other channels.

Another selection style is *switching*, which is a dual process: I choose this and that and a third or more, but not everything else. In other words, switching means watching multiple programs simultaneously without particularly emphasizing on one program. This is possible when television programs are redundant and progress slowly (as in soap operas, which were specifically designed for incidental viewing along with other activities), when only the highlights are of interest (as in sports broadcasts, which often switch between multiple locations), or when they are reruns. Probably every viewer knows that it is possible to watch two or three programs (or even more) in parallel by alternating between them with the remote control. The relationship between programs connected through switching is thus one of addition rather than negation, as the viewer is no longer selecting or deselecting a particular program but rather selecting these few here and not those others there. Switching can also be connected to the other selection styles of grazing and zapping. For example, the group of programs being followed at the same time is the product of a preselection, which is created through grazing. It can also be broadened or narrowed, depending on what else is being offered, and the commercial breaks can provide opportunities to switch over from one program to another.

The fourth and final selection style is *channel hopping*, in which the viewer switches ahead almost arbitrarily. It is also characteristic of channel hopping that the viewer is switching not to a particular channel but rather merely to the next channel in the series with the help of the corresponding button. She remains there until she has had enough, which can take a long time or a short time, and then she switches ahead again. Commercial breaks might serve as occasions to switch ahead, as with zapping, only in this case the viewer does not switch back. It is also possible that the viewer switches ahead more or less regularly when her attention span is exhausted. This style also involves negation, as the viewer is constantly rejecting each channel in favor of the next one. It is also possible for this style to intersect with all other possible styles. Operations of negation (which choose between all channels, no channels, and one particular channel), operations of addition (which choose between this channel, that channel, and again another channel), operations of alternation (which choose between multiple channels), and operations of revision (which change or return to a previous choice) all combine in the various selection styles and their intersections with one another, and they do this in the continuously parallel flow of program sequences on perhaps 30 or 130 channels. And it has not yet been considered that the composition of the group in front of the television can also change or be characterized by a plurality of expectations, likes, and dislikes.

## Contingency and Latency

Given all this, it is important to determine the specific status of what appears on the screen in relation to what does not appear, and vice versa. We have already seen that what is deselected using the remote control does not simply disappear, as even necessarily contingent deselections set conditions on what is selected. It could appear at any time and replace what is contingently present (on the screen). Our attention is also phenomenologically and aesthetically always with what we do not see and, depending on the selection style, is distributed to varying degrees and over a varying number of alternatives. The use of the remote control thus no longer involves the binary logic of being and nonbeing or yes and no. Every image is operative—even those that are unseen—because they all influence one another through the remote control, which allows every image to be selected and deselected from every other image. In order to clarify the relationship between what appears and what does not appear, it is not enough to differentiate the real from the imaginary. Unselected images really exist in the same way that a room really exists when it is not being used—and not only through the imagination. Moreover, unselected images do not exist in another time or place but rather precisely here and now. What I am not watching nevertheless watches me.

At the start of our considerations, we already encountered a similar question when we discussed the act of switching the television on (see Chapter 1 in this volume). This involved the status of images that I could potentially see but do not (yet) actually see because the television is still switched off. We already determined there that these images are already present in their potentiality, yet they still remain hidden or *latent*. After the television is switched on, these latent images then become *manifest*. The availability of latent images is displayed on the television through the—usually red—diode in "stand by" mode. It is thus natural that "latency" is also the technical concept for the condition of an apparatus while it, as we say about computers, "boots up." With many television sets, the diode changes to another color during this phase, such as yellow or orange. In connection with the remote control, Winkler also used the distinction between latent and manifest to refer to the visible images on the screen as well as the invisible and unconscious contents of dreams, which the process of switching exposes without showing them. But this distinction between latent and manifest does not seem suitable to describe the relationship that switching creates between the selected and the deselected programs, as this distinction is precisely what connects the latent images, which are still enclosed and registered in the television when it is switched off, to the manifest images, which appear on the screen when it is switched on. Their latency ceases once they become manifest. The light diode then changes color, which is modal-theoretically significant and consistent, and it usually glows green. When the manifest phase is over, the images once again become latent. Manifestation and latency thus do not involve different images but rather the same images, which are sometimes manifest and sometimes latent.

This is not the case with the remote control, as the images that the remote control navigates between and around are all manifest. And unlike the relationship between manifest and latent images, which are the same only in another modality, the relationship between selected and deselected images is one of mutual interdependence. The selection of an image shifts not only that image but all other images into another state of being. To be more precise, it enables the emergence of numerous existential and operating modes of images, which are slightly different and in transition. The deselected images, which nevertheless see me, do this in different ways, which is shown in the selection styles and their transitions. For example, switching highlights one image and allows all of the others to recede; however, this back and forth occurs between a small number of channels, and others do not or hardly ever emerge. Grazing, on the other hand, sweeps arbitrarily across the range of offerings, and all of the alternatives that are not selected at a given moment are equal. Channel hopping introduces a sequence. The transition between these various selection styles also allows mixed and transitional modalities of images to emerge.

## The Actual and the Virtual

Deleuze employed the terms *actual* and *virtual* to refer to the relationship between images, which he characteristically finds in film (Deleuze 2013: 71–101). In modern film, according to Deleuze, images of the real and the imaginary (such as images that represent dreams, memories, and visions) are no longer necessarily detached from one another. Even flashbacks no longer retain any special markings (Deleuze 2013: 48–56). Besides Deleuzian film theory, one can also think here of the recent practice of "unreliable" or subjunctive narration. Deleuze's argument thus introduces a typically transrepresentational turn that is no longer based on what images represent, as images no longer distinguish between the real and the possible. The suspension of this distinction also applies to the images themselves, as it is just as difficult to distinguish between images of the real and the possible as it is to distinguish between real and possible images.

This distinction between the real and the possible is replaced by the distinction between the actual and the virtual (Deleuze 2013:73f.). All images show the real, but they only show what is actually real in the here and now (in contrast to the virtually real, such as memories or flashbacks in film). All of the images of a film, including those that cannot be seen, are also equally as real, although only one of them is actual at any given moment. In contrast, images that have already been seen yet are no longer visible and images that are possible but have not yet appeared are virtual. (Perhaps even images that are not seen or contained in the film are nevertheless virtual and thus also real.) This is demonstrated, for example, by mirror images in film (Engell and Fahle 2002: 222–45; see also Engell and Fahle 2008: 57–70): in contrast to that which is directly or actually looked at when watching a film, that which appears in a mirror (within the film) is "only" the object of a virtual image. In modern film, there are more and more shots that cannot initially be recognized as mirror images and are thus actual images (such as when the frame of the mirror cannot be seen and no mirrored gestures are discernible). If the camera rises up or pans around, however, then the same image turns into a virtual image in relation to the now visible scene taking place before the mirror. Something similar can also be assumed for unreliable narration, as a variant initially appears actual, but it becomes virtual with the appearance of others, with the important addition that this movement is reversible. Both of these variants, or others, can be actualized at any time, as they oscillate in a liminal zone where they become different yet indistinguishable from one another.

This idea can be considered a model for the relations between television images under the conditions of the remote control. As in Winkler's shock thesis, however, the television viewer is no longer only exposed to and called upon to synthesize the oscillation between the actual and the virtual, as is the case with film; rather, she can also join in the game itself. The viewer's own *switching* joins a strange and possibly higher *ruling*. It is not the images themselves that produce the oscillation of the television image; rather, the viewer does this by playing with the images. It is important to remember, however, that the viewer is not an entity that is separate from the image; rather, she is an anthropo-mediatic relation that extends between and is entangled in the techno-aesthetic body of the television and the biological body sitting before it. As a supplementary intermediating medium, the remote control intensifies this entanglement or coupling, as it converts the act of merely watching into the act of switching (by pressing buttons). Like the virtualization of an image, the actualization of an image passes through the viewer's body and is charged with the contingency that the process requires. Just as a mirror image in a film (and thus a movement and time image) changes from an actual to a virtual condition through a lens or camera movement, so too does this occur in television through switching. One image is actualized, and another that is not seen is conversely virtualized. At any time, however, the switch can reverse these relations again. An oscillation zone emerges between the selected but deselectable image and the deselected but selectable images, and within this zone actuality and virtuality are constantly suspended and capable of changing places. In addition to what she sees, the viewer also sees what she does not see, and what she does not see once again sees her.

Deleuze also mentioned that the gap between the actual image and the (or even its) virtual image can vary (Deleuze 2013: 56; 71f.). The gap is very slight in the case of a mirror image in a film, as it is apparent that if one image disappeared then the other would also disappear. The gap is larger in the case of subjunctive narration, in which two exclusive variants are shown but are thought of as equally present—that is, as different yet indistinguishable in the sense that neither one is marked as more correct, probable, or real than the other. The reality is then the oscillation between them. However, unlike the mirror image, which can be seen at the same time as the actual image, both variants can no longer appear in one and the same image. The gap is even wider in the case of a memory sequence or a flashback. The image of the past is just as present as the image of the present, which is its virtual image and vice versa. Nevertheless, they are far apart and out of reach for one another, and what emerges from and in their oscillation is time.

Deleuze's idea is also closely related to Bergson's philosophy of time, which already described time as an oscillation between actual and virtual images (Bergson 1988: 141–8). This idea was encapsulated in his famous image of the "cone of time" (*Zeitkegel*), which stands on its tip (Bergson 1988: 160–71). The cone keeps getting wider the further it extends into the past because, according to Bergson, the gap between an actual image and its virtual image becomes larger. The cone becomes narrower as it approaches the present, which nevertheless encompasses the entire past, until it finally contracts to a point, in which the actual image and the virtual image coincide to form the present moment. In the case of television images under the conditions of the remote control, this present moment is reached in the moment of switching itself, as the actual image and the virtual image come into contact and become indistinguishable through the pressing of a button. The cone of time would correspond to the periods between the switches, when it is unclear whether the selected or the deselected image is more important and which one is the actual or the virtual image. The image that is selected and then deselected is by no means no longer available. It moves into the past as a virtual image of the present actual image, yet it still remains selectable and present at any time through another keystroke. The present actual image also remains deselectable, so it always operates as a virtual image of the other image, which it sees as a virtual image. The present actual image is thus always affected by or charged with its virtual image, and in this sense it is always already past. What we watch with the remote control are images that are charged with the past, when they are selected, and images that are still affected by the present actual image even if they have been and remain deselected. In other words, what we watch with the remote control is the oscillation between the poles of the actual and the virtual.

This applies even more when the oscillation space involves not merely two images, as in the case of a mirror image, or a manageable number of images, as in the case of memory or subjunctive narration, but rather an unbelievably vast quantity of images. However, the image of the cone is also instructive here. The tip of the cone represents the moment of switching, in which the selected and deselected images are related to each other only through the process of switching itself. The process of selection thus constitutes the narrowest circle of oscillation between the actual and the virtual. However, the recurring actualization of previously selected images, which is characteristic of switching between a limited number of channels, moves into a wider ring of the cone of circulating images. The space of oscillation expands even wider in the case of grazing, and it eventually encompasses images that are not selected during the course of a single television evening but are nevertheless still present and included. It is also possible to transition between these expanded rings, just as it is possible to transition between selection styles, so television with a remote control can move through the entire cone. In a sense this even happens when the viewer foregoes the use of the remote control and pauses on a single program for an extended time, such as a feature film or a sports broadcast. Even in this case, the deselected images are anything but excluded, as they are still looking back at me along with the actual image, and they are still watching what I watch with me over my shoulder, thus charging the actual image with virtuality.

## The Indexical World

We have here observed the sustained effect of the remote control on television through the trajectory of intensification, but the dimension of expansion also comes into play. The previous considerations show that a basic property of the electronic pixel image extends from the microscopic level to the macroscopic level. As we already determined earlier, the tube image is always a virtual image, as it is absent yet still operative and, in this sense, real. Strictly speaking, this only applies to the basis of the image itself, like the digital pixel images that followed the tube image. In other words, the basic element of the point, from which television can be thought of as being built, is itself a virtual element. In mathematics the point is presented as an "ideal element" that is completely extensionless, but it must expand as soon as it is actualized in the physical world, and it thus stops being a point. The same also applies to the points in an image, as they are already planes. What holds true in geometry also holds true in time, which similarly involves extensionless events in the temporal order of *Aion* that must cross over into the extended time of *Chronos* in order to be able to persist in the (actual) world. *Aion* also conversely stabilizes the collapsing time of *Chronos* by setting limits and anchoring it in the virtual (Deleuze 2004: 186–93; see Chapter 6 in this volume). The remote control extends this principle to the level of complexity and contingency of entire programs, and the *switching point* expands through the "fancy transitions" of televisuality. Double contingency allows the switching point to stabilize the expansion of individual program lines, which is in danger of collapsing (through constant self-interruption and self-repetition), and it also enables an expansion of its own order—namely, the television evening. The incorporation of switching points into running programs lends actuality to the purely virtual switching point implemented by the remote control, as they articulate the limitless extension of the running program, which is anchored and thus stabilized by the virtual.

In the switching point implemented by the remote control, moreover, both of the images—that is, the (still) actual image and the (still) virtual image—are not only distinguished from but also coupled to and in contact with one another. The remote control and the implicit remote control of televisuality intensify the fundamentally tactile nature of the switch image. This is not only metaphorical: the finger physically touches the button, and the switching contact physically connects two conductors. It is also interesting that to this day the remote control must be directed at the television (and other remote controls must be directed at other devices). The viewer must take aim, although this is not as obvious as the "Flash-Matic," which looked like a pistol and required a direct hit with the light beam. Nevertheless, the remote control remains technically as well as semiotically an instrument of addressing and showing, and its purpose is to make selections and produce long-distance effects. Its function is not iconic, like the classical image, but rather *indexical*. According to Charles Sanders Peirce, indexical signs are causally connected to the objects that they represent, such as a weathervane, which indicates the direction of the wind, or a photograph, which is caused by a chain of physical-optical and chemical processes that can be attributed at least partly to the object it represents (Peirce 1998: 274–92). All signposts, detectors, indicators, addresses, traces, and imprints can thus be considered indexical signs. Measurements are also indexical signs in two ways, such as when the column of mercury in a thermometer is caused by the temperature being measured and again when it is ascribed a numerical value on a scale. These are both indexical operations.

Even though the remote-control signal lies in the infrared range, which remains invisible to humans (and dogs), it is nevertheless a sign that is caused and has an impact on the image on the television screen. The instantaneously visible change in the image on the screen indicates that the corresponding button on the remote control has been pressed, and in this sense it is a sign of a pressed button. Whereas iconic signs (a category that includes all images) configure the world according to relations of similarity, indexical signs thematize causality and causation. Indexical signs always point not only to a cause, such as the wind or the foot that left behind a footprint, but also to *causality*—that is, to causation itself. They denote not only specific objectives, as in the case of signposts and addresses, but also pathways, and they denote not only effects but also causal relations. For Pierce, they are always *double* signs (Peirce 1998; see also Engell 2013a). Alfred Gell developed this into the assumption that indices produce effects and causal relations by inducing their users and observers to ascribe causes, effects, and even intentions to them (Gell 1998: 28–51). *Artworks* and design objects particularly function as indices in this sense, as the act of observation ascribes a special cause to them as things that were made and not simply grown. According to Gell, effects are also ascribed to artworks—namely, effects on the observer, such as the specific emotion evoked by a painting. These effects are either intentionally elicited by the artist, who uses the artwork as a vehicle, or they operate as "intentio operis," which is not intended by the artist. In complex arrangements they can also come about as non-monocausal causal relations that emerge from the constellations that sustain them.

Gell primarily focuses on *magical objects*, such as wands, fetishes, totems, and masks, which similarly function as indices because regardless of what they do they also thematize above all the *process of causation* (Gell 1998: 96–258). They conceive of the world as an interrelation of effects, and their function is to imply causal relations and induce attributions of power. The remote control certainly belongs to and occupies a prominent place in this series of *indexical objects*. Its relationship to magical operations, which led to names like the "Mystery Control," was already pointed out at the beginning of this chapter. It is also clear from the bodily gesture it requires that the remote control is a pointing tool, and it extends the causal connection from the fingertip to the screen. This also applies to the implicit remote control and the televisuality of neotelevision. The self-reflexive stylistic awareness that characterizes this type of television also shows that television images are selected, arranged, and contingent on the production side. In contrast to the world of iconicity, which is structured by relations of similarity through the medium of the image, and the world of symbolicity, which is regulated by conventions based on the medium of language, the remote control leads to a world of selectability, which is an indexical world of cause-and-effect relationships, direction and directionality, addresses and traces, and lastly numbers. The word "digital" is derived from the Latin word "digitum" or finger and thus from pointing and triggering (Engell 2013a). In a paradigmatic way, the remote control solidifies this connection between magic, bodily gesture, and technology, which extends from pointing and addressing to counting, indexicality, and digitality.

## References

Bellis, Mary. 2018. "The Television Remote Control: A Brief History." In: *ThoughtCo*, December 24, 2018. Accessed August 28, 2019. https://www.thoughtco.com/history-of-the-television-remote-control-1992384.

Benjamin, Walter. 1999. "Little History of Photography." In: *Walter Benjamin: Selected Writings. Volume 2. 1927–1934*, ed. by Michael W. Jennings, Howard Eiland, and Gary Smith, pp. 507–31. Cambridge, MA, London: Harvard University Press.

Bense, Max. 1969. *Einführung in die informationstheoretische Ästhetik*. Reinbek: Rowohlt.

Bense, Max. 1979. *Die Unwahrscheinlichkeit des Ästhetischen und die semiotische Konzeption der Kunst*. Baden-Baden: Agis.

Bergson, Henri. 1988. *Matter and Memory*. New York: Zone Books.

Berkner, Jörg. 2013. "'Diener Ihrer Bequemlichkeit'. Die Geschichte der Fernseh-Fernbedienung." In: *Scriptum. Publikation des Historischen Archivs der Infineon Technologies*, February 2013. Accessed August 28, 2019. http://www.joerg-berkner.de/Scriptum/pdf/HA_Scriptum_IFX_23_Fernbedienung_d_2013_02_08s.pdf.

Brauns, Jörg. 2004. ". . . eine stets zu erneuernde Welt. Zur Einführung des Supermarkts in Deutschland." *Zeitschrift für Mediengeschichte* 4: 117–27.

Bühler, Karl. 1990. *Theory of Language: The Representational Function of Language*. Amsterdam, Philadelphia: John Benjamins Publishing Company.

Caldwell, John T. 1995. *Televisuality: Style, Crisis, and Autohority in American Television*. New Brunswick: Rutgers University Press.

Casetti, Francesco, and Roger Odin. 1990. "De la paléo- à la néo-télévision." *Communications*, 51: 9–26.

Certeau, Michel de. 1988. *The Practice of Everyday Life*. Berkeley, Los Angeles, London: University of California Press.

Davis, Dennis K., and Stanley J. Baran. 1981. "A History of our Understanding of Mass Communication and Everyday Life." In: *Mass Communication and*

*Everyday Life: A Perspective on Theory and Effects*, ed. by D. K. Davis, and S. J. Baran, pp. 19–52. Belmont: Wardworth.
Deleuze, Gilles. 2004. *The Logic of Sense*. London, New York: Continuum.
Deleuze, Gilles. 2013. *Cinema II: The Time-Image*. London, New York: Bloomsbury Academic.
Dienst, Richard. 1995. *Still Life in Real Time: Theory after Television*. Durham: Duke University Press.
Early Television Museum. n. d. "Postwar American Television. Zenith Flashmatic." Accessed August 28, 2019. https://www.earlytelevision.org/zenith_flashmatic.html.
Eco, Umberto. 1985. "TV – La transparence perdue." In: Umberto Eco. *La guerre du faux*, pp. 190–9. Paris: Grasset et Frasquelle.
Eco, Umberto. 1989. "Chance and Plot: Television and Aesthetics." In: Umberto Eco. *The Open Work*, pp. 105–22. Cambridge, MA: Harvard University Press.
Engell, Lorenz. 1989. *Vom Widerspruch zur Langeweile. Logische und temporale Begründungen des Fernsehens*. Frankfurt/M., New York: Peter Lang.
Engell, Lorenz. 2003. "Tasten Wählen Denken. Genese und Funktion einer philosophischen Apparatur." In: *Medienphilosophie. Beiträge zur Klärung eines Begriffs*, ed. by Stefan Münker, Alexander Roesler, and Mike Sandbothe, pp. 53–77. Frankfurt/M: Fischer.
Engell, Lorenz. 2013. "The Tactile and the Index: From the Remote Control to the Hand-Held Computer. Some Speculative Reflections on the Bodies of the Will." *NECSUS. European Journal of Media Studies*, 2. Accessed August 28, 2019. https://necsus-ejms.org/the-tactile-and-the-index-from-the-remote-control-to-the-hand-held-computer-some-speculative-reflections-on-the-bodies-of-the-will/.
Engell, Lorenz, and Oliver Fahle. 2002. "Film-Philosophie. Mit einer Analyse zu 'Winterschläfer.'" In: *Moderne Film-Theorie*, ed. by Jürgen Felix, pp. 222–45. Mainz: Bender.
Engell, Lorenz, and Oliver Fahle. 2008. "Gilles Deleuze." In: *Philosophie in der Medientheorie von Adorno bis Zizek*, ed. by Alexander Roesler, and Bernd Stiegler, pp. 57–70. München: Fink.
Faatz, Michael. 2001. *Zur Spezifik des Fernsehtextes. Eine Untersuchung zu Inhalten, Präsentationsformen und Perspektiven; dargestellt anhand des MDR-Textes und des Sat.1-Textes*. Fernsehwissenschaft Vol. 4. Köln: Teiresias.
Flusser, Vilém. 2014. *Gestures*. Minneapolis, London: University of Minnesota Press.
Gell, Alfred. 1998. *Art and Agency: An Anthropological Theory*. Oxford: Clarendon.
Gupta, P. Sen, Meher H. Engineer, and Virginia Anne Shepherd. 2009. *Remembering Sir J.C. Bose*, pp. 106. Bangalore: Indian Institute of Science, World Scientific.
Jakobson, Roman. 1960. "Closing Statements: Linguistics and Poetics." In: *Style in Language*, ed. by Thomas A. Sebeok, pp. 350–77. Cambridge, MA: The MIT Press.

Kracauer, Siegfried. 1960. *Theory of Film: The Redemption of Physical Reality*. New York: Oxford University Press.

Lasswell, Harold D. 1948. "The Structure and Function of Communication in Society." In: *The Communication of Ideas: A Series of Addresses*, ed. by Lyman Bryson, pp. 32–51. New York: Harper & Brs.

Luhmann, Niklas. 1981. "Über die Funktion der Negation in sinnkonstituierenden Systemen." In: Niklas Luhmann. *Soziologische Aufklärung, Vol. 3: Soziales System, Gesellschaft, Organisation*, pp. 35–49. Opladen: Westdt. Verl.

Luhmann, Niklas. 1990a. "Meaning as Sociology's Basic Concept." In: Niklas Luhmann. *Essays on Self-Reference*, pp. 21–79. New York: Columbia University Press.

Luhmann, Niklas. 1990b. "The Work of Art and the Self-Reproduction of Art." In: Niklas Luhmann. *Essays on Self-Reference*, pp. 191–214. New York: Columbia University Press.

Luhmann, Niklas. 1995. *Social Systems*. Stanford: Stanford University Press.

Luhmann, Niklas. 2000. *Art as a Social System*. Stanford: Stanford University Press.

O'Neill, John J. 1944. *Prodigal Genius: The Life of Nikola Tesla*. New York: McKay.

Peirce, Charles S. 1998. "A Syllabus of Certain Topics of Logic." In: *The Essential Peirce: Selected Philosophical Writings*, edited by The Peirce Edition Project, Vol. 2, pp. 258–99. Bloomington: Indiana University Press.

Radiomuseum. n. d. "Mystery Control." Accessed August 28, 2019. https://www.radiomuseum.org/r/philco_mystery_control.html.

Shannon, Claude. 1948. "A Mathematical Theory of Information." *Bell System Technical Journal* 27: 379–423 (July), 623–56 (October).

Spigel, Lynn. 1992. *Make Room for TV, Television and the Family Ideal in Postwar America*. Chicago, London: University of Chicago Press.

Winkler, Hartmut. 1991. *Switching-Zapping. Ein Text zum Thema und ein parallellaufendes Unterhaltungsprogramm*. Darmstadt: Häuser.

Wired. 2007. "1956: Zenith Space Commander Remote Control." In: *Wired*, October 23, 2007. Accessed August 28, 2019. https://www.wired.com/2007/10/vg-greatestgadget/.

Yuste, Antonio Perez, and Magdalena Salazar Palma. 2005. "Scanning the Past from Madrid. Leonardo Torres Quevedo." *Proceedings of the IEEE* 93, no. 7: 1379–82.

Zenith: Remote Background. n. d. "Six Decades of Channel Surfing: History of the TV Remote Control." Accessed November 14, 2019. https://www.zenith.com/remote-background/.

Ziemann, Andreas. 2011. *Medienkultur und Gesellschaftsstruktur. Soziologische Analysen*. Wiesbaden: Springer VS.

Zubayr, Camille, and Heinz Gerhard. 2017. "Tendenzen im Zuschauerverhalten. Fernsehgewohnheiten und Fernsehreichweiten im Jahr 2016." *media perspektiven* 3: 130–44.

# 9

# Second Screens

From the beginning, these considerations have been based on classic tube television. The first part used the classic picture tube to develop the definition of television as a switch image. The main feature of the switch image as an ontographic medium and the ontographic mode of being that television inscribes into its world also emerge from the functioning of classic tube television. The same applies to its entangled and relational-operative anthropology, which was described as an anthropo-mediatic relation in connection with McLuhan's concept of television as a *cold medium*. The foundational quality of liveness, which gives rise to seriality and *flow*, also stems from the technical conditions of the cathode ray tube. Even though the structure of the switch image as both an apparatus and a *dispositif* has never been stable since its emergence and introduction, I have argued that its basic operativity comes from the picture tube.

The second part represented the transformational movements, which were understood as extensions, amplifications, intensifications, and inversions of the switch image. The instant replay, the flight to the moon, and the remote control made the switch image into something else, and we have recognized the medium's actual properties and variable mode of being in these profound and interconnected transformations, which are in line with its basic conditions—that is, its ontographic qualities and its basis as a switch image. Its switchability has expanded dramatically, and its ontographic mode of being still determines the dynamic that television itself introduced through its non-suspendable variability, its fundamental diachrony, and its low object stability (*Gegenstandfestigkeit*). Television only exists in the course of its processing. This applies primarily to the writing of the cathode ray, and it also applies to its diachronic development on a large scale. Television cannot be strictly defined, neither in terms of its basic technical image nor its large-scale evolution as a mass medium. It is never what and where it is. All of this has been deduced here from the cathode ray tube.

## Expanded Television

In the 1990s, however, television acquires a new kind of screen, a second screen after the first one—namely, the liquid-crystal display (LCD), whose functions are entirely different from those of the cathode ray tube. Even before that, though, and increasingly since then, television began to proliferate across countless screens, which expanded, supplemented, and ultimately dissolved if not delimited the classic living room *dispositif*. It thus liquified the distinction between inside and outside in classic television theory. This distinction can be understood as a boundary or shield, as in Stanley Cavell's work, or as coupling and transmission, following Nipkow's definition (Cavell 1982; Hickethier 1998: 15; see also Chapters 1 and 2 in this volume). In both cases, however, it becomes difficult to distinguish between interior and exterior space when the migration of the screens to the outside leads to even more screens to be encountered in the exterior space than in the interior space. Following the implementation of the internet and the computer monitor as a second screen, television was under pressure to compete with digital and network-based forms of image circulation, to which it must be and is related. Internet television, streaming services, and online platforms already exponentially increased the number and presence of images. They put so much pressure on television that it is often assumed that television no longer exists. The second great wave of digitization after *neotelevision* and *televisuality* thus seems to deform the switch image to such a degree that it is no longer possible to talk about television as an objective fact, and it will soon no longer be possible to talk about it in terms of an institution or of user practices (Cassetti and Odin 1990; Caldwell 1995; see also Chapter 8 in this volume).

The following chapter will show that this is by no means the case. Gene Youngblood already argued in the 1970s that an essential feature of television was its extension beyond its borders (Youngblood 1970). He thus conceived of television as an expansion of the moving image—namely, as "expanded cinema." According to Youngblood, this expansion then led television even beyond itself through videotape technology, such as when video enters galleries and other art spaces, when it is incorporated into social and political activism, or when it is used in the home as a supplement to and a repetition of television (Youngblood 1970: 257–344). Television *is* then the movement of (self-)transcendence of the switchable image. In contrast to what is being said about the disappearance of television, the visuality of switching, the ontography and unique anthropology of television, and its live and serial nature are being further developed on a massive scale. They are expanding and becoming more complex. They include large sectors of image circulation, even though it no longer occurs through cathode ray tubes or terrestrial broadcasting. The vast number of digital images in circulation is still ontographic switch images, irrespective of their technical evolution and their second digitization, and they are thus television. Furthermore, they often and perhaps mainly involve a greatly expanded and enhanced form of television, even though their users can no longer describe their activities as television when streaming news, *binging* series on online platforms, or using websites like YouTube

The third part of the study will focus on this second television or television 2.0. This chapter will first establish the foundation for this discussion through the observation of the second screen, to which the switch image extends in its most recent transformation to date; more precisely, it extends to the multitude of second screens, to which it is transferred and as whose relation it is sustained. We can take a perfectly arbitrary yet typical situation as a starting point: the Hyatt Hotel in Chicago. Here, dozens of flat screens hang next to each other in an unbroken chain above the roughly thirty-meter-long hotel bar. Such screens also hang above the roughly twenty tables in the vast space in front of the bar, each one looking down at one of the two long sides of the table below. The bar is located on the balcony of the hotel's spacious and multi-story lobby, throughout which more screens are distributed. The same uninterrupted television program can be seen simultaneously on all of the more than fifty large screens, and it is usually a sports broadcast or occasionally a news program. Visitors thus find themselves in an interior space that emulates an exterior space through its size and transparency, like a shopping mall or an airport terminal. At the same time, however, this lounge area turned inside out transports them into a screen environment. They are enclosed or even engulfed by the oversized, multi-part, and completely synchronous switch image. Even when they are also hotel guests or bar patrons, and they behave as such, they are at the same time viewers or even agents of television, whether they like it or not.

Whether they are operated concurrently in a large mass or independently and dispersed, the development of second screens is mainly found in two dimensions. First, the LCD gives the television image an entirely new technical foundation, which enables flatness, enormous size, and an increased optical density. At the same time, it is also based on an entirely different operating principle than the old cathode ray tube, which we will return to at length. Second, the number of screens also increases to an enormous extent. Third and lastly, they migrate from their traditional environments, such as the home or living room, to places that are often still private yet publicly accessible. They can be interior spaces, exterior spaces, or a strange hybrid of both, as in the example given earlier. In order to begin with this last-mentioned transformation, it was already introduced much earlier, before the invention of the LCD, and it can even be seen in the classic phase of paleotelevision before 1980. In the early 1950s, for example, television began to develop a second screen beyond the first one at which viewers could stare individually or as a group. This is verified by a rather bizarre television set from the early 1950s that was never successful on the market. It was already clear at this time that there is no ideal television viewer, just as there is no homogeneous mass audience; rather, they both had to be manufactured by television itself in the course of its work, and the viewers who were being manufactured had to collaborate actively in this process. This was already established by Günter Anders, and it was discussed earlier in connection with the concept of "anthropomediality" (Anders 1956a: 102ff.; see also Chapter 5 in this volume). From the beginning, however, the creation of viewer-subjects as individuals and as a collective also involved a differentiation between individual users and groups, an intermittent addressing of ever more precise targets, and generally speaking a *singularization*.

## The Family of Television

Viewers were initially differentiated according to very simple criteria—namely, gender and generation. They were not so much differentiated according to class, race, religion, and culture. This was because early television mainly counted on and targeted the family unit, which it itself manufactured (in the form of the modern nuclear family with a single breadwinner, a housewife, etc.) and ideally enclosed in a (privately owned) home. This process has been accurately described by Lynn Spigel and John Hartley (Spigel 1992; Hartley 1999: 92–111). The family was thus dogmatically conceived and formed as a unit according to class, race, religion, and culture, but according to this ideologically conservative position it was not unified with regard to gender and generation; on the contrary, it was an organizational form designed to bridge differences of gender and generation. Despite its compulsory homogenization, therefore, the family was still always conceived as a form of "diversity management," and television also had to perform this organization of difference. We already encountered this fact and its close connection to the system of consumption in a society of overproduction in the analysis of the soap opera as a typical daytime television format that was addressed to housewives and thus reproduced them as a specific form of existence.

In order for the family to function, differences of gender and generation had to be simultaneously bridged and reproduced; otherwise, television would no longer contribute anything to society. Joshua Meyrowitz already showed in the 1980s how television linked and blurred cultures of gender and generation by analyzing how the behavior of men and women tends to converge in television, but this argument is even more convincing with regard to generational roles. As Meyrowitz assumes, it is possible to observe in many areas how children and adult behavior converges in the entertainment formats of television, such as quiz shows and variety shows (Meyrowitz 1985: 88f.). At the same time, however, television must also exploit differences in order to make them economically useful. The development of specialized programs for women and men is not enough to maintain and uphold these differences. It also requires an instrumental basis, a device, or a device configuration that can articulate the differences of gender and generation. At the same time, however, these differences must also be absorbed into the collective and simultaneous activity of television.

The aforementioned device from the early 1950s was called the "DuMont Duoscope." It was an apparatus with two screens, and it was thus a very early version of a second screen (Spigel 1992: 71). Each screen had its own receiver, and in this sense they were independent of one another, but they were housed in the same cabinet, which had a triangular base. The tubes were arranged at right angles to one another on two sides of the cabinet and were operated simultaneously. Both images were then cast through a polarized and semi-transparent mirror to another glass screen that filled the front side facing the viewers. The images were thus superimposed, but they could be optically separated again with the help of polarized glasses. Depending on the polarization, viewers would only be able to see one of the images. If two pairs of glasses were used, then two viewers could peacefully sit side by side, look at one and the same screen, but watch two different programs. In other words, they could watch television together without watching the same thing. The device was intended so that a woman could watch a love story and a man could watch a boxing match on the same screen at the same time. The woman and the man were supposed to be positioned and coordinated together as a married couple, but they were supposed to be addressed separately according to their *gender*. Television is then neither the love story nor the boxing match nor their consecutive sequence in the program schedule; rather, it is their simultaneity and their technically based spatial coordination. More precisely, it is the foundation of this space through the arrangement of the (simultaneously) coexistent, as with Leibniz.

Later arrangements with the same goal moved away from the unity of the living room and beyond it by merely enabling parallel viewing on different screens in different rooms within the same home. Even if television was not able to unify the living room, it was still able to keep the household together. This began with television in the kitchen, such as its installation in the wall as a "TV stove" (Spigel 1992: 73f.). This was supposed to allow the housewife to watch cooking shows on a second screen while the main news was on in the living room. As an alternative, she could also purchase a dishwasher in order to avoid standing in the kitchen after the meal and instead watch the same thing with everyone else in the living room, or at least this is what advertisements suggested (Spigel 1992: 93). A swapping of roles or functions was never foreseen.

The introduction of second screens within the home gained momentum with the development of small portable televisions. Richard Sapper's legendary design from 1962 sums up this development and articulates it in the material and formal vocabulary of contemporary modern design, such as the use of plastic and bright colors. These devices could be placed anywhere, even in children's rooms, because they were small and had their own antennas, and parallel simultaneous viewing could thus become a dispersed activity within the home. Television here already begins to be not what viewers do with it (and what it does with them) but rather what happens in their separate but synchronous, parallel, and interconnected activities. At the same time, however, portable television was precisely that—portable—which means that it was movable in space. This marked the beginning of its migration into mobility and its detachment from a fixed location (such as the location B in Nipkow's definition). This mobility was not limited to the home: as long as it could reach a power source, it could penetrate spaces that had never before been exposed to television, beyond the apartment, the home, and the family. Large television sets soon followed the portables into these spaces. They remained connected to specific locations, as they were not portable, but precisely their size made it possible to transform any arbitrary location into a location or zone of television viewing.

When television was first introduced in Europe, and especially in Germany, it had already appeared in public spaces, such as restaurants or the display windows of electrical appliance stores that sold televisions. The living room *dispositif* then became more prevalent as prosperity increased, but television later returned to public or exterior spaces in the 1970s. Television sets infiltrated schools and recreational areas, and they could also be found in train stations, airports, bus stations, and even busses. They also appeared in cultural institutions, like theater lobbies and stages, as well as in supermarkets and grocery stores.

## Ambient Television

This development toward a multiplicity of second screens beyond the single screen at home, as television was initially conceived, was particularly characteristic of the 1980s and 1990s but obviously continues today. Anna McCarthy described this in her book *Ambient Television*, which is crucially important for the viewing of second screens (McCarthy 2001). According to McCarthy, television migrates, and like all migrants it is highly adaptable to changing environments and habitats outside of its home. This often leads to a proliferation, such as the emergence of numerous identical screens and even entire video walls or, like the Chicago Hyatt, rows of screens in bars, malls, and other public spaces. According to McCarthy, however, television also appears to be highly technologically diverse in that it connects a wide variety of image sources (direct-to-home, videotape, DVD, etc.) to a wide variety of screen formats with different functions and design forms. Added to this is the wide variety of distribution technologies, which includes the terrestrial antenna signal as well as cable and satellite TV (and today the internet). Television does not have to choose between these technologies; rather, it can use all of them, depending on their availability. In fact, McCarthy argues that it combines them into a mixture or "blend" (McCarthy 2001: 14). Television still always performs this mixing by switching and interconnecting. "Ambient television" thus becomes a second-order switch image, which no longer appears as a single specific sample image or functions as a particular imaging or distribution technology, such as the cathode ray tube or broadcasting. The individual screen image currently shown is always related to the images on other second screens, to which it refers, which it repeats, in which it is reflected, from which it is differentiated, and to which it conveys the image.

This happens in two ways. First, television grows into a more or less complete habitat. In other words, it is the space in which we live (and not only us), as it is an inescapable condition of life. We already encountered this ubiquitous moment in our discussion of the primary mediasphere of television—namely, the electric and electromagnetic environment—but it now crystallizes into a large-scale and tangible environment of screens. Second, the ubiquitous appearance of television as a technical device also results in the entanglement of different habitats, which were previously separate from one another and which required or gave rise to different behaviors, to form a single environment that is precisely television. Habitats thus develop flexible regimes of behavior that are differentiated from one another, such as the regime of the home, the workplace, or public space. Hotels, factories, theaters, and living rooms produce and reproduce entirely different modes of behavior and existence. They also pass through single individuals, but they are normally connected to specific media and medial habitats. The cinema produces a different kind of human than the computer. Even though the switch image pervades and intersects these niches and habitats equally by means of second screens and ambient television, thereby blending them into a total environment, they nonetheless do not abandon their specific modes of behavior and existence. Television in a school adapts to the school, television in a hotel adapts to the hotel, and television in a living room conforms to the living room without alteration. However, the environment of television no longer allows particularly privileged modes of behavior and existence to become large general structures, such as the living room of the nuclear family; rather, it limits them selectively or specifically to certain areas of behavior, and users are thus constituted as students, guests, and couch potatoes under the conditions of television. However, each of these areas is also visibly or invisibly marked as one of many, just as television itself always appears as one of many other forms and sites of television viewing.

In the characteristic style of Bruno Latour's actor-network theory, an agent can be seen in the television of second screens and ambient television, but it is once again an agent of another order (McCarthy 2001: 1; Engell et al. 2014; Engell 2013, 2015; see also Chapter 5 in this volume). Beyond the mere behavior, action, or even embodiment of agency, this agent distributes and organizes different forms of agency and relates them to one another in their difference. The multiplied television image also allows each of the other habitats to appear, such as by selecting them and presenting them on the screen—be that as fiction or as report—in the same way that television as a screen image can and does appear in them: it is always already present in what it shows. This is an aspect that completely eludes McCarthy, as she is not interested in the images of television. It produces an amalgam of multiple locations, and this amalgam is precisely the location of television, as it can be situated anywhere. If the soap opera mirrored the living room in the living room, and other formats showed all possible exterior spaces in the living room, then all locations and rooms were now carried to all other locations and rooms. The reflection, duplication, projection, or coupling of a room to the same room is thus still possible, such as televisions that show a range of products or sales activities in a store (McCarthy 2001: 163–71). The spaces are visible at another or the same location, which is essential for television according to Nipkow, and the image makes them operationalizable—that is, switchable—through their visibility. However, this transmission does not make them uniform and standardized; rather, they are only held together in that they are all screen-based and controllable. The space of television thus tends to be the image of diversity, as it visualizes all of the diverging modes of behavior found at all of the different locations. It becomes a switching point that connects any habitats or niches, which have nothing in common other than the fact that televisions and screen images are there. Following the rise of second screens, it is no longer possible to talk about the homogeneous spaces, events, actions, or modes of behavior of television. This particularly applies when we turn from the heterogeneous materiality of second screens to their respective locations, niches, and habitats. Television enables the articulation of heterogeneity in general—namely, in the connections and networks that are operationalized through switching. Television tends to make every connection possible, regardless of the different origins of those being connected—and this does not only apply to connections between the supermarket and the living room.

From this point on, the distinction between interior and exterior space, which was once decisive for television, starts fading away. According to McCarthy, it is replaced by the operation of scaling or the insertion of one dimension into another dimension. Through scaling, television binds something all-encompassing and global to something particular and local, thus synchronizing them both with one another. McCarthy emphasizes that the scale, according to which the diversity of spaces is to be experienced, is a *physical quality* (McCarthy 2001: 15). An example shows what this shift illuminates and how it is also related to time. In airports, for example, the regime of a globally networked schedule management (including departure times, arrival times, time differences, and time zones) is coupled with a televisual poetics of the moment, in which those waiting here and now are sporadically suspended and then released (McCarthy 2001: 195ff.). Something similar can be found in relation to sports broadcasts in bars. In the case of the Chicago Hyatt bar, this even occurs twice, as the bar is connected and synchronized to the expanse of the sports stadium and each individual screen is also connected and synchronized to all of the other screens and thus to a second expanse—namely, the enormous interior space of the lobby. Space is described no longer in terms of interior and exterior but rather in terms of contraction and expansion.

It can thus be said that television increasingly takes place on multiple screens, which are arranged within sight and range of one another, and these screens are so pervasive that television ultimately merges with its environment. It is deterritorialized and relocated from the center to the periphery—entirely in line with Deleuze and Guattari's concept of "schizophrenic capitalism" (Deleuze and Guattari 2000: 231ff.). From there it actually establishes a "despotic" regime, as it becomes inescapable and overpowering; as a mere image carrier and surface, the screen itself replaces the image with its spatial and referential depth. In a certain sense, which we will describe more precisely, it wants to be "read" instead of watched (Deleuze and Guattari 2000: 206). The overflowing, excessive, or proliferating growth of screens is thus associated with a loss at the level of meaning and a gain at the level of intensity and transformation (Deleuze and Guattari 1986: 13). However, the movement of screens to the periphery is ultimately reversed, as television becomes a reterritorialization that looks inward and makes new localizations and determinations there. In an open space, which was initially foreign to television, it lays down a defiant articulation (Deleuze and Guattari 2000: 257–60).

## Becoming Flat, Becoming Space

Even the two-dimensionality of the image is transformed, and this extends far beyond pure size ratios. On the one hand, the screens themselves have now become entirely flat, and they no longer take up space like the classic tube television and its enormous depth. They thereby lose their three-dimensional thingness or furniture-like quality. They can no longer be conceived as a relation between thing and space, as with McCarthy. As a pure surface, they become part of the wall or even the wall itself—an idea that already appeared earlier in the development of the device. In their multitude, however, they simultaneously form—precisely as walls do—a three-dimensional space into which they then look. This particularly applies when they are arranged at right angles, like walls. While classic screens were curved outward, the concentrated flat screens are turned inward. The screen thus transforms from a convex extension into exterior space to a concave encapsulation of interior space.

In order to understand this process more clearly, it seems logical to consider Roger Caillois' idiosyncratic theory of mimicry (such as the mimicry of insects) (Caillois 1935). Caillois says that mimicry is driven by the animal's desire to become one with its environment. Screens also seem to become one with the space surrounding them, as they vanish into it and no longer appear as addressable, contourable, and space-filling things, just like animals camouflaged in nature. Sometimes, though not predominantly, a screen actually adapts to its environment and becomes imperceptible. For example, screens in hospital waiting rooms can provide medical and pharmaceutical advice and show doctors, assistants, and patients, or screens in hardware stores and supermarkets can present images of products and sales stands. The colors and shapes on these screens thus adapt to the spatial environments in which they are found. According to Caillois, however, insects that assume the color and form of a leaf or a flower are not imitating or adapting to their environments in order to deceive or deter predators; rather, these actions are motivated by an instinct for self-dissolution, the renunciation of individuality, and the desire to merge with space. Caillois argues not only that this reflects a weak sense of self, which is also encountered in the human psyche and which he labels "psychasthenia," but that space itself generates the force or attraction that absorbs and entices the individual toward self-dissolution (Caillois 1935: 8–9). This could also apply to an individualized technical object in its technosphere, as the pervasiveness of at least certain technologies could be related to the fact that technospheric space exerts such an attraction on the device (Simondon 2017: 53–6; see also Simondon 1989; Deforge 1994). In any case, we can clearly observe how the television set went from being a heavy three-dimensional piece of furniture to a flat and weightless part of the wall. It warped the entire space and even the entire home around it, positioned its users as well as the other pieces of furniture in the room, and then expanded the space of its own range. Now it is no longer a thing, as it has become space itself. The tendency toward singularization postulated earlier has here found a complementary tendency.

What at the same time distinguishes the pervasiveness of flat screens from insects mimicking their environment is that the switch image also transforms this three-dimensional space, which clings to the built space and even acts like a built space. Flat screens now project other and preferably larger spaces into their locations, such as images transmitted from stadiums, studios, and streets. In contrast to mimicry, it produces a mixed space as an amalgam of the here and the elsewhere. Television also places its users in this space, while at the same time they are patients, customers, or patrons at a bar. They are doubly spatialized, as they move in two areas of action simultaneously, and it is precisely in this simultaneity that the television of multiple second screens possesses a specific dimension of its agency. This agency consists in relating the highly different and diverse possibilities of both amalgamated environments to one another and thus enabling new, complex, and contradictory conglomerations of behaviors (McCarthy 2001: 17). For example, the arrangement of screens above eye level is what makes a sports bar or a news bar different from a video diner, which is defined by small screens on individual tables. Something similar applies to laundromats and waiting rooms, which has far-reaching consequences for the possible behaviors, social structures, or presumed modes of existence in these televisually mixed environments (McCarthy 2001: 222). The enormous opening, diversity, contingency, and unpredictability of the medium is always obtained, ideologized, contracted, subjected to systems of control, and reterritorialized. Each of the amalgamations realized through second screens presents itself as necessary or almost natural, like a flat screen above a bar. This serves to obscure and conceal the fact that all of these highly flexible amalgamations are contingent, that everything could look completely different, and that the connection could be supplied in a different way.

## Discontinuity

Even more far-reaching, however, is the other transformation of the switch image—namely, the creation of a new technical substrate for television with the introduction of a screen that is not only flat but also high-resolution and nonlinear. We already discussed the transformation of its spatial conditions, but the screen also functions entirely differently than the cathode ray tube, as it eliminates the previously compulsory, linear-continuous ontographic mode of writing of the screen image. The plasma screen, which was first developed in 1997, replaces pixels with tiny hollow cavities filled with a plasma that glows when electrically activated. These cavities are divided into three parts, and each of these parts or cells glows in one of the three primary colors. They each have separate addresses and can be controlled or activated individually regardless of their position on the screen; the activation sequence is thus nonlinear, and it can jump back and forth across the surface. This obviously occurs so quickly that it remains under the threshold of perception for the human eye, and the neurological system still reads the image as a unified whole. But there is no longer a cathode ray that is projected from a central source and that writes the image in a continuous line following a specified sequence. The metaphor of writing is thus no longer valid. This is the reason why the depth of the tube can be omitted, as the screen is now a (thick) pane of glass. The number of image cells can also be increased. The screens can thus be significantly larger and produce the wall effect mentioned earlier.

The distance between the cells on a plasma screen is also much smaller than the distance between the pixels on a cathode ray tube, so the density of image points can be increased and the image tends to be high-resolution. This has almost dramatic consequences for the television image. We can first think of McLuhan's paradigmatic definition of television as a "cold" medium whose images are so fragmentary that they must constantly be supplemented or completed through the neurological and neuronal activity of the viewer (McLuhan 1964: 344–6; see also Chapter 5 in this volume). According to McLuhan, television viewers are thus always active, even below the threshold of perception or consciousness. If the plasma screen eliminates this activity, then according to McLuhan this would be a "heating up" of the medium (McLuhan 1964: 36–44). McLuhan was interested in the "heating up" or "cooling down" of a medium because it produces large-scale cultural changes, but it also alters the fundamental anthropology of the medium by shifting the anthropo-mediatic relation between the human organism and the technical image. Viewers no longer need to fill in any gaps, as the number of image points tends to be greater than the number of photoreceptors in the retina, and the image thus looks complete to the human sense of sight with its capacity for resolution. This will be examined in more detail in the third part of the study.

There is another important consideration here. Since the screen cells are activated separately, the image loses its technically conditioned linear continuity. The writing of the image now consists in the activation of individual cells that are freely distributed over the surface of the screen. The line or line scan image of the cathode ray tube thus becomes an image of points that operate freely on the surface. The only thing that persists is that the cells fade after a short time if they are not reactivated. The instability of the image thus remains, as it is never truly "present" and it only exists if and as long as it is produced and reproduced before the eyes of the viewer. It is still ontographic, but its ontography now becomes discontinuous. It changes from a continuous form to an event form: the flowing sequence is replaced by an instantaneous flash from anywhere on the screen surface, even though it is imperceptible to the human eye. The coherence of the surface as an image arises no longer only through a temporal succession but also through an aggregation of discontinuity on the picture plane. This ontography thus differentiates itself from all of the metaphors of writing and drawing. It functions more like a kaleidoscope or a temporal mosaic that is constantly changing. The image is detached from the continuity of the signal stream and the electrical current, to which the cathode ray tube was connected. At the macroscopic level, television still registers the world as a temporal process but no longer as a continuum of lines, surfaces, and spaces. It is no longer rewritten fifty times per second but rather instantaneously reassembled and recomposed as an aggregate of points. Any point in the image can change at any time and thus affect the entire configuration. Vilém Flusser already conceived of the technical image in general (since photography) as a "computation" or consolidation of points that was beyond the linearity of writing, although he was thinking of the grains of light-sensitive film on celluloid strips, which is hardly convincing (Flusser 2011). Television strangely plays no role for Flusser, as he only considers the shift from analog to digital photography (Flusser 2011: 6; 128f.). However, this idea does apply to television's transition from a continuous ontography that consists of lines to a discontinuous ontography that consists of points distributed over a surface.

# Analogism

The contours of discontinuous ontography can be further elaborated using the work of ethnologist Philippe Descola, who distinguishes between various culturally formative image practices that he describes as "ontologies" because they generate the world and being (Descola 2010a, 2013). He specifically identifies four main ontologies, two of which seem relevant here—namely, naturalism and analogism. A consideration of these ontologies in relation to television is insightful even though, as we have repeatedly seen, television proceeds not ontologically but rather ontographically, as it remains an integral part of what it itself writes. A naturalistic ontology distinguishes between ensouled and unsouled beings, such as between humans and animals or other living things (Descola 2010b, 2013: 172–200). For Descola, being ensouled means having a form of "interiority," such as a mind or consciousness, whereas the unsouled world refers to the physical, external world. Because it is external, the reality of the unsouled world can be completely imaged, described, and measured (from an ontrographic perspective, it consists of nothing other than these drawings, writings, and measurements, like those of television). According to Descola, there are two ontologies that are opposed to naturalism: the ontology of animism, which considers all of nature to be equally ensouled and thus makes distinctions based on physical, external characteristics, and the ontology of totemism, which is based on units that are composed of the interior and the exterior (Descola 2013: 129–43; 144–71).

The ontology of "analogism" is particularly relevant for our purposes (Descola 2010c, 2013: 201–31). According to Descola, analogistic cultures do not distinguish between interior and exterior or spiritual and physical characteristics of organically connected bodies; rather, they break bodies down into elements or events of any kind—material or immaterial—and they view the world as a mutable multitude of constellations of such points. These arrangements follow similar patterns and form analogies and thus systems that cut across fixed entities. Different scales also intersect, and their differences often become unimportant. For example, there can be an analogy between the stamen of a flower and a constellation in the sky. They can also cut across the usual distinctions of naturalism, such as an analogy between a face and the bark of a tree. In addition, analogism must not provide any further explanation for the similarities in the sense of causal relations. The fundamental parallel between the ontology of analogism and Flusser's idea of the universe of technical images is clear (Flusser 2011: 148; 151). According to Flusser, digital apparatuses dissect the (visible) world into image points and then reassemble them in configurations. This parallel applies all the more since for Descola these ontologies particularly crystallize in image practices, such as the technical images of photography and cinematography for naturalism and the creation and use of fetishes and totems for animism and totemism. The discontinuous plasma image of television would thus be based on the tradition of naturalism, but it would also be in the sphere of analogism at the same time.

However, there is an important distinction between analogistic image practices and flat screen technology, which is related to the difference between ontology and ontography. If the ontology of analogism is detached and "dizzying," then an ontography always remains implied (Descola 2013: 201). Television would then be an *analogistic ontography* that switches from the observable, precursive, fixed, and detached constellation to the continuous operation of constellating. It would also take place not outside the world as its mere observation but rather always operatively as an intervention in the world, to which it itself belongs. This is precisely what the plasma screen does for the visible world: it initiates the process of constellating points of light to form flat configurations that are connected to one another through different kinds of analogies. The world is neither captured by nor detached from the image; rather, it is dissected, constellated, and arranged according to shifting analogies. This recalls the process of switching from deterritorialization to reterritorialization and from "diffusion" to "disassembly," which Deleuze and Guattari discuss in connection with their reading of Kafka. This rapturous expansion can also be described as a form of serialization or the expansion of seriality (Deleuze and Guattari 1986: 13f., 48; for more on serialization, see 53–62; see also Chapter 10 in this volume). We will come back to this.

## Without a Studio

The changes to television aesthetics and to television as a *dispositif*, which are induced by the plasma screen, also have epistemological and ontographical consequences. This can be traced using the example of television news. Until the 1990s, television news was characterized by alternate switching between three spaces: the interior spaces of the studio, which included live moderation; the various exterior spaces, from which reports came in; and the inserted or computer-generated maps, infographics, logos, names, and photographs. The interior spaces could also be subdivided (such as when there was more than one speaker or anchorperson), graphics and photographs could appear as part of the image in the background, and the reports from exterior spaces could be live or recorded. Live reports usually featured a speaker, who looked into the camera against the background of the original location, whereas recorded reports were broadcast later and featured images of the original location with a voice-over commentary. The exterior spaces thus referred to an interior space—namely, the studio from which they were coordinated. This affected not only space but also time. Within an expanded present—that is, the actuality of the news broadcast itself—the already seen was differentiated from the currently seen. News broadcasts thus touched on question of what would presumably happen next, which produced expectations. In the case of memorial days, anniversaries, and holidays, on the other hand, there were brief retrospectives, which often included original documentation from the archive of television itself (Engell 2014). Future and past times were thus coordinated from the here and now, and this entire construction was projected onto the relationship between the space of the viewer—that is, the home—and that of the studio (Feuer 1983). This relationship was characterized by the simultaneity of the live broadcast and especially by the anchorperson's direct address of the viewer while gazing into the camera. Each switch to another space, which always occurred in the present before the eyes of the viewer, resulted in the superimposition of the viewer's space and the studio space. These superimpositions unfolded in a linear-temporal sequence that was carried along by the broadcast.

This spatial and linear-temporal configuration was fundamentally transformed by digitization in the age of the flat screen, as the studio disappeared. As happens so often, the disappearance of the studio as the coordination center was already announced long beforehand. It is interesting to observe the concealment, appearance, and disappearance of the studio on the screen. In early television, the studio was a space without any visible boundaries, and it was thus never emphasized as an active production space. News broadcasts always suggested that the anchorperson was located in an enclosed room, whose boundaries coincided with those of the screen. However, this changed with the modernization of television. We already saw with the example of *Moonlighting* how a fictional television series in the 1980s suddenly broke the illusion by incorporating the studio into the image (see also Chapter 3 in this volume). But studio sets and technologies already appeared in the image much earlier in the 1970s, such as the German sports program *Das aktuelle Sportstudio* (*The Current Sports Studio*) on the second German public television station ZDF, which opened with a long shot that showed the entire lighting system, the studio set, the cameras, the camera operators, and the assistants (Wehmeier 1979). This practice occasionally finds its way into news broadcasts, such as when two anchorpeople are shown making notes on their scripts a few seconds before the broadcast begins or talking with one another or leaving the studio after the broadcast is over.

Now there is no longer a studio, or rather the studio is no longer a space but rather an image that only exists in the computer. Like the living room of classic television, it has dissolved into the second screen. The furnishings do not exist as material objects, such as the extended counter at which the moderator stands, and the rear wall only consists of a long chain of additional images(like the screens in the hotel bar) that are computer-generated and already show the key situations, symbols, or actors of the news report.

Although a studio space is simulated here, the world-forming configuration is obviously different, as individual images from the chain of screens in the background (or from other points and surfaces within the image, depending on the aesthetic style of the program) exceed their frames, expand even further, and ultimately coincide with the primary image of the studio itself. Viewers no longer switch to another space, which they observe; rather, they are directed to another screen, which is precisely a second screen. In other cases, exterior images are incorporated into the image using the split-screen process, and the use of split screens and picture-in-picture has greatly increased in news broadcasts. Parts of the image are thus always already somewhere else or refer to a different point in time. This replaces central perspective, which was essential to the cathode ray tube, which distinguished between the background and the foreground as well as between the middle and the periphery. Viewers now switch to spaces that appear as images in and from other images and then disappear again.

## Transparency Spaces

Another essential element of the high-resolution screen plays an important role. The image is now perceived as clear due to the high number of image cells. This means that the contour lines between the different color fields, which represent different bodies, are now precise. There is no impression of interference and overlapping between them, which was common with the cathode ray tube. In principle, even optical blurriness in the depth of the image disappears, as it can simply be subtracted. Blurred perspective thus disappears, as the most distant leaf on a tree can look just as sharp as a leaf in the foreground. Unlike the cathode ray tube, which possessed a certain depth or thickness of its own, the flat screen appears to be a device with no body, and its images also appear to be flat and surface-like. Everything is coordinated with everything else, and the interplay between the multitude of images does not create any space. They are either arranged next to each other, or they are laid or stacked on top of one another like *transparencies*, which represents an entirely new way of creating space. They can entirely or partly conceal one another, and they can also emerge from any position in the stack or sequence of transparencies. If the image space is a site of multiple images, then it is not flat in the strict sense; however, it lacks the expanded and structured depth of classical perspective, such as the use of foreground, middle ground, and background. Instead, the various image layers, which are each almost entirely flat, relate to one another like superimposed or overlaid photographs, a stack of papers, or obviously windows on a computer screen.

What we already observed as a principle and a tendency following the return of the image from the moon to the earth effectively prevails in the age of the flat screen (see also Chapter 7 in this volume). Access to an event in the world changes from an arrangement of spaces in time to a constellation of screens, and the central studio is now just one screen among many. Distinctions between interior and exterior, center and periphery, or "still" and "no longer" lose their structuring and orienting power. Reported world affairs basically contract into a huge simultaneity, and the individual events can appear as configurations anywhere on the surface. Any part of the image can become the next center in this discontinuous ontography, and the other images can be organized around and encircle any image within the image. The perspective from which the viewer navigates all of this is also defined as and by an arrangement of screens, which in the case of the bar in the Chicago Hyatt at the same time also constitutes the actual walls of the location where the viewer is situated. The *second screens* of the image habitat thus localize the viewers, no matter where they are, and at the same time arrange the events and situations that they show into constellations. The world is no longer phantom and matrix, as it was for Günter Anders; rather, it is now transparency and constellation.

## Becoming a Switch

The switch image undergoes another spectacular shift with a further technological evolution of the screen. Today plasma televisions are only used in very specific contexts, as they have largely been replaced by LCD screens (for this and the following, see Kawamoto 2002; Dunmur and Sluckin 2011; Gross 2018). The first LCDs were used for digital clocks and calculator displays in the early 1970s. In the early 2000s they quickly caught on as computer monitors and from 2003 on as televisions, and nearly all of the screens manufactured since 2010 have been LCD screens. LCD screens share many of the same qualities as plasma screens, as they are also flat, high-resolution, clear (in the way described earlier), and scalable (they can be almost any size). In addition, the image pixels do not have to be illuminated in a specific sequence according to their linear arrangement, as the image cells can also be addressed independently. However, they are no longer activated in the same way. Unlike plasma cells and the traditional pixels of the cathode ray tube, the image cells no longer glow when they are contacted or addressed; rather, they are switches that allow light to pass through or block it. These cells are filled with a liquid crystal whose molecular structure forms a three-dimensional grid pattern. Liquid crystals can change the structure of this grid by turning it 90 degrees so that it is either upright or horizontal. As a result, the light that penetrates the individual liquid-crystal cells at each of these positions, independent of their sequential arrangement in rows and columns, can be polarized so that segments of light waves only penetrate horizontally or vertically. This change is activated by an electrical impulse that can access the cells freely at any controllable position on the image surface, so it is discontinuous like the plasma screen. It is also possible to activate intermediate positions by varying the current, like the positions of the blades on window blinds. In this sense, the LCD image is not a completely digital image, as the variation of the current and the duration of the activating impulse, which are analog variables, still play a role in its production (Wang et al. 2004).

If two such crystals are overlaid like windows blinds—one with vertical and the other with horizontal blades, as is the case in the LCD screen—then all light waves or light pulses can be prevented from penetrating and thus be switched off (or nearly all: LCD screens are never entirely black when they are in operation) (Sluyterman et al. 2005). The technical condition of the image is also shaped by the transparency-like layering or stacking of images, which we already observed earlier in relation to the aesthetics of television's second screen using the example of news broadcasts. Every perceptible image point also consists of three cavities for the three primary colors of the image. The light is emitted not from the liquid-crystal cavities themselves but rather from behind the arrangement like an additional light surface (or like the window behind the window blinds), which is usually a LED display that glows continuously like a lamp as soon as the device is switched on. The interplay of both crystal lattices determines how much light from which colored cavity passes through and emerges from the external layer of the arrangement—that is, the actual tangible screen. The image that is perceptible to the human eye emerges from these switched image cells.

This represents a deep intervention into the technological condition of the television image, as it is now an arrangement of switches. In other words, it is no longer an object that is switched; rather, being more than ever a switch image, it emerges from an aggregate of switches and becomes a switch itself. With the cathode ray tube and the plasma screen, viewers could still operatively distinguish the fleeting image from the switches or the writing process from its control and interruption. The plasma image could also still be understood in terms of writing or drawing, even though this process became discontinuous. In the case of the LCD screen, however, the entire image relies on complex switching operations. The discontinuous writing or drawing of the image and the switching of the image technically coincide. The image no longer consists of a linear flowing process that allows for interventions via switching, such as interruptions, insertions, or recursions; rather, it itself consists of a constellation of switching operations that are constantly changing and thus form a sequence that is visible to the human eye as change, movement, and time. The incorporation of switching into the image is also expressed by the technical term "in-plane switching," which was used for one of the most important patents in the development of the LCD screen (U.S. Patent US3834794 (A) 1974; see Becker 2005).

There is another fact that clarifies this overlapping of drawing and switching processes in the LCD screen and its emergence from the logic of the second screen: the LCD screen was originally developed for the remote control in order to display additional information about the selected program or the volume settings. The remote control would have thus provided graphic information about the current settings or switches via the small LCD, and the switching process could have been visualized and controlled through feedback to the remote control itself. As with videotext, additional program-related information could have been passed to the LCD of the remote control, which would have then functioned as a real second screen, although this principle did not catch on.

## From Ontography to the Ontogram

In addition to introducing a new version of the television image as a nonlinear configuration of switching operations, the LCD screen also brought another fundamental change. The flow of light emanating from the LEDs in the background continues for as long as the device is in operation, and it is entirely independent of the switching configuration of cells. This initially continues the principle that we already observed at the beginning of tube television: in addition to the electrical current, with which the device is always connected, and the electromagnetic wave event, in which the device is always already embedded, the light of the LEDs is another constant that works through the device. Moreover, once they have assumed a particular state, the liquid-crystal cells can maintain that state as long as they are not switched, which means that each image point no longer fades or changes until it is switched. In other words, the image cells only need to be controlled if they are supposed to change; otherwise, they remain in the same switched state. If nothing happens (besides the glow of the background light), then the screen configuration persists, which is a sharp and fundamental contrast to all previous screens. The switch image thus acquires something stable, even though the difference is not initially apparent to the human eye, as it changes from an ontography, which only exists during the process of writing or drawing, to an *ontogram*, which remains intact. For the first time, the television picture is now capable of change *and* stasis or instantaneity *and* duration at the same time. More precisely, its being-switch (*Schaltung-Sein*) oscillates between ontographic and *ontogrammatic* operations (as a switch that cannot change is not a switch). It thus becomes something between the process of drawing and its product, the drawing itself, and its operativity consists in its oscillation between these two states. It is perhaps similar to the page of a book on which the text does not continue to be written, so that it appears and disappears, but rather varies or replaces its individual letters, so that a constantly changing text emerges in the middle of a persistent text. At the technical-microscopic level, the switch image now recalls the shift to an infinitely expanding middle without beginning and end (Deleuze and Guattari 1986: 13f.). As a threshold value, the text also has a definite possibility that it did not have with the cathode ray tube—namely, to remain still. This once again has visible consequences for the epistemology and aesthetics of television, as something in the image can now remain still and flicker-free, unlike with picture tubes, while something else in the same image changes.

Even before the implementation of the LCD screen, Belgian video artist David Claerbout already explored the astounding aesthetic operativity of an image that is resting and moving at the same time (Bellour et al. 2008). For example, he produced a still image—a snapshot—that showed a schoolyard with children playing, and all movement was frozen except for the trembling and swaying of leaves in the wind. Another image combines slow motion and fast motion by showing a figure covering a table on a terrace and then gradually approaching the camera in a decelerated movement as the day goes by in an accelerated movement of clouds and light changes. In the case of the switch image, however, the thematizing or at least analogizing of the simultaneity of duration and change takes other forms. We have already seen earlier how flat screen television switches no longer between spaces but rather between surfaces, which it no longer arranges according to an outside-inside scheme but rather overlays like transparencies. Switching makes one of these transparencies emerge from behind the others, as if it had already been there the whole time, or a section of the image is highlighted and enlarged. Switching operations between spaces thus become switching operations in and on the image itself, and the image becomes both the operational chain and the operational basis of this switching. What emerges is no longer the visual or referential nature of images but rather their operative nature as image-internal switching. According to television theorist Daniela Wentz, the images become diagrams—or, more precisely, diagrammatic images (Wentz 2017, 2019).

## Ontogram and Diagram

Wentz is referring here to Charles Sanders Peirce's peculiar concept of diagrams or diagrammatics. For Peirce, diagrams are graphic orderings that not only represent ideas and make them comprehensible but also set them in motion and implement them. Logical or geometrical facts and relations and even entire arguments can thus be diagrammatically developed. Television images whose aesthetics incorporate, analogize, or thematize the conditions of the flat screen are diagrammatic in precisely this sense, and Wentz thus reads them as "diagrammatic images." She particularly observes the dynamic sequence of diagrammatic images in the fictional format of the television series, and she is primarily interested in the media-aesthetic, narratological, and epistemographical aspects of the format (Wentz 2017: 181-0). She clarifies this idea using television series like *House, M.D.* or *Sherlock*, which foreground the title characters' powers of deduction and evoke this ability through diagrammatically deductive images (Wentz 2017: 181–234; see also Chapter 10 in this volume). We could also go back once again to the images of television news broadcasts or announcements. These images implement a process of argumentation through the succession of texts, graphics, photographs, and film clips embedded within them, as a set of facts is gradually developed from one embedded image to another before the eyes of the viewers. For example, changes in unemployment statistics over the last year can become a moving pie chart, which is then followed by a filmed commentary and explanation given by an expert. The captions and titles to the image provide accompanying information so that the facts finally emerge before the eyes of the viewers as a sequence of visualizations. The facts are made plausible or even evident through this mathematical construction, yet the various kinds of images or signs (graphics, animation, interviews, texts, numbers, etc.) exist on the screen not only as a sequence but also at the same time, like the arrangement of overlapping or coordinated transparencies. None of them can claim to represent the horizon of reference or the referential reality for the others; rather, this only arises from the succession or rapid sequence of actualizations. In other words, the facts represented on television *exist* in a sequence of simultaneous and continuous visual operations. Already for Peirce, therefore, the concept of the diagram is characterized by its arbitrary oscillation between (complex) visual signs, such as the "available" drawings or graphics, which are resistant to time, and the construction and reconstruction of graphics in the course of their drawing or "reading," which is diagrammatic. The diagram is both of these operations at the same time. As diagrammatic images, flat screen images are strictly speaking no longer observed but rather "read" and in this sense scanned.

Deleuze and Guattari already referred to this transition in connection with the movement of deterritorialization, although it was not applied to television (Deleuze and Guattari 2000: 206).

Wentz insists, however, that the television image is both an image and a diagram (Wentz 2017: 31ff.). It constantly oscillates between its status as a fixed image and sign and the operation of "reading" and (thereby) writing or drawing. Already for Peirce, the concept of the sign merges with the process of drawing as a semiographic operation. Signs *are* at the same time also constructions of signs. Peirce thus assumes, first and foremost, that all being coincides with being represented (*Repräsentiertsein*) in and through the continuous process of the sign (Peirce 1983: 76–7; 87). Different phases and states of the sign process or "sign thematics" represent different modes of being or "reality thematics" (Peirce 1958: 220–45; see also Bense 1976). Second, however, Peirce also assumes that every sign (which he strictly understands as a relation) has a material sign carrier and that it always implies (paradoxically) an object, which is independent of the sign and represented through a second object provided by the sign. Although there can be no reality outside of the represented being of signs, it is nevertheless represented by means of a second object, as if this were precisely the case.[1] Third, Peirce also assumes that the sign process is not consciously performed; rather, consciousness itself is a product of the sign process (Peirce 1983: 116–18; see also Wentz 2019: 188–9). Like the medium in the assumptions of a medial ontography, Peirce's sign is thus also a third that is not preceded by anything. Lastly, according to Peirce, the diagrammatic sign process also exhibits an unavoidable temporality. Signs are not only fundamentally relational but also operative. Signs arise from and return to material reality (physical as well as social), which also applies precisely to the process of ontography. The sign process also continues indefinitely, although Peirce allows for an operation of discontinuation or interruption for pragmatic reasons (the "pragmatic maxims") (Peirce 1960: 252–65).

While the concepts of "ontography" and the "ontogram" never appear in Peirce's writings (though his concept of "phaneroscopy" appears to mediate between phenomenology and ontography) (Peirce 2016a,b), Wentz argues that Peirce's semiotics and particularly his diagrammatics still follow a very similar project (Wentz 2019). There is nevertheless still a difference between them, as the sign remains fundamentally connected to representation, which is not true of ontography and the ontogram. Ontographies do not occupy a second level of abstraction above that of the concrete facts; rather, they themselves operate as facts on the same level. Ontograms do not represent something; rather, they are something—namely, a part of (and a process in) the reality that they revise. What is important here, however, is that the switch image of the LCD screen oscillates between the ontogram and ontography in the same way that the diagram in Peirce oscillates between sign-character (*Zeichenhaftigkeit*) and operativity. This will be further explained in the third part of the study by means of the "new series" of television and the genre of "reality television."

## Pervasive Switch Images

As we have seen, the LCD was tested early on as an element of the remote control. The use of the LCD as a television screen was then taken from the computer monitor, just as older tube monitors had been equipped for decades with screen technology taken from television. Computer screens and television screens have always shared their basic technology. What was new about LCD screens was that they could be any size—from very small to very large—and that they could be installed anywhere and integrated into any device surface due to their lack of depth. The television image thus became more ubiquitous and pervasive than ever before, particularly due to its miniaturization. Television can now be viewed on television sets as well as mobile phones, tablets, laptops, and all computer screens. This introduces a further development of the second screen, which supplements and reverses the extension of television to the screen environment of ambient television. This development involves the use of additional screens at the same time that the television screen is in operation, and the concept of "second screens" is mostly used in this narrower sense. While watching television, for example, viewers can now chat, text, email, surf the internet, or even follow a second television program streamed over a wireless network. Television has obviously always been a medium of incidental viewing that is used during other accompanying activities, as we observed in the example of the soap opera, and additional uses of the medium (such as telephoning over television) were also already established much earlier. With the arrival of second screens, however, the status of television as a mere background activity becomes even more pronounced. It now constitutes more than ever a horizon, habitat, or niche that serves as a backdrop against which other screen-based digital communication processes take place, whether they be textual, visual, or auditory. Just as ambient television creates an exterior space into which it disappears, so too does television create an interior space that serves as a habitat for other image streams. Television thus becomes a form of everyday audiovisual noise that grounds other screen activities.

This can be seen as the disappearance of television; however, Markus Stauff's study of this phenomenon comes to a different conclusion, as he refers to second screens as an "assemblage" (Stauff 2015). He first summarizes the state of empirical communication research on media use, which shows that the large television set and its broadcasts constitute not the backdrop but rather the communicative focus of the other image processes running simultaneously on second screens. For example, text messages or emails sent during a television program often refer to the program, which synchronizes the reception of the same running image by two (or more) partners watching television at different locations at the same time. Second screens thus facilitate a function that was always inherent to television. Websites are also frequently visited using smart phones or tablets in order to supplement or expand on the program running on television at the same time, such as by providing biographies of the actors, summaries of the previous episodes of a series, or detailed information about a news story. This is even supported by television networks, which use captions or moderators to refer to the offerings related to the program that they themselves maintain on the internet. This also includes the use of information on second screens as program guides in order to organize the course of the television evening by browsing the wide range of alternative program options available at the same time. A smart phone or mobile computer interacts with the remote control to organize (through the selection of programs), synchronize (such as with other viewers), and annotate (through follow-up communications) the event on the large screen. This also involves a deterritorialization of television, and in this sense the designation of the (other) screen as "secondary" is justified (Stauff 2015: 127–9).

According to Stauff, however, the actual process of the television evening then becomes the organization, synchronization, and annotation of television, and the television evening thus extends beyond the boundaries of the interior space (i.e., the living room) (Stauff 2015: 128–30). Television viewing now means distributing, organizing, and synchronizing image and communication flows over multiple devices. In other words, it means no longer looking at a television set but rather establishing and regulating a multi-stream flow over and across diverse screens and modes of communication. The primary stream—the television program—can thus be overlaid, extended, diverted, or even reversed, such as when the media library of the broadcaster is accessed through websites or digital platforms that enable the time-shifted viewing of previously broadcast images. Television is now no longer something that takes place on the large screen; rather, it is the constantly shifting relations between things that take place on different screens. It resides not on these screens but rather between them.

## Prosumer and Patient

This is intensified by further technical and economic changes. For example, the streaming function allows the internet to be used as a distribution technology for live television programs. Television broadcasters and streaming services like Netflix or Amazon also offer databases, which include feature films as well as television series and entertainment shows that can be accessed freely outside of regularly scheduled programming. The digital program offerings of pay TV and other forms, which Stauff persuasively labels "new television," are nothing other than databases that are made public (for a fee) through various access technologies (cable, satellite, internet). Television reception is thus detached from linear and schedule-based programming, as every viewer tends to be able to watch whatever they want and whenever they want. The idea of the viewer as an allegedly passive "couch potato"—the addressee of a one-way flow of television—is thus replaced by the idea of the viewer as an active "prosumer," who accesses and creates what she wants to watch by herself. This obviously applies not only to database television but also to all televisual processes involving second screens.

Stauff offers a convincing analysis of the relationship between this development and the neoliberal control of processes of subjectification and forms of appropriation, which we already encountered in our earlier discussion of the media anthropology of television and *interconnection* (Stauff 2005; see also Chapter 5 in this volume). He particularly identifies four tendencies. First, television sees and sells itself in neoliberalism as optimizable, as it is advertised as having more comprehensive coverage, as being more perfect, and above all as offering more control by means of increasingly better navigational tools. In the meantime, however, the internet is expected to have established itself as the decisive navigational medium of television, as we have seen. Second, according to Stauff, this navigation presents itself as a question of access, as access is its primary operation. In the context of the switch image, one could add that this access is always performed as switches. One could also add that Deleuze's famous essay on societies of control already emphasized that questions of information access replace the regulation of physical inclusion and exclusion, which Foucault associated with modern disciplinary environments (i.e., schools, prisons, factories, barracks, hospitals, etc.) (Deleuze 1992). Third, television is now designed as an individualized experience instead of a group phenomenon or even a synchronization implemented society-wide on a massive scale. Lastly, all of these tendencies obviously serve to intensify the economization of television, which underlies the meaning of all neoliberal change. Stauff shows that early digital television already performed a function that we are now perfectly familiar with from the internet and social media platforms: the image looks back at its viewers by identifying user profiles and presenting individualized offerings. Viewers thus become individual economic subjects who are supposed to express themselves, be creative, and act independently. In short, they become entrepreneurs (Stauff 2005:

254–7). One could add that they are also supposed to manage and control themselves.

More detailed consideration is needed to determine whether this is actually true of television with second screens. We already established that the localization and specification of the viewer in terms of a schematic division between active and passive or "actor" and "patient" does not work for classic tube television, and instead we developed an entangled model of the viewer as "agent" (see Chapter 5 in this volume). These considerations can also be applied to the relations of television with second screens. Stauff at least admits with regard to, say, the mere devotion to the flow of what runs its course that the passive mode of being of the "couch potato" already contains within it the appearance of subversion in a situation in which individual freedom no longer grants the critique of a cultural technology whose productivity comes precisely from this freedom (Stauff 2005: 259).

## Computer Television

This development of subjectification, individualization, and economization is also not entirely new, and it cannot be attributed to digitization alone; indeed, the opposite may even be the case. It was first introduced with the implementation of videocassettes and videorecorders, which were marketable descendants of the AMPEX image recording technology that we already encountered in our discussion of the instant replay, and it continued with the implementation of DVDs. The DVD also enabled the infamous practice of "binging," in which all of the episodes of a television series are watched in the same evening, often with a group as a communal event. However, the principle of liveness by no means disappears. Live streams, such as the broadcasting of sports, political debates, musical performances, or quiz shows, are nothing more than live television using other distribution channels and sometimes, but not always, other content providers. Television still involves what Nipkow described as making an event at location A visible at another location B at the same time. Live streaming is therefore not an alternative to television; rather, it is television. It is also revealing that streaming services like Netflix increasingly employ forms of usage that correspond to the classic usage of television. For example, a new series is always released on a specific date, and whoever wants to be there must be there at a certain time on a certain day. It is also possible to make an appointment to watch a series episode, film, or other online offering together at the same time but in different locations, which imitates the program effect of television. If a great many viewers (particularly younger viewers) report that they do not watch television but instead typically stream from the internet, then this is related to the earlier form of television as a more or less compact and individual activity rather than the accelerated or intensified forms of television. These accelerated or intensified forms include the migration of television to other screens, its expansion into habitats, its miniaturization in all of the contexts of life, its adaptation to practices derived from other media, and above all its new function to organize the diverse and diversified communication flows in terms of their temporality, sequentiality, synchronicity, and simultaneity.

It is often claimed that television disappears in the computer or the internet, but it can just as well be claimed that television uses the computer and the internet to expand and refine itself to an almost excessive degree. It increasingly becomes one with diverse habitats that enclose, invert, and permeate one another, like the living room, shopping mall, or hotel bar. It thus retains its original function as an articulation and liquification that has a society-wide effect or as the synchronization and simultanization of audiovisual event chains, from which all of the complications and evolutions of the switch image unfold. It also retains its operational basis as a switch image. Its mode of being can also still be understood as an ontography, even though it has shifted and is now a process that alternates between ontography and the ontogram. This also applies when it involves the operative entanglement of other screen activities on other devices at the same time, which are mutually dependent on this entanglement and would be imperceptible without it. This represents a continuation of what the early research on intermediality already determined: media are defined by their relations to other media, so a medium is what it is only in connection with what it is not. Television is thus a relation, an operation of coordination and blending, and a process of merging and separating again. It connects and amalgamates what is not television but is nothing without television.

## Note

1  It needs to be determined whether Peirce mediates between correlationism and (speculative) realism and thus also between the two versions of ontography contrasted here.

## References

Anders, Günther. 1956a. "Die Welt als Phantom und Matritze." In: Günther Anders. *Die Antiquiertheit des Menschen, vol. 1: Über die Seele im Zeitalter der zweiten industriellen Revolution*, pp. 97–211. München: Beck.

Becker, Michael E. 2005. "Kristallmanufaktur—Schritte auf dem Weg zum sehrichtungsunabhängigen LC-Schirm." *c't-Magazin* 22: 222–6.
Bellour, Raymond, Francoise Parfait, Dirk Snauwaert (eds.). 2008. *David Claerbout: The Shape of Time*. New York: JRP Ringier.
Bense, Max. 1976. *Die Vermittlung der Realitäten. Semiotische Erkenntnistheorie*. Baden-Baden: Agis.
Caillois, Roger. 1935. "Mimétisme et psychasthénie légendaire." *Minotaure* 7: 4–10.
Caldwell, John T. 1995. *Televisuality: Style, Crisis, and Authority in American Television*. New Brunswick: Rutgers University Press.
Casetti, Francesco, and Roger Odin. 1990. "De la paléo- à la néo-télévision." *Communications* 51: 9–26.
Cavell, Stanley. 1982. "The Fact of Television." *Daedalus 111*, no. 4: 75–96.
Deforge, Yves. 1994. "L'évolution des objets techniques." In: *Gilbert Simondon. Une pensée de l'individuation et de la technique*, pp. 173–83. Paris: Albin Michel.
Deleuze, Gilles. 1992. "Postscript on the Societies of Control." *Oktober* 59: 3–7.
Deleuze, Gilles, and Félix Guattari. 1986. *Kafka: Toward a Minor Literature*. Minneapolis, London: Minnesota University Press.
Deleuze, Gilles, and Félix Guattari. 2000. *Anti-Oedipus: Capitalism and Schizophrenia*. Minneapolis: University of Minnesota Press.
Descola, Philippe, ed. 2010a. *La fabrique des images: Vision du monde et formes de la représentation*. Paris: Musée du quai Branly/Somogy éditions d'art.
Descola, Philippe, ed. 2010b. "Un monde objectif." In: *La fabrique des images: Vision du monde et formes de la représentation*, ed. by Philippe Descola, pp. 73–100. Paris: Musée du quai Branly/Somogy éditions d'art.
Descola, Philippe, ed. 2010c. "Un monde enchevêtré." In: *La fabrique des images: Vision du monde et formes de la représentation*, ed. by Philippe Descola, pp. 165–84. Paris: Musée du quai Branly/Somogy éditions d'art.
Descola, Philippe, ed. 2013. *Beyond Nature and Culture*. Chicago, London: University of Chicago Press.
Dunmur, David, and Tim Sluckin. 2011. *Soap, Science, and Flat Screen TVs*. Oxford, New York: Oxford University Press.
Engell, Lorenz. 2013. "Über den Agenten. Bemerkungen zu einer populären Figur der Dia-Medialität." In: *Paradoxalität des Medialen*, ed. by Jan-Henrik Möller, Jörg Sternagel, and Lenore Hipper, pp. 41–58. München: Fink.
Engell, Lorenz. 2014. "Jenseits von Geschichte und Gedächtnis. Historiographie und Autobiographie des Fernsehens." *montage a/v* 14/1: 60–79.
Engell, Lorenz. 2015. "Agentur." In: *Essays zur Film-Philosophie*, ed. by Lorenz Engell, Oliver Fahle, Vinzenz Hediger, and Christiane Voss, pp. 17–62. München: Fink.
Engell, Lorenz, and Carina Jasmine Englert, Natascha Kempken, Dominik Maeder, Jo Reicherzt, Jens Schröter, Daniela Wentz. 2014. "Das Fernsehen als Akteur und Agent." In: *Die Mediatisierung sozialer Welten. Synergien empirischer Forschung*, ed. by Friedrich Krotz, Cathrin Despotović, and Merle-Marie Kruse, pp. 145–65. Wiesbaden: Springer VS.

Feuer, Jane. 1983. "The Concept of Live Television: Ontology as Ideology." In: *Regarding Television*, ed. by E. Ann Kaplan, pp. 12–21. Frederick: University Publications of America.

Flusser, Vilém. 2011. *Into the Universe of Technical Images*. Minneapolis, London: University of Minnesota Press.

Gross, Benjamin. 2018. *The TVs of Tomorrow: How RCA's Flat Screen Dreams Led to the First LCD's*. Chicago, London: University of Chicago Press.

Hartley, John. 1999. *Uses of Television*. London, New York: Routledge.

Hickethier, Knut. 1998. *Geschichte des deutschen Fernsehens*. Stuttgart, Weimar: Metzler.

Kawamoto, Hiroshisa. 2002. "The History of Liquid-Crystal Displays." *Proceedings of the IEEE* 90, no. 4: 460–500.

McCarthy, Anna. 2001. *Ambient Television*. Durham: Duke University Press.

McLuhan, Marshall. 1964. *Understanding Media: The Extensions of Man*. London, New York: Routledge.

Meyrowitz, Joshua. 1985. *No Sense of Place: The Impacts of Electronic Media on Social Behavior*. New York, Oxford: Oxford University Press.

Peirce, Charles S. 1958. "To Lady Welby." In: Charles S. Peirce. *Collected Papers of Charles Sanders Peirce. Volume VIII: Reviews, Correspondence, and Bibliography*, ed. by Arthur W. Burks, pp. 220–45. Cambridge, MA: Harvard University Press.

Peirce, Charles S. 1960. "How to Make Our Ideas Clear." In: Charles S. Peirce. *Collected Papers of Charles Sanders Peirce. Volume V: Pragmatism and Pragmaticism*, ed. by Charles Hartshorne, and Paul Weiss, pp. 248–71. Cambridge, MA: The Belknap Press of Harvard University Press.

Peirce, Charles S. 1983. *Phänomen und Logik der Zeichen*. Frankfurt/M.: Suhrkamp.

Peirce, Charles S. 2016a. "Phaneroscopy; Or: The Natural History of Concepts." In: Charles S. Peirce. *Prolegomena to a Science of Reasoning: Phaneroscopy, Semeiotic, Logic*, pp. 65–76. Frankfurt/M.: Peter Lang.

Peirce, Charles S. 2016b. "Phaneroscopy." In: Charles S. Peirce. *Prolegomena to a Science of Reasoning: Phaneroscopy, Semeiotic, Logic*, pp. 77–94. Frankfurt/M.: Peter Lang.

Simondon, Gilbert. 1989. *L'individuation psychique et collective*. Paris: Aubier.

Simondon, Gilbert. 2017. *On the Mode of Existence of Technical Objects*. Minneapolis: Univocal.

Sluyterman, A. A. S. and E.P. Boonekamp. 2005. "Architechtural Choices in a Scanning Backlight for Large LCD-TVs." In: *SID05Digest 2005*, pp. 996–9.

Spigel, Lynn. 1992. *Make Room for TV, Television and the Family Ideal in Postwar America*. Chicago, London: University of Chicago Press.

Stauff, Markus. 2005. *Das neue Fernsehen. Machtanalyse, Gouvernementalität und digitale Meiden*. Münster: Lit.

Stauff, Markus. 2015. "The Second Screen: Convergence as Crisis." *Zeitschrift für Medien- und Kulturforschung* 6, no. 2: 123–44.

Stauff, Markus. 2016. "Taming Distraction: The Second-Screen Assemblage, Television, and the Classroom." *Media and Communication* 4, no. 3.

US Patent US3834794 (A). 1974. 1974-09-10 (*Liquid Crystal Electric Field Sensing Measurement And Display Device*).

Wang, Haiying, Thomas X. Wu, Xinyu Zhu, and Shin-Tson Wu. 2004. "Correlations between Liquid Crystal Director Reorientation and Optical Response Time of a Homeotropic Cell." *Journal of Applied Physics* 95, no. 10: 5502–8.

Wehmeier, Klaus. 1979. *Die Geschichte des ZDF: Entstehung und Entwicklung 1961–1966*. Mainz: v. Hase und Köhler.

Wentz, Daniela. 2017. *Bilderfolgen. Diagrammatologie der Fernsehserie*. Paderborn: Transcript.

Wentz, Daniela. 2019. "Existential Graphs as Ontographic Media." *Zeitschrift für Medien- und Kulturforschung (ZMK)* 10/1: 177–89.

Youngblood, Gene. 1970. *Expanded Cinema*. London: Studio Vista.

Part III

# Television 2.0

The electric switch image, television 1.0, was always pcesent and live, exactly now and there. With the instant replay, however, it created an expanded present, in which time was capable of flowing upstream without leaving the stream. It could now switch back and forth, seamlessly mediating between different directions of the flow, between passing and persisting, or between movement and stasis. Television thus transformed from an image that was always already switched before it reached the screen to an image that could be switched on the screen on which it was received by means of the remote control, as it could be replaced and combined with other images. Then, as an image, television effectively left this screen, observed it from outside, returned to it, projected itself onto it, doubled, and proliferated. It flew to the moon and turned its gaze back on the Earth. It abandoned its original location—namely, the television set—and distributed itself over countless screens, between which it now constantly migrates back and forth. It thus spread outward into the environment (in the form of ambient television) as well as inward into the hands of viewers (in the form of mobile phones). It transformed into a configuration of devices that no longer constituted a permanently integrated apparatus but rather occurred as a constant configuring and reconfiguring of images on different screens. It developed into a more or less closed environment. It is still a live image, but it now synchronizes the screens, times, and spaces between which it ontographically extends.

Television finally became a switch—or, more precisely, a constellation of many switches—which made the operative image itself an operation. It is now not (only) switched; rather, it is the switching, changing, or maintaining of an arrangement of switching positions, and it shows what it shows precisely through switching operations. This new switch image, television 2.0, is also no longer an image that is continuously written, like the cathode ray tube image; rather, it has become a discontinuously and kaleidoscopically changing image. Its image points are no longer scanned linearly, one after the other, in a fixed sequence; rather, they can be addressed and accessed arbitrarily. Television has also simultaneously transitioned from a naturalistic or representational ontography to an analogistic ontography that traces constellations and makes them readable. The instant replay and the liquid-crystal screen thus transformed an image that was only present in the course of its drawing or writing into an image that can also remain, and it thus oscillates back and forth between its production as ontography and its persistence as an ontogram. And in all of this, the switch image is always its own transformation, and its initial conditions (liveness, flow, seriality, etc.) not only continue but are also carried along in this transformation. The earlier version of the switch image is not gone; rather, it has been amalgamated with the later version. Television 2.0 does not simply follow and replace television 1.0; rather, they are adjacent and even tangential to one another.

Television not only experiences and manages all of these developments; rather, it also observes them, shows them, thematizes them, repeats them, applies them recursively to itself, and turns them into another standard. The location where this occurs, and the form that it takes, is once again the *television series*. It also develops its own new space of reality. It no longer (only) observes, affects, or moves itself and us into this space; rather, it (also) produces this space, and it thus deals with its production rather than only its results. Because it extends into its environment, it can now envisage an exterior space in which it always already exists or is embedded. It relates to this space ontographically as well as ontogrammatically, and this new reality of television acquires its own program segment or format, which is known as the *reality show*. However, the new reality concept of television comes into effect through its access to history. Television 2.0 also develops a changed anthropology—namely, one in which viewers stop being the agents of the switch image and the switch image stops using them. On the one hand, the images now encircle the viewers, incorporating them and looking (and switching) more intensely back on them. On the other hand, image operations also enable viewers in the first place, provided that viewers interrupt these operations and thus become switches themselves. They ultimately either switch the television off or they are switched off—it no longer makes any difference.

# 10

# The Series (2)

We already described the classic television series primarily as the interaction between the episodic principle and the continuation principle (see Chapter 3 in this volume). Series are fundamentally generative, and both of these principles, which constitute the main forms of the series, are thus plastic in different ways. However, the dual nature of the serial is also at work beyond the distinction between the episode and the continuation. As we developed earlier with reference to Gilles Deleuze, every series is based on two series that arise from the same elements, whether they are images, characters, settings, or events (Deleuze 2004: 44–50). The same image or character can thus function in the first series (which Deleuze calls the series of signifiers) as well as the second series (which Deleuze calls the series of signifieds). The first series is unstable and produces ruptures, whereas the second is stable and produces analogies. Each of these series is finite in and of itself, but their interaction is necessarily infinite, as the first is closely related to the second. Their interaction also forms episodic series, when analogies are favored, and continuing series, when ruptures are favored.

This interaction changes, however, in the discontinuous and analogistic ontography of television 2.0. Both series are still at work, but they become indistinguishable and coalescent, and they stop being infinite. This gives rise to a new type of series, which still can be observed and described alongside the distinction between the episodic series and the continuing series but which no longer finds its paradoxical "logic of sense" in these forms. This new type already began to develop in the 1990s, but it gathered momentum in the decades after 2000, and it was observed from early on, addressed as the "new series," "neo-series," "complex series," "quality series," or "transmedial series" (Kelleter 2012; Engell 2019).

## The Forensics of the Series

An example is *CSI: Crime Scene Investigation*, which is one of the most successful series since 2000. This series is not only the most important representative of an entirely new series type—namely, the *forensic series*

(Allen 2007; Englert and Reichertz 2016)—but also one of the most prolific episodic weekly series of all, as it ran for 15 seasons and had a total of 336 episodes. It also generated two additional long-running spin-offs: *CSI: Miami* and *CSI: New York*. The expansion of the image, which we discussed in the previous chapter, thus contracts here back into television itself (and not for the first time).[1]

What is more important than its tremendous success, however, is that it shows the transformation of material reality into images. The actual theme of the series is the closing off of the world through screens and the movement and distribution of images over countless screens. This closing off occurs in stages. After the opening scene and the opening credits, every single episode begins with the crime scene, which is marked off by the iconic barrier tape. This tape separates the victim of the crime and his immediate surroundings, in which the investigators act, from the spectators, just as the stage where the actors perform is marked off from the audience in a theater. The investigators then convert the entire scene and everything that belongs to it—often including the spectators—into images. This is primarily accomplished through cameras, the sounds of which provide a rhythm that acoustically punctuates the entire opening sequence (Lury 2007: 120). Moreover, physical objects, things, material traces, or particles, such as weapons, pieces of clothing, nuts and bolts, clumps of dirt, chemical substances, splinters, body parts and fluids, or even entire corpses, are then brought from the crime scene to the laboratory, where they serve as evidence. However, the transfer of physical objects is only a detour to visualization. The physical objects are not immediately investigated but rather first transformed and transcribed into visual or visualized data sets (Hollendonner 2009: 29). According to the ontology of evidence on *CSI*, only that which can be visualized exists (Nohr 2014: 29). All sorts of different high-tech laboratory processes are mobilized for this purpose, such as spectral analyses, microphotographic recordings, fingerprint impressions from the surfaces of objects, the visualization of temperature or climate data, and oscillograms of recorded voices from answering machines. The virtuosity of the investigators lies precisely in the ingenious use and combination of these visualization processes, which are often combined with or connected to one another in chains or series. *CSI* thus involves the transmission of the facts encountered at the crime scene from the materiality (one could also say medium) of physical "reality" to another materiality or medium—namely, that of the electronic image or monitor (Turnbull 2007: 30).

This work takes place in a closed image environment. There is no exterior space, and even the light itself comes from apparatuses, glass cabinets with exhibits and utensils, or at best through window blinds that make it resemble screen light. Unlike the original material, the image material is also almost arbitrarily shapable, as it is highly plastic and malleable, and it possesses its own dynamic. It can also be displaced, which is characteristic of digital images. Television on *CSI* becomes a shell medium that contains all other image types, and the television series becomes the medium in which all of these images can circulate and connect to one another to form series. The investigators resemble image engineers like those who create the television picture for us and whom we cannot see. It is also no coincidence that "CSI" and "CGI" (computer-generated images) sound confusingly similar. Hence, the crime laboratory is also only a post-production (Turnbull 2007). This excess of visibility or evidence also replaces human psychology, which the investigators of earlier criminal plots used to expose perpetrators.

The experimental laboratory processes, as performed here by the investigators, in themselves also follow the series form. Every scientific experiment must be reproducible in order to be verifiable, and these reproductions constitute an identical series, which follows the principle of the identical series. In order for knowledge to advance, however, an experimental setup also involves a series of procedural steps with minor differences, which follows the principle of the differential series. On *CSI* this dual seriality of experimental science is projected onto the individual episodes of a television series, and it also at the same time serves to expand the image over countless screens. *CSI* thus asserts nothing less than the idea that the expansion of the television image into the environment beyond television follows a serial logic.

## Multiplication and Finitude

*CSI* thus illustrates the characteristics of the new series of television 2.0 in two ways. First, it involves the classic style of an episodic series with a self-contained plot, but the seriality of the continuing series is incorporated into the individual episodes. Paradoxically enough, the infinitude of the serial thus arises from the finitude of the episode. This is why the limited time frame is also a narrative constant on *CSI*, as viewers are repeatedly told that the first hours are crucial to solving the crime.

The team basically only has twenty-four hours because after that it is extremely unlikely that the solution will be found. It is for this reason that there are two shifts on *CSI*—a day shift and a night shift—which again represent two series that are different yet indistinguishable (there is always artificial light in the laboratory, so the difference between day and night is negligible). The collaboration and competition between these two series may drive the plot and occasionally also give rise to asynchronies.

This new relationship between the finite and the infinite is an important feature of the new series. This is quite clear in cases like *24* or *Flash Forward*, in which the plot moves relentlessly toward a chronologically fixed time or calendared date when a catastrophe will occur. The idea of an external time limit as a condition for internal infinitude is particularly evident in *Flash Forward*, in which the investigators not only attempt to prevent the inexorably approaching catastrophe but also have a vision at the beginning of the series (at the same time as everyone else) that allows them to see the exact moment of the coming catastrophe. These visions are recalled in more and more extended detail as the series continues, and the flashbacks (which are also flash forwards) constantly intervene in the ongoing events. Here there is no longer an infinitely expanding middle with no beginning or end but rather an acutely temporal framing that constantly returns within itself, moving backward and forward and thus filling up the middle. As Daniela Wentz has shown, this unfathomable form of infinitude also dominates the episodic series *House, M.D.*, which in its form follows the simple episodic principle but in which the always absurd reasoning of the title character follows a pattern of recursion, iteration, and hence seriality that constitutes the core of each episode (Wentz 2017: 181–90). Seriality thus returns here in the episode, which contributes greatly to the absurdity of the series. The new principle of finitude is also inherent in *The Sopranos*, however, in which the plot strands of the frame narrative, which shows Tony Soprano at the psychologist, converge with the primary action as a story within the story. *Breaking Bad* also functions (at the beginning and again at the end) on the basis of finitude, as the main character Walter White has a fatal illness and must solve his problem before and ultimately through his death. In both of these cases, as well as in *House of Cards*, the difficulty consists in the fact that the anticipated endpoint is not actually the real endpoint, as the original time frame is exceeded (Walter White is cured, Underwood becomes president) and the series has to change its internal logic and find a new endpoint. As we will soon see, the earliest example of this new type of series, *Twin Peaks*, also had to solve this problem in the transition from the first to the second and third seasons.

Second, on *CSI* seriality is especially identified as an event that accompanies the internal proliferation of screen images and their movement across a wide variety of screens and screen technologies. *CSI* is paradigmatic in this regard, but the replication of images is also noticeable on *24* through the prominent use of split screens. The face of the running clock is also additionally set into the images of the four partial screens, which explicitly connects image multiplication with temporal limitation. What was described earlier as the expansion of images thus becomes the concentration of images (within images), which is again conceived as serialization. Series are the carriers, and seriality is the continuous form of the proliferation processes of screen images. The identification of seriality as an event is also evident on *Lie to Me*, in which laboratory sequences and diverse imaging or at least diagrammatic processes of visualization, such as from the voices or bodily functions of test subjects, play a crucial role. It is interesting that there are hardly any digital images on *Flash Forward*; instead, there is a relentless proliferation of completely analog sign carriers, such as pieces of paper, Polaroids, maps, and other photographic and diagrammatic documents and traces. They are combined on an enormous pinboard in the office of the investigators, and they are also connected to each other with red threads, which creates a sense of structure. As the series progresses, this structure becomes increasingly dense and complex. It is also interesting that the main character already foresaw the state of this pinboard on the day of the catastrophe in his vision. The pinboard is thus a serial signifier, which reflects the changing situation and the progress of the investigation, as well as a fixed signifier, which contains the solution to the mystery. It is also the serial signified to which the repeatedly inserted vision images refer, as these images remain constant while the pinboard always appears new and different (due to the changing relationship between the images in the vision and those in the real world).

Furthermore, on *CSI* the process of serialization is already conceived as the intersection and interaction of the involved (sub-)series of signifiers and signifieds, and it is even repeated and brought into the image (see Chapter 3 in this volume). A number of dual series arise outside of and embedded in the actual investigation of the images, as a second series of images is juxtaposed with and activated by the serial images generated from the laboratory processes (Fahle 2011). This second series consists of computer-generated and animated images of a speculative kind. These images do not appear on the screens of the investigators; rather, they are only visible to the television viewers. And they do not show what actually happened but rather only what could have happened during the crime, such as how the knife could have pierced the pot, how the bullet could have penetrated the brain, how the poison molecule could have interacted with other molecules in the stomach, or how the car could have grazed the corner of the house. In this respect they are subjunctive or hypothetical and thus fictional or imagined images (Hollendonner 2009: 33–5). These images are also taken from a purely imaginary perspective that is more or less physically impossible, such as from the interior of a heart or the path of an electron, as in a Whiteheadian world (Hollendonner 2015: 108–10; see also Whitehead 1978: 119–20). These internal and aerial images, whose persuasive power is no less than that of images from actual laboratories (such as the images used on scientific programs), are located in the imaginations or brains of the investigators, as they are visualizations of their hypotheses (Adelmann 2011: 326). As imagined, hypothetical, or fictional images, however, they are at least triggered—if not created—in the brains of the investigators by the technical-indexical images seen on their screens. This involves new chains of signifieds, as the transfer of materiality corresponds not to the transmission of electronic images but rather to the biologically and neurologically created imaginary images of the investigators. They are then externalized once again as signifiers and made visible to viewers through television. These images are thus created by other images, and the investigators effectively become image carriers.

## Second Series

An additional series runs counter to this second series that is juxtaposed with the laboratory images. As Oliver Fahle and Deborah Jermyn demonstrate, there is also another series of images that show the pale and motionless corpses of the victims laid out on the metal surfaces of the morgue (Fahle 2011; Jermyn 2007: 75). These images do not reveal any movement or convey any knowledge. They are not connected to the images of other series but rather form their own sequences with their own structures. They constitute a chain of constant signifieds—namely, of the bodies whose deaths the episodes are about. In contrast, the animated hypothetical images of the possible progression of events are the changing signifiers that illustrate the various ways in which these bodies could have died. The second chain—that of the dead bodies as the last signifieds of the investigation—is oriented not toward knowledge but rather toward affect and affixation, respect and compassion. They thus prevent the bodies from being visualized as pure objects of research and instead grant them their own inactive yet still very present mode of existence.

*CSI* even integrates these different series—that is, the constant series that constitutes the chain of signifieds and the variable series that constitutes the chain of signifiers—in explicit images that once again form their own series. This happens when two image sequences are juxtaposed on the screens of the investigators and on the viewers' screens, such as when the investigators search for a fingerprint or a projectile in a database. The trace (the fingerprint or the projectile) remains constant on one half of the screen, while the sequence of possible perpetrators or gun owners passes rapidly on the other half. If there is no match, then the series moves on to the next portrait. In other words, the trace (the signifier) remains unchanged while the (potentially) corresponding person (the signified) keeps changing, which means that the constant series shifts to the side of the signifiers while the variable series shifts to that of the signifieds. Despite their persistent differences, therefore, signifieds and signifiers become indistinguishable and coalescent. They are literally adjacent to one another on the same level—namely, that of the screen.

Furthermore, the photographs of suspects are superimposed over one another in quick succession so that they appear like a film. This sequence results not in a chain but rather in a cross-section of individual faces that recalls Francis Galton's experiments with composite photography, in which the images of faces were superimposed to form an average face, out of which the main identity-establishing features of a particular family, for instance, would emerge. These experiments inspired Ludwig Wittgenstein's concept of "family resemblance," according to which resemblance involves not consistent and divergent features but rather the proliferation and non-proliferation of certain features from one family member to another in long serial configurations (Wittgenstein 1999: 30$^e$–6$^e$). And what is true for family members is also true, according to Wittgenstein, for concepts and conceptual identities in general. We will come back to this in more detail, but for now it will suffice to note that the logic of family resemblance through serialization also occurs on *CSI* through the comparison between the static image on one half of the screen and the rapid sequence on the other half. This sequence suddenly freezes when a successful "match" is found, and it is not uncommon for the portrait to change its color or begin to blink in order to mark the event of a coincidence as well as the individual matching features. These static images can occur in whole series, and they thus punctuate the progress of knowledge through their own series of events. The individual image here does not prove anything at all; rather, it is only the sequence of images that gives the individual image its specific, sudden, and eventful character. The non-recurring once again does not exist (Anders 1956: 180–1).

Every single episode of *CSI* thus unfolds as a fluid, time-based, and time-generating network of different serialization processes. The episodes are also entirely self-contained, like those of a classic episodic series, as they are not connected to each other through references to prior events or continuing plotlines (apart from a few double episodes). However, they themselves emerge from the interaction between numerous converging and diverging, repetitive and differential serializations, such as those of the signifiers and the signifieds, which are indistinguishable from one another.

The new series of television 2.0 was established at around the turn of the century, but *Twin Peaks* already functioned as a groundbreaking precursor to the new series in the mid-1990s. This series is particularly relevant not only because it was created by one of the most prominent postmodern filmmakers, David Lynch, but also because it introduced the renegotiation between finitude and infinitude that we already encountered in *CSI*. There were obviously a number of earlier series that did not continue indefinitely but instead had a clear ending, such as *The Fugitive*, the remarkable early-evening German series *Percy Stuart*, and the globally successful Brazilian *telenovelas*, but *Twin Peaks* is different. There is a narrative goal—namely, the solving of the murder of Laura Palmer—and the individual episodes also undeniably build on one another and come after one another in time, unlike those of *The Fugitive* and *Percy Stuart*. With regard to the solving of the crime, however, there is no progress from one episode to the next. The linearity of time appears to be kept in an incredibly decelerated, suspended, and uncanny simultaneity in which every advance in the investigation becomes a circle or a dead end. Everything refers to everything else, and everything begins to become different yet indistinguishable from everything else. *Twin Peaks* thus thematizes the paradoxes and instabilities that constitute the logic of seriality itself (according to Deleuze, all series are derived from the *regressus ad infinitum* or infinite regress). This particularly applies to the second season, as the series reached its conclusion with the solution to the murder of Laura Palmer at the end of the first season (even though the evil force embodied in the form of Bob moved on). Due to its success, though, new seasons were drafted, and it became necessary to define a new narrative goal. This occurs gradually within the series itself, and this is precisely what the chess game between Agent Cooper and Windom Earle is actually about. The goal finally emerges shortly before the end of the third season, although it always already existed in advance: Cooper changes sides, and everything can start over again.

## Resemblance 1: Epistemology

If the new series is characterized by the coalescence and indistinguishability of the two series through which it emerges, then *Twin Peaks* gives it a describable epistemic and aesthetic form—namely, that of resemblance. Its description can be oriented toward Michel Foucault, whose historical epistemology identifies an order of knowledge that he dates between the fifteenth and seventeenth centuries, when the world was organized by the imagination of resemblance (Foucault 2002: 19–50). According to Foucault, there were four primary relations of resemblance that were thought to hold the world together in the knowledge of this period, and all of these relations can be seen to be at work in *Twin Peaks*. The first is *convenientia* or convenience, which refers to the joint appearance or emergence of two different things or events at the same location (Foucault 2002: 20). The resemblance here is based on the fact that the location of a thing or event is relevant, as locations impress their own qualities onto the things or events that are situated there. All of the things at a particular location thus share these qualities and resemble each other as well as the location itself. They can assimilate one another under the influence of the location, or they can emerge together since they are similar to each other and to the place anyway (Foucault 2002: 21). This is precisely what occurs on *Twin Peaks*, as the characters always appear in pairs at the same locations, such as Bob and Mike or the room service waiter and the giant.

The second relation of resemblance is *aemulatio* or emulation, which refers to the doubling or mirroring of a thing at another location in space or the recurrence of an event in time (Foucault 2002: 21ff.). It plays a dominant role on *Twin Peaks*, as there are numerous uncanny relations of reflection and doubling. This includes pairs of characters, such as Laura and her reincarnation Maddy, Annie as Caroline's revenant, the two Coopers, and the character of Bob, who is only visible in mirrors (a reversal of the vampire tradition). It also includes locations like the black-and-white lodges or the twin peaks above the city (which gives the series its title). There are also images that reflect relations of emulation, such as the two R's in the Double R Dinner and especially *Invitation to Love*, the series within the series that doubles and mirrors *Twin Peaks* itself. For example, the two sisters on *Invitation to Love* reflect the dual character of Laura and Maddy, and when a character is murdered on television (within the diegesis) Leo is also shot down. Events also mirror one another, such as Laura's death and Maddy's death. It is interesting that the Latin word *aemulatio* also means jealousy, which suggests that the binary relation of mirroring gives rise to a triangular relation. The plot features jealousy and love triangles, which appear in entire series of their own and which can also intersect.

The third relation of resemblance is *analogia* or analogy (Foucault 2002: 23-6). We already encountered this form in another context—namely, in the sense of Descola's analogistic, constellative ontography of the screen. It is based not on things or events but rather on the structure, proportion, rhythm, and function of their arrangements—that is, their orderings and the relations they arrange in a particular context. For example, murders are connected through an analogy of the circumstances of the crimes, such as the murders of Teresa Banks and Laura Palmer or the vagrant and Caroline. There is also an analogy between the chess game and the struggle between Cooper and Earle, and the two series *Twin Peaks* and *Invitation to Love* are connected through analogy—namely, through the rhythm of broadcasting and the viewing arrangement of television.

The fourth and final relation of resemblance is *sympathia* or sympathy, which refers to the force of attraction that allows the things it connects to adapt to one another (Foucault 2002: 26ff.). Sympathy enables all forms of convergence and thus all movement in the universe, and its effects extend over any distance, such as that between the sun and sunflowers. Agent Cooper's Tibetan bottle experiment is a dramatic case of sympathy, as he throws stones at bottles that represent various suspects while the deputy sheriff concentrates on the person concerned and a suspicion is justified when a bottle is smashed (this experiment is ultimately successful, as Leo Johnson becomes the focus of the investigation and is exposed as a criminal). Cooper's ability to read body language is also based on sympathy. Evil is particularly attractive, and sympathy can only be controlled and limited by its counterforce, which is repulsion or antipathy.

Each of these resemblances can and will replace or represent another, as they are interrelated (Foucault 2002: 28–33). They even form entire series so that one resemblance can serve as a key to and a recognition of another. According to Foucault, they are signatures of one another (Foucault 2002: 28f.). Every visible resemblance can point to an invisible resemblance lying behind it, and it can thus become a signifier for another resemblance, which then assumes the position of the signified. Both resemblances glide over and under one another, to take up Deleuze's formulation. Knowledge and that which is known become intertwined elements of the same order, which makes them indistinguishable. The question as to whether knowledge represents or produces the relations between things or events—that is, whether resemblance is ontically or epistemically significant—thus has no foundation (it obviously involves an ontographic operation that records and at the same time generates beings). The various types of resemblance are thus connected not to other resemblances of the same type (self-referentially) but rather to resemblances of other types: every relation of resemblance encodes another relation of another type. This also happens on *Twin Peaks*. The letters pulled from under the fingernails of the dead stand via convenience for the analogy of the crimes and at the same time via emulation for the names of the murderer. The resemblance of sympathy between the stone and the bottle in the Tibetan bottle experiment signals the resemblance of convenience between Leo Johnson's crime and the murder of Laura Palmer. Resemblances themselves are also based on resemblance. The metaphor of the smiling bag is also simultaneously a resemblance of convenience that refers to Jacques Renault's corpse and a resemblance of emulation that refers to Bob. At the same time, this chain also constitutes a resemblance of analogy of the sympathy between Cooper and the giant.

But the series of resemblances on *Twin Peaks* already exceeds the limits of just this series and the television screen on which it is shown. After entire seasons of television shows began to be sold on DVD in the 1990s, complementing or following their broadcast, the series became the preferred object of a form of television use that went beyond and was detached from television itself. This new form of television use was called "binging," as it involved viewing entire seasons over a long night or a weekend as a party-like event. With *Twin Peaks*, the computer network was added. There were still no social networks or digital platforms in 1995, but speculation concerning the progress of the plot, the individual parts of the mystery, and especially the endlessly expanding referential chains, which often led deep into film and television history, was conducted over email in a collective mailbox with sometimes as many as 20,000 participants. With the continued development of digital platforms and second screens, this first approach to the proliferation of the series then led within a decade to *transmedia storytelling*, in which a series extends beyond television or is supplemented with additional discussions and other contributions through different media (Jenkins 2006; Branch and Phillips 2019; Denson and Mayer 2012; see also Beil et al. 2016). The accumulation of narratives and information that branch out from the series also allows viewers to participate, as they can place additional content about the content of the series, which results in *user-generated content*. The series *Lost* highlights this development, as it was a mystery series that expanded significantly from the television screen to numerous second screens in the collective mediasphere (Beil, Schwaab, and Wentz 2017). It also gave rise to *Lostpedia*—a digital encyclopedia that ordered and unfolded the obviously completely fantastic knowledge concerning the world of the series. Like *Wikipedia*, *Lostpedia* was also based on open participation, and it thus constituted a form of *user-generated content*.

## Resemblance 2: Family Resemblance

Besides the precursor series *Twin Peaks*, the characteristics of the new series can also be described as a change in the regime of serial resemblance. This applies once again to the expansion of television over a multitude of screens as well as to the dynamic of the television series itself as the coalescence and indistinguishability of two series—that is, a constant series and a variable series or a series of signifiers and a series of signifieds. This is clear when we shift from the concept of resemblance in Foucault's historical epistemology to another version of the phenomenon of resemblance and its dynamic— namely, Wittgenstein's concept of *family resemblance* (Wittgenstein 1999: 1$^e$– 33$^e$, here: 30$^e$–3$^e$; see also Gründler 2008: 79–90; Schulte 1992: 150f.; Engell 2016).

Wittgenstein does not explicitly discuss the concept of the series; however, the idea of family resemblance, which he developed in the context of his *Philosophical Investigations*, describes the phenomenon of serialization. He was initially interested in the insufficiently precise distinctions and definitions of concepts. It is impossible to produce a complete and conclusive list of the features that define something as a game, for example, as there is no universally valid definition of what constitutes a game. There are always games that do not exhibit one or more of these features but are still games, and there are other things that possess all of these features but do not fall under the concept of games. It is even possible that two different games could share none of the same features with one another, yet they could nevertheless both be counted equally as games. Among each other, games are only related by resemblances. As in a family, games are held together not by a strictly defined concept but rather by a "complicated network of similarities overlapping and criss-crossing: sometimes overall similarities, sometimes similarities of detail" (Wittgenstein 1999: 32$^e$). And what applies to games also applies to colors, numbers, pages, or chairs—that is, to all concepts. However, this imprecision is not a disadvantage; rather, it is a condition for both the dynamism and stability of concepts, much like (interestingly) blurriness in photography.

The model of the series is already encountered here. In his thoughts on genre as medium as opposed to cycle, Stanley Cavell initially conceived of genre in the same way that Wittgenstein conceived of family. As a cycle, a genre would have a fixed set of attributes, but it would remain incapable of developing. As a medium, a genre would arise as a flexible network of relations of conformance and deviation. Cavell also applied these ideas to the television series, which was always cyclical, controlled by characters, and thus sterile. As we saw earlier, this was already an insufficient definition of early television series, which could unfold as a medium in Cavell's sense. The television series can also be understood with Wittgenstein as a complex network of overlapping and intersecting resemblances. This will become clearer when we observe the four main characteristics of family resemblance (Gabriel 1980).

First, resemblance is an aesthetic category that is dependent on (visual) perception (*Anschauung*). Resemblance must be observed and attributed, whether externally or internally. Second, the attribution of resemblance always involves three elements or members of a family or series. In other words, resemblance always requires three poles or family members— namely, the two elements that resemble one another and the aspect in which they resemble one another, which in the case of family resemblance must be performed by a third element. Two episodes alone do not constitute a series. Only the addition of a third episode provides the template for the resemblance, as it shows that each of the two episodes share features with one another that do not appear in a third. The third episode can also, conversely, share different features with one of the other two episodes, which the other two episodes do not share with each other. A third episode can always arise between two episodes (unlike nonserial sequences), which results in the possibility of a series that acts as an infinitely expanding middle with no beginning or end, like the soap opera. Only the emergence of a third episode between two other episodes ensures the transition between them and thus constitutes the aspect through which they resemble one another. Third, this process ensures a temporal dynamic, as a third family member always arises between two other family members, and this third produces the resemblance between the other two precisely like the episodes of a television series. Every episode is assigned a place in a sequence (Gabriel 1980; see also Goeres 2000: 272ff.). Lastly, individual family members (or series episodes) no longer have any features in common when they are far enough away from one another, as all of the earlier features were lost in the developmental process. They still share something with their predecessors (and successors), but it is not necessarily the same. Essential or recurring and added or mutable properties thus become indistinguishable.

The characters in television series provide an obvious example of this. The characters in every kind of series can change, whether it is an episodic, continuing, or new series, and this often leads to complications, such as the disappearance and return of Bobby Ewing on *Dallas*, which caused enormous dramaturgical problems. However, these changes can also be integrated into the series itself, as in the case of *Mission: Impossible*, each episode of which began with a more or less arbitrary selection of characters. The replacement of the entire cast can also occur gradually, such as on a soap opera like *Guiding Light* (probably the queen of the genre), where none of the characters from the beginning were present any longer at the end. The main characters were also replaced on *CSI*, entirely in the sense of family resemblance, as there were episodes in which characters could say goodbye or be welcomed. This also applies to sets and settings or types of events. A series can switch from structural elements like implicit or explicit finitude to structural infinitude, which is the case with *Twin Peaks*, *Breaking Bad*, and other series. Series involve the passing on and elimination of features rather than their continued existence, which makes them plastic and capable of development. This also explains the crucial function of the cliffhanger, which thematizes the possible passing on and non-passing on of a string of events. More precisely, the cliffhanger simultaneously describes and writes the processuality of the series itself as a dynamic process of family resemblance (Fröhlich 2015; see also Engell 2016: 25f.). If the cliffhanger is implemented as a freeze frame, then it also negotiates the inability to distinguish the finitude of the episode or series from its infinitude.

## Resemblance and Its Medium

All of this applies to seriality in general, as series always involve the handing down and non-handing down of features, elements, and properties; conversely, Wittgenstein's families always form series or are arranged serially. These findings can also be easily connected to Cavell's observations on genre: again like experiments, series are continued negotiations and tests of what exactly constitutes each series—namely, this specific continued and interminable (though not actually infinite) negotiation and testing (Wentz 2017: 174–9; Engell 2009; see also Lyotard 2003, 2012; on Lyotard's critical reading of Wittgenstein, see also Goeres 2000: 296). Against this background, two profound changes arise for the new series of television 2.0. The first change is temporal. We have already seen earlier that many new series have a time limit that leads to a kind of internal infinitude or iterability, which is related to the technique of splitting and dividing the image that characterizes the liquid-crystal screen. The production of resemblance does not have to proceed in an ordered line; rather, it can also become detached from this line and proceed in loops or lateral movements. This means that in the new series the linear process of family resemblance becomes a winding, looping, and thus two-dimensional arrangement. The processes also multiply, as there is no longer only one two-dimensional transmission from episode to episode but rather more (and there tend to be many more). All of these two-dimensional processes now lie on top of each other like transparencies, which results in a new kind of family resemblance that arises or shines through them.

Ulrich Richtmeyer's media-philosophical reading of Wittgenstein pointed out that something similar can already be found in Wittgenstein's work, as his concept of family resemblance was inspired by his experiments with so-called "average" or "composite" photography (Richtmeyer 2009), following Francis Galton. Galton overlaid standardized photographs of numerous people's faces as diapositives, which resulted in an image of common facial features or the "average face." These features did not recur in every face (as is the case with family resemblance), and there could have even been images in the stack that did not match any of them. However, they gave rise to a common face that above all changed whenever one or more images were removed from the stack and replaced with others. Galton thus attempted to capture the resemblances between the members of a family, and Wittgenstein tested this method himself using photographic images of the faces of the members of his own family, as he was clearly fascinated by genealogical questions. This observation not only shows convincingly that Wittgenstein's idea of family resemblance was derived from a visual impression as well as the operation of a technical medium—namely, composite photography. It also has far-reaching consequences, which are now related to the new series of television 2.0 as a process of resemblance. The positions of the individual photographs in Galton and Wittgenstein's stacks of transparencies do not play an important role, as the order of the images is irrelevant to the result. The transfer of features is discontinuous, as it is possible for resemblances to emerge between the face of a younger family member added later to the top of the stack and that of an older family member added earlier to the bottom of the stack. Resemblance moves not only forward but also backward or even transverse to the linear arrangement of time.

This is precisely what happens on the new series of television 2.0, although it happens under different technical conditions than Galton's composite photography. We have already noted the multiplication of images within the episodes of a series as well as the transparency-like arrangement of the images on liquid-crystal screens. The images are not really transparent, but they nevertheless show that other images are also present, whether through the multiple screens within the image (as on *CSI*) or through the emergence of overlaid frames, as on news broadcasts or computer screens with graphical user interfaces. An image can come forward and fill the screen, be obscured or pushed back, and then withdraw again at any time. Earlier episodes can accordingly be pulled forward by later episodes, reread, and then reinserted back into the series once again. This happens in a very crude way with the previously mentioned return of Bobby Ewing on *Dallas*, but it is the driving principle of serialization on *Twin Peaks*. Narrative progress on *House, M.D.* is also characterized by the overriding of earlier assumptions within the same episode, and on *Flash Forward* the same images are repeatedly pulled forward and surrounded by new images. The images on *Homeland* (such as surveillance images) are also constantly compared and related to other images from the stack; new images can be pulled forward at any time, which changes everything, and a large part of the plot consists precisely in these image operations. This also extends to the characters who can change to the other side of bipolarity, corruption, or terrorism at any time and then change back again, just as the images of the series are constantly being reconfigured.

Christoph Menke has shown that Walter White's (double) transformation on *Breaking Bad* is particularly connected to the finitude of the series (which manifests in two ways, as he initially faces certain death by cancer and at the end, when he has long been cured, he eventually dies in a gunfight like a proper criminal) (Menke 2016). According to Menke, White's constantly changing identity once again reflects the logic of seriality itself (for us, the logic of the new series of television 2.0) as a double discontinuity, as White breaks a habit—that is, seriality—and the series arises only from this rupture. In other words, the discontinuous and mutable relations between serial images generate family resemblances that constitute the series itself. This can also relate to the possible series within the series (*Twin Peaks*, *The Sopranos*) and even television within the series. Menke has also shown that shots of drugs and money on *Breaking Bad* provide the crucial motivation for White—that is, they lend dynamism to the series from the background (Menke 2016: 6–8). The same applies to a certain extent to *Mad Men*, be that in the rebroadcasting and rereading of earlier television recordings (such as Kennedy's assassination) or the back story (of the protagonist's changing identity). The new series of television 2.0 expands not only forward and backward from the middle, like the soap opera, but also in dynamic loops that can intervene, conclude, or provide new beginnings for the existing narratives at any time. Flashbacks, repetitions, and decelerations occur in and between the episodes (which is particularly evident on *Breaking Bad*), making the entire narrative of the series inherently unreliable: at any time everything (i.e., every individual point in the now two-dimensional temporal arrangement) can not only become different but even be shown to have always already been different. This also includes the paradox of the theater, which is a variant of the paradox of the liar who tells the truth when he lies. Frank Underwood repeatedly demonstrates this by gazing directly into the camera on *House of Cards*: within the diegetic world he is only performing the role of a politician, just as he performs politics, and politics is thus shown to be nothing more than a performance. When he winks at the viewer, the series also reveals itself as a stack of transparent images that shine through one another.

## Qualities without Objects

With the two-dimensional expansion of time, the series as cycle becomes indistinguishable from the series as medium (in Cavell's sense). In his analysis of *Breaking Bad*, for example, Menke describes how the serial narrative as an episodic habit (i.e., cycle) turns into plasticity (Menke 2016: 10f.). This now occurs between and within the episodes not once or twice but rather repeatedly. This dynamic is entirely independent of the protagonist, such as the blatant example of the episode filmed from the perspective of a fly, which interrupts the flow of the narrative. White is not the cause but rather the product of the plasticity of the series. Insofar as chemistry is the practice of transforming substances, *Breaking Bad* can thus be understood as a chemical series. Although it involves an asymptotically terminable combinatorics of a finite number of available transparencies, as the series has an endpoint (in other examples, like *House, M.D.*, the case of the cycle can resemble or even be mistaken for the classic case), there is nevertheless an interminable and unforeseeable dynamic of appearing and disappearing resemblances, as with Wittgenstein. This is also related to the second way in which the new series of television 2.0 (read as a process of family resemblance following Wittgenstein) represents a highly remarkable and effective shift. What was negotiated and tested in earlier series was the passing on and non-passing on of features (such as characters, plots, and settings), which produced the identity of the series itself (in Wittgenstein's terms, the family, such as the family of games, or the concept, such as the concept of a game). Now, however, this process, which drives the series and to which it owes its existence, moves to a deeper level, as it affects no longer (only) the identity of the series but rather that of the features themselves. What is negotiated is no longer the respective episode at the level of its constituent elements but rather the family resemblances between the elements themselves, such as what constitutes a character, relationship, setting, crime, or object. Each of these elements is also not identical but rather similar to itself and the others. This is clearly shown on *Mad Men* in relation to objects, as nearly every episode negotiates the identity—or, more precisely, the plasticity, malleability, and transformability—of an object to be advertised, such as a cigarette, slide projector, or brassiere.

The principle on which this functions can be clarified by returning once again to composite photography, which is the medial practice on which the concept of family resemblance is based. It is impossible to determine in advance what will or will not emerge as a common or defining feature in the "average face" that appears in composite photographs. It is not certain whether the prominent features will be light or dark; whether they will be planes, lines, or configurations; or whether they will only appear in the light of photography (like shadows) or coincide with features like eyebrows or the curved line of the lips. The features that can constitute a face must first expose themselves in the truest sense of the word. The qualities and potentials of the medium (such as the ability of photography to reproduce something in a brighter or darker, sharper or fuzzier way) are thus inextricably interfused with those of the face (such as the ability of certain features to reflect light in striking ways), and the same is true for the intertwining of attributions and facts. What is tested in the new series of television 2.0 is what constitutes a feature, person, location, or plot in a constantly changing context, from which the progressive form of the series is derived. Characters like Walter White, Carrie Mathison, Claire and Frank Underwood, Tony Soprano, and even already Ally McBeal not only have serial identities, which are open to redefinition and constantly subject to renegotiation, but also—at best—resemble themselves, as they are characteristically plastic and undergo transformational processes (unlike earlier heroes, who learn something or develop) to which they also subject everything else, or vice versa. Locations like Albuquerque, Washington, Boston, Berlin, and Bagdad as well as laboratories and offices or props and scenery are also constantly reconfigured as serial images. The ontography of analogistic and discontinuous configurations and reconfigurations, which we noted earlier as a feature of the liquid-crystal screen, thus returns here at the level of diegetic and semantic functions.

## Resemblance 3: Icon and Diagram

In addition to Foucault's notion of epistemic resemblance, which we discussed using the example of *Twin Peaks*, and Wittgenstein's notion family resemblance, which we discussed above all using the example of *Breaking Bad*, there is yet a third operational form of resemblance in the new series of television 2.0, which involves *iconicity* (see Wentz 2017: 47–63). This is a concept borrowed from Charles Sanders Peirce's theory of semiotics, and it refers to signs that are connected to the objects that they represent through resemblance (unlike indexicality, in which the connection is a causal relation, such as traces, or symbolicity, in which the connection is based solely on agreement, habit, or regularity, such as verbal language). Iconic signs function in that they identify their own qualities as those of the objects to which they refer, such as color, form, sound, texture, material, weight, size, or duration (for time-based images) (see Wentz 2017: 50). This generally applies to images, and Peirce thus insists that it is irrelevant whether the represented objects actually "exist." For example, iconic signs can also refer to fictional or imaginary objects, which do not exist outside of their representations and whose state of being is always already ontographic to some extent (even though the movement of the ongoing recording must be included for a fully developed ontography). A television image is also iconic insofar as it is an image, and a television series is a complex iconic sign if it is read as a representation of characters, events, and objects.

However, the switch image is not only—and possibly not primarily—an image in this sense. First, it is from the beginning more of a haptic image than an optical image, and its switchability operates through the touching of buttons. Second, it itself became a switch following the transition to the liquid-crystal screen. The main characteristic of the switch image is thus its operativity rather than its visual resemblance to the objects it displays or creates. However, iconicity is still the prominent semiotic mark of switch images. In addition to images, for example, Peirce also identifies a second particularly important type of iconic sign, which is that of the *diagram* (Wentz 2017: 50f.). Diagrams are of an iconic nature, but they resemble neither objects nor their qualities (in the most general sense as objects of representation and thus also characters); rather, they represent and produce relations between objects and between qualities. As iconic signs, they are also self-referential, like images, as they show all of the relations that they themselves represent or produce, and this is precisely what comprises their resemblance. Moreover, according to Peirce, diagrams contain everything needed to understand them, and they are thus self-explanatory.

Hence, the basic liquid-crystal screen can already be read as a diagram for various reasons. First, as we have seen, it is based on the configuration or constellation of image points—that is, of switches and their positions—and therein lies its ontographic analogism. As diagrams, switch images are based "on a distribution of points and their relations to one another, on arrangements, accumulations, directions, or metric relations and the like [. . .] which work by means of contrasts, distances, omissions, etc." (Heßler and Mersch 2009: 33). The switch image is thus, if anything, an image not of objects but rather of relations. Second, it produces these relations by and in itself, and in this sense the switch image is operative and self-referential as a diagram. Third, however, the diagrams of the switch image constantly change with their changing switch positions. They are time-based, time-critical, and by no means purely two-dimensional (or spatial) arrangements. They represent and produce relations not only in space but also in time, such as relations of succession, synchronicity, simultaneity, or parallelism in ongoing processes. In addition to relations of resemblance, this is precisely an essential aspect of the diagram for Peirce, as diagrams are changeable. On the one hand, they are very stable, such as maps, plans, design drawings, or statistical diagrams, and we already used this ability of liquid-crystal images to discuss ontograms (instead of ontographies). On the other hand, however, diagrams function in time—namely, through their implementation, whether it involves recording (*Aufzeichnen*) or analyzing (*Nachzeichnen*). For Peirce, diagrams are not only representations but also manipulations or modifications of relations. They not only show established facts, insights, or ideas, but also embody thought processes, through which insights and knowledge are first generated. They visualize thought processes at work in that they themselves produce these processes. This is precisely how they are original and generative as iconic signs, according to Peirce, as they produce new insights and new knowledge through the manipulation or experimentation that they themselves enable and perform (Stjernfelt 2007: 90).

## Serial Ontogrammatics

This second, diagrammatic variant of iconicity now appears in the new series of television 2.0 on a macroscopic scale. Signs were already serial for Peirce, as every sign necessarily produces another sign, which he calls the interpretant, but we are particularly concerned here with diagrams. As Daniela Wentz has extensively shown, many of the new series are characterized by the emergence of numerous diagrams within the series images. Maps and floorplans (on *Lost*), white board sketches (*House, M.D., Numb3rs*), and pinboards (*Flash Forward*) often play an important role, and on *Sherlock* the screens of computers and mobile phones are incorporated into the images as diagrams that are performed as diagrammatic operations through the addition of text and graphic elements, such as highlighting, lines, or arrows, that embody Sherlock Holmes' thought processes. We have already discussed the diagrams on the screens of the investigators on *CSI*. Photo walls, whiteboards, and pinboards appear in nearly all detective series, and they often fill the image. They show in a paradigmatic way how diagrams resemble relations, as the relationships between people, clues, locations, and so on are represented by lines, arrows, and groupings. These relations are also frequently represented as mere hypotheses (irrespective of their relationship to the truth and reality), and they can thus always be rearranged to form new variants.

In recent years these walls have been increasingly made of glass, and sometimes the glass even has a grid. The wall thus becomes a diagram not only of each individual case but also of the screen itself or even of the episode or the series as a whole. The famous pinboard on *Flash Forward* is a special case that actually accompanies, documents, and guides the investigation, as it already contains the final outcome in the main character's vision of the future and must only be completed. In other words, everything needed to understand the mystery—that is, the course of the entire series—is already contained in this diagram, including what is needed to understand the diagram. This is what makes the diagram an ontogram, as everything that happens on *Flash Forward* becomes a product of the diagram, including the diagram itself and its deciphering. The world is an extension or continuation of the diagram by other means, as the mere diagram extends into three-dimensional space (within the diegesis) and merges with the world. This draws attention to other examples, such as the famous "top shots" produced by aerial cameras looking down at large cities that resemble bustling and moving city maps, as in numerous *Law and Order* series. Oliver Fahle has explicitly pointed to the staging of the city as a game plan or playing field, like the diagram of a board game, which is also an example of the operativity of a diagram (Fahle 2007, 2010). This also applies to the game of chess on *Twin Peaks*. And lastly, the switch image itself is diagrammatic: on *24*, for example, the screen is divided into four segments (plus a clock), the arrangement of which denotes as well as produces the relation of simultaneity.

The city as an overflown and moving map, the constantly reconfigured pinboard, the time-based split screen, and the writing of text over the image are not only intra-diegetic diagrams that embody and convey the characters' thoughts or inferences; rather, they are iconic and at the same time dynamic (i.e., serial) signs that resemble something they themselves always also are and produce (which was part of Peirce's definition of the diagram). They thus constitute serial ontograms—that is, ontograms of the seriality of the series itself and of television in general, insofar as seriality is the core of televisual processes. What emerges in the diagrams of the series is what we, following Deleuze, identified at the beginning of the chapter as the distinguishing mark of this new type of series: the two (sub-)series that produce them— that of change and rupture and that of stability and analogy—become indistinguishable. The diagrams (or ontograms) of the series are their game plans, as they represent the playgrounds as well as the rules of the games, both stable and distinct, and the course of play, which is unstable and constantly changing. Yet these aspects resemble one another to such a degree that it is impossible to know if a diagram (such as the pinboard on *Flash Forward*, the whiteboard on *House, M.D.*, the street grid of Manhattan on *Criminal Intent*, or the painting in Cooper's office on *Mad Men*) functions in the series of conditions or signifieds or in the series of moves or signifiers. In the course of the series, it folds back on itself and revises its plans, rules, and fields of play, and this process constitutes the course of the series itself. In this respect, the new series of television 2.0 also remains true to television's fundamental temporal regime—namely, the principle of simultaneity and synchronicity established by live television. Everything occurs as it is shown—or rather viewers watch time itself as it arises from the interaction between the series.

## Sitcom

The switch image can then even profit from unraveling the moebius-like paradox of such seriality at specially designated locations, as there are also serial formats that do not participate in any of this but instead remain virtually unchanged and resistant to renewal (see Schwaab 2008; Beil et al. 2016: 149–96). They stoically implement an earlier type of classic seriality in its simplest form—that is, the episodic series—without any experimentation and with an anachronistically small investment in imaging technologies. They do not feature images within the image, split screens, flashbacks or flash forwards, or digital or real diagrammatics. Everything is performed on a stage, as in the live television series of the early 1950s, and the cutting mostly operates according to the three-camera principle. The archaic series forms of television 1.0 are thus not completely gone; rather, they still persist on television 2.0. And they persist not only in the form of expanded reruns (or media libraries), through which older series can be watched again and again; rather, they also continue to be produced with tremendous success.

This applies above all (but not only) to the format of the sitcom, as represented by *Friends, The Big Bang Theory, Two and a Half Men, How I Met Your Mother, It's Always Sunny in Philadelphia, Grace and Frankie*, and others. Apart from their adjustments to the changing aesthetics of everyday life and to the multiplicity of life forms, they structurally continue what *I Love Lucy* began in the 1950s, as the clear separation between stasis and progress remains unchanged. They usually even still play the same laugh track, which suggests the presence of a real audience and allows viewers to share interpassively in the simulated pleasure of others (Pfaller 2000, 2008). In doing so, the sitcom serves as the outside of the new seriality of television within television. The clear-cut distinction between standstill, on the one hand, and advance, on the other hand, continues to prevail here unaltered. This is not only a form of constancy that perpetuates (inter) passive reception; rather, the new environment, which is now dominated by other forms of seriality, nonetheless contains the entire development of the series and all of its earlier forms in all of their ramifications, which can be switched into, next to, or over one another. They thus once again negotiate their relations (i.e., their differences and analogies) by means of family resemblance through always new (and serial) superimpositions. Depending on their arrangement, they may reveal common traits that ultimately constitute the series itself.

# Note

1  Television series often split and divide into such spin-offs, such as *Dallas* and *Knots Landing* or *Law and Order, Law and Order: Los Angeles, Law and Order: Criminal Intent*, and *Law and Order: Special Victims Unit*.

# References

Adelmann, Ralf. 2011. "Mars-Viskurse. De- und Rekontextualisierungen von wissenschaftlichen Bildern." In: *Blickregime und Dispositive audiovisueller Medien*, ed. by Nadja Elia-Borer, Simon Sieber, and Georg Cristoph Tholen, pp. 311–35. Bielefeld: Transcript.

Allen, Michael, ed. 2007. *Reading CSI: Crime TV under the Microscope*. New York: Tauris.

Anders, Günther. 1956. *Die Antiquiertheit des Menschen, vol. 1: Über die Seele im Zeitalter der zweiten industriellen Revolution*. München: Beck.

Beil, Benjamin, Lorenz Engell, Dominik Maeder, Jensch Schröter, Herbert Schwaab, and Daniela Wentz 2016. *Die Fernsehserie als Agent des Wandels*. Münster: LIT.

Beil, Benjamin, Herbert Schwab, and Daniela Wentz, eds. 2017. *LOST in Media*. Münster: LIT.

Branch, Frank, and Rebekah Phillips. 2019. "An Ontological Approach to Transmedia Worlds." In: *The Routledge Companion to Transmedia Studies*, ed. by Matthew Freeman, and Renira Rampazzo Gambarato, pp. 383–91. New York: Routledge.

Deleuze, Gilles. 2004. *The Logic of Sense*. London, New York: Continuum.

Denson, Shane, and Ruth Mayer. 2012. "Bildstörung. Serielle Figuren und der Fernseher." *Zeitschrift für Medienwissenschaft* 7: 90–102.

Engell, Lorenz. 2009. "Fernsehen mit Unbekannten. Überlegungen zur experimentellen Television." In: *Fernsehexperimente. Stationen eines Mediums*, ed. by Michael Grisko, and Stefan Münker, pp. 15–46. Berlin: Kadmos.

Engell, Lorenz. 2016. "Die Kunst des Fernsehens. Ludwig Wittgensteins 'Familienähnlichkeit' und die Medienästhetik der Fernsehserie." In: *Kunst/Fernsehen*, ed. by Klaus Krüger, Christian Hammes, and Matthias Weiß, pp. 19–38. Paderborn: Wilhelm Fink.

Engell, Lorenz. 2019. "On Series." In: Lorenz Engell. *Thinking Through Television*, pp. 189–200. Amsterdam: Amsterdam University Press.

Englert, Carina, and Jo Reichertz, eds. 2016. *CSI. Rechtsmedizin. Mitternachtsforensik*. Wiesbaden: Springer.

Fahle, Oliver. 2007. "Die Stadt als Spielfeld. Raumästhetik in Film und Computerspiel?." In: *Spielformen im Spielfilm. Zur Medienmorphologie des Kinos nach der Postmoderne*, ed. by Rainer Leschke, and Jochen Venus, pp. 225–38. Bielefeld: Transcript.

Fahle, Oliver. 2010. "Die Nicht-Stadt im Tatort." In: *Tatort Stadt. Mediale Topographien eines Fernsehklassikers*, ed. by Julika Griem, and Sebastian Scholz, pp. 69–79. Frankfurt/M., New York: Campus.

Fahle, Oliver. 2011. "Das Bild und das Sichtbare und das Serielle. Eine Bildtheorie des Fernsehens angesichts des Digitalen." In: *Blickregime und Dispositive audiovisueller Medien*, ed. by Nadja Elia-Borer et al., pp. 111–33. Bielefeld: Transcript.

Foucault, Michel. 2002. *The Order of Things: An Archaeology of the Human Sciences*. London, New York: Routledge.
Fröhlich, Vincent. 2015. *Der Cliffhanger und die serielle Narration. Analyse einer transmedialen Erzähltechnik*. Bielefeld: Transcript.
Gabriel, Gottfried. 1980. "Familienähnlichkeit." In: *Enzyklopädie Philosophie und Wissenschaftstheorie*, ed. by Jürgen Mittelstraß, Vol. 1, pp. 473f. Tübingen: Metzler.
Goeres, Ralf. 2000. *Die Entwicklung der Philosophie Ludwig Wittgensteins unter besonderer Berücksichtigung seiner Logikkonzeption*. Würzburg: Königshausen und Neumann.
Gründler, Hana. 2008. *Wittgenstein. Anders sehen. Die Familienähnlichkeit von Kunst, Ästhetik und Philosophie*. Berlin: trafo.
Heßler, Martin, and Dieter Mersch. 2009. "Bildlogik, oder: Was heißt visuelles Denken?." In: *Logik des Bildlichen. Zur Kritik der ikonischen Vernunft*, ed. by Martina Heßler, and Dieter Mersch, pp. 8–62. Bielefeld: Transcript.
Hollendonner, Barbara. 2009. "Der Zauber der Präsenz. Evidenzproduktion in CSI: Crime Scene Investigation." *Zeitschrift für Kulturwissenschaften*, 1: 27–40, Topic "Sehnsucht nach Evidenz."
Hollendonner, Barbara. 2015. "Der Blick nach Innen." In: *Medien in Zeit und Raum. Maßverhältnisse des Medialen*, ed. by Ingo Köster, and Kai Schubert, pp. 107–16. Bielefeld: Transcript.
Jenkins, Henry. 2006. *Convergence Culture: Where Old and New Media Collide*. New York, London: The University of New York Press.
Jermyn, Deborah. 2007. "Body Matters: Realism, Spectacle, and the Corpse in CSI." In: *Reading CSI: Crime TV under the Microscope*, ed. by Michael Allen, pp. 79–89. New York: Tauris.
Kelleter, Frank, ed. 2012. *Populäre Serialität: Narration – Evolution – Distinktion. Zum seriellen Erzählen seit dem 19. Jahrhundert*. Bielefeld: Transcript.
Lury, Karen. 2007. "CSI and Sound." In: *Reading CSI: Crime TV under the Microscope*, ed. by Michael Allen, pp. 107–21. New York: Tauris.
Lyotard, Jean-François. 2003. "Wittgenstein 'After.'" In: Jean-François Lyotar. *Political Writings*, pp. 19–22. London: UCL Press.
Lyotard, Jean-François. 2012. "Philosophy and Painting in the Age of Their Experiment." In: Jean-François Lyotard. *Textes dispersés I: esthétique et théorie de l'art. Miscellaneous Texts I: Aesthetics and Theory of Art*, pp. 147–75. Leuven: Leuven University Press.
Menke, Christoph. 2016. "Breaking Bad. Versuch über die Befreiung." *West End. Neue Zeitschrift für Sozialforschung* 2: 3–24.
Nohr, Ralf. 2014. *Nützliche Bilder. Bild, Diskurs, Evidenz*. Münster: LIT.
Pfaller, Robert, ed. 2000. *Interpassivität. Studien über delegiertes Genießen*. Berlin: Springer.
Pfaller, Robert. 2008. *Ästhetik der Interpassivität*. Hamburg: Philo Fine Arts.
Richtmeyer, Ulrich. 2009. "Vom Bildspiel zum Sprachspiel – Wie viel Kompositphotographie steckt in der Logik der Familienähnlichkeit." In:

*A Selection of Papers from the International Wittgenstein Symposium in Kirchberg am Wechsel*, ed. by Volker A. Munz, Klaus Puhl, and Joseph Wang, n.p. Accessed August 25, 2015. http://wittgensteinrepository.org/agora-alws/article/view/2828/3380.

Schulte, Joachim. 1992. *Wittgenstein: An Introduction*. Albany: State University of New York Press.

Schwaab, Herbert. 2008. "Stanley Cavell, King of Queens und die Medienphilosophie des Gewöhnlichen." In: *Ästhetik und Alltagserfahrung*, ed. by Deutsche Gesellschat für Ästhetik. Accessed December 12, 2019. http://www.dgae.de/downloads/Herbert_Schwaab.pdf.

Stjernfelt, Frederik. 2007. *Diagrammatology: An Investigation at the Borderlines of Phenomenology, Ontology, and Semiotics*. Dodrecht: Springer.

Turnbull, Steven. 2007. "The Hook and the Look: CSI and the Aesthetics of Television." In: *Reading CSI: Crime TV under the Microscope*, ed. by Michael Allen, pp. 15–32. New York: Tauris.

Wentz, Daniela. 2017. *Bilderfolgen. Diagrammatologie der Fernsehserie*. Paderborn: Transcript.

Whitehead, Alfred North. 1978. *Process and Reality: An Essay in Cosmology*. New York: The Free Press.

Wittgenstein, Ludwig. 1999. *Philosophische Untersuchungen. Zweite Auflage. Philosophical Investigations*. 2nd edn, trans. by G. E. M. Anscombe. Oxford, Malden: Blackwell Publishers.

# 11

# Reality and History

At the end of the 1990s an entirely new genre or kind of television caught on—namely, the *reality show* or *reality television*. *Reality TV*—exactly like *history TV*—is distinguished by the fact that television here presents its own operativity and also extends into a reality or history that it itself nevertheless already is. We will begin with the format of the reality show, which was pioneered by predecessors that it partly surpassed and partly inverted, was experimentally implemented and heavily debated in the 1990s, was then rapidly accepted worldwide, and today constitutes a large share of the emerging television programming around the world (Biltereyst 2004). Reality TV comes from television documentaries and reportage, the live show as an entertainment format, smaller genres like *Candid Camera*, as well as non-televisual forms developed on the newly emerging internet (Clissold 2004). However, reality TV is not just the integration of these forms; rather, it functions entirely differently than a news report or reportage, as it is live, serialized, and without any recourse to filmic and documentary forms. Reality TV exposes the ontographic form of television 2.0, and it first and characteristically comes about (apart from its predecessors) when television meets, relates to, and installs itself in other media—namely, the internet and live streaming.

First, the switch image as reality TV intervenes in reality and simultaneously reports on this intervention so that the report *is* the intervention itself. Imagine the following scenario: a live television camera appears in a public square that is not too busy, and the attention it arouses or the crowd it produces is the sole subject of the broadcast. This presupposes that reality is accessible to such an intervention at all (which is one of the differences between a given reality and the reality of reality TV). Second, television reality is specifically prepared for this transformation of reality into reality TV in that television intervenes in it while and by performing it. In the previous example, attention would be drawn to the arousal of attention and the production of the crowd in such a way that the arousal *is* the attention and the production *is* the crowd (which is similar to Elias Canetti's idea that the formation of the crowd is already the crowd, only in this case it exists not directly and immediately but rather only through the switch image, and it is thus switchable, flexible, diverse, and distributed) (Canetti 1981: 16f.). Third, reality TV explores the unclear and new ontological status of television reality through its own form of experience and operativity. Television reality is at the same time image and operation, condition and alteration, produced and given, an intervention and what is being intervened into, a report and what is being reported on, *switching* and *ruling* (Engell and Siegert 2020). Reality TV thus attempts to understand itself again operatively through an intervention—that is, through switching.

## Ontography and Simulation

One of the biggest peculiarities is that there seems to have already been a well-developed theory of this new form, informed by theory (instead of television), before it emerged. It was already apparent early on that television 1.0 had a special relationship to reality due to its power to put reality into the image and by doing so calling reality into being in the first place—that is, the reality of television itself. We already encountered this idea at the beginning in connection with the live broadcast, and we suggested that the mode of being of the cathode ray tube, as a product of the televisual apparatus, is already ontographic (see Chapter 2 in this volume). It only exists as it is being written, and it imposes its own medial condition (i.e., its ontographic mode of being) on everything that passes through it. Even that which appears recognizable in the screen images of a live broadcast is shown by television as if it always already involves an ontographic reality that only exists as it is being written by television itself, in that it appears on the screen. Live television is the *writing of events*, as it writes the sequence of events as they occur and helps them to become a progressive form as a sequence (Pasolini 2005; see also Engell 2012). It feeds the course of the world to the world, yet it is also simultaneously part of the world as well as its description or distortion. It is the medium that possesses and uses reality in order to write itself.

When it proceeds in the mode of television reality, the ontographic writing of reality becomes a counter-actualization. We already extensively encountered Deleuze's concept of counter-actualization in connection with the instant replay and the repetitive formats of television, and it initially referred to the reality-positing (*wirklichkeitssetzende*) incorporation of the extensionless (and thus not real) moment into the extended (and thus real) duration (see Chapter 6 in this volume). A counter-actualization thus occurs in the medium of reality. It is an intervention from an immeasurable and entirely heterogeneous exterior, but it is also coextensive to and indistinguishable from reality, just as a parody is indistinguishable from what it parodies. The counter-actualization is indistinguishable from reality, and according to Deleuze it reduplicates the duplication. This also appears to apply to the reality of television. Reality repeats television, and television repeats this repetition (Deleuze 2004: 192).

In the context of theories of representation, which assume a vertical distinction between image and reality, it is difficult to conceive of the ontography of television as counter-actualization or as anything other than deviation and disruption. We have already seen this by means of Daniel Boorstin's concept of the "pseudo-event" (Boorstin 1992; see also Chapter 2 in this volume). According to Boorstin, there are also events that are only caused by television yet nevertheless have an existence independent of television, if television reports them like other external events, and in this sense they are not really "real." Jean Baudrillard took this idea even further by claiming that these events do not exist at all, such as the Gulf War of 1990–1991 with its concentrated live coverage (Baudrillard 1995); rather, according to Baudrillard, these events are merely *simulations*, which are performed above all through television. "Real" events or incidents can thus no longer be distinguished from stagings or images. Baudrillard already developed this idea much earlier in the 1970s using various examples, including a television program that can be recognized today as a precursor to the reality show (Baudrillard 2010: 27–30). For half a year the Loud family allowed their everyday lives to be observed and then shown on a weekly program. Cameras were installed throughout their home, and there were rounds of interviews with the members of the family. Baudrillard was not interested in the shocking disclosure of intimate details; rather, he postulated that even before their supposedly unaffected private life was recorded and broadcast, it was already completely permeated and structured by the criteria and schemata of television, such as the family series and advertising. It did not need to change in order to become a television program, as it was always already programmed by television. Television was thus watching itself, as the family did not have a non-televisual or nonpublic life that could have subsequently been made public.

Baudrillard could have found a similar idea in Horkheimer und Adorno's *Dialectic of Enlightenment*, which claimed that the faces of teenagers in Texas were already naturally typed according to the models of the film industry (Horkheimer and Adorno 2002: 112). By adhering to this distinction, however, they overlook the fundamental nature of the duplication of reality in the medium of reality and particularly that of the (ontographic) counter-actualization as the reduplication of this duplication in terms of Deleuze's logic of sense. According to Baudrillard, in contrast, adherence to this distinction precisely confirms the simulation. Television, in turn, does everything to conceal this nondistinctness (if necessary, by lamenting its loss), which Baudrillard calls *dissimulation*. Drama and scandal help, as the Louds get divorced and the family falls apart. The breakup of the family thus conceals its simulated nature, particularly when a critical gaze "reveals" that it was only a result of television's intrusion into their private life. This phase of simulation and dissimulation also occurred in Germany much later in the very successful series *Die Fußbroichs*, which was particularly popular in Cologne. It began as a television documentary about the everyday life of a working-class family, and it continued as a series that was an early form of reality TV. This also led to a quarrel and even criminality, which was attributed to television and the disastrous effect of its constant presence and its creation of celebrities. What is identified as a disclosure, however, is merely the normal course of a soap opera. Television thus continues to claim that the events it shows have a certain weight or even an independent existence, or that this is at least possible, such as the dramatic events in the lives of these families; as simulations, however, these events are neither existent nor nonexistent. Without this claim to a persistently possible reality, according to Baudrillard, television would lose its power, which is based on simulation and is itself a simulation: it does not *exist* at all.

This argument is highly problematic and even cynical when applied to crises and wars that cost many lives and lead entire regions of the world into a state of constant misery and continuous catastrophe (such as the Gulf Wars, which Baudrillard claimed did not take place); however, it is also difficult to sustain as a theory in the context of television 1.0's ontographic mode of operation. Television 1.0's ontography of reality precisely does not change the reality of ontography, including its power, effectivity, and potential violence. The ontographic process does not claim that there is no reality; rather, it claims that it is part of reality and operates on the same level. Television images are not simply simulations of reality; rather, they are inscribed in reality and are themselves real, as they have real effects.

The concept of the reality show is evidently connected to the *dispositif* of surveillance. According to Baudrillard, however, this connection can be understood as the "end of the panopticon"—that is, as an inversion and atomization of the surveillance system described by Foucault using the famous passage on the panoptic prison in Jeremy Bentham's plans (Foucault 1995: 195–228; Baudrillard 2010: 29ff.). This prison had a central observation tower, from which all of the other rooms, cells, and corridors of the prison were visible; in the reality show, however, this imbalance is omitted or reversed, as there is now a central room that can be seen from anywhere, such as the home of the Louds, later the living container on *Big Brother*, and other rooms. For Foucault it is irrelevant whether the observation tower is actually manned, as it could be manned at all times but it is not visible from the cells. The gaze from the tower is therefore only possible—or, more precisely, virtual; in any case, it will still discipline the behavior of the prisoners even when they are not actually being observed. According to Baudrillard, the same effect applies to the simulation, although it is doubly reversed: not only can the central room be observed from all of the cells but all of the cells can also be the observed room at the same time. The cells are thus no longer organized around a central tower; rather, they mutually control one another, and the inhabitants of the cells all behave as if they are being observed (in the same way that they observe the other cells) even when they are not actually being observed. In short: they behave like television personalities. As a result of this atomization, according to Baudrillard, the imbalance and effects of power realized in Foucault's structure collapse: power no longer "exists." This is also the basic condition of the switch image since the flight to the moon, as every image after Apollo 11 is basically seen from the perspective of one or many other images (see also Chapter 7 in this volume). This does not erode its power or change it to the register of simulation; rather, it changes its physical state and how it is perceived. Like the switch image in general, it is no longer visually coded but rather tactile, and it arises no longer from the gaze and the image but rather from switching. We will come back to this through a closer examination of *Big Brother*.

## Ontography and *The Reality of the Mass Media*

Niklas Luhmann developed another theory of the reality of television in his book *The Reality of the Mass Media*, which was published shortly before the spectacular breakthrough of reality TV with *Big Brother* (Luhmann 2000a). The thesis that is central in this context can easily be connected to the examples of the Louds and others, such as *The Real World* and *Die Fußbroichs*, even though they do not appear in the book. For Luhmann, one of the characteristics of television reality among others is that it comes about through the attribution of information (i.e., events with news value) to individuals (Luhmann 2000a: 71–5). This occurs through news reports, which trace events back to the human actors involved, as well as advertising, which emphasizes the individual, decisive, rational, and practical identity of consumers (which is paradoxical, as a consumer's decisions are also obviously supposed to be limited and controlled expressly by the advertising); however, the televisual construction of the individual, personal "human existence" (*Menschsein*) particularly takes effect in forms of entertainment, such as television dramas, feature films, live shows, and sports broadcasts. The addressing of individuals and the emphasis on individuality also became a distinguishing feature of the dominant formats of reality TV after 2000. According to Luhmann, this happens above all through dramatizations, such as dramatic tension.

Also according to Luhmann, the evidentiary power, affectivity, and multiperspectivity of film and television images strengthen the viewers' adoption of the experiences and expectations of fictional characters. Fictional and real experiences are thus mixed, and this mixture is even also incorporated and thematized in the fictions themselves—as in Don Quixote, only more efficiently (Luhmann 2000a: 81f.). In other words, the boundary between fiction and reality, which is one of the fundamental differentiating features of mass media according to Luhmann, is incorporated into the fiction. This becomes even more intense and confusing in the age of visual media, as fictional realities and real fictions are formed. The reality show, which appeared shortly after the publication of Luhmann's book, seems to confirm this diagnosis precisely. Luhmann also blames the dominance of real fiction for the rise of simulation theory, which was contemporary at the time, and he thus sees television as the condition for the development and boom of simulation theory.

According to Luhmann, however, the crucial characteristic of the televisual construction of reality is that television's own criteria and processes, such as individuation and real fiction, are not subjected to those same criteria and processes (Luhmann 2000a: 88–94). Its mechanisms of selection are not subject to selection. It views them as part of a never spoken yet always presumed background knowledge. This *reality of the construction* is itself always constructed as a self-evident and unquestionable consensus, and it thus constitutes a second reality that observes and comments on the first. An example of this is that televised election debates are evaluated not on the basis of the programs or the expertise, presentation skills, and advantages of the actors but rather on the basis of the candidates' presumed effects on viewers. This second reality is the actual *reality of the mass media*. It is largely removed from observation, and it does *not require consensus* (Luhmann 2000a: 93f.). This fundamentally distinguishes it, almost disturbingly, from all of the realities that preceded it. In order to participate it is only necessary to have any opinion whatsoever, which does not have to be true. It also justifies the public's general distrust of the reality of television. What is shown on television must be presumed to be known because it is shown on television. Even if individual viewers do not acknowledge that it is real, as they do not believe it themselves, they must still acknowledge its value, as they believe all of the other viewers believe it.

According to Luhmann, this still works even when one understands the mechanisms through which it works. These paradoxes point to the second level of the *reality of the construction of reality*, in which viewers do not use television to observe reality but rather observe the production of reality through television—albeit following certain given formal specifications and from a level established by television itself. According to Luhmann, though, television does not engage in a final paradox; admittedly, it observes its observers (which particularly applies to reality TV), and it can also be observed while it is observing. It does not consolidate these observations, however, so from Luhmann's perspective it does not pose the question of the subject of observation (Luhmann 2000a: 117–22). It does not make clear to viewers that wherever they may observe television's makings they are in a feedback situation that forces them to look at television according to the directives of television itself. Unlike a work of art, therefore, television never appears as an object (or a system) that can only be observed on the condition that self-observation (or at least the capability of self-observation) is ascribed to it. In this sense, it does not permit *second-order cybernetics*, and this is precisely what distinguishes the self-observation of society through the mass media from the self-observation of society through the social sciences. Even if this latter observation is irrefutably true, however, its justification in the present context is nevertheless not convincing. Indeed, television does not allow second-order cybernetics due to the lack of a second level or an external observation post, and this is precisely its essential ontographic feature. In the case of television reality, however, the reality of the construction of reality precisely proceeds in the medium of reality and as reality—namely, as a counter-actualization that reduplicates the duplication (Deleuze 2004: 192).

## Reality 2.0

In the context not of the singled-out event (such as Mary Ann Doane's notion of crisis and catastrophe) but rather of the everyday flow of events (or "information"), something else occurs with television 2.0 (Doane 1990). It has three aspects, which are all related to the fact that television does *not* deal with an event on two distinct levels, such as those of facts and observations, of first-order and second-order observations, or of first-order and second-order cybernetics. (This was also diagnosed by Luhmann, although he assumed that it was a defect.) On the contrary, television and its reality fundamentally operate on one and the same level, which is compulsory for ontographies. This is now articulated in three ways under the conditions of television 2.0, which motivated the development of reality TV. With television 2.0, the switch image of second screens becomes a more or less closed and self-contained environment (see also Chapter 9 in this volume). Wherever it looks and reaches, it encounters a world that already includes television and that already relates to television in the same way that television relates to it. This does not mean (or at least it no longer means) that there is no longer any reality or that reality is a *construction* of television, as Luhmann assumes, as the reverse also applies. Even if it did mean this, it would not change the reality of the construction. Television has also not extinguished reality by replacing it with its own processes or simulations.

In the age of second screens, however, reality is always equipped and entangled with television, and it must arise from and as constellations of screens and switch images. The reality of television is therefore the relationship between reality and television. Luhmann's convincing insight is that this reality is *doubly addressed*—not on two different levels but rather on the same level at the same time in one go. This addressing first occurs as reality, which is always already related to television (it is not possible for it to be unrelated), and it then occurs as the representation, recording, or writing of television reality, which is different yet indistinguishable from reality itself. Like reality, television 2.0 also occurs twice, as it first occurs as an environment (or part of an environment), and it then inhabits this environment as a television show. The question of how television relates to reality and how reality relates to television thus becomes not only an object of critical and theoretical observation in sociology, media theory, and aesthetics but also above all a regular program component of television itself, which again operates at the same level. As the inhabitant of the environment of television, it also develops its own new programming category—that is, the consequentially named reality show, in which television 2.0 experiments with the reality of television itself.

The emergence of the reality show as a specific achievement of television 2.0 is derived not only macroscopically from the ubiquity and omnipresence of screens (and thus of television) but also microscopically from the operating principle of LCD screens or television 2.0. As we have already seen, the switch image can now encounter itself not only externally but also internally as an ontogram, as the liquid-crystal screens glow permanently and are able to maintain programmed constellations (see also Chapter 9 in this volume). By recording and retaining constellations of pixels, to which it can revert, the switch image is able to single them out as sustained and resilient ontograms from the constant ontographic flow of new drawings and redrawings. This occurs at a microscopic-technical level, which is hardly discernible for human vision, but it has advantages with regard to the technology of transmission, as the only signals that must still be transmitted are those that implement changes. These changes thus take effect as changes on and in something that remains otherwise unchanged rather than as changes on and in something that already and only exists as changeable.

This can also be observed macroscopically by means of the television series. The radical peculiarity of the series form, as we saw earlier, is that what is real and essential for the series is not the consistent (i.e., the referent) but rather the changeable (Deleuze 2004: 44–50, here:46f.; see also Chapter 9 in this volume); however, the new series of television 2.0 incorporates the ontogram not only at a microscopic-technical level but also explicitly and noticeably within the diegesis, such as in the diagrams that appears as images within the images of the series.

The series now oscillates between ontographic and ontogrammatic processes, which not only intersect but also merge with one another. This once again raises the question of their reality, but this question is examined not only in and through the series but also in the domain of live broadcasting, which is still foundational for television despite all of the changes it has undergone. The reality show thus experiments with its relationship to reality, and this experiment is not exclusively but still primarily live, including the different inflection forms of live, near to live, and live on tape. As we will see, it also always plays with the relationships and transitional forms between ontography and the ontogram.

Third, television 2.0 no longer functions in the context of a naturalistic and representationalistic ontology (to use Descola's concepts again); rather, it forms an analogistic ontography, which operates with relations of resemblance rather than relations of representation (Descola 2013: 172–231, 2010b,c). We have also seen this microscopically by means of the operating principle of the digital screen and macroscopically by means of the series (see also Chapters 9 and 10 in this volume). The reality show proceeds in precisely the same way, only now in a fundamentally live rather than serial medium. Its experiments are performed not on representations or the relationships between reality (such as real people) and representations (such as roles or characters) but rather on arrangements and constellations (including people, such as contestants, residential groups, or families, and things, such as institutions, facilities, or tools). It thus always also involves the inclusion or integration of television into reality as a configuration as well as the location of reality in the configuration of television.

## *Big Brother*

The first format of the new programming category of the reality show was *Big Brother*. It was first produced and broadcast in the Netherlands in 1999, followed by Germany in 2000, and later in more than sixty countries around the world (for more on this and the following, see Balke, Schwering, and Stäheli 2000). Numerous spin-offs and further developments are still being produced worldwide, including a new season that is currently being prepared in Germany to celebrate the twentieth anniversary of the format. The basic principle of the program is already extravagant: a number of people (between twelve and sixty, depending on the season) selected from a large number of applicants live together for a few months (up to a year) in a shared house that is sealed off from the outside world and completely monitored by television cameras. There is minimal privacy and no television reception. The daily broadcasts and evening recaps then chronicle the life of this community. At the end of each week there is also a large evening live show filmed in a television studio, during which the audience votes over the internet to determine which person should leave the house, and the last remaining person is the winner. In order to increase the pressure, the inhabitants are also subjected to difficult conditions, such as food shortages. They are also required to perform tasks and solve riddles, sometimes collectively and cooperatively and sometimes in competition with one another, and these tasks are announced by a recorded voice, which is precisely the voice of "Big Brother." They also make daily "confessions" to a camera in a private room, where they cannot be overheard by the others.

*Big Brother* is thus not simply a program or a series but rather a wide-ranging constellation of programs and formats—what McLuhan would call a large-scale "charge of the light brigade" (McLuhan 1964: 341; 357). In the early years it also included a weekly evening show as well as daily live windows and montages, which were given fixed time slots and distributed over multiple channels. In other words, it makes use of everything the classic programming categories of television had to offer—from the raw form of sheer surveillance television (in the sense of Cavell's monitoring) to the glamorous and directorially controlled live show (Cavell 1982). *Big Brother* thus combines the format of the live show with that of the series as well as the format of the entertainment show with that of the magazine program (Kava and West 2004). From the beginning, *Big Brother* also extended into the internet and later into live streaming. An expensive public relations campaign (another parallel to the television coverage of the flight to the moon in 1969) ensured that *Big Brother* was heavily discussed and debated on other programs and in other media. These discussions initially focused on scandal and outrage, and they even extended to considerations of a ban (in Germany at least), which of course was very profitable to the format. *Big Brother* also led to diverse analyses in communication and media theory. On one of the evening shows, a professor of media studies was even allowed to provide a critical explanation of the format.

*Big Brother* thus brought everything developed by classic and modern television to the screen, as if it were the last great performance of television 1.0. In this respect, it was exactly like the vision of television presented in the 1998 feature film *The Truman Show*. This film featured a television studio that included an entire town that was situated on an island covered by a dome that functioned as an artificial sky; it was so big that it could even be seen from space. This studio was dedicated to the production of a daily television show, and the protagonist of this show (and the film) was Truman, who had spent his entire life in the town. Truman believed that the town was authentic, but he was actually being observed continuously by hidden cameras and microphones, and all of his fellow human beings were actors, who followed the instructions of an all-powerful studio director. In the best Hollywood style, the film chronicles Truman's gradual realization of his situation, his exit from immaturity, and the end of the show, which was accompanied by the frenetic applause of its viewers.

## Early Forms and Constellations

However, *Big Brother* was not only a brilliant (or shabby) presentation of television's combined capabilities and means; rather, it was also bracketed and almost presented by another type of television—namely, television 2.0—from which it is impossible to exit (unlike feature films or television 1.0). We already determined earlier that television 2.0 does not replace but rather overwrites television 1.0. This is already clear from the overlapping of traditionally distributed television and internet television—that is, the first screen and the second screen. After all, *Big Brother* was accompanied at almost the exact same time by the first internet-based experiments with everyday existence and the public. The earliest and most famous of these experiments was *JenniCam* (Lane 2000: 252–6). With the help of a webcam, a student (and later web designer) named Jennifer Ringley recorded an image of her apartment every three minutes and posted it on the internet for twenty-four hours a day. This idea was inspired by the internet site *FishbowlCam*, which posted twenty-four-hour recordings of an aquarium. Television stations had already broadcast uninterrupted live images of aquariums in the 1980s after the close of the day's programming. Ringley later installed more cameras and increased the image frequency until she was able to produce flowing, television-like live images. The object of the broadcast was also her love life, and it was sharply disputed and is still seen as an early form of live pornography on the internet. Ringley eventually monetized her program by adding an access fee, which was very successful.

She finally closed *JenniCam* in 2003, after she had inspired hundreds of imitators worldwide.

Unlike *Big Brother* and *JenniCam*, other contemporary experiments made radical artistic claims. In his experiment *Quiet: We Live in Public*, for example, internet entrepreneur Josh Harris, apparently inspired by *The Truman Show*, had roughly 100 people live together in a house in New York for a month without any contact with the outside world (see also Smith 2019). Surveillance cameras were installed in every corner of the house, and the images (switched automatically from camera to camera) were transmitted over a twenty-four-hour live stream on the internet. The participants also slept in "pods" equipped with monitors that played the live stream, so all of the pods were visible to everyone. The experiment ended in hygienically and psychologically catastrophic conditions and was finally terminated by the police on January 1, 2000. Harris subsequently continued this experiment in a different form with the title *weliveinpublic*, in which he monitored and transmitted his own private live and his relationship with his partner. The relationship ended after a few months, not least because of the pressure of their uninterrupted live observation on the internet and the accompanying loss of intimacy.

In the surveillance *dispositif* of reality TV, television, internet, and film (if one thinks of the model of *The Truman Show*) form an inherently contradictory configuration, in which television is distributed and situated and which is also simultaneously television itself. The possibilities and realities of television are presented and discussed in and through television and this changes the state of television, which is then performed on *Big Brother* as television on a large scale. However, it is performed not as second-order television or metatelevision but rather simply as television, which is then distributed over numerous screens and *dispositifs* as a switch image. Without already being a self-parody, reality TV infiltrates and undermines itself. The principle of public exposure is wholeheartedly affirmed, for example, yet for this purpose it must also be exposed. Following Horkheimer and Adorno, though, this exposure does not nothing to change the humiliation or self-contempt of the candidates, who freely accept it (Horkheimer and Adorno 2002: 123f.). At the same time, however, the cultural devaluation of television reflected in this critical diagnosis is registered in the format itself as a kind of affirmative self-contempt of the medium.

## Experimental Television

Even in this already presumptuous self-degradation, *Big Brother* still has all of the traits of an experiment and is thus, as suggested earlier, comparable to (and almost an inversion of) the greatest of all television experiments—namely, the 1969 flight to the moon (about this and the following, see Engell 2009a). Even before the beginning of the first season, the rules of the program, the technical design, and the floor plan of the house or so-called container were made known—a process that was clearly reminiscent of the television coverage of the flight to the moon. Despite the clear differences between these programs, *Big Brother* was also an experimental setup that served above all to investigate television itself. The space program might appear more successful and important at first glance, and this was also how it was communicated, while *Big Brother* was apparently a completely inconsequential and unimportant form of entertainment; however, the latter similarly marked a transition to a new phase of television in the age of its experimentation (Lyotard 2012). Among other things, *Big Brother* very much like the space program required the creation of a self-contained outpost and the exposure of a group of individuals to extremely harsh conditions, which similarly served to test and later distribute a new type of television. It was an inversion of the flight to the moon, however, because the gaze was directed inward rather than outward and because the essentially televisual nature of the experiment was revealed rather than concealed behind an allegedly humanistic project. Nevertheless, the aim of both of these experiments was to use televisual operations to determine what television is, and the process and outcome of these experiments changed the development of television itself.

In light of this comparison, it is obviously interesting that television is not permitted within the container itself. This fundamentally distinguishes the *Big Brother* house from the capsule of Apollo 11 as well as the pods in *Quiet: We Live in Public*, which were all equipped with television. The candidates thus cannot select and watch their own condition of being watched. As the only place without television—that is, the only place where the program cannot be selected or watched—the *Big Brother* house is also specifically marked as the last refuge of a reality without *Big Brother*—that is, without television. All of the subsequent spin-offs and other reality TV formats also follow this model. At first glance, this emphasis might appear to contain another double inversion and thus double confirmation of Baudrillard's simulation thesis. According to Baudrillard, for example, Disneyland is explicitly flagged and framed as an artificial world, and its function is to reinforce the belief that there is still a real, natural world from which it can be distinguished (Baudrillard 2010: 12f.). Disneyland thus distracts from the fact that the unidentified, undefined, and unmarked reality of the city of Los Angeles is just as artificial as the amusement park that it surrounds. In other words, the simulatedness of Disneyland dissimulates the true simulacrum, which is Los Angeles.

The group in the *Big Brother* house obviously know and affirm that they are being watched, like an attraction at Disneyland or a zoo; this is the entire purpose of their presence. What is special about the container, however, is not that it can be selected and watched from any other location but rather that it is possibly the only remaining location where no other location can be selected and watched, including the location itself. Every room outside of the panopticon is a control room, like the Mission Control Center in Houston, Texas; the only exception is the *Big Brother* house. In terms of Nipkow's original definition of television, it would be the location A that is selected and made visible at another location B (Hickethier 1998: 15; see also Chapters 2 and 7 in this volume); however, its special function is not that it can be selected from all other locations but rather that it itself can select nothing. It comes into play as a negative location B or a location non-B, which is defined by the fact that it cannot access any location A.

This difference becomes clear when we return to the example given at the beginning of this chapter—that is, a live camera placed in a public square. It would be easy to play the live images at the square by means of a feedback loop, which would increase its self-sustaining attraction. This is already a standing practice of television, such as when images of or close-ups from a crowd are shown live on giant screens in soccer stadiums, which provokes reactions in the audience that are also captured by cameras and shown live on the screens. On *Big Brother*, however, this precisely does *not* happen; instead, this feedback structure, which is nothing but a concentrated form of television itself, is exposed and reversed. This confirms the existence of a gap between the viewers and the candidates, which is also a gap between the actual (the candidates and the house are visible) and the virtual (the viewers remain invisible). While they may be indistinguishable, they are nevertheless different. The gap is also reversed or shifted—namely, from visibility to the ability to see and switch (i.e., the viewers can see and switch, but the candidates can't). The viewers' homes and the container are also similar in that their occupants cannot select and watch themselves. This confirms the status of the viewers, whose position at location B (i.e., their homes, which cannot be selected and watched) mirrors that of the candidates at location A (i.e., the *Big Brother* house, which also cannot be selected and watched by its own occupants). In both cases, therefore, the referent is inaccessible to itself.

According to Baudrillard, this is also a prominent feature of the simulation: it protects the long-lost referent (i.e., reality) by preventing access to it. Baudrillard extensively shows this using the example of a group of indigenous people living in complete isolation on a remote island in the Philippines, who for protective purposes are not allowed to be visited and harassed—even by ethnologists (Baudrillard 2010: 7–11; see also Engell

1994). The primary reality to be studied is thus made inaccessible. This pattern is repeated on *Big Brother*, although it is simultaneously shifted and inverted. In the case of *Big Brother*, intimacy is protected by making it directly and bluntly available to the gaze and disposal of others but preventing the people involved from looking at themselves—or the gaze of others. It thus consists of an interruption of self-reference. The referent is what cannot refer or (in terms of television technology) connect to anything beyond itself. As the basic form of self-reflexivity, however, self-observation is traditionally the foundation of subjectivity and reflexivity in general. If the *Big Brother* house is deprived of this possibility, then it is also claimed as a simple, primary, unreflective, and unselfconscious reality, which wants to be looked at (unlike Foucault's prisoners) but cannot look back.

## Celebrity: Ontography of Prominence

The unconventional ontographic status of the reality of reality TV is particularly readable when it is condensed as the way of life, form of existence, and mode of being of the participants—namely, as prominence (on the sociology of prominence, see Ziemann 2011: 59–114, here: 63–5). Winning on *Big Brother,* and comparable formats, obviously consists in a monetary prize, but this is merely incidental. What is more important is that the winner is singled out, appears longest on the screen, and possibly continues to be under observation afterwards. In other words, the real prize consists in the opportunity to become prominent and to appear on television outside of the show itself. The phenomenon of prominence has been well researched in sociology and is often conflated with other forms of public attention, such as recognition and fame (Ziemann 2011: 63f.; see also Wenzel 2000). Unlike these forms, however, prominence is not related—or does not refer—to anything outside of itself. There are no criteria for prominence other than that of prominence itself. A person can be recognized or famous for something specific, such as an ability, performance, or experience, but this is not necessary for prominence. It is nevertheless necessary to distinguish between the prominence and the celebrity of television reality. The term "celebrity" refers to a person as well as a quality—or, more precisely, a mode of existence. It is also always located in the process of its production, which in the case of the reality show is simultaneously the content as well as the progressive form of the program, and it only exists in the course of its implementation in the dynamic of emergence, execution, and elimination (Holmes 2004).

The borderline between the condensation of the ontographic status of reality in individual people and its transformation through the phenomenon of prominence has been thoroughly and extensively explored by the diverse formats of reality TV that followed *Big Brother*. This includes the *Next Top Model* format, which is supposed to produce models. It began with Tyra Banks' *America's Next Top Model* in 2003, and similar shows have since been produced in over a hundred countries (Stehling 2015). Another important format is the *Pop Idol* genre, which is supposed to produce pop stars. It was first developed by Simon Fuller in Great Britain in 2001, and it has since been produced and widely distributed internationally (in Germany under the title *Deutschland sucht den Superstar*). The *Next Top Model* format features not daily live broadcasts but rather weekly recaps and live shows, during which the steps in the selection process take place (i.e., the elimination of individual applicants from the field). The *Pop Idol* format is mainly based on live shows that feature the performances of the applicants and the decisions of the jury. Despite these differences, they are both considered reality TV formats because they involve actual interventions in the actual lives of the applicants, which actually (or possibly) have significant consequences, as they are supposed to produce prominence (Biressi and Nunn 2005: 144–55).

Depending on the format, the decision of the jury can be replaced or supplemented by the participation of the public, so viewers are able to intervene in the course of the program. Unlike *Big Brother*, a gift (such as beauty or voice) or an ability (such as strength, cleverness, or performing skill) is actually demanded, but the criteria according to which these gifts and abilities are measured are those of television itself, such as the telegenic appeal of the applicants or their survival under the conditions of the live broadcast. Other requirements involve not the abilities of the individuals but rather their compatibility with the special conditions of the entertainment industry. In other words, what matters is not their performance but rather their (conceivable yet still pending) success, as success already presupposes success. This is particularly evident when the jury consists of people who owe their own success to the reality TV format. What is on trial in the program is the suitability of the applicants to become manufactured, and the production of a public persona is already this persona.

## Celebrity, Scripted Reality, Makeover Show

Other format types expand the field. On living history shows, for example, candidates perform reenactments in historical settings, such as life in a Black Forest house around 1900. Dating shows, such as *The Bachelor* and *The Bachelorette*, involve the formation of couples, which is strongly sexualized on *Love Island*. Candidates can also return, just as a few television stars in the making are able to migrate between different series. This entire effort is accompanied not only by offers on the internet and other electronic media but also numerous talk shows and society magazine shows, in which successful and rejected applicants are questioned about their experiences and the impact of becoming prominent, as well as quiz and variety shows, in which they appear again. *Big Brother* also developed a sub-format, *Celebrity Big Brother* (in Germany, *Promi Big Brother*), which features candidates who are far from famous or influential but are nevertheless already caught up in the machinery of prominence. The prominence manufactured by television is here exposed to ridicule yet at the same time also validated and cured. Last but not the least, the originally British show *I'm A Celebrity—Get Me Out of Here!* (in Germany, *Ich bin ein Star–Holt mich hier raus!*) gathers together people whose prominence has suffered considerably (as proven by recent appearances on television). Their prominence is then manufactured once again by spending time in a "jungle camp," where they experience numerous humiliations and impositions, like a repentance ceremony. A further turn of the screw brought *Ich bin ein Star–Laßt mich hier rein!* (I'm a Star, Let Me In), in which the prize is that the winner (Brigitte Nielsen) is given the opportunity to participate in the jungle camp and to allow herself to be humiliated in order to recover her prominence.

In the context of television 2.0 and reality TV, however, something is added to the mere construction, reinforcement, circulation, consumption, and restoration of prominence. Prominence means not only being able to move from one format to another; rather, it is also at the same time the individuation, personalization, and thus embodiment of television reality—namely, the relationship of television to reality, which it inhabits and in which it always already appears (Ziemann 2011: 63). Prominence appears twice in the environment of television: once as its part, and thus a condition of life, and once as an individual, who comes from this environment, faces it, and is realized in it. In this respect, prominence is the condition to which it itself is subject. The relations between the mode of existence and the environment are exchanged and reversed in the reality of the reality show, as the reality of television constitutes an environment inhabited by individuals who embody the conditions faced by this reality. McLuhan's notion of media as "the extensions of man" is doubled and mirrored in the condensation of the environment in the individual (McLuhan 1964: 45–52), and the narcissism that McLuhan attributes to technical and medial existence is also reversed. When the human mode of existence faces its own techno-mediatic environment of apparatuses, according to McLuhan, it believes that it is looking at an external and foreign environment, with which it is fascinated and almost falls in love; however, human existence is actually only facing itself as a mirror image through the technological extensions of its own body. This is reversed on reality TV, as the television environment observes human individuals who seem external and foreign but are actually condensations, if not extensions, of itself.

Other derivatives of reality TV switch, at least to some extent, from the individuality of (prominent) candidates to the *singularity of (sensational) events*. This includes the once again highly controversial pseudo-live formats in which cameras accompany police, fire, and rescue services—preferably to scenes of accidents (Jermyn 2004). A classic early example is *COPS*. A German parallel was produced in 2019 as a two-hour live broadcast in real time under the title *Bundespolizei Live* (Federal Police Live). As with prominence, the sensational event condenses the environment of television into a temporal object that functions in this environment. Reality TV is also associated with the formats of scripted reality shows, in which actors act amateurishly as they play amateurs who get into fictional situations (Korte 2020). In other words, they act like amateur actors who are attempting to act like even less professional people would when accompanied by a camera in their everyday work, such as investigative work with the police, and their doubly unprofessional unprofessionalism is supposed to demonstrate the reality of the script. Reality TV also includes the formats of makeover shows, in which people who are having difficulty coping with their lives receive help from television personalities, who are also occasionally celebrities in the context of a television program (Oliva 2013; Lewis 2009; see also Lancioni 2009). The switch image intervenes and doubles this intervention as an image, such as in very simple before-and-after dramaturgies. Their essentially ontographic nature is particularly characterized by an extended present, as these programs often show slow-motion close-ups of the participants observing images of their own astonishment at the sight of the change or surprise. In addition to slow-motion replays, elements of live, pseudo-live, and live on tape can also appear, and this particularly applies to shows in which the appearance of the participants is freely revised (Morreale 2007; see also Chapter 6 in this volume). The encounter of the televisual habitat with itself as an inhabitant, which is condensed into an individual body, is developed here into its own format. What is most important is how television shows the intervention that it performs on individual bodies while it is being performing, and that is precisely what constitutes the intervention itself. There is also the serial format of the broadcast, which has its own temporal dynamics of classification and distinction.

## Television Reality: Ontography and Self-Reference

To sum up: television negotiates its relationship to reality in the reality show, and it differentiates itself from various conflicting and complementary views and practices. First, there is the view of reality as a horizon of reference, to which images and statements visually or semantically refer. Television undermines this by producing the reality to which it refers. Second, there is the view of reality as a simulacrum and dissimulacrum. Television is obviously based on this, but it significantly deviates from, doubles, and reverses it. Television reality as the reality of television 2.0 is no longer something that does not exist outside of television and whose nonexistence is hidden from view. It is not something inaccessible that the switch image can access, as we saw earlier in the example of the container on *Big Brother*. On the contrary, it is entirely internal to television itself, which cannot access it and from which nothing is visible or switchable—not even itself. It is also not the televisual construction of reality, although one can see the construction of a reality in a format like *Big Brother*—namely, that of prominence. Under ontographic conditions, however, the construction (or registration) is the same as reality. This is clear in the phenomenon of prominence, which cannot be observed without producing it. Like the model of second-order observation or second-order cybernetics, the idea of the televisual construction of reality fails because reality performs, produces, and propels its own construction from the start. There is no second level and thus actually no observation.

What the reality show experimentally explores is ultimately the relationship between ontography and *self-referentiality*. Not every form of self-reference or self-thematization is self-referential; rather, this only applies to processes and operations that themselves generate the conditions on which they are based (Luhmann 1995: 9ff.; 99f.; 129ff.; 144; see also Kirchmann 1993). For example, systems produce and reproduce the elements and relations on which they are built, just as an organic body does with cells. This also seems to apply to television reality—one need only think once again of the phenomenon of prominence and the sensational aspect of sensational events, which are obviously self-reflexive and self-reinforcing in this way. In the case of the reality show, however, the operation of ontography is at odds with self-reference for various reasons. The first indication of this is that the ontographic operation is accompanied by interruptions of self-reference and self-reinforcement, which we saw earlier in the comparison between the *Big Brother* container and the sports stadium. This also applies to casting shows and shows in which camera crews follow the police. In contrast to candid camera shows, it is not the cameras but rather the screens that are hidden. The candidates are only confronted at most with the effects of the broadcast, such as when they are deselected by the audience. The cycle of self-reference is thus interrupted by an intervention or deferral. This does not apply to the ontographic process, which has no posteriority but instead takes place simultaneously—or, more precisely, simultaneously with itself. Prominence is more or less closely linked to a person's presence on television, so people are (or can once again become) prominent to some extent only as long as they appear (or appear again) on the screen.

This is related to another important distinction that we have already encountered several times: unlike self-reference and self-observation, ontography does not involve a second level. It does not look down at itself; in fact, it is not an observation at all but rather an implementation that produces something (like a sign). Ontography is also not related to that which it produces in the same way that an organism is related to its cells—that is, at a higher level. The ontographic process obviously has different conditions of complexity, organization, density, and degree of coupling, but they are not sorted on two distinct levels; rather, these conditions merge indistinguishably into one and the same process, which now proceeds sequentially in time. If we have repeatedly distinguished here between macroscopic and microscopic perspectives, such as that of the cathode ray or the pixels, which cannot be perceived by viewers, and that of the configurations on the screen, which are visible to human observers and users, then this does not actually involve absolutely separate levels but rather different scales of observation. These perspectives always still refer to the same level in the image, and they are only differentiated by the relative proximity of the observation to the image. In filmic terms, the change from a macroscopic to a microscopic perspective always refers to the focal length or resolution of the image.

Lastly, ontography is always a technical operation that requires apparatuses, devices, and tools, and it is thus subject to material and physical conditions. This is precisely what the suffix *-graphy* is supposed to indicate. Ontographic processes cannot proceed without writing and drawing materials. They are not abstract and immaterial but rather concrete and material, and they are thus of the same ontological order as that which is produced by writing and drawing (see also Engell, Hartmann, and Voß 2013). In this respect, they resemble the category of *work*, which is also no less real than what it produces. Ontography possesses a technical-artifactual body and is itself a corporeal event performed by technical-physical as well as biological bodies; in fact, it is itself a body, from which it is indistinguishable. This is particularly clear in the case of the switch image because its ontography consists of material switches and switching processes. The medium of television reality is also always already the reality of a televisual body, which intervenes in it and in which it intervenes, and this televisual body constructs and reconstructs reality as a counter-actualization.

All of this does not apply to self-reference, however, as it is a relationship (like the underlying reference) and a logic (in increased complexity). It exists at best between entities or bodies, such as in biology, and it also participates in their reproduction. As a theoretical model, however, it is always detached from bodies and by no means coincides with them. Regardless as to whether it occurs inside or outside of television, its development is always the same. Even if it is crystallized and embodied in technical or organic feedback *dispositifs*, it is always conceived as an abstract schema that is detached from them. It is thus related to ontography in the same way that logic is related to the switch: while logic is conceived as abstract and disembodied, even when it is implemented by bodies (such as brains or circuits), switches actually implement switching, and they are thus of the same order as that which they switch.

## From Reference to Operation

This applies not only to self-reference but also to reference, as ontographic processes do not refer to something but rather are something. They cannot distinguish between self-reference and hetero-reference. When they represent something, they produce it, and when they stop, it disappears again. The German word for "representation" (*Darstellung*, which literally means "placing there") encompasses both of these ideas. In the language of cameralists, for example, amounts of money that need to be raised for investments are "represented." In the language of physicians, a body part that is anatomically laid bare during an autopsy is also "represented." In this sense, representation (or reference) can also be an ontographic process. Ontographies do not consist of references or relations, however, as they are implemented in and by operations. In the case of the switch image, these operations are articulated in and by switching. In other words, reference and self-reference are relations, while ontography is implemented as an operation. Therefore, the interesting overlapping area between (self-)reference and ontography or between (self-)relation and self-realization is precisely that of causality—or, more precisely, indexicality. In indexical relations, for example, a reference coincides with its material cause (Gell 1998: 13; 35ff.). While (self-)reference distinguishes between causes and effects, the ontographic process does not separate them; instead, they form a single closed indexical chain that intervenes in itself.

With television 2.0 it became possible to interrupt this process. As we have seen, the image points on liquid-crystal screens can be retained or preserved.

They cannot leave the flow of ontography, but they can stop it. The image then becomes an ontogram, and the operativity of ontography transforms into the relationality of ontograms. In this sense, ontograms are comparable to chronophotographs and photograms (i.e., the single frames of a film), only the process of their emergence is reversed: while a motion picture arises from the photograms on the celluloid film strip in the course of their projection on the screen, televisual ontograms are special conditions of the flowing image from which they arise—namely, as freeze frames. Televisual ontograms also do not form a separate level; rather, they arise as special conditions of ontography in the dimension of referentiality. Televisual ontograms are thus constellative and diagrammatic, and they always represent relations in the broadest sense (and not objects). Operativity and referentiality converge in the ontograms of the switch image. They can be activated, but they are no longer switchable—at least not without changing and becoming different ontograms. If we switch to the macroscopic scale, then we can see that the *Big Brother* house, the operative *dispositif* of the reality show, and the weekly or daily recaps and retrospectives are all ontogrammatic. As recaps embedded within an ongoing process, for example, they refer to actual or presumptive preceding processes and events in the container. At the same time, they are also phases of the ontographic process to which viewers have not attended (such as because they were never broadcast). Temporal and causal relations are thus renegotiated in these televisual transitions between ontography and ontogrammatics, and television reality extends beyond the unity of presence and self-presence—or, more precisely, self-emergence.

## Television History: The Attack of the Present on the Rest of Time

The extension of the reality of television beyond the present is confirmed by the fact that in the mid-1990s—at precisely the same time as the emergence of reality shows—it was condensed into its own program genre—namely, history shows. Both of these genres overlapped in the already mentioned format of living history shows, but television history also claims to its own independent value. *History Channel*, which has been developed globally, can be taken as an example (Gray and Bell 2013). Another leader is the BBC, which produces and exports numerous series on the history of not only Great Britain but the entire world on a vast scale. *Discovery Channel* also produces reports on history (among other things) that are distributed worldwide. In Germany the series *ZDF History* is the flagship of this genre, but channels like *ntv* also broadcast daily and extensive contributions on historical themes (Lersch and Viehoff 2007). History has obviously always been a program component in fictional as well as documentary formats since the beginning of broadcasting (see Knopp and Quandt 1988; Erll and Nünning 2004; Gray and Bell 2013). For example, history was thematized on historical television dramas, science programs, and reports on the results of the latest research or currents exhibitions with historical content. (History is here used in the conventional sense shaped by Western positivism—namely, as an inventory of facts concerning relevant events in the past.) Around 2000, however, the number of so-called *history shows* grew considerably, and the format was increasingly marked as a separate genre. Television history differs from what is traditionally understood as history in the same way that television reality differs from reality, as television's intervention in an environment in which it already exists or which it itself is and creates plays a major role in both genres.

In order to trace the ontographic practice of television history, it is useful to start by establishing an ontographic or more precisely *historiographic* understanding of history. According to this view, history is by no means what happened, and it does not consist of a causal chain of events, actions, and relations (on this and the following, see among others Engell 2019a). It arises not from events but rather from writing—namely, the writing of history—which is understood not as a description but rather as the writing of the events themselves. Without the writing of history, there would be no history. Even unwritten history is only a reversal of the writing of history. It thus does not exceed but rather expands the horizon of the present, which is characteristic of ontographic operations in general, as they always take place in the present. The writing of history operates not from the depths of the past but rather in the present and for the purposes of the present, such as the attempt to give or create meaning to the present (Luhmann 1978, 1995: 79f.). The writing of history explains why things are the way they are with reference to their past, origin, creation, and development. This also includes an increased awareness of contingency, as the writing of history confronts the present with what was once possible and what could have been an alternative future to the past and thus a different present. The present is enriched, as it procures a past for itself by the writing of history, whether it confirms or questions itself in this past. In the sense of Deleuze's theory of time, history thus involves a paradigmatically chronological time (Deleuze 2004: 186f.).

According to this understanding of history, the "attack of the present on the rest of time" that Alexander Kluge associates with the reign of television already began long ago in the modern scholarly writing of history (Kluge 1985). If on top of this the switch image now operates as the medium of historiography, then it provides a first historiographic ontography, in which it intervenes and which it overwrites through its own ontographic process. Historiography can also be read as the operation of differentiating between before and after, which is fundamentally repeated and duplicated in the switching process. The "attack of the present" can then obviously also be seen as an intervention and even as the intervention of the extensionless, external now moment of the differentiation into what is being differentiated—namely, extended time, which also includes history (Deleuze 2004: 190–2). It thus develops a paradoxical, often counterfactual, and in any case self-positing counter-actualization of history, again in the Deleuzian sense of the concept. The most blatant example of this is an experiment performed by the Discovery Channel in 2004 under the title *Virtual History* (see also Engell 2009b,c). A two-hour historical documentary was broadcast, which focused on the attempt to assassinate Adolf Hitler on July 20, 1944. It also included historical film footage, in which Winston Churchill, Franklin D. Roosevelt, and Joseph Stalin appeared. What was spectacular about this documentary was that the producers compensated for the lack of archival footage by using computer-based imaging processes to generate film footage that could not be found in the archives. This involved digitizing all of the available films and photographs of these historical figures as well as images of interiors and as many documentary color photographs from the period as possible. The scenes needed, such as from Hitler's "Wolfsschanze" (Wolf's Lair), Roosevelt's train, and the Kremlin, were filmed with actors and then altered by algorithmic processes so that they resembled the motion patterns and facial expressions calculated from the historical documents. The "look" of the footage was thus revised in the same way, and it also incorporated artificial traces of use and decay, to which materials from film archives can be exposed. The Discovery Channel documented all of the steps in this process in detail, and the documentation of the production of the program was disseminated widely, including on the internet. It even took up more time than the two-hour historical vision, which suggested a high degree of transparency.

That is not enough: in reference to the extensive scholarly archival research that went into the preparation of the project, in which a number of historians and so-called experts participated, it was argued that the only artificial documents that should be produced are those that could have been found in the archives, if they had only been recorded—or perhaps even those that had existed at one time but had since been lost (Engell 2009b,c). From the perspective of the producers, the program thus involved artificial but probably possible documents, which were derived from "real" documents through a process of interpolation, intervention, interposition, and hence forms of switching. These documents were not imitations of existing footage;

rather, they themselves were of the nature of artificial originals. They were connected to the "real" events of July 20, which were already familiar as historical facts, by a seamless though multistep indexical chain of causes and effects, and they could thus claim to be the closest traces to the reality of the events.

## Hyperreality and Historical Ontography

Discovery Channel's approach would seem to correspond to what Umberto Eco already described in the late 1970s as a trip into the realm of hyperreality (Eco 1986). He saw evidence of the hyperreal in American popular museums, such as a diorama in a California museum that presented a wax figure of a model sitting in a painter's studio. The painting on the easel in this diorama is easy to recognize, as it is the Mona Lisa (Eco 1986: 18f.). The scene is elaborately authenticated by an extensive explanation (the copy of the portrait is based on a photographic reproduction, etc.), and it is identified as the scene that must have presented itself when Leonardo da Vinci painted his image. Although it was derived from the painting ex post, Eco notes that this scene still must have come before the painting itself, and it thus seems more real than reality. The situation is different in the case of *Virtual History*, however, as the process is once again ontographic. The object of the representation is neither an object nor a representation, and it involves neither an original that came before the original (as in hyperreality) nor the processes of precedence and reproduction; rather, it involves the watching of something while it happens. First, viewers watch the people in action as the event is happening, such as Hitler, Roosevelt, and Stalin. Second, viewers watch the process of producing (any desired) originals on the basis of the operative nature of the televisual switch image. In other words, viewers do not watch representations of the past from the past; rather, they watch the past as it is written in the present (and only as long as it is written). The imaging process and its methodological and scholarly legitimation and authentication ensure that the historiographically produced reality of the events is overwritten once again, although this time it simultaneously changes from the medium of conventional historiography to the medium of television. The actual theme of the program is not the historical event itself but rather the use of imaging technology and, what is more, how the techniques of representation make history producible and plastic and how the producibility of televisual documents is brought about in seamless indexical chains. The historical event is operatively overwritten through its relation to television, and this relation consists in the operation of overwriting itself. In short: viewers are able to watch how history becomes television history.

Even more: television locates itself as an image in the presence of a historical place and time (Engell 2009b: 410). Through the intricate interaction of iconic and indexical relations in technical images, the artificial document suggests no less than the "authentic" document from the archive that there must have been or at least virtually was a recording apparatus at precisely this location and time. The process of "virtual history" thus means at least asymptotically that any documents of any events can complement the existing archive of images. The ubiquity and omnipresence of television in the age of television thus ultimately extends to all of time, as the archive of television can produce documents of all of history. Within the archive of television, in other words, history lives on as television history. This also means that the archive of television documents and extends the history of television itself. As television history, it now becomes coextensive with history in general. Whatever might have happened—from prehistoric times to the Anthropocene—television was virtually, if not actually, there. Television does not live in history; rather, history lives in it.

# Being There Is Everything: The Iconicity of Television History

This applies not only to the radical experiment of *Virtual History*, which incidentally failed—that is, was discontinued—due to the extremely high production costs (in 2004 at least). *Virtual History* only marked the tip of the iceberg, as the individual operations and elements of the condensed process shown here might be found on any history show in varying constellations and levels of intensity.

The forms used on history shows are mainly visual documents and images of documents, the testimony of an interviewee (the so-called contemporary witness) or of a place of an event, and the reconstruction or "re-enactment" of historical scenes (Sieber 2016). Visualizations, such as maps and animations, are also used. These explanatory images are closely related to the (usually off-screen) commentaries or representations of experts. The organizational role of montage should also be mentioned, as it coordinates the assemblage of the various material and formal elements. Individual history programs do not necessarily use all of these forms, and they differ greatly in how they use them; nevertheless, significant commonalities can be noted. For example, history programs use all kinds of technical images, such as photographs, documentary film clips, and other archival material from television itself, as well as computer-generated images and animations. They are complemented by filmic restagings and commentaries from experts. Close-ups of other archival documents are also used, such as historical documents or objects from museums. Through their interaction in the medium of the switch image, these fundamentally different yet interconnected types of images once again give rise to a seamless indexical causal chain, which is authenticated by the experts and which inversely demonstrates that what the experts say is true.

What is interesting, however, is that these images also fulfill a manifestly iconic function—namely, that of participation (Peirce 1983: 64ff.; see also Engell 2019b). An example is the heightened reality of the footage of Nazi atrocities and warfare during the Second World War. This stems from the fact that the images not only document crimes and violence but also indicate that something and someone—the apparatus and its operator—must have been present in the scenes they depict. The images themselves are thus not only testimonials but also witnesses, as they report their presence at the event and always carry it with them (Didi-Huberman 1992; Schwarte 2011). Viewers are also synchronized with these testimonies. The same applies to less drastic cases, in which objects that were possibly present at an event are placed before the camera like material witnesses. Sometimes the images also show documents, which usually cannot be deciphered but which convey the impression of age and often feature signs of authentication, such as seals or signatures.

They are not content to show the viewer what it was allegedly like to be there; rather, they show how it must have been to be present at the event, as mediated to viewers by the presence function (*Gegenwartsfunktion*) of the continuous ontography. The images are identified as both a product of a historical occurrence—that is, causally derived from it as a trace or index—and a part of the original event itself, as the camera was at least virtually there, following the possibility of its possibilities. They thus authenticate the event through their participation in it. They produce what they show in that the spatial and temporal situation that the events inhabit is the same spatial and temporal situation in which the images are also embedded (see Ziemann 2013). This produces a large and (in a Deleuzian sense) chronographic simultaneity, in which the viewers are synchronized with history. Lastly, televisual history seeks out original locations. Nearly every case of historical documentation on television includes images of the buildings and places where the event being reconstructed originally took place or could have taken place, and they are shown as they appear today, even if there is nothing left but ruins. In this spatial and temporal order, television switches to the location of the event and thus to the event itself as a kind of universal live broadcast. At the same time, this historical liveness is divided once again, as the location is always somewhere else—that is, not here but rather there (otherwise, television would not be a medium of transmission)—and it is no longer the same, which can also be shown through historical footage. The location itself is thus television history, as it is always already a relation between different images.

## Beyond History and Memory

The format of television history also undermines another established distinction—namely, that between history and memory (see also Engell 2019b: 172-4). One of the basic assumptions of Maurice Halbwachs' theory of memory, which has since evolved and been further developed, is that history emerges from the separation of the past from the present (Halbwachs 1992,n. d.; A. Assmann 2011; J. Assmann 2011). History is separate or cut off from the present, and it tends to be inaccessible because it is no longer part of everyday life, habits, and living traditions. Through this separation, the present becomes open to change and the past becomes open to retrospective, objectifying, and distancing reconstructions. The past is made available as an isolated fact, but it is also exposed to more or less random access. This access enables all of the activities associated with historical scholarship, including archives, museums, and academic research, as well as mass media popularizations, including the history industry. On the other hand, memory applies to events that are not forgotten and are thus treated as precisely not separate but rather always still present. While history confronts the present with distance and difference, memory operates with identity and proximity. Memory operations are identity-forming, and they privilege space over time, such as the "mnemotope" or the "lieux de mémoire" (J. Assmann 2011: 27; 45ff.; Nora 1984, 1986, 1992). This also applies when they are not individual, physiological, or psychological (and presumably even then) but rather take place through recording and storage technologies, which are always already external to the human body. It particularly applies when they are publicly or collectively available and then function as collective or cultural memory.

The transcription of history into memory also occurs in the overwriting and counter-actualizing of history through television history and the incorporation of the historical into the interior space of television, as described earlier. The subject of this memory is neither the individual nor the collective, such as a nation, class, or other identity formation, but rather television itself (Halbwachs n. d.:50f.). As we have repeatedly established, television is not a delimitable medium with a core identity; rather, since at least television 2.0, it consists of operative relations between a wide variety of screens, which makes it more constellative and variable. It nevertheless has and is a memory, and it is actually the most extensive technical memory of all. This does not necessarily apply to the archive of television as storage memory, even though its storage capacity and accessibility are constantly increasing; rather, it particularly applies to television as functional memory and thus as the site where remembering is distinguished from forgetting (Esposito 2002: 260–6; see also Chapter 3 in this volume). Through television history, television also registers itself in this memory everywhere, as if it were always already there and its own past were as extended as the entirety of the past, in the same way that it encounters itself in its own environment as television reality. It basically ontographs all of history as its own autobiography, with which it also spends its entire present as a counter-actualization of its own and all of history.

# References

Assmann, Aleida. 2011. *Cultural Memory and Western Civilization: Functions, Media, Archives*. Cambridge: Cambridge University Press.
Balke, Friedrich, Gregor Schwering, and Urs Stäheli, eds. 2000. *Big Brother: Beobachtungen*. Bielefeld: Transcript.
Baudrillard, Jean. 1995. *The Gulf War Did Not Take Place*. Bloomington, Indianapolis: Indiana University Press.
Baudrillard, Jean. 2010. "The Precession of Simulacra." In: Jean Baudrillard. *Simulacra and Simulation*, pp. 1–42. Ann Arbor: The University of Michigan Press.
Biltereyst, Daniel. 2004. "Reality TV, Troublesome Pictures and Panics: Reappraising the Public Controversy Around Reality TV in Europe." In: *Understanding Reality TV*, ed. by Su Holmes, and Deborah Jermyn, pp. 91–110. London: Routledge.
Biressi, Anita, and Heather Nunn. 2005. *Reality TV: Realism and Revelation*. London: Wallflower Press.
Boorstin, Daniel. 1992. *The Image: A Guide to Pseudo-Events in America*. New York: Vintage.
Canetti, Elias. 1981. *Crowds and Power*. New York: Continuum.
Cavell, Stanley. 1982. "The Fact of Television." *Daedalus* 111, no. 4: 75–96.
Clissold, Bradley D. 2004. "Candid Camera and the Origins of Reality TV: Contextualising a Historical Precedent." In: *Understanding Reality TV*, ed. by Su Holmes, and Deborah Jermyn, pp. 91–110. London: Routledge.
Deleuze, Gilles. 2004. *The Logic of Sense*. London, New York: Continuum.
Descola, Philippe. 2010b. "Un monde objectif." In: *La fabrique des images: Vision du monde et formes de la représentation*, ed. by Philippe Descola, pp. 73–100. Paris: Musée du quai Branly/Somogy éditions d'art.

Descola, Philippe. 2010c. "Un monde enchevêtré." In: *La fabrique des images: Vision du monde et formes de la représentation*, ed. by Philippe Descola, pp. 165–84. Paris: Musée du quai Branly/Somogy éditions d'art.
Descola, Philippe. 2013. *Beyond Nature and Culture*. Chicago, London: University of Chicago Press.
Didi-Huberman, Georges. 1992. *Ce que nous voyons, ce qui nous regarde*. Paris: Minuit.
Doane, Mary Ann. 1990. "Information, Crisis, Catastrophe." In: *Logics of Television: Essays in Cultural Criticism*, ed. by Patricia Mellencamp, pp. 222–39. Bloomington, Indianapolis: Indiana University Press.
Eco, Umberto. 1986. "Travels in Hyperreality." In: Umberto Eco. *Travels in Hyperreality: Essays*, pp. 1–58. San Diego, New York, London: A Harvest Book, Harcourt Inc., A Helen and Kurt Wolf Book.
Engell, Lorenz. 1994. *Das Gespenst der Simulation. Ein Beitrag zur Überwindung der "Medientheorie" durch Analyse ihrer Logik und Ästhetik*. Weimar: VDG.
Engell, Lorenz. 2009a. "Fernsehen mit Unbekannten. Überlegungen zur experimentellen Television." In: *Fernsehexperimente. Stationen eines Mediums*, ed. by Michael Grisko, and Stefan Münker, pp. 15–46. Berlin: Kadmos.
Engell, Lorenz. 2009b. "Virtual History Die Geschichte als Fernsehen." *Zeithistorische Forschungen* 2009/3, Jg. 6: 391–412.
Engell, Lorenz. 2009c. "Virtual History. Falsche Spur und lückenloses Gedächtnis: Wie das Fernsehen sich behauptet." In: *Goofy History: Fehler machen Geschichte*, ed. by BUTIS BUTIS/Marion Herz, Alexander Klose, Isabel Kranz, and Jan Philip Müller, pp. 280–94. Köln, Weimar, Wien: Böhlau Verlag.
Engell, Lorenz. 2012b. "Kommentar." *Zeitschrift für Medien- und Kulturforschung (ZMK)* 2: 91–7.
Engell, Lorenz. 2019a. "Narrative: Historiographic Technique and Narrative Spirit." In: Lorenz Engell. *Thinking Through Television*, , ed. by Markus Stauff, pp. 145–70. Amsterdam: Amsterdam University Press.
Engell, Lorenz. 2019b. "Beyond History and Memory: Historiography and the Autobiography of Television." In: Lorenz Engell. *Thinking Through Television*, pp. 171–88. Amsterdam: Amsterdam University Press.
Engell, Lorenz, Frank Hartmann, and Christiane Voß. 2013. "Einleitung." In: *Körper des Denkens. Neue Positionen der Medienphilosophie*, ed. by Lorenz Engell, Frank Hartmann, and Christiane Voß, pp. 7–8. München: Fink.
Engell, Lorenz, and Bernhard Siegert. 2020. "Schalten und Walten. Editorial." *Zeitschrift für Medien- und Kulturforschung (ZMK)* 1: 7–12.
Erll, Astrid, and Ansgar Nünning, eds. 2004. *Medien des kollektiven Gedächtnisses. Konstruktivität – Historizität– Kulturspezifizität*. Berlin, Boston: De Gruyter.
Esposito, Elena. 2002. *Soziales Vergessen. Formen und Medien des Gedächtnisses der Gesellschaft*. Frankfurt/M.: Suhrkamp.

Foucault, Michel. 1995. *Discipline and Punish: The Birth of the Prison*. New York: Vintage Books.
Gell, Alfred. 1998. *Art and Agency: An Anthropological Theory*. Oxford: Clarendon.
Gray, Ann, and Erin Bell. 2013. *History on Television*. London, New York: Routledge.
Halbwachs, Maurice. 1992. *On Collective Memory*. Chicago, London: The University of Chicago Press.
Halbwachs, Maurice. n. d. *The Collective Memory*. New York et al.: Harper & Row.
Hickethier, Knut. 1998. *Geschichte des deutschen Fernsehens*. Stuttgart, Weimar: Metzler.
Holmes, Su. 2004. "'All you've Got to Worry About is the Task, Having a Cup of Tea, and Doing a Bit of Sunbathing': Approaching Celebrity in *Big Brother*." In: *Understanding Reality TV*, ed. by Su Holmes, and Deborah Jermyn, pp. 111–35. London: Routledge.
Horkheimer, Max, and Theodor W. Adorno. 2002. *Dialectic of Enlightenment. Philosophical Fragments*. Stanford: Stanford University Press.
Jermyn, Deborah. 2004. "This is About Real People: Video Technologies, Actuality and Affect in the Television Crime Appeal." In: *Understanding Reality TV*, ed. by Su Holmes, and Deborah Jermyn, pp. 71–90. London: Routledge.
Kava, Misha, and Amy West. 2004. "Temporalities of the Real: Conceptualising Time in Reality TV." In: *Understanding Reality TV*, ed. by Su Holmes, and Deborah Jermyn, pp. 136–53. London: Routledge.
Kirchmann, Kay. 1993. "Zwischen Selbstreflexivität und Selbstreferentialität." *Film und Kritik* 2: 23–37.
Kluge, Alexander. 1985. *Der Angriff der Gegenwart auf die übrige Zeit*. Frankfurt/M.: Syndikat/EVA.
Knopp, Guido, and Siegfried Quandt, eds. 1988. *Geschichte im Fernsehen*. Darmstadt: Wissenschaftliche Buchgesellschaft.
Korte, Jule. 2020. *Zwischen Script und Reality. Erfahrungsökologien des Fernsehens*. Bielefeld: Transcript.
Lancioni, Judith, ed. 2009. *Fix Me Up: Essays on Television Dating and Makeover Shows*. New York: McFarland.
Lane, Frederick S. 2000. *Obscene Profits: The Entrepreneurs of Pornography in the Cyber Age*. New York: Routledge.
Lersch, Edgar, and Reinhold Viehoff, eds. 2007. *Geschichte im Fernsehen: Eine Untersuchung zur Entwicklung des Genres und der Gattungsästhetik geschichtlicher Darstellungen im Fernsehen 1995–2003*. Berlin: VISTAS.
Lewis, Tania. 2009. "Changing Rooms, Biggest Losers and Backyard Blitzes: A History of Makeover Television in the United Kingdom, United States and Australia." In: *TV Transformations. Revealing the Makeover Show*, ed. by Tania Lewis, pp. 7–18. New York: Routledge.

Luhmann, Niklas. 1978. "Temporalization of Complexity." In: *Sociocybernetics: An Actor-Oriented Social Systems Approach*, ed. by Felix R. Geyer, and Johannes van der Zouwen, pp. 95-111. Leiden: Nijhoff.
Luhmann, Niklas. 1995. *Social Systems*. Stanford: Stanford University Press.
Luhmann, Niklas. 2000. *The Reality of Mass Media*. Cambridge: Polity Press.
Lyotard, Jean-François. 2012. "Philosophy and Painting in the Age of Their Experiment." In: Jean-François Lyotard. *Textes dispersés I: esthétique et théorie de l'art. Miscellaneous Texts I: Aesthetics and Theory of Art*, pp. 147-75. Leuven: Leuven University Press.
McLuhan, Marshall. 1964. *Understanding Media: The Extensions of Man*. London, New York: Routledge.
Morreale, Joanne. 2007. "*Faking It* and the Transformation of Identity." In: *Makeover Television: Realities Remodeled*, ed. by Dana Heller, pp. 95-106. London: Tauris.
Nora, Pierre. 1984. *Les lieux de mémoire. I. La République*. Paris: Gallimard.
Nora, Pierre. 1986. *Les lieux de mémoire. II. La Nation*. Paris: Gallimard.
Nora, Pierre. 1992. *Les lieux de mémoire. III. Les France*. Paris: Gallimard.
Oliva, Mercè. 2013. *Telerrealidad, disciplina e identidad. Los Makeover Shows en Espana*. Barcelona: Editorial UOC.
Pasolini, Pier Paolo. 2005. "The Written Language of Reality." In: Pier Paolo Pasolini. *Heretical Empiricism*, ed. by Louise K. Barnett, pp. 197-222. Washington, DC: New Academia Publishing.
Peirce, Charles S. 1983. *Phänomen und Logik der Zeichen*. Frankfurt/M.: Suhrkamp.
Schwarte, Ludger. 2011. "Bilder bezeugen, was nicht ausgesagt werden kann. Überlegungen zur visuellen Performanz." In: *Bild-Performanz. Zur Kraft des Visuellen*, ed. by Lena Stölzl, and Ludger Schwarte, pp. 137-60. München: Fink.
Sieber, Gerald. 2016. *Reenactment. Formen und Funktionen eines geschichtsdokumentarischen Darstellungsmittels*. Marburg: Schüren.
Smith, Andrew. 2019. *Smith: Totally Wired. The Rise and Fall of Josh Harris and the Great Dotcom Swindle*. New York: Groove Press, Black Cat.
Stehling, Miriam. 2015. *Die Aneignung von Fernsehformaten im transkulturellen Vergleich. Eine Studie am Beispiel des Top-Model Formates*. Wiesbaden: Springer VS.
Wenzel, Harald. 2000. "Obertanen. Zur soziologischen Bedeutung von Prominenz." *Leviathan* 4, no. 28: 452-76.
Ziemann, Andreas. 2011. *Medienkultur und Gesellschaftsstruktur. Soziologische Analysen*. Wiesbaden: Springer VS.
Ziemann, Andreas. 2013. "Zu Philosophie und Soziologie der Situation. Eine Einführung." In: *Offene Ordnung? Zu Philosophie und Soziologie der Situation*, ed. by Andreas Ziemann, pp. 7-18. Wiesbaden: Springer VS.

## 12

# Switch-Off-Images

## The Endings of Television

Since we began our study with the operation of switching on, it should rightfully conclude with that of switching off. However, it is not so easy to switch off television—be that in the short terms of everyday life or the long terms of media history. On the one hand, everyday experience shows that television makes it difficult for viewers to turn it off. This obviously also applies to other media, such as computer games; however, television is fatiguing in a different way. Television evenings can drag on for a long time, and viewers often fall asleep in front of the television and wake up when it is switched off. It is possible, of course, to analyze how television is precisely structured for continued viewing, which Neil Postman calls the "now...this" mode of discourse (Postman 2006: 99–101), but there is also another reason. Television prevents viewers from switching it off not through activation, like a game, but rather through a strange form of deactivation. This form is also at work in web-based television, such as streaming and browsing, and it is especially apparent in the practice of binging. The viewing of television on other devices also illustrates the apparent difficulty of switching off television in terms of media history. Although it may have been superseded long ago, it is still here, even in an expanded and intensified state. How is this possible?

A preliminary answer could be that television is difficult to switch off because it is always already switched off—or, more precisely, it is never really there. This already applies to the earlier form of the cathode ray tube. We will come back to this at the end of the chapter. However, our reflections on switching off begin elsewhere and at a more recent point. Our previous discussion of reality TV revealed that television 2.0, as a medium and a constellation of screens and screen events, develops a material environment that it simultaneously inhabits and transmits as a show or broadcast. Viewers live in this environment, and it cannot be easily switched off. As a program component or format, the concrete individual show and its protagonists and celebrities are also detached from this environment or medium of a television reality that is always already permeated by screens and switch images. Each individual show (and its cast) thus individuates from this environment and can only then be switched off, which is difficult enough, but at the same time it extends and migrates over diverse image and program types. It is thus distributed once again, and it merges back into the environment from which it emerged without being switched off. In other words, it arises from the environment and then sinks back into it, which is a genuinely ontographic process. This even applies to the historical dimension in the form of television history, as the history that viewers encounter and experience through television becomes the counter-actualization of history in general. Television itself also appears as a show that arises from history and then sinks back into it again. It is thus impossible to switch off the environment of television reality, but it is possible to localize it in certain images—including images of people—that can in principle be switched off.

## Flow 2.0

For various reasons the idea of an environment that cannot be switched off brings us back to the televisual concept of flow, which we encountered in our discussion of television 1.0 (see Chapter 4 in this volume). Flow is also an emergent phenomenon, as it is an effect that cannot (or at least not only) be traced back to the individual images from which it emerges. Like an environment, it is also all-encompassing and without anything external. It is only effective through the persistence of the images as a whole, even though it emerges as an effect from the individual fragments of the broadcast event. Flow is also associated with immersion insofar as the neurological apparatus and thus the body of the viewer is linked to and immersed in the flow and its rhythm. On the other hand, however, the flow of television 1.0 was by no means condensed into individual formats or images that then reappeared in the flow itself, as applies to the reality show in the medium of television reality. In other words, the flow of television 1.0 was not recursive because there were no images of the flow embedded within it, through which it could reencounter itself.

The reason for this was once again primarily technical. As we have extensively discussed, the classical cathode ray tube was a constant and uninterrupted process of activating, deactivating, and reactivating passive image points in a fixed linear sequence. A concrete image was never delineated and suspended, yet the continuous image flow was nevertheless switchable, like the electrical current, as it could be and was interrupted. This also applied at a macroscopic level to the flow of images that could be visually perceived by the viewer. It could also be viewed from the perspective of the programs, as in Raymond Williams' conception of television as an organized structure that formed units of meaning from distinct programs, sequences, and shots. The originally structureless signal and current flow was thus articulated by diverse switching operations (Williams 1992: 85f.). This applied, for example, to the practice of switching to another location, to an advertisement, or to the next program. It also applied to references to the program's website, to parallel streams, or to the broadcaster's media library. However, the screen event could also be seen conversely as a dense sequence of preexisting switches. From this perspective, television already consisted of interruptions, and it no longer made sense to talk about interruptions at all, as there was nothing continuous that could be interrupted. Williams also identified this aspect of the flow of television 1.0 (Williams 1992: 84). However, a coherent flow emerged from this dense sequence of switches. The entire structure of program-controlled units of meaning and perception thus disappeared, as it merged into the bodily sensation of a rather neurological, physical flow. It could also be assumed that the individual shows dissolved into the television reality of their environment or medium in the same way.

All of this applies to the flow of cathode ray tube television or television 1.0, but it changes with the development of television 2.0. As we saw, the switch image of the LCD screen is active, discontinuous, and flat (see Chapter 10 in this volume). It is active because the image now glows steadily instead of only when it is stimulated by the cathode ray, and the switches are incorporated into the screen and thus into the image itself. While the cathode ray tube image faded after a split second and had to be constantly rewritten in order to remain the same, the LCD image can remain in the same state without having to be rewritten. In other words, it is time-resistant because the writing can be simply suspended, the flow of images can be arrested, and the image as a whole can remain entirely unchanged. The LCD image can even be externally paused at the push of a button, and it can later continue in the same way, differently, or not at all. In this case the interruption triggered by a human observer through the remote control is articulated and visualized in the medium of the image, and it continues on the screen. In the context of television 2.0, it could thus make sense to talk once again of interruptions, articulations, units, and structures. At a macroscopic level, as we already saw using the example of the series, television 2.0 also furnishes arrested ontograms that are parallel to and embedded in the continuous ontographic process. Through this interrelationship between ontography and ontogrammatics there are now images that proceed ontographically in the flow, and thus constitute the flow itself, but that also visualize and arrest it ontogrammatically.

On the other hand, however, every pixel of the picture is now its own switch and as such already an interrupter. There is no longer any ray that is carried along its predetermined, uninterrupted, and endless path. While the cathode ray tube image was characterized technically and microscopically as continuously flowing and completely predictable lines of activated (or non-activated) image points, the liquid-crystal image of television 2.0 is discontinuous and flat. Already at a microscopic level, therefore, the liquid-crystal image is far more than a single interruption event. Each of these switches also has its own address, so it can be reached individually instead of only as a location in a specified scanning sequence. Generally speaking, it is impossible to predict which image point will light up next (or not). The image points nevertheless set conditions on each other, as the switching of one pixel increases or decreases the probability of another pixel being switched. The microscopic flow accordingly also becomes two-dimensional, as it extends no longer only linearly but rather in all directions and even potentially over the entire screen. The image is completely incoherent at a microscopic level, as any image point can be switched at any time instead of only the next point in the scanning sequence. It can continue in the same way or differently, here or elsewhere, kaleidoscopically and chaotically. If viewers perceive these points as an image at the macroscopic level, then the image could already be described as a flow-like effect—namely, as an emergent whole that is more than the sum of its parts.

Lastly, the image can now appear on countless screens of almost any reduction or magnification in size and at almost any location. On the one hand, screens shrink to the dimensions of mobile device displays, which can distribute television everywhere and which are themselves transportable. The flow thus becomes movable in space and makes space itself plastic. Even though this may seem absurd or metaphorical at first—all movement, even that of flow, fundamentally occurs in and through space, which itself remains constant—it is just as true as the incorporation of movement into the image in the case of motion pictures. On the other hand, liquid-crystal screens also spread out into all other spaces due to their flatness and their almost arbitrarily variable expansion. It eventually culminates in dense, coherent, and unstructured image environments and their concentration into closed image environments. The flow no longer only covers *one* screen (i.e., that of the television set); rather, it proliferates over a very large number of screens. It spans a space, surrounding, or environment—namely, a coherent, placeless, ubiquitous, and recursive television reality.

The complex relationship between coherence and articulation, discontinuity and discontinuity, and interruption and duration thus changes in many ways with the rise of television 2.0, and this also changes the flow that is characteristic of television. This does not mean that the classical flow of television 1.0 disappears; rather, as we already determined elsewhere, a second type of flow emerges under the conditions of television 2.0, and this neo-flow transforms the basic relationship of continuity and discontinuity that constitutes the flow itself.

## Henri Bergson: The Materiality of Images

In order to understand this neo-flow more precisely, it is helpful to consult a theory that focuses on the relationship between continuity and interruption in the system of images. This theory also provides some further considerations that we will be able to develop later. It involves Henri Bergson's famous description of the world of images in his book *Matter and Memory* (Bergson 1988). Gilles Deleuze already used this text as the starting point for his philosophy of film as a system of images (Deleuze 2013: 1–78; here: 1–13). As we have repeatedly observed, however, the image relations of television as a switch image are fundamentally different from those of film, so we can at best follow Deleuze's reconstruction in order to replace it.

Bergson begins with a thought experiment: what if the whole world consisted exclusively of images that appeared as soon as we opened our sensory organs and disappeared again as soon as we closed them (Bergson 1988: 17)? If we want to apply this suggestion to the world of switch images, then we must first bracket the question of the sensory organs of the human body. The nature of the image as a switch is crucial for television, so we can substitute sensory organs with switches and assume that the images appear as soon as the device is switched on and disappear as soon as it is switched off. However, Bergson also uses the concept of the image in a highly idiosyncratic way. First, he does not further differentiate the concept of the image, and under the simple terms of the image he conceives of entities that are clearly differentiated from one another. In the following we will therefore attempt to differentiate between them using additional terms, such as material-images, differentiation-images, and object-images. Second, for Bergson images are not linked to certain carriers (such as screens), which would be mandatory for a media-theoretical approach and which we have also presumed so far. In other words, he does not conceive of images as technical artifacts, and he does not differentiate between them on the basis of their material conditions. They are also not defined by their flatness and their framing in the sense of conventional image theory or by their representational function and their ability to make something appear (Schulz 2005: 61ff.; 122ff.). Instead, Bergson conceives of images in two ways. First, he defines them ontologically as a special form of existence, as they are characterized by a peculiar mode of being. They are ontologically "less" than a thing but "more" than a mere idea or representation (Bergson 1988: 9). Images occupy an intermediate existence halfway between things and representations. For Bergson, therefore, the world consists of images that are not illustrations or representations and that are also indistinguishable from things. Insofar as representation also always requires subjectivity or consciousness, images are thus a mixture or hybrid of object and subject. They have a mixed existence.

At the same time, however, the image in Bergson is the entirety of material reality as such; simply everything that exists in the world is an image (Bergson 1988: 9). Images are not images of something, such as things; rather, they themselves are something. Nothing precedes the mixture that constitutes the image. The real world thus consists not of things but rather of images. This assumption poses few difficulties for the world of television, and we have explicitly followed this premise from the beginning. As we determined early on, the images of television constitute a mixed zone. They are not identical with the visible things from which they are iconically and indexically derived, and they are also not detached, external things, as they are "cold" images (in McLuhan's sense) that show nothing without the help of the human perceptual apparatus (McLuhan 1964: 24–35; 344–6). On the other hand, they are indissolubly linked to the environment by the signal current, which is particularly clear in the case of live images, and they cannot be seen as pure, detached representations that simply reproduce something that is fundamentally different from them. This elimination of a detached level of representation is precisely the point of the ontographic process. Bergson's equation of things and images—that is, of matter and the materiality of images—is thus initially helpful for television theory; however, it is challenged once again when he describes the image as a hybrid existence between thing and representation (Bergson 1988: 9). This wording implies that there are things and representations that are fundamentally different from one another and that lie outside of the mixed image. This contradiction can only be resolved by taking into account that the things Bergson indirectly assumes are beyond images only arise out of mixed or material-images. The same would then also apply to representations as well as subjectivity and consciousness. Bergson thus implies that subject and object both emerge from prior mixed relations. We already encountered an analogous process between a physical object and a human subject, which only became separable after their prior entanglement, with the concept of anthropo-mediatic relations (Voß 2010; see also Chapters 1 and 5 in this volume).

For Bergson, however, images are not only ontologically mixed relations between the objective level of things and the semantic level of representations and meanings; rather, they are also incessantly mixing or, more precisely, interacting with one another (Bergson 1988: 17). The world of images vibrates, as all images move and change, and every movement or change has a direct effect on the images adjacent to them. The adjacent images absorb these effects and immediately pass them along. Every movement of an image continues in another image and eventually in all other images. All images are thus constantly moving and changing with one another as a whole, a system, and a world. They follow strict laws of causality and determinacy, which according to Bergson are the laws of nature (Bergson 1988). The wind makes the trees sway, fruit falls down, animals are attracted; water flows, turbines turn, current is generated, motors run, streetcars go. Everything in the world is thus predictable and calculable, provided that the laws of nature are understood correctly. Bergson criticizes this view, however, because there is no future in the world of natural laws that would not be an extension, continuation, or extrapolation of the present. This is the world of nineteenth-century scientific positivism described by Auguste Comte and Herbert Spencer, who claimed that positive research begins with empirical observation and data collection, continues with the deduction of the causal laws governing what is observed, and concludes with reliable predictions of future developments and phenomena (Spencer 2019, 1974; Comte 2009). And this is precisely the world that Bergson rejected in his polemics against Comte and Spencer.

## Perception-Images

For Bergson, this description of the interaction between images according to positivist laws is fundamentally wrong. It is incomplete, and it ignores an essential phenomenon of the world of images—namely, their ability to produce the unpredictable. The reason for this, according to Bergson, is that images are dependent on perception. After the ontological localization of images as mixed existences, we thus come to Bergson's other essential and aesthetic element of the image: images are always embedded in perceptual relations, and they are thus always determined and ordered precisely by perception (Bergson 1988: 17). Perception should not be understood as a relationship between images and viewers, however, as the world of images consists of nothing but images, and even the viewers of images are images. Perception should thus be understood as just another relationship between images, but quite a special one that transcends the mechanistic force of causal relations. This special relation produces images, which then produce perception. Even the perception of images, which need images in order to be images, is a product of images. Images are always perceived images that set conditions on perception so that they can only be perceived when their perceivedness is also perceived.

This actually marks a striking resemblance between the Bergsonian concept of the image and artistic images—particularly technical and moving images. Stanley Cavell has shown this extensively in relation to film (Cavell 1979: 16–22; 126–32). For television, of course, the concept and phenomenon of perception must always be replaced by that of switching. Like perception for Bergson, switches are relations between images—even between switch images. To characterize them in a Bergsonian way, switch images are distinguished by the fact that they are determined and ordered by switching, and even their own switchability can be switched. LCD images are switches, for example, so if they are switched on or over then their switchability is being activated or transferred from one switch to another.

There is yet another possible reformulation of the peculiar recursivity between image and perception for Bergson, which brings us back to the opening question concerning the environment that cannot be switched off. The relationship between the image world and perception can be seen against the background of the interaction between the environment and the individual: just as a living being engages in and depends on its environment, so too does it participate in its emergence. We already encountered this based on television as an environment using the example of television reality. In contrast, it seems more difficult to accept the idea of a vibrating and constantly interactive materiality of images in the case of television.[1] Bergson speaks of linear causality and determinacy according to law-like processes, in which the effects of one image are passed on to the next. This includes feedback effects, reciprocal effects, and circular causalities, and it could presumably even extend to remote effects. In the case of television, however, we are dealing not with causality in a strict sense but rather at most with probabilities and conditionalities. This applies microscopically to the elementary level of image points, as the sequence in which they are written is necessary but the activation of one point is not determined by that of the previous point. In this respect, one cannot speak of the effect of one image point on the others, yet they still set conditions on one another.

This applies a little less to the sequence of images in the flow of movement. As with film, it appears that there are relations of cause and effect between the images, such as the shot/reverse shot pattern, in which one image shows the cause and the other shows the effect. Gilles Deleuze identified this as the "action-image" in his Bergsonian philosophy of film (Deleuze 2013: 179–97). At the nonrepresentational level being discussed here, one image is thus the cause of the other and not merely the representation of this cause. A conditioning also occurs if the position of individual programs in the program sequence is taken into account, as the function, value, and even meaning of the images is assessed according to their relative positions in the program schedule. If the non-semantic and nonrepresentational image material vibrates, then this particularly occurs in the movement of flow; however, flow is not characterized by a determinate and causal relationship but rather emergent. It also involves not the relationship between individual images but rather the relationship between all of the images—or, more precisely, it *is* this possible relation. In this respect, it once again corresponds very precisely to Bergson's concept, though it is not determinate and predictable. Flow has no temporal direction; rather, it is suspended in an extended present. With the increasing transformation of television, it is thus also possible to speak of a vibrating materiality of images in Bergson's sense. For example, the instant replay rerecords the chain of forwards and backwards determinations of the images, and the remote control places all programs under the direct or indirect influence of the other programs running in parallel. However, these are also not determinations according to natural laws of causality; rather, as we saw, they involve a complex interplay and interaction of the virtual and the actual. The flow is thus doubled, as the sequence of images and programs in the course of the broadcast gives rise to another flow that is produced by the viewer's switching operations between the various flows of the various programs with the help of the remote control. And this doubling is overtaken by a second, if the flow moves across various screens and becomes an environment.

Hence, although the assumption of the determinacy of the interactions between images is only very conditional for television, the flow of television nevertheless involves a kind of vibrating, constantly changing, and interrelated image material. This difference between Bergson's world of images and the process of the switch image also concerns another fundamental difference between them—namely, the function of interruptions and thus differentiations as well as pauses or delays.

## Interruption-Images

In addition to the immediate interaction between images and the vibration of image material, Bergson next introduces two additional operations that challenge the positivist assumption of a universe of images that is limited to immediate interactions. The first additional operation is that of *interruption* and thus amazingly, in our sense, switching (Bergson 1988: 18). Some of the images in the system are in a position to interrupt the infinite chain of effects, and this constitutes their specific characteristic. They do not seamlessly pass on what they have received, and their reactions are no longer mechanical, automatic, and immediate but rather delayed. They switch, stop, and steer things differently. They particularly work with the moment of the *delay*. They are no longer merely mechanical continuations of the received effects; rather, they counter the effects with stagnation, resistance, or at least difference instead of allowing them to pass through without consequences. They thus differentiate themselves from the surrounding images, stand out from their vibrations through *pauses*, and articulate themselves in this way. They insert a third between stimulus and response, which interrupts the connection between them by marking their difference or differentiation. In other words, stimulus and response can only be differentiated from one another through the interruption. The entire logic of causality and determinacy can be observed here for the first time, as causes and effects can only be separated from one another through the intervention of the interruption. Bergson also refers to the difference between received and transmitted effects, which emerges in the interruption as a delay or *affect* (Bergson 1988: 18ff.; 50–9; here: 51ff.). These pausing differentiation-images are *affected* by the images that act on them, as they allow these images to work on them without immediately passing on their effects, and they thus halt the blind chain of stimuli and responses. In this sense, the affect is the articulation of the differentiation-image and can be seen as *subject*-forming, although Bergson does not use these terms.

The second additional operation beyond mere interaction is that of *selection* (Bergson 1988: 18f.). According to Bergson, interruption-images are able to pause, and they can thus affect other images in many possible ways, from which they can *choose*. After they have differentiated themselves from other images, they can apparently also differentiate between the various responses available to them—according to whatever criteria, from the purely accidental to the goal-oriented. Mechanistically interactive images cannot do this, as they are too brief and lack the necessary *time*. Images capable of differentiation and interruption, which we can also designate as switch images, select different and not always predictable movements and effects in response to the same stimulus. For Bergson, these images are the only source of innovation in the system of images precisely because their responses are indeterminate and unpredictable. Something new is only able to enter the system through the unpredictable behavior of images of this type, and this enables a real future that is surprising and not always exhaustively laid out by what is already there.

Interruption-images can also differentiate between the surrounding images, and they can then affect this or another image in this or another way. In addition to the affect that differentiation-images more or less *are*, there is thus also a second difference—namely, the difference between the totality of all possible effects as a consequence of the stimulus received and the one particular response or handing down that is selected, specified, and actually implemented after the interruption is over. Bergson defines this difference as the *object* (Bergson 1988: 21). The object is thus also an image, but it is neither a primary and immediately interactive material-image nor an individuated and subjective differentiation-image; rather, it *reflects* all of the possible ways that it can be affected *back* to the interruption-image. The interruption-image, in turn, experiences this reflection as *perception*. A *subject-* and *object-*image as well as *affect* and *perception* thus arise from the mere interruption, delay, and modified continuation of the chain of effects. In the case of the switch image, however, this perception is not visual or optical but rather tactile. As we have repeatedly seen, switch images do not watch but rather touch one another precisely through switching, and viewers also feel the images, whether it is with their eyes or with the remote control.

Despite all of these analogizabilities, however, television 2.0 seems to turn Bergson's world of images upside down, as it *is* always already an *interruption-image*, and it only consists of interruption processes and images. Interruption is nothing special for switch images. Unlike the affection and perception effects of Bergson's interruption-images, however, switch images cannot pause without interrupting each other again in that very pause. Television is stabilized as an extended and structureless duration both at the macroscopic level in the emergent mode of *flow* and at the microscopic level in the *ontogram* of the LCD screen, which is below the threshold of perception.

Whereas Bergson's vibrating materiality of images is abuzz with constant interaction, there can be no interaction in the case of television 2.0 because it is always already interrupted and redirected before it can even take effect. And whereas Bergson's interruption-image interrupts, stops, and suspends the material process for a brief moment, a switch image must perform the opposite function, as it interrupts the interruption.

Are there switch images that suspend the switching function of the image—no matter how temporarily? At the beginning of this chapter we already looked into the possibility that the *flow* might recursively reappear as an image in the stream of images—that is, in the chain of interruptions—and we previously encountered this recursion as the relation between television reality and the reality show or more generally between the environment and the individual. Can there be switch images that interrupt the environment of interruptions and thus reflect this environment so that they themselves are individualized? Do switch images also include switch-off-images in this sense?

## Cliffhanger, Freeze, Instant Replay

The series cliffhanger is the first obvious candidate for a switch-off-image that also has a semantic effect (Fröhlich 2015; see also Chapters 3 and 10 in this volume). The cliffhanger was initially introduced as a halt and pass-on-image at the end of an entire season, and in many cases it was also used at the end of every episode. The former had to bridge the interval between the seasons, which lasted for several months, and the latter had to bridge the interval between the episodes, which lasted a week. With the development of television 2.0 and its complex narrative strands, which intersect and penetrate one another in quick succession, cliffhangers are also incorporated into the individual episodes. The cliffhanger does not dramaturgically or semantically synthesize and conclude a plotline—that is, a causal relation—in the sense of a (large or small) finale; rather, it breaks off that which preceded it. In other words, it switches off the season, episode, or narrative strand. However, it does not stop them forever (this would be an ending); rather, it simultaneously promises their continuation. We already conceived of the cliffhanger as a switch in connection with the neo-series and the theory of *family resemblance*, which differentiates between the handing down and non-handing down of characteristics. The function of the cliffhanger is to suspend this differentiation for a certain period of time, which can last from a few seconds to a few months. The switching process still takes place, but it is delayed or extended over time (to a greater or lesser degree).

Even though the prospect of that which follows—that is, a continuation after the interruption—seems to arise only as a psychological expectation or tension in the perceptual apparatus or consciousness of the viewer, Bergson's concept of the image nevertheless states that this prospect— namely, stopping and keeping open—is already a function of the image. The cliffhanger continues through expectation or tension. Real end-images, which completely conclude a plotline, do not do this. The flow of images and movement, which the cliffhanger stops, generates pressure and leads to excess. It produces lingering images that are perhaps invisible yet nevertheless perceptible to the viewer. This excess branches off, separates, and continues, even if the sequence of images has since been interrupted by other switch images. In the context of Bergson's philosophy of the image, this can be seen as another functional equivalent, as the pressure or excess is related to the switch-off-image in the same way that affect is related to the subjective, delaying interruption-image. It affects the cliffhanger and thereby makes it what it is. It lasts until the interrupted connection is resumed, which can take minutes, days, or months.

Interestingly, as we already noted, the stopped narrative or image flow usually does not resume at the same place where the cliffhanger interrupted an interruption. When the narrative begins again, such as in the following episode, it does not begin at the same place where it was suspended by the cliffhanger. It does not confirm the long-held expectation, or at least not precisely but rather at best vaguely. The image interrupts the expectation once again, breaks it off, or even allows it to collapse all of a sudden. It is as if the cliffhanger unleashes a multitude of possibilities to which it might later be connected, and only one of these possibilities can then be incorporated into the continuing series. This suggests that the difference between the horizon of possible connections and the actually selected and visible images can be viewed as the site where the series itself comes into effect in all of its seriality. The cliffhanger perceives the series or makes it perceptible as an object. The series as a whole is thus encapsulated once again in an image that is also part of the series itself. With the cliffhanger, in other words, an image arises from the midst of the chain of the coordinated (and uncoordinated) interruption-images, which interrupt one another, and this image is itself an interruption that nevertheless suspends interruptions by stopping them. It thus makes the flow that arises from these interruptions—namely, the series itself—perceptible as a whole.

The nature of the cliffhanger as a switch-off-image is particularly clear when it is implemented as a freeze frame. The image suddenly stands still, even if it was in motion just a moment before. This stops not only the narrative but also the elementary sequence of images, which is nothing other than a sequence of interruptions or switching processes. The freeze frame tends to condense the ontographic stream of interruptions into an ontogram, which enables it to revert to itself. This circumstance leads to another arrested and arresting image—namely, the slow-motion image—particularly when it is slowed down to a standstill. The instant replay operates even more clearly as a delay and stop-image that interrupts the interruption (i.e., the switch image). In the case of the instant replay, what is arrested is not the basic televisual form of the series but rather the still preceding form of the *live broadcast*. In this sense, the moment of increasing tension between the continuing live stream of events and event-images and the rewinding and arresting repetition-image, which we already encountered, establishes an affect. This affect is the difference between what occurs and what follows from it, as the image material resists its continuation. Insofar as the events themselves are always intermittent and extensionless interruptions that differentiate between a before and after, the live stream is also a dense chain of interruption events that is interrupted by the instant replay. Like the cliffhanger, however, the instant replay gives rise to a second stream of images, this time even visible images, that can be superimposed over the ongoing events, pushed to the side, or completely suspended. An object-like perception can also occur here, as it is impossible to predict where in the ongoing live flow the instant replay will end. The live nature of the continuous live broadcast as a switch image is registered here in the difference between all of the possible times when the instant replay can switch back to the ongoing event and the precise moment when this actually occurs.

The fact that the examples of the cliffhanger and the instant replay refer to the earlier development of television 1.0 does not refute the idea that they also apply to television 2.0. If anything, this shows that recursive images of the flow could already be found in the flow itself in the earlier phase of television. Both types of switch images coexist and interact with one another, and they cannot be clearly demarcated like strictly separated epochs. The long and sustained process of transformation, in which the instant replay and the remote control intervened, already shows that there is an overlapping of both types of switch images. And just as the images of television 1.0 continue to have an effect on recent television, so too do elements and functions of television 2.0 already appear much earlier, at a time when the digitization of screens and distribution channels had hardly begun.

## Memory

The example of the cliffhanger also points to another feature of Bergson's system of images—namely, *memory* (Bergson 1988: 48–50; 59ff.). We have already extensively developed the link between seriality and memory (see Chapter 3 in this volume). For example, functional memory switches between remembering and forgetting (Esposito 2002: 24ff.; Luhmann 2000: 21; 33; 38; see also von Foerster 1985), and television operationalizes this switching function in the differentiation between the open-ended episodes of the continuing series and the closed episodes of the episodic series as well as their hybrid formats. Within the continuing series, in which the cliffhanger functions, the interplay between the passing on and non-passing on of features repeats the function of switching back and forth between remembering and forgetting as well as the keeping open and the excess of possibilities that are implemented by the differentiation. In addition to perception and affect, memory also has a crucially important function in Bergson's world of images. While it is traditionally assumed to be a central activity of consciousness, however, Bergson sees it in the opposite way: like perception, memory also arises not from the assumed interiority of consciousness but rather from the system of image material. That is precisely why he titled his book *Matter and Memory*.

The differentiation-image, which for Bergson suspends the constant and immediate interaction between the material-images, needs the past. It must select one response from all of the possible responses that can follow a received stimulus, and for this purpose it must somehow already have these responses at its disposal as mere possibilities. In other words, it must have access to responses and effects—in short, operations—that it does not implement. In particular, it must be able to differentiate between operations that it has already performed and those that it has not yet performed and that emerge from the former by means of deviation, variation, intersection, and opposition. The differentiation-image must assume the iterability and variability of its own operations, and it must therefore be able to differentiate between repetition and reinvention and thus between remembering and forgetting. Operations that have already been performed, such as the responses that followed earlier stimuli, have thus not disappeared or passed in the sense of an inaccessible absence, as they are still effective.

We already observed the transcendence of linear time and the linear chain of effects in our discussion of the cliffhanger, and we traced it back to the *Zeigarnik effect* produced by the retention of interrupted connections (Zeigarnik 1927; see Chapter 3 in this volume). According to Bergson, the present moment does not truncate the past; rather, they both coexist and are equally real, although one is actual (i.e., the actually performed operation) and the other is virtual (i.e., possibility and past). Earlier operations are not absent or nonexistent, nor are they the representational content of a prior or assumed consciousness; rather, they exist to some extent "out there" as virtual images, which are just as real as operations in the present. The past has not passed, as it is still present in the exterior space of the differentiation-image and it can also be perceived with the help of memory as a sensory organ (Bergson 1988: 61). Memories are thus in no way internal or inward, since they are not located in the interiority of an assumed consciousness, brain, or subject; rather, they are found in the exterior space of the image material, and consciousness, brain, and subject emerge from them. In other words, subjectification is an effect of remembering and memory, rather than the reverse, and memory is a function of the image material, as it arises from its processuality and operativity.

In the system of the switch image, delays are caused not by interruptions but rather by halting the interruptions and keeping them open through the suspension of the context of interruptions. The cliffhanger and the instant replay are prominent examples of the performance of memory, as it is driven by such images. It is possibly more apparent in the case of the instant replay that the memory function arises from the internal properties and relations of images, as the techno-material nature of the image is more strongly emphasized in the instant replay and it thus refers more clearly to the visual materiality (or material visuality) and operative origin of the memory function. Like every other switch image, the image of the instant replay interrupts the image; however, it also reverses, decelerates, and freezes the image, and it assimilates this process seamlessly into the live flow of the ongoing events, which it interrupted and to which it eventually leads back. As an interruption, the instant replay intermittently suspends the interruptions of the switch image and thus gives rise to the past. The cliffhanger does the same thing in relation to the series that the instant replay does in relation to the live broadcast. If the series uses the memory of the viewer, as we described in connection with television 1.0, then the reverse is true in the context of television 2.0, as the memory of the viewer occupies a space that is genuinely generated by the image.

## Fancy Transitions and Test Patterns

In the period of television's transformation between analog and digital images, another interruption-image emerged that interrupted the interruptions and differentiated itself from differentiation—namely, *fancy transitions*, which are no longer or rarely seen today. Fancy transitions are images that acquire their own time and employ their own aesthetic processes to transition from one image to another. The images no longer simply replace one another on the screen; rather, they transform into one another through all kinds of video editing tools. For example, an image contracts to the size of a dot against the background of a new image, or an image arises from the middle of a prior image and gradually expands until it fills the screen. Images twist into each other, tilt toward one another, or become blurry and dissolve into non-semantic fields of pixels, from which new images emerge. These images also suspend the interruption that they themselves are, and their asemanticity particularly points to their technical materiality. They thus reflect their visual-material foundation in a Bergsonian sense. They are not representations but rather purely functional images that first emerge from representations, and they make this process perceptible by capturing it in images.

*Test patterns* are a very special case from the early period of television (Engell 2008). They were broadcast at the end of the day's programming and before it began, as programs were not yet broadcast to fill up the entire day. They were static and completely abstract screens on which various basic patterns and degrees of resolution were arranged next to one another in circular sectors, rectangular areas, or stripes. Test patterns looked exactly like the test charts used for the white balance and focus adjustment of the electronic tube cameras in the studio before the beginning of the day's programming. Test patterns also included a constant high-pitched pilot tone and some form of station or channel identification, and they were later furnished with the three primary colors of color television. They had a purely technical function in the period of terrestrial reception, as they were supposed to facilitate the adjustment of antennas and optimize the fine-tuning of the frequency setting of the receiver. If every part of the image was free of blurring, overlapping, shadows, and static, and if the sound was clear, constant, and free of noise, then the antenna was adjusted correctly and the tuning of the receiver was precise. Beyond this purely phatic function, which focused on the equipment and the reception of the technical communication channel, test patterns also indicated that something was transmitted but not sent in the sense of a program or program content (Jakobson 1960). The uninterrupted sequence of switch images was thus interrupted by a perpetually frozen image, and the pilot tone particularly drew attention to its uninterrupted and all-pervasive nature, as it was hard to bear for humans. The test pattern was thus an image of the conditions of possibility of television, as it demonstrated television's purely material-visual technicity, and it was quite simply the switch-off-image of television 1.0 (and it was actually switched off as soon as possible, if everything was adjusted correctly, in order to stop the extremely annoying pilot tone).

With the advances of television 2.0, however, these switch-off-images disappeared. There are various interrelated reasons for this. New receiver technologies, particularly cable reception, made the adjustment of antennas superfluous. Receivers also had program search functions that automatically optimized the reception and adjusted the focus on the basis of frequency and signal parameters that were completely independent of human vision. In other words, the test pattern effectively became invisible. The programming day was also extended for economic reasons that were also rooted in technology. The preferred times for broadcasting test patterns—namely, in the morning and early afternoon, when technicians were adjusting television sets and antennas—were then reserved for programs. In the 1990s, though, there were still periods of time that were not reserved for regular programming, particularly in the case of public-service broadcasters, and these periods were filled with images that can now be identified as switch-off-images in their purest form. These images were practically or entirely uninterrupted by any switching processes, such as footage of aquariums and fireplaces, recordings of train journeys through the windshield of a locomotive, or only slightly structured dashboard camera recordings of the hundred most scenic highway intersections, which were shown for hours or nights on end. The particularly impressive satellite recordings of the earth from space also pointed to the fundamental entanglement of television with space travel, which was consolidated in the Apollo Project, and visualized the environment-forming function of television as a mediasphere. Television was thus confronted by the all-encompassing environment of television perhaps most clearly here as an image on television. The flow contracted into an image within the flow, which interrupted and inhabited the flow itself, and then expanded again.

These images ran without interruptions, (almost) nothing happened, there were no events or operative interventions, and there was no switching to give them structure. These images obviously recall Cavell's concept of monitoring, particularly if one considers that they did precisely what Cavell assumed of television images—namely, they confirmed that nothing was happening outside (particularly at night, when it was important that everything was quiet) but that the world still existed in a sedentary or steady state (Cavell 1982). These images thus showed, accompanied, and created the world's sleep by interrupting the daily operation of interrupting. We already encountered this state of television prior to all interruption—namely, before and while television is switched on—at the beginning of this study, and we associated it with the concept of *latency* or the difference between the *latent* and the *manifest* (see Chapter 1 in this volume). As we saw, an apparatus is latent in a technical sense when it is in an intermediate state between being switched on and being on or having its full functionality, such as during the process of starting up and shutting down. These perpetual nightly images were in a similar but reversed state of latency in the sense of fading out or shutting down.

However, these exceptional and long-lasting switch-off-images have largely disappeared since the rise of television 2.0. That is because they always functioned as an external position to regular television that simultaneously continued and recursively observed and commented on the internal broadcast event after it was switched off, but television 2.0 forms a dense and ineluctable environment that makes such an external position no longer appropriate or even possible. Switch-off-images must now emerge from the interior of television, but all switch-off-images—from the instant replay to the cliffhanger to the nightly fireplace and even satellite images from space—display what resides inside television as well as what it resides in, and only as a whole. This is precisely what distinguishes the flow of television as well as that of television reality. Switch-off-images not only contain the entire world—from the smallest things, like image resolution or the details in a freeze frame, to medium-sized things, like fish in an aquarium or trains on railways, to the largest things, like the universe; rather, they also contain, condense, and reflect the structureless totality of all television images in a special image released from within this totality.

## The Light-Emitting Diode

The highest degree of condensation that the switch-off-image can experience is that of a single point of light—namely, the light-emitting diode (LED), which we already encountered in connection with the process of switching on. The LED glows constantly and without interruption in "stand by" mode, and it thus indicates the continued availability of the device and the readiness of its operating conditions (i.e., the electrical and signal current). Its glowing is at best weakly structured by the change of color, depending on its operating state (on some television sets, the shift from the latent state of being turned on—that is, of television reflecting its own status—to the manifest state of being operative is indicated by a change in color from red to green). Precisely through its glowing, the LED is also a switch-off-image that highlights the switched-off state of all images (albeit temporarily), which are still present through this difference. The LED is obviously not unique to the television set, as it can also be incorporated into any device capable of remaining in a latent "stand by" mode. This shows again how the properties of the switch image can detach from television. They migrate from television to any device capable of showing moving images, as they are all switch images and therefore they all come from television, and from there they proliferate to many other types of devices.

The fact that the LED is a switch-off-image and an image of switching off that cannot itself be switched off refers back once again to Bergson's system of images (Bergson 1988: 18). As we have seen, this system consists of interactions between material-images, and it contains special interruption-images that generate affect, subjectivity, perception, objectivity, as well as memory; however, these interruption-images also have another unusual feature, which is that they cannot be switched off. Bergson begins his description of this system with the following thought experiment: What if the world consisted of images that appeared as soon as we opened our senses and disappeared as soon as we closed them? In the context of the switch image, we have read this thought experiment in terms of the process of switching on and off. However, all of these images can now be perceived—and that means that they are images—by one of these images, which is itself capable of perception, and the interruption-image is one of these. The Bergsonian interruption-image is thus the image that allows all of the images to exist and that is also capable of switching them off. To apply this idea to switch images, the relations must be reversed: the switch-off-image is the only one that can allow the images to be present or absent. According to Bergson, however, the interruption-image *cannot be switched off*. Every interruption-image perceives itself proprioceptively as uninterrupted because it is uninterruptedly affected by the possibility of its own operativity, even if it switches off its external contacts and no longer perceives anything. In the case of television, however, this inability to switch itself off corresponds not to the interruption-image but rather only to the suspending switch-off-image. It is potentially only impossible to switch off switch-off-images, and the LED is such an image.

For Bergson, the express type of interruption-image is the living organism and especially the human body, as the organism always perceives and registers itself (with itself) as uninterrupted. The analogy between the system of switch images and Bergson's system of images ends here for the time being, as the technical body of the switch image registers not with itself but rather with the viewer through the glow of the LED. Even when it is not switched on, the body of the technical device obviously still affects itself through technical feedback processes and thus ineluctably and proprioceptively registers itself, but the LED, of all things, is completely unnecessary for this. The technical feedback of the device in "stand by" mode, which is a liminal state between being switched on and off, is not conveyed through imagery in the sense of visual units of visibility; if anything, it involves invisible images, such as amperage, voltage, or measured values. The LED only signals this technical proprioception externally and shows that the technical body of television does not switch itself off and that it is continuous and uninterrupted from the start.

While the LED is not technically necessary, it nevertheless connects the half-sleep of the device to its viewers and thus to the human body, thus once again exceeding the technical device. This gives us reason to reconsider the relation of the technical and human-organic body and thus the anthropomedial relation of television 2.0 and above all of the switch-off-image. It appears not only that the LED is the closest and most concentrated reification of the switch-off-image but also that most of the switch-off-images we have encountered are linked in a peculiar way to the organic and mainly the human body. Furthermore, this link is not only functional but also perceptible to the human organism (i.e., the viewer). Human proprioception and technical switch-off-images thus anthropomedially approach one another. Both of these materialities—that is, the materiality of the human interruption-image according to Bergson and the materiality of the technical switch-off-image of television—complement and are entangled in one another.

## The Technical Body and the Human Body

This is already clear from the examples of switch-off-images that we already briefly discussed in this chapter. It occurs when the structure and function of the image moves to the semantic level and is thus made visible as the visual content or properties of the image. We already saw something similar in the case of television series that project the structural and functional properties of their seriality into the content of their images and narratives (see Chapter 3 in this volume). The cliffhanger is once again an example of this. It is significant that it frequently includes close-ups or freeze frames of human faces. For example, viewers might first see an object and then a close-up of a blank face before it begins to show any signs of a reaction. Or, conversely, viewers might see a facial reaction in a freeze frame but not the shot of what this face has beheld. The cliffhanger thus interrupts the stimulus-response chain, and this interruption is projected onto a human face such that the visual-technical interruption caused by the pausing of the image is superimposed over the delaying interruption performed by the human organism. In other words, the switch-off-image (i.e., the freeze frame) and the interruption-image that complements it (i.e., the facial expression) effectively overlap, as they perform the same delaying function. It can even be said that the pause is performed twice, as it first performed functionally by the switch-off-image and it is then performed fictionally by the interruption-image that constitutes the human body.

Something more intricate occurs in the instant replay (see Chapter 6 in this volume). In many if not all cases, instant replays play around with causal relations—or rather their limits—and they thus focus on unpredictable moments. As the examples here show, delays can take three different visual or semantic forms. First, the magnifying or zooming function of the instant replay can apply to an object or an objectification. Viewers see how a ball sinks into the net of a soccer goal or how a blown-up building collapses into a cloud of dust. This can also affect human bodies if they are treated as objects. Second, the instant replay can also apply to a subject or subjectification by tracing the occurrence of an affect (such as the stunned expression of a prizewinner at the moment of her success) or the performance of an action (preferably the surprising and unforeseen action of a human actor, which includes athletes as well as other television characters). The subject-pole and the object-pole can also be combined into one and the same image, such as when viewers see how a human body affects an object (a brilliant pass, a decisive gesture, etc.). Objectification and subjectification are then active at the same time. Third, the instant replay can also apply to the relations between affect and action and to the interruption of the automatic interruptions between them. By slowing the image down, the instant replay shows that nothing happens for a brief moment, and viewers then experience the prolongation of this moment. According to Bergson's theory of the system of images, this delay is precisely what enables affect, action, and objectifying perception. The instant replay thus extracts the switch image from the chain of interruptions by reversing, decelerating, and stopping it. It also simultaneously explores how the objects depicted expose relations of influence primarily between people and things. There are also recordings that are not occupied by human bodies but rather only show relations between objects, such as catastrophe reports (Doane 1990). Affect, subjectivity, and unpredictability are then also extended to things that are normally viewed and treated as objects.

As for test patterns and LEDs, it is ultimately irrelevant what they show as images. They are entirely functional, and they intervene in the linking of human and image directly without any reference to possible image semantics, as we have already seen. The images of aquariums, fireplaces, train journeys, and satellite recordings at the end of the day's programming are a particularly interesting case, as the filling or semanticization of the suspension occurs here through images of the suspension of the filling or semanticization. The images have no significance; if anything, they refer to the end of all references. For example, a fireplace does not mean anything other than what it itself is. However, this example reveals another characteristic, which is related to the sociality of the switch image. The attraction of the fireplace or the view of (or from) the starry sky (such as the moon) is that it is seen by each individual subject but it is assumed to be seen simultaneously by all, many, or at least some absent others. This viewing is thus the experience of communicationless communication through a collective yet at the same time separate perception of the same thing. This is precisely the reason for the group- and community-building function of fireplaces (and various technical kinds of light and sensory effects, from beacons to church bells to shining satellites in the sky at dusk). This leads to the formation of a community that is purely assumed, as its members are absent, unknown, and unable to communicate with one another. However, this is precisely the basic structure of classical mass communication. The participants share nothing with one another other than their individual relation to a broadcast source and the knowledge that they are assuming the existence of others with whom this relation is shared. Considering the peculiar sociality of mass communication, which does not require copresence, switch-off-images thus also condense the whole of television into a single image (Luhmann 2000: 93f.).

# Anchor-Images: Anthropic Casting and Tactical Operations

As interruption-images, switch-off-images are thus furnished with people and semanticized with human looks and faces in an operation of anthropic casting. However, they are also aimed at people (i.e., viewers), whom they orient and direct toward themselves in a tactical operation. Following the Greek concept of *taxis*, the term "tactical" here means directing or guiding in the sense of orientation (see Voß 2010). *Taxis* refers the deployment or directing of an army, such as giving marching orders and especially aiming lances in a uniform direction. *Taxis* was later used to refer to attraction in biology, such as the sense of direction of plants that are attracted by light or water (Dusenbery 1992; see also Dusenbery 2009; English 2009). Just as the remote control is a tactical (i.e., directional) device that gives direction to viewers through the exercise of a tactile or causal movement so too are there directional switch images of addressing, such as the test pattern or the LED. However, most of these tactical images are also subject to the operation of anthropic casting.

This bring us to another particularly important type of switch-off-image—namely, the *anchor-image*, which involves *anchorpeople*, such as speakers, announcers, moderators of news and sports broadcasts as well as magazine formats, and hosts of talk shows and innumerable other shows. Anchorpeople address viewers as well as the other people on the screen. The changes in perspective between the anchor-images on the screen and between these images and the viewers are thus superimposed in a kind of suture, but it is very different from the kind of suture between the gazes of the viewers and characters in film (Oudart 1978; Dayan 1974; Heath 1978; Žižek 2001). This is already clear from the fact that characters in film avoid looking directly into the camera because it breaks the illusion—a rule that is only transgressed for specific purposes or special effects (Vernet 1988). Characters in film are thus usually unaware that they are being watched, and the technology also separates them completely from the viewers, as films are recordings. In the case of live or pseudo-live anchor-images on television, however, there is no comparable illusion to protect; rather, these images constitute a tactical orientation. Anchor-images (or anchorpeople) know that they are being watched, and they communicate this knowledge through gestures of address or tactical behavior in the sense of *taxis*.

Anchorpeople thus primarily look directly into the camera (i.e., at the viewers). Even though this frontal gaze and direct address to the viewers has always existed on television, such as during announcements or newscasts, it increasingly and characteristically expands with the transition to television 2.0. In news coverage, for example, reporters today are always shown from a frontal perspective, and they speak directly into the camera. In the case of television 1.0, in contrast, they still looked (slightly) past the camera, such as at a monitor on which their interlocutor actually appeared. This particularly applies to the anchorperson in the studio, who now actually turns away from the viewers at the beginning of a recording but is then seen once again from a frontal perspective, which is shot from a second camera. The exchange of glances between the reporter and the anchorperson thus passes through the body of the viewer, who functions anthropo-mediatically as a switch or a Bergsonian interruption-image between both of the faces on the screen.

Anchorpeople are connected to test patterns and LEDs by their tactical direction, and they are connected to freeze frames and cliffhangers by their anthropic casting. In other respects, however, they can still be counted as switch-off-images that arrest the televisual interruption events that make them possible—namely, through their recurrence. They are highly recurrent and not subject to change. They are only surpassed in this regard by the object-images of advertising, and it would be worth considering to what extent and in which cases advertising images might also be conceived as switch-off-images that then assume the function of subjectification in the interaction between images. It could also be further examined whether advertising images are not switch-off-images but rather switch-over-images, as they commonly trigger switching or zapping by means of the remote control (to avoid advertising), but that must remain a speculation here. In any case, the recurrence of anchorpeople still surpasses that of series characters, who are embedded in a different image mechanics, which can already be seen in the divergent forms of the suture, such as the different regimes of use or avoidance of a frontal perspective.

Anchorpeople and anchor-images are anchors precisely because they seem to stabilize and center the images surrounding them, and they often semanticize the switching and interruption processes ("we now switch from Buenos Aires to . . .") and direct them ("let's look again at the playground . . .") although without making themselves addressable or fungible. They intervene, yet they themselves are not subject to interventions. In this sense, they are always in a switched-off state, as the general interruption event does not affect them.

## The Dionysian Switch

The interaction between the semantic, iconic operation of anthropic casting and the tactical, indexical operation of addressing thus forms a special kind of anthropo-mediatic relation, which is stabilized by the third operation of recurrence, condensed into an image, and removed from interruption. These images displace the body of the viewer by assuming the position of the interrupter between two or more switch images. They connect them to and integrate them into the image world of television, and they also endow them with affections, subjectification capabilities, degrees of freedom (such as that of switching), memory functions (such as in the differentiation between self-contained and open-ended episodes), and object perception. As we have seen, however, they are also functional switch-off-images or televisual pauses; regardless as to what they show, they remain untouchable, and they thus persist and suspend the dense sequence of interruptions that constitute the switch image. The dual operations of these semanticized and especially anthropocized switch-off-images are inextricably linked, and they simultaneously involve bridging and interrupting, switching over and switching off, continuity and discontinuity.

We thus come back to the moment of the flow, which we encounter in anchor-images and in all switch-off-images as a recursive image within the flow itself. In our discussion of the flow, this duality was described using the metaphor of the Dionysian switch (Voß 2013; see also Chapter 4 in this volume), which enables the change between a Dionysian state (i.e., an ecstatic flow of images) and an Apollonian state (i.e., a structured sequence in the program mode of perception). It seems as if this distinction collapses with the rise of television 2.0, however, as both states now exist together and in parallel. To take Christiane Voß's formulation even further, the Dionysian switch deteriorates into the failure mode of a loose connection that no longer enables a clear switch (Voß 2013: 129). As a result, the ecstatic and structuring properties of the switch image amalgamate or coalesce. The viewer also becomes a switch with a loose connection that stays in an intermediate mode, as the viewer belongs to the system in the intermediate space between body and image and is thus both at the same time. The viewer is situated between LED and remote control, between pixel and image, between flow and structure, between the characters on television, and between them and others. The viewer can only perceive her function in the system of switch images as that of an interruption and a connection as well as an amalgam of them both at the same time. The viewer is thus simultaneously switched on and off, and this is precisely what constitutes her anthropo-mediatic form of existence.

This also brings us back to a polarity of television that is represented by the basic concepts of Stanley Cavell and Marshall McLuhan (Cavell 1982; McLuhan 1964: 24–36; 341–4), which we already encountered in our discussion of the operation of switching on (see Chapter 1 in this volume). While Cavell assumes that television separates the viewer from the world, as the world is disconnected from the viewer, McLuhan assumes that television functions as a switching-on into the image and the world, as it engages the viewer in the image and the world as an intervention or operation. In light of switch-off-images, however, this polarity seems to dissolve, as switching-off is also an intervention or operation that presupposes the operation of switching on, just as switching on inevitably entails and simultaneously always is switching off. The switch that constitutes the television image is always in an intermediate or simultaneous mode. The viewer's withdrawal from the world (according to Cavell) even necessitates her engagement in the world (according to McLuhan), and the latter cannot suspend the former. Television thus oscillates between an ontography of separation, like the one stipulated by speculative realism (in the present context, this means ontogrammatics), and an ontography of connection and combination, which can be developed, for instance, with Maurice Merleau-Ponty's phenomenological position and Michel Serres' media philosophy (Harman 2010: 124–35; Blanc 2000; Serres 2008). However, television obviously proceeds according to an ontographic rather than ontogrammatic principle, as it allows them to change into one another and it performs them both at once in one constant movement: like the flow and switching off, the ontography of television combines—or, more precisely, amalgamates—connection and disconnection as well as coherence and interruption.

## Boredom

Voß develops the idea of the Dionysian switch particularly in the context of her studies on the phenomenon of humor; however, it appears here in the context of another special state that is existential and relevant for existence in general (Harman 2010: 114–17). More specifically, it is accompanied by a characteristic and exceptional experience that has been addressed as both a *mood* and a special ontological mode that has a specific access to being—namely, *boredom* (see Engell 1989: 233–324, 2019). Boredom is the environment of television and the mode of existence of those who inhabit it. Switch-off-images also reflect boredom as an individuated, addressable, and experience-forming image from the midst of boredom itself. This is evident in the images shown at the end of the day's programming, such as aquariums and fireplaces, as well as LEDs, if they are viewed as images. Boredom is present in these images because nothing happens in them, they are not preceded by anything, they do not have any consequences, and they are not interrupted. Boredom is also present in anchor-images in an indirect and almost accelerated way. These images only consist in having something precede or succeed them, or they interrupt something to which they are entirely related, and in this respect they propel the sequence of the event. At the same time, however, they also delay the event and separate what precedes and follows them in order to insert themselves into the emerging gap. They are completely empty, even as information. They show something, but they usually have nothing to say, and this nothingness gives rise to boredom.

It is not only the switch-off-images of television that are boring but also television in its entirety, which is reflected in switch-off-images. In other words, television is not more or less boring depending on its formats and aesthetics or the personal preferences and interests of its viewers; on the contrary, it meets the requirements of boredom in different ways and thus presents boredom as a richly facetted mode of existence. We can assume counter-intuitively that the activity of television is not actually an activity or a collaboration but rather the avoidance of activity precisely through switching-off. The constellations of images that we analyzed as television 2.0 and as second screens make even the most active prosumers of digital images inactive and immobile precisely through their activity. Television stops and suspends itself and its viewers. It moves between affection and action, emergence and immersion, environment and individual. As a switch, it oscillates or remains poised (which amounts to the same thing) between the Apollonian, discursive meaning of structured programming and the Dionysian, corporeal nonmeaning of programming flow. It shifts its users to this intermediate state of existence that it itself operates, and this is apparently a state that viewers prefer. In other words, viewers use television not to escape boredom but rather to experience it.

Boredom is first and foremost a fundamental experience and form of time. If time is the raw material of television, then boredom is its product, as television effectively transforms time into boredom. It incorporates boredom as flow and articulates it through diverse switching processes. Through these switching processes, it inserts events as interventions that it itself links and forms into sequences. It then slows them down and reverses them. It serializes, reproduces, multiplies, and coordinates the time sequences. It allows the event chains to flow recursively back into themselves and interconnects them so that they stop. At the macroscopic level of the viewer's experience, this process manifests as a diversion, but it would be a mistake to assume that this diversion involves the avoidance of boredom. Diversions dispel not boredom but rather time, and what remains after time has been successfully dispelled is precisely boredom (Mattenklott 1987).

This dispelling of time is what television itself first produced live, serially, as functional memory through repetition and memorization techniques and the control of expectation. It now undoubtedly functions as the agent of a digital image society and its economic system, which in turn relies on the televisual form of time in order to function. This time should be understood as an order of events that television operatively produces, and it does this twice: once through lifting it out of the stream of time and once through the operation of this articulation itself—namely, through switching. As an operation, switching itself is an intervention and thus an initially extensionless event that differentiates between a before and after. Every production of an event—namely, through switching—is itself an event. Through further treatment with the techniques of the switch image, this doubled linear succession of the heterogeneous, which is the first main form of televisual time, can then experience and mediate condensation and pressure as well as expansion, recursion, and interference. The second main form of televisual time arises from the multiplication of temporal flows, particularly in the form of multiple channels. This leads to the horizontal juxtaposition of the heterogeneous, which enables and enforces synchronization between events and generates increasing levels of complexity, and the remote control then makes it switchable. The third main form of televisual time is the extended duration of the present, also in the form of dense repetition, such as in the episodic series. At a microscopic level, the pausing of the image on the LCD screen is also such a form of duration. It marks the period of time during which future events can be planned and predicted and decisions that have already been made can still be revised. This duration serves as a contrasting foil to the events and makes them visible for the first time.

The switch image then dispels and undermines its own time by arresting, delaying, and keeping it open. The enduring and extended present is no longer framed with regard to or in opposition to a before and after. The horizontal juxtaposition becomes an intermediate space, in which neither one nor the other is the case, and the linear succession is so expanded or compressed that it becomes indistinguishable from simultaneity. This is precisely a successful diversion, whose strongest instrument is television. As a result, it frees the present from the burdens of time and gives rise to a pure, enduring present, which is not contrasted with any other dimensions or structures of time and which allows nothing to be expected and remembered; it even allows all opposites and oppositions to be forgotten. Planning, projecting, and previewing can be dispensed with, and recapitulating and reviewing become superfluous, as coordination of the parallel events and direct communication with others dissolves. Even the automatic doubling of the events through switching processes, which the events first produce and which are themselves events, is suspended, as the switches are now kept open. They are no longer extensionless but rather occupy time as switch-off-images, like the announcements between programs, such as test patterns or LEDs.

Boredom is thus associated with the dissolution of the structure of ends and means or causes and effects. As a structure of the absence of structure, it is experienced not only as a lack of temporal orientation but also as a palpable loss of meaning, concern, and interest. At a macroscopic level, television can thus present itself collectively as the experience of boredom, but it also represents a basic form of the loss or dissolution of meaning beyond causality and finality.

## The Logic and Existence of Switching Off

Gilles Deleuze revealed that precisely the loss or dissolution of meaning is also the logic of sense (Deleuze 2004: 78–85; here: 81f.). This is obviously diametrically opposed to the conventional concept of meaning in hermeneutics or sociology (see, for example, Keppler 2015). Other than humor, which we already encountered, it is the paradoxes, parodies, absurdities, and serializations of literature in particular that first sublate meaning and thus allow it to be suspended, according to Deleuze. This occurs precisely when the incorporeal moment of differentiation enters into extended duration (Deleuze 2004: 191f.). Apart from the fact that television is also shaped by paradoxes and especially serializations, boredom can now also align itself with television in this series of counter-actualizations. Like the flow, boredom is also an emergent effect that is reflected not in the details but rather in the entirety of television, yet it is nevertheless encountered in the switch-off-images of television 2.0. Switch-off-images are obviously temporary, and they are often quite brief; like the experience of the islands of the absurd, the range of parodies and states of boredom usually (but not always) end at some point. Like moments, however, they are infinite in their duration for as long as they endure.

Martin Heidegger extensively showed and proved that boredom is an existential experience—or, more precisely, an experience of existence (Heidegger 1995). Instead of using the concept of experience, however, he focused on the mood of boredom in order to do justice to its emergent and physical rather than discursive or cognitive nature (Revers 1949: 57–73). As Heidegger formulated it, boredom delays us and thus leaves us empty (Heidegger 1995: 86f.). While Heidegger did not explicitly discuss television, Paddy Scannell already used his work to call attention to the existential dimension of television—particularly in connection with switching on (Scannell 2014: 62–4; see also Chapter 1 in this volume). We now encounter them again in connection with switching off, as the delay and emptiness of boredom is a suitable description of the difficulty of switching off the television that we already mentioned at the beginning of this chapter. In Heidegger's characteristic style, it could be said that television's mode of existence is precisely its non-switch-off-ability (*Nicht-Abschalten-Können*).

Heidegger also distinguished between three forms of boredom. The first is "becoming bored by something" (*Gelangweiltwerden von etwas*), such as when an anticipated event does not take place and another event does not take its place. The directed expectation then transforms into mere waiting, in which impatience itself disappears (Heidegger 1995: 83ff). The second is "being bored with something" (*Sichlangweilen bei etwas*), such as with the repetitive (and perhaps even accelerated) flow of ongoing events, in which no structure, development, or meaning crystallizes; this would be comparable to a diversion (Heidegger 1995: 90f.). The third is, lastly, "profound boredom" (*tiefe Langweile*), which is not related to any particular event. Linear time disappears, including subjects, objects, causalities, and themes. This form of boredom is related not to time but rather to *temporality* (*Zeitlichkeit*) and not to subjectivity but rather to *existence*, which is based on temporality. Instead of allowing access to individual objects or beings (*das Seiende*), this form of boredom allows existence to access what Heidegger calls "being as a whole" (*Sein im Ganzen*), which is revealed in boredom precisely because it is withheld (Heidegger 1995: 150).

As we have seen from the beginning of our study, however, this ontological difference—that is, the difference between mere beings and being as a whole—is undermined and replaced by the ontographic process of television. In the case of television, in other words, boredom is not an ontological but rather an ontographic event. In contrast to Heidegger's fundamental ontology, this is precisely what constitutes television's logic of sense in a Deleuzian sense: television begins where the incorporeal series of differentiations (for Deleuze, this is the "now-moment") enters into its extension (for Deleuze, this is the continuity of past, present, and future), each of which could not exist separately (Deleuze 2004: 190f.). The differentiation-image of television thus always has a body, as it is never a purely immaterial or ontological difference and it is also not subject to such a difference. It is never detached from concrete conditions, things, or image material, like an abstract structure of existence; rather, it is always inevitably implemented in technical bodies, biological-organic bodies, or image material that connects technical and biological bodies. What is switched off on television are not beings (*das Seiende*) but rather their difference from a being (*Sein*) that would exceed and transcend them. The boredom of television thus applies not to being as a whole (*Sein im Ganzen*) but rather to television as a whole, and it does not apply to existence per se but rather to a special form or mode of existence—namely, televisual existence.

Like the images through which it is encountered, this mode of existence is characterized by switching off. We thus assumed at the start that television cannot be switched off because, in a narrow sense, it is never really there.

The switch-off mode can be differentiated from disconnection in the same way that a device in "stand by" mode can be differentiated from a device that is not connected to a power supply. This would metaphorically be a state of unconsciousness or even death. Television can only operate in the switch-off mode when it is connected. When it is awakened from "stand by" mode—a state of sleep that is only induced when the device is switched on—the mode of operation changes, and the device goes from being asleep to half asleep. What changes is thus the process and relation but not the fact of switching off. The switched-on switch-off mode might also be subjectively and physically perceptible, at least in the course of a longer viewing, as a liminal state between waking and sleeping—that is, as a state of half-sleep or even as an alternative to sleep. Switching off then becomes ontographic even before the apparatus is operational. This is significant, as users can only be immersed in its switch-off mode of existence through the ontographic process, like the entire environment in which it is embedded and which it simultaneously spans. And it is difficult to switch off the switch image precisely because it is always already switched-off when it is switched-on, just as it turns the viewers and the world both on and off at the same time. But switching it off is also obviously unnecessary, as it is always already switched off and it switches itself off to the same extent that it is switched on. Television thus claims its historically strange and media-philosophically essential place as the switch-off mode of switched-on switch images.

## Note

1  Jane Bennett introduces the concept of "vibrating matter," which is inspired by Deleuze and Bergson but does not explicitly refer to *Matter and Memory* (Bennett 2010).

## References

Bennett, Jane. 2010. *Vibrant Matter: A Political Ecology of Things*. New York: Combined Publishers.
Bergson, Henri. 1988. *Matter and Memory*. New York: Zone Books.
Blanc, Sébastien. 2000. "L'ontographie ou l'écriture de l'être chez Merleau-Ponty." *Les Etudes philosophiques* 3: 289–310.
Cavell, Stanley. 1979. *The World Viewed: Reflections on the Ontology of Film*. Cambridge, MA: Harvard University Press.
Cavell, Stanley. 1982. "The Fact of Television." *Daedalus* 111, no. 4: 75–96.

Comte, Auguste. 2009. *A General View of Positivism*. New York: Cambridge University Press.
Dayan, Daniel. 1974. "The Tutor-Code of Classical Cinema." *Film Quarterly* 23, no. 1: 22–31.
Deleuze, Gilles. 2004. *The Logic of Sense*. London, New York: Continuum.
Deleuze, Gilles. 2013. *Cinema I: The Movement-Image*. London, New York: Bloomsbury Academic.
Doane, Mary Ann. 1990. "Information, Crisis, Catastrophe." In: *Logics of Television: Essays in Cultural Criticism*, ed. by Patricia Mellencamp, pp. 222–39. Bloomington, Indianapolis: Indiana University Press.
Dusenbery, Daniel. 1992. *Sensory Ecology*. New York: Freeman.
Dusenbery, Daniel. 2009. *Living at Micro Scale*. Cambridge, MA: Harvard University Press.
Engell, Lorenz. 1989. *Vom Widerspruch zur Langeweile. Logische und temporale Begründungen des Fernsehens*. Frankfurt/M., New York: Peter Lang.
Engell, Lorenz. 2008. "Drei kleine Theorien des Testbilds." In: *Modernisierung des Sehens. Sehweisen zwischen Künsten und Medien*, ed. by Mattias Bruhn, and Kai Uwe Hemken, pp. 299–322. Bielefeld: transcript.
Engell, Lorenz. 2019. "Boredom and War: Television and the End of the Fun Society." In: Lorenz Engell. *Thinking Through Television*, ed. by Markus Stauff, pp. 131–42. Amsterdam: Amsterdam University Press.
English, Stephen. 2009. *The Army of Alexander the Great*. Barnsley: Pen & Sword Military.
Esposito, Elena. 2002. *Soziales Vergessen. Formen und Medien des Gedächtnisses der Gesellschaft*. Frankfurt/M.: Suhrkamp.
Foerster, Heinz von. 1985. "Gedächtnis ohne Aufzeichnung." In: Heinz von Foerster. *Sicht und Einsicht*, pp. 133–75. Braunschweig et al.: Vieweg.
Fröhlich, Vincent. 2015. *Der Cliffhanger und die serielle Narration. Analyse einer transmedialen Erzähltechnik*. Bielefeld: Transcript.
Harman, Graham. 2010. *The Quadruple Object*. Winchester, Washington, DC: Zero Books.
Heath, Stephen. 1978. "Notes on Suture." *Screen* 18, no. 4: 48–76.
Heidegger, Martin. 1995. *The Fundamental Concepts of Metaphysics: World, Finitude, Solitude*. Bloomington, Indianapolis: Indiana University Press.
Jakobson, Roman. 1960. "Closing Statements: Linguistics and Poetics." In: *Style in Language*, ed. by Thomas A. Sebeok, pp. 350–77. Cambridge, MA: The MIT Press.
Keppler, Angela. 2015. *Das Fernsehen als Sinnproduzent. Soziologische Fallstudien*. Berlin: de Gruyter.
Luhmann, Niklas. 2000. *The Reality of Mass Media*. Cambridge: Polity Press.
Mattenklott, Gert. 1987. "Tödliche Langeweile." In: *Merkur. Deutsche Zeitschrift für europäisches Denken* 41: 91–103.
McLuhan, Marshall. 1964. *Understanding Media: The Extensions of Man*. London, New York: Routledge.

Oudart, Jean-Pierre. 1978. "Cinema and Suture." *Screen* 18, no. 4: 35–47.
Postman, Neil. 2006. *Amusing Ourselves to Death: Public Discourse in the Age of Show Business*. New York et al.: Penguin Books.
Revers, Wilhelm Josef. 1949. *Die Psychologie der Langeweile*. Meisenheim: Hain.
Scannell, Paddy. 2014. *Television and the Meaning of Live*. Cambridge: Polity Press.
Schulz, Martin. 2005. *Ordnungen der Bilder: Eine Einführung in die Bildwissenschaft*. Paderborn: Fink.
Serres, Michel. 2008. *The Five Senses: A Philosophy of Mingled Bodies (I)*. London, New York: Continuum.
Spencer, Herbert. 1974. *The Evolution of Society: Selections from Herbert Spencer's Principles of Sociology*. University of Chicago Press.
Spencer, Herbert. 2019. *First Principles of a New System of Philosophy (1867)*, Withorn: Anodos.
Vernet, Marc. 1988. *Figures de l'absence. De l'invisible au cinema*. Paris: Cahiers du cinema, coll. Essais.
Voß, Christiane. 2010. "Auf dem Weg zu einer Medienphilosophie anthropomedialer Relationen." *Zeitschrift für Medien- und Kulturforschung (ZMK)* 1/2: 170–84.
Voß, Christiane. 2013. "Der dionysische Schalter. Zur generischen Anthropomedialität des Humors." *Zeitschrift für Medien- und Kulturforschung (ZMK)* 1: 119–32.
Williams, Raymond. 1992. *Television as Cultural Form (1973)*. Middletown: Wesleyan University Press.
Zeigarnik, Bljuma. 1927. "Das Behalten erledigter und unerledigter Handlungen." *Psychologische Forschung* 9: 1–85.
Žižek, Slavoj. 2001. *The Fright of Real Tears. Krzysztof Kieślowski Between Theory and Post-Theory*. London: bfi publishing.

# Bibliography

Abelman, Robert, and David J. Atkin. 2002. *The Television Audience: The Art and Science of Watching TV*. Cresskill: Hampton Press.

Abramson, Albert. 1974. *Electronic Motion Pictures*. New York: Arno Press.

Adelmann, Ralf. 2011. "Mars-Viskurse. De- und Rekontextualisierungen von wissenschaftlichen Bildern." In: *Blickregime und Dispositive audiovisueller Medien*, ed. by Nadja Elia-Borer, , Simon Sieber, and Georg Christoph Tholen, pp. 311–35. Bielefeld: Transcript.

Allen, Michael, ed. 2007. *Reading CSI: Crime TV under the Microscope*. New York: Tauris.

Anders, Günther. 1956a. "Die Welt als Phantom und Matritze." In: Günther Anders,. *Die Antiquiertheit des Menschen, vol. 1: Über die Seele im Zeitalter der zweiten industriellen Revolution*, pp. 97–211. München: Beck.

Anders, Günther. 1956b. *Die Antiquiertheit des Menschen, vol. 1: Über die Seele im Zeitalter der zweiten industriellen Revolution*. München: Beck.

Anders, Günther. 1970. *Der Blick vom Mond. Reflexionen über Weltraumflüge*. München: C. H. Beck.

Ang, Ien. 1993. *Watching Dallas: Soap Opera and the Melodramatic Imagination*. London et al.: Routledge.

Aristotle. 2005. *The Physics. Books I-IV*, with an English Translation by Philip H. Wicksteed and Francis M. Cornford, Cambridge, MA, London: Harvard c Press.

Assmann, Aleida. 2011. *Cultural Memory and Western Civilization: Functions, Media, Archives*. Cambridge: Cambridge University Press.

Assmann, Jan. 2011. *Cultural Memory and Early Civilization: Writing, Remembrance, and Political Imagination*. Cambridge et al.: Cambridge University Press.

Augustine. 2016. *Confessions II. Books 9–13*, ed. and trans. by Carolyn J.-B. Hammond. Cambridge, MA, London: Harvard University Press.

Bachelard, Gaston. 1984. *The New Scientific Spirit*. Boston: Beacon Press.

Balke, Friedrich, Gregor Schwering, and Urs Stäheli, eds. 2000. *Big Brother: Beobachtungen*. Bielefeld: Transcript.

Barnouw, Erik. 1990. *Tube of Plenty: The Evolution of American Television*. Oxford, New York: Oxford University Press.

Baudrillard, Jean. 1994. *The Illusion of the End*. Stanford: Stanford University Press.

Baudrillard, Jean. 1995a. *The Gulf War Did Not Take Place*. Bloomington, Indianapolis: Indiana University Press.

Baudrillard, Jean. 1995b. "The Gulf War Will not Take Place." In: *The Gulf War Did Not Take Place*, pp. 23–8. Bloomington, Indianapolis: Indiana University Press.

Baudrillard, Jean. 2007. "Requiem for Media." In: Jean Baudrillard. *Utopia Deferred*, pp. 70–93. New York: Semiotext(e).

Baudrillard, Jean. 2010. "The Precession of Simulacra." In: Jean Baudrillard. *Simulacra and Simuluation*, pp. 1–42. Ann Arbor: The University of Michigan Press.

Bazin, André. 1997. "A Bergsonian Film: *The Picasso Mystery*." In: André Bazin. *Bazin at Work. Major Essays & Reviews from the Forties & Fifties*, pp. 211–19. New York, London: Routledge.

Bazin, André. 2004. *Was Ist Film?*. Berlin: Alexander.

Bazin, André. 2005a. "Theater and Cinema." In: André Bazin. *What Is Cinema ? Vol. 1*, pp. 76–124. Berkeley, Los Angeles, London: University of California Press.

Bazin, André. 2005b. "Painting and Cinema." In: André Bazin. *What Is Cinema ? Vol. 1*, pp. 164–9. Berkeley, Los Angeles, London: University of California Press

Bazin, André. 2014a. "Television Is Unbeatable for Live Coverage." In: André Bazin. *André Bazins New Media*, ed. by Dudley Andrew, pp. 48–50. Oakland: University of California Press.

Bazin, André. 2014b. "What Is Live? Preserve our Illusions." In: André Bazin. *André Bazins New Media*, ed. by Dudley Andrew, pp. 51–3. Oakland: University of California Press.

Bazin, André. 2014c. "Looking at Television." In: André Bazin. *André Bazins New Media*, ed. by Dudley Andrew, pp. 67–74. Oakland: University of California Press.

Becker, Michael E. 2005. "Kristallmanufaktur—Schritte auf dem Weg zum sehrichtungsunabhängigen LC- Schirm." *c't-Magazin* 22: 222–6.

Beil, Benjamin, Lorenz Engell, Dominik Maeder, Jens Schröter, Herbert Schwaab, and Daniela Wentz. 2016. *Die Fernsehserie als Agent des Wandels*. Münster: LIT.

Beil, Benjamin, Herbert Schwab, and Daniela Wentz, eds. 2017. *LOST in Media*. Münster: LIT.

Bellis, Mary. 2018. "The Television Remote Control: A Brief History." In: *ThoughtCo*, December 24, 2018. Accessed August 28, 2019. https://www.thoughtco.com/history-of-the-television-remote-control-1992384.

Bellour, Raymond, Christine van Assche, Francoise Parfait, Dirk Snauwaert. 2008. *David Claerbout: The Shape of Time*. New York: JRP Ringier.

Benjamin, Walter. 1999. "Little History of Photography." In: *Walter Benjamin: Selected Writings. Volume 2. 1927-1934*, ed. by Michael W. Jennings, Howard Eiland, and Gary Smith, pp. 507–31. Cambridge, MA, London: Harvard University Press.

Benjamin, Walter. 2006. "The Work of Art in the Age of Its Technological Reproducibility." In: Walter Benjamin. *Selected Writings. Volume 4. 1938-1940*, ed. by Howard Eiland, and Michael W. Jennings, pp. 251–83. Cambridge, MA, London: Harvard University Press.

Bennett, Jane. 2010. *Vibrant Matter: A Political Ecology of Things*. New York: Combined Publishers.
Bense, Max. 1949. *Technische Existenz*, Stuttgart: DVA.
Bense, Max. 1969. *Einführung in die informationstheoretische Ästhetik*. Reinbek: Rowohlt.
Bense, Max. 1976. *Die Vermittlung der Realitäten. Semiotische Erkenntnistheorie*. Baden-Baden: Agis.
Bense, Max. 1979. *Die Unwahrscheinlichkeit des Ästhetischen und die semiotische Konzeption der Kunst*. Baden-Baden: Agis.
Bergson, Henri. 1889. *Essai sur les données immédiates de la conscience*. Paris: Felix Alcan.
Bergson, Henri. 1988. *Matter and Memory*. New York: Zone Books.
Berkner, Jörg. 2013. "'Diener Ihrer Bequemlichkeit'. Die Geschichte der Fernseh-Fernbedienung." In: *Scriptum. Publikation des Historischen Archivs der Infineon Technologies*, February 2013. Accessed August 28, 2019. http://www.joerg-berkner.de/Scriptum/pdf/HA_Scriptum_IFX_23_Fernbedienung_d_2013_02_08s.pdf.
Bernet, Rudolf. 1999. "The Phenomenon of the Gaze in Merleau-Ponty and Lacan." *Chiasmi International* 1: 105–20. Topic "Merleau-Ponty: L'Heritage Contemporain. The Contemporary Heritage. L'Eredità Contemparanea."
Biltereyst, Daniel. 2004. "Reality TV, Troublesome Pictures and Panics: Reappraising the Public Controversy Around Reality TV in Europe." In: *Understanding Reality TV*, ed. by Su Holmes, and Deborah Jermyn, pp. 91–110. London: Routledge.
Biressi, Anita, and Heather Nunn. 2005. *Reality TV: Realism and Revelation*. London: Wallflower Press.
Blanc, Sébastien. 2000. "L'ontographie ou l'écriture de l'être chez Merleau-Ponty." *Les Etudes philosophiques* 3: 289–310.
Bogost, Ian. 2012. *Alien Phenomenology, or What It's Like to Be a Thing*. Minneapolis, London: University of Minnesota Press.
Boltanski, Luc. 1999. *Distance Suffering: Morality, Media and Politics*. Cambridge: Cambridge University Press.
Boorstin, Daniel. 1992. *The Image: A Guide to Pseudo-Events in America*. New York: Vintage.
Bootdiskerror. 2019. *Mondlandung - ARD-Übertragung vom 20./21.07. 1969*. Accessed July 31, 2019. https://www.youtube.com/watch?v=q6i6MTUYjjM.
Bourdieu, Pierre. 1984. *Distinction: A Social Critique of the Judgement of Taste*. London, New York: Routledge.
Branch, Frank, and Rebekah Phillips. 2019. "An Ontological Approach to Transmedia Worlds." In: *The Routledge Companion to Transmedia Studies*, ed. by Matthew Freeman, and Renira Rampazzo Gambarato, pp. 383–91. New York: Routledge.
Brand, Stuart, ed. 1970. *Whole Earth Catalog*. New York: Portola.

Brauns, Jörg. 2004. "... eine stets zu erneuernde Welt. Zur Einführung des Supermarkts in Deutschland." *Zeitschrift für Mediengeschichte* 4: 117–27.

Brecht, Berthold. 2003. "The Radio as an Apparatus of Communication." In: *New Media. Theories and Practices of Digitextuality*, ed. by Anna Everett, and John T. Caldwell, pp. 29–31. New York, London: Routledge.

Bühler, Karl. 1990. *Theory of Language: The Representational Function of Language*. Amsterdam, Philadelphia: John Benjamins Publishing Company.

Büttner, Elisabeth, and Marc Ries. 1997. "Deleuze und die Natur des Ereignisses im Kino." In: *Der Film bei Deleuze / Le cinéma selon Deleuze*, ed. by Oliver Fahle, and Lorenz Engell, pp. 350–60. Weimar, Paris: Verlag der Bauhaus-Universität Weimar.

Buxton, David. 1990. *From "The Avengers" to "Miami Vice": Form and Ideology in Television Series*. Manchester et al.: University Manchester Press.

Caldwell, John T. 1995. *Televisuality: Style, Crisis, and Authority in American Television*. New Brunswick: Rutgers University Press.

Caillois, Roger. 1935. "Mimétisme et psychasthénie légendaire." *Minotaure*, Paris, 7: 4–10.

Canetti, Elias. 1981. *Crowds and Power*. New York: Continuum.

Cantor, Muriel, and Suzanne Pingree. 1983. *The Soap Opera*, New York: Sage.

Casetti, Francesco, and Roger Odin. 1990. "De la paléo- à la néo-télévision." *Communications* 51: 9–26.

Cassin, Barbara, ed. 2004. *Vocabulaire européen des philosophies. Dictionnaire des intraduisibles*. Paris: Seuil/Le Robert.

Cavell, Stanley. 1979. *The World Viewed: Reflections on the Ontology of Film*. Cambridge, MA: Harvard University Press.

Cavell, Stanley. 1982. "The Fact of Television." *Daedalus* 111, no. 4: 75–96.

CBS News. 2019. *Apollo 11 Moon Landing 50th Anniversary, Live Stream*. Accessed July 31, 2019. https://www.youtube.com/watch?v=QBdyzTvA 3oA.

Certeau, Michel de. 1988. *The Practice of Everyday Life*. Berkeley, Los Angeles, London: University of California Press.

Clayton, Philip. 2006. *Mind and Emergence: From Quantum to Consciousness*. Oxford: Oxford University Press.

Clissold, Bradley D. 2004. "Candid Camera and the Origins of Reality TV: Contextualising a Historical Precedent." In: *Understanding Reality TV*, ed. by Su Holmes, and Deborah Jermyn, pp. 91–110. London: Routledge.

Comstock, George. 1991. *Television in America*. London: Sage.

Comte, Auguste. 2009. *A General View of Positivism*. New York: Cambridge University Press.

Csíkszentmihályi, Mihály. 1985. *Beyond Boredom and Anxiety: The Experience of Play in Work and Games*. San Francisco, London: Jossey-Bass.

Daniel, Eric D., Dennis C. Mee, and Mark H. Clark. 1999. *Recording: The First Hundred Years*. London: Wiley-IEEE Pr.

Davidson, Donald. 1980. *Essays on Actions and Events*. Oxford: Oxford University Press.

Davidson, Donald. 1984. *Inquiries into Truth and Interpretation*. Oxford, New York: Oxford University Press.
Davis, Dennis K., and Stanley J. Baran. 1981. "A History of our Understanding of Mass Communication and Everyday Life." In: *Mass Communcation and Everyday Life: A Perspective on Theory and Effects*, ed. by D. K. Davis, and S. J. Baran, pp. 19–52. Belmont: Wardworth.
Dayan, Daniel. 1974. "The Tutor-Code of Classical Cinema." *Film Quarterly* 23, no. 1: 22–31.
Dayan, Daniel, and Elihu Katz. 1987. "Performing Media Events." In: *Impacts and Influences: Essays on Media Power in the Twentieth Century*, ed. by James Curran, Anthony Smith, and Pauline Wingate, pp. 174–97. London, New York: Methuan.
dcmdcmdcm. 2006. *Zidane knockt Materazzi aus - und bekommt ROT*. Accessed September 2, 2018. https://www.youtube.com/watch?v=K9owfWFzdnQ.
Debord, Guy. 1994. *The Society of the Spectacle*. New York: Zone Books.
Débray, Regis. 1991. *Cours de médiologie générale*. Paris: Gallimard.
Deforge, Yves. 1994. "L'évolution des objets techniques." In: Gilbert Simondon. *Une pensée de l'individuation et de la technique*, pp. 173–83. Paris: Albin Michel.
Deleuze, Gilles. 1969. *Logique du sens*. Paris: Les Editions de Minuit.
Deleuze, Gilles. 1986. "Le cerveau, c'est l'écran. Entretien avec Gilles Deleuze." *Cahiers du cinema*, no. 380 (1986/2): 25–32.
Deleuze, Gilles. 1988. *Bergsonism*. New York: Zone Books.
Deleuze, Gilles. 1992. "Postscript on the Societies of Control." *Oktober* 59: 3–7.
Deleuze, Gilles. 1994. *Difference and Repetition*. New York: Columbia University Press.
Deleuze, Gilles. 2004. *The Logic of Sense*. London, New York: Continuum.
Deleuze, Gilles. 2013a. *Cinema I: The Movement-Image*. London, New York: Bloomsbury Academic.
Deleuze, Gilles. 2013b. *Cinema II: The Time-Image*. London, New York: Bloomsbury Academic.
Deleuze, Gilles, and Félix Guattari. 1986. *Kafka: Toward a Minor Literature*. Minneapolis, London: Minnesota University Press.
Deleuze, Gilles, and Félix Guattari. 2000. *Anti-Oedipus: Capitalism and Schizophrenia*. Minneapolis: University of Minnesota Press.
Denson, Shane, and Ruth Mayer. 2012. "Bildstörung. Serielle Figuren und der Fernseher." *Zeitschrift für Medienwissenschaft* 7: 90–102.
Derrida, Jacques. 1982. "Signature Event Context." In: Jacques Derrida. *Margins of Philosophy*, pp. 307–30. Chicago: The University of Chicago Press.
Descola, Philippe, ed. 2010a. *La fabrique des images: Vision du monde et formes de la représentation*. Paris: Musée du quai Branly/Somogy éditions d'art.
Descola, Philippe, ed. 2010b. "Un monde objectif." In: *La fabrique des images: Vision du monde et formes de la représentation*, ed. by Philippe Descola, pp. 73–100. Paris: Musée du quai Branly/Somogy éditions d'art.

Descola, Philippe, ed. 2010c. "Un monde enchevêtré." In: *La fabrique des images: Vision du monde et formes de la représentation*, ed. by Philippe Descola, pp. 165–84. Paris: Musée du quai Branly/Somogy éditions d'art.

Descola, Philippe, ed. 2013. *Beyond Nature and Culture*. Chicago, London: University of Chicago Press.

Dewey, John. 2008. "Art as Experience." In: John Dewey. *The Collected Works of John Dewey, 1882–1953. The Later Works, 1925–1953, Vol. 10: 1934*, ed. by Jo Ann Boydston. Carbondale: Southern Illinois University Press.

Didi-Huberman, Georges. 1992. *Ce que nous voyons, ce qui nous regarde*. Paris: Minuit.

Dienst, Richard. 1995. *Still Life in Real Time: Theory after Television*. Durham: Duke University Press.

Doane, Mary Ann. 1990. "Information, Crisis, Catastrophe." In: *Logics of Television: Essays in Cultural Criticism*, ed. by Patricia Mellencamp, pp. 222–39. Bloomington, Indianapolis: Indiana University Press.

Dreyfus, Hubert L. 1997. *What Computers Still Can't Do: A Critique of Artificial Reason*. Cambridge, MA, London: The MIT Press.

Dunmur, David, and Tim Sluckin. 2011. *Soap, Science, and Flat Screen TVs*. Oxford, New York: Oxford University Press.

Durkheim, Émile. 1953. *Sociology and Philosophy*. Glencoe, IL: Free Press.

Durkheim, Émile. 1966. *The Rules of Sociological Method*. New York: Free Press.

Dusenbery, Daniel. 1992. *Sensory Ecology*. New York: Freeman.

Dusenbery, Daniel. 2009. *Living at Micro Scale*. Cambridge, MA: Harvard University Press.

Early Television Museum. n. d. "Postwar American Television. Zenith Flashmatic." Accessed August 28, 2019. https://www.earlytelevision.org/zenith_flashmatic.html.

Eco, Umberto. 1985. "TV—La transparence perdue." In: Umberto Eco. *La guerre du faux*, pp. 190–9. Paris: Grasset et Frasquelle.

Eco, Umberto. 1986. "Travels in Hyperreality." In: Umberto Eco. *Travels in Hyperreality. Essays*, pp. 1–58. San Diego, New York, London: A Harvest Book, Harcourt Inc., A Helen and Kurt Wolf Book.

Eco, Umberto. 1989. "Chance and Plot: Television and Aesthetics." In: Umberto Eco. *The Open Work*, pp. 105–22. Cambridge, MA: Harvard University Press.

Elias, Norbert. 2007. *Involvement and Detachment. The Collected Works of Norbert Elias, Vol. 8*. Dublin: University College Dublin Press.

Ems -Dollart Media. 2016a. *MONDLANDUNG- Livesendung, WDR 20./21Juli 1969 Teil 1*. Accessed July 31, 2019. https://www.youtube.com/watch?v=30QA1xwEiZg.

Ems -Dollart Media. 2016b. *MONDLANDUNG- Livesendung, WDR 20/21.JULI 1969 Teil 2*. Accessed July 31, 2019. https://www.youtube.com/watch?v=tfZLFZoQ6Bg.

Engell, Lorenz. 1987. "Wechselwirtschaft und vertauschte Ansprachen." *Tumult. Zeitschrift für Verkehrswissenschaft* 11: 102–15.

Engell, Lorenz. 1989. *Vom Widerspruch zur Langeweile. Logische und temporale Begründungen des Fernsehens*. Frankfurt/M., New York: Peter Lang.
Engell, Lorenz. 1994. *Das Gespenst der Simulation. Ein Beitrag zur Überwindung der "Medientheorie" durch Analyse ihrer Logik und Ästhetik*. Weimar: VDG.
Engell, Lorenz. 1996. "Das Amedium. Grundbegriffe des Fernsehens in Auflösung: Ereignis und Erwartung." *montage a/v*, 5/1: 129–53.
Engell, Lorenz. 2000a. "Schwierigkeiten der Fernsehgeschichte." In: Lorenz Engell. *Ausfahrt nach Babylon. Essais und Vorträge zur Kritik der Medienkultur*, pp. 89–108. Weimar: VDG.
Engell, Lorenz. 2000b. "Die Liquidation des Intervalls. Zur Entstehung des digitalen Bildes aus Zwischenraum und Zwischenzeit." In: Lorenz Engell. *Ausfahrt nach Babylon. Essais und Vorträge zur Kritik der Medienkultur*, pp. 183–205. Weimar: VDG.
Engell, Lorenz. 2003. "Tasten Wählen Denken. Genese und Funktion einer philosophischen Apparatur." In: *Medienphilosophie. Beiträge zur Klärung eines Begriffs*, ed. by Stefan Münker, Alexander Roesler, and Mike Sandbothe, pp. 53–77. Frankfurt/M: Fischer.
Engell, Lorenz. 2008a. "Drei kleine Theorien des Testbilds." In: *Modernisierung des Sehens. Sehweisen zwischen Künsten und Medien*, ed. by Mattias Bruhn, and Kai Uwe Hemken, pp. 299–322. Bielefeld: transcript.
Engell, Lorenz. 2008b. "Das Mondprogramm. Wie das Fernsehen das größte Ereignis aller Zeiten erzeugte und wieder auflöste, um zu seiner Geschichte zu finden." In: *Medienereignisse der Moderne*, ed. by Friedrich Lenger, and Ansgar Nünning, pp. 150–71. Darmstadt: Wiss. Buchges.
Engell, Lorenz. 2009a. "Fernsehen mit Unbekannten. Überlegungen zur experimentellen Television." In: *Fernsehexperimente. Stationen eines Mediums*, ed. by Michael Grisko, and Stefan Münker, pp. 15–46. Berlin: Kadmos.
Engell, Lorenz. 2009b. "Virtual History Die Geschichte als Fernsehen." *Zeithistorische Forschungen*, 2009/3, Jg. 6: 391–412.
Engell, Lorenz. 2009c. "Virtual History. Falsche Spur und lückenloses Gedächtnis: Wie das Fernsehen sich behauptet." In: *Goofy History. Fehler machen Geschichte*, ed. by BUTIS BUTIS/Marion Herz, Alexander Klose, Isabel Kranz, and Jan Philip Müller, pp. 280–94. Köln, Weimar, Wien: Böhlau Verlag.
Engell, Lorenz. 2010. "'Are You in Pictures?'—Ruhende Bilder am Ende bewegter Bilder, besonders in Ethan und Joel Coens 'Barton Fink." In: *Freeze frames. Zum Verhältnis von Fotografie und Film*, ed. by Stefanie Diekmann, and Winfried Gerling, pp. 172–91. Bielefeld: Transcript.
Engell, Lorenz. 2011. "Erinnern/Vergessen. Serien als operatives Gedächtnis des Fernsehens." In: Serielle Formen. *Von den frühen Film-Serials zu aktuellen Quality-TV- und Online-Serien*, ed. by Robert Blanchet, Kristina Köhler, Tereza Smid, Julia Zurtavern (=Zürcher Filmstudien, Bd. 25), pp. 115–33. Marburg: Schüren.

Engell, Lorenz. 2012a. "Folgen und Ursachen. Über Serialität und Kausalität." In: *Populäre Serialität: Narration - Evolution - Distinktion. Zum seriellen Erzählen seit dem 19. Jahrhundert*, ed. by Frank Kelleter, pp. 241–58. Bielefeld: transcript.

Engell, Lorenz. 2012b. "Kommentar." *Zeitschrift für Medien- und Kulturforschung (ZMK)* 2: 91-7.

Engell, Lorenz. 2013a. "The Tactile and the Index: from the Remote Control to the Hand-Held Computer. Some Speculative Reflections on the Bodies of the Will." *NECSUS. European Journal of Media Studies* 2. Accessed August 28, 2019. https://necsus-ejms.org/the-tactile-and-the-index-from-the-remote-control-to-the-hand-held-computer-some-speculative-reflections-on-the-bodies-of-the-will/.

Engell, Lorenz. 2013b. "Über den Agenten. Bemerkungen zu einer populären Figur der Dia-Medialität." In: *Paradoxalität des Medialen*, ed. by Jan-Henrik Möller, Jörg Sternagel, and Lenore Hipper, pp. 41–58. München: Fink.

Engell, Lorenz. 2014. "Jenseits von Geschichte und Gedächtnis. Historiographie und Autobiographie des Fernsehens." *montage a/v* 14/1: 60–79.

Engell, Lorenz. 2015a. "Der Film zwischen Ontografie und Anthropogenese." In: *Mediale Anthropologie*, ed. by Lorenz Engell, and Christiane Voss, pp. 63–82. München: Fink.

Engell, Lorenz. 2015b. "Agentur." In: *Essays zur Film-Philosophie*, ed. by Lorenz Engell, Oliver Fahle, Vinzenz Hediger, Christiane Voss, pp. 17–62. München: Fink.

Engell, Lorenz. 2016. "Die Kunst des Fernsehens. Ludwig Wittgensteins 'Familienähnlichkeit' und die Medienästhetik der Fernsehserie." In: *Kunst/Fernsehen*, ed. by Klaus Krüger, Christian Hammes, and Matthias Weiß, pp. 19–38. Paderborn: Wilhelm Fink.

Engell, Lorenz. 2019a. "Bilder aus dem All. Das 'Anthropische Prinzip' und der Planet Erde als medienanthropologische Inszenierung." In: *Medienanthropologische Szenen. Die Conditio Humana im Zeitalter der Medien*, ed. by Christiane Voß, Katerina Krtilova, and Lorenz Engell, pp. 15–30. München: Fink.

Engell, Lorenz. 2019b (expected). "'Seither' und 'Immer Schon'. Zwei Zeitfiguren bei Friedrich Kittler." In: *Kittler 1985/1986*, ed. by Till A. Heilmann, and Jens Schröter. n. p.: Springer.

Engell, Lorenz. 2019c. "Boredom and War. Television and the End of the Fun Society." In: Lorenz Engell: *Thinking Through Television*, ed. by Markus Stauff, pp. 131–42. Amsterdam: Amsterdam University Press.

Engell, Lorenz. 2019d. "Narrative: Historiographic Technique and Narratrive Spirit." In: Lorenz Engell. *Thinking Through Television*, ed. by Markus Stauff, pp. 145–70. Amsterdam: Amsterdam University Press.

Engell, Lorenz. 2019e. "Beyond History and Memory: Historiography and the Autobiography of Television." In: Lorenz Engell. *Thinking Through Television*, ed. by Markus Stauff, pp. 171–88. Amsterdam: Amsterdam University Press.

Engell, Lorenz. 2019f. "On Series." In: Lorenz Engell. *Thinking Through Television*, ed. by Markus Stauff, pp. 189–200. Amsterdam: Amsterdam University Press.

Engell, Lorenz, Carina Jasmin Englert, Natascha Kempken, Dominik Maeder, Jo Reichertz, jens Schröter, and Daniela Wentz.. 2014. "Das Fernsehen als Akteur und Agent." In: *Die Mediatisierung sozialer Welten. Synergien empirischer Forschung*, ed. by Friedrich Krotz, Cathrin Despotović, and Merle-Marie Kruse, pp. 145–65. Wiesbaden: Springer VS.

Engell, Lorenz, and Oliver Fahle. 2002. "Film-Philosophie. Mit einer Analyse zu 'Winterschläfer'." In: *Moderne Film-Theorie*, ed. by Jürgen Felix, pp. 222–45. Mainz: Bender.

Engell, Lorenz, and Oliver Fahle. 2008. "Gilles Deleuze." In: *Philosophie in der Medientheorie von Adorno bis Zizek*, ed. by Alexander Roesler, and Bernd Stiegler, pp. 57–70. München: Fink.

Engell, Lorenz, Frank Hartmann, and Christiane Voß. 2013. "Einleitung." In: *Körper des Denkens. Neue Positionen der Medienphilosophie*, ed. by Lorenz Engell, Frank Hartmann, and Christiane Voß, pp. 7–8. München: Fink.

Engell, Lorenz, and Bernhard Siegert. 2020. "Schalten und Walten. Editorial." *Zeitschrift für Medien- und Kulturforschung (ZMK)* 1: 7–12.

Engell, Lorenz, and Bernhard Siegert, eds. 2010. *Zeitschrift für Medien- und Kulturforschung (ZMK)* 1/1, Topic "Kulturtechnik."

Engell, Lorenz, and Bernhard Siegert, eds. 2012. *Zeitschrift für Medien- und Kulturforschung (ZMK)* 2, Topic "Kollektiv."

Engell, Lorenz, and Joseph Vogl. 1999. "Vorwort." In: *Kursbuch Medienkultur: die maßgeblichen Theorien von Brecht bis Baudrillard*, ed. by Claus Pias, Lorenz >Engell, Oliver Fahle, Britta Neitzel, and Joseph Vogl, pp. 8–11. Stuttgart: Deutsche Verlags-Anstalt.

Engell, Lorenz, and Christiane Voß. 2011. *Aufhören/Weitermachen: Zur Polarität des Humors*. Accessed June 12, 2019. https://www.uni- weimar.de/fileadmin/user/fak/medien/professuren/Philosophie_Audiovisueller_Medien/Downloads/ Ringvorlesung-Engell-Voss_compr.mp3.

Englert, Carina, and Jo Reichertz, eds. 2016. *CSI. Rechtsmedizin. Mitternachtsforensik*. Wiesbaden: Springer.

English, Stephen. 2009. *The Army of Alexander the Great*. Barnsley: Pen & Sword Military.

Erll, Astrid, and Ansgar Nünning, eds. 2004. *Medien des kollektiven Gedächtnisses. Konstruktivität—Historizität—Kulturspezifizität*. Berlin, Boston: De Gruyter.

Esch, Deborah. 1999. "No Time Like the Present." In: Deborah Esch. *In the Event. Reading Journalism, Reading Theory*, pp. 61–70. Stanford: Stanford University Press.

Esposito, Elena. 2002. *Soziales Vergessen. Formen und Medien des Gedächtnisses der Gesellschaft*. Frankfurt/M.: Suhrkamp.

Faatz, Michael. 2001. *Zur Spezifik des Fernsehtextes. Eine Untersuchung zu Inhalten, Präsentationsformen und Perspektiven; dargestellt anhand des MDR-Textes und des Sat.1-Textes*. Fernsehwissenschaft Vol. 4. Köln: Teiresias.

Fahle, Oliver. 2005. "Das Bild und das Sichtbare. Eine Bildtheorie des Fernsehens." In: *Philosophie des Fernsehens*, ed. by Oliver Fahle, and Lorenz Engell, pp. 77–91. Paderborn: Fink.

Fahle, Oliver. 2007. "Die Stadt als Spielfeld. Raumästhetik in Film und Computerspiel?." In: *Spielformen im Spielfilm. Zur Medienmorphologie des Kinos nach der Postmoderne*, pp. 225–38, ed. by Rainer Leschke, and Jochen Venus.

Fahle, Oliver. 2010. "Die Nicht-Stadt im Tatort." In: *Tatort Stadt. Mediale Topographien eines Fernsehklassikers*, ed. by Julika Griem, and Sebastian Scholz, pp. 69–79. Frankfurt/M., New York: Campus.

Fahle, Oliver. 2011. "Das Bild und das Sichtbare und das Serielle. Eine Bildtheorie des Fernsehens angesichts des Digitalen." In: *Blickregime und Dispositive audiovisueller Medien*, ed. by Nadja Elia-Borer, Simon Sieber, and Georg Christoph Tholen, pp. 111–33. Bielefeld: Transcript.

Fahle, Oliver, and Lorenz Engell. 2005. "Einführung." In: *Philosophie des Fernsehens*, ed. by Oliver Fahle, and Lorenz Engell, pp. 7–19. München: Fink.

Feuer, Jane. 1983. "The Concept of Live Television: Ontology as Ideology." In: *Regarding Television*, ed. by E. Ann Kaplan, pp. 12–21. Frederick: University Publications of America.

Flasch, Kurt. 1993. *Was ist Zeit? Augustinus von Hippo: Das XI. Buch der Confessiones*. Frankfurt/M: Klostermann.

Flusser, Vilém. 2011. *Into the Universe of Technical Images*. Minneapolis, London: University of Minnesota Press.

Flusser, Vilém. 2014. *Gestures*. Minneapolis, London: University of Minnesota Press.

Foerster, Heinz von. 1949. *Circular Causal, and Feedback Mechanisms in Biological and Social Systems*. New York: LLC.

Foerster, Heinz von. 1985. "Gedächtnis ohne Aufzeichnung." In: Heinz von Foerster. *Sicht und Einsicht*, pp. 133–75. Braunschweig et al.: Vieweg.

Foerster, Heinz von. 1993. "Epistomologie der Kommunikation." In: Heinz von Foerster. *Wissen und Gewissen. Versuch einer Brücke*, pp. 269–81. Frankfurt/M.: Suhrkamp.

[Formula 1 San Marino 1994]. n. d. Accessed September 14, 2018. https://www.youtube.com/watch?v=fCrUdyPY02k.

Foucault, Michel. 1995. *Discipline and Punish. The Birth of the Prison*. New York: Vintage Books.

Foucault, Michel. 2002. *The Order of Things: An Archaeology of the Human Sciences*. London, New York: Routledge.

France Automobile. 2017. *GP de Saint-Marin 1994*. Accessed November 17, 2019. https://www.youtube.com/watch?v=z7Mam-wRbZk&t=2329s.

Franck, Georg. 1998. *Eine Ökonomie der Aufmerksamkeit. Ein Entwurf*. München: Hanser.

Freud, Sigmund. 1961. "Homour." In: Sigmund Freud. *The Standard Edition of the Complete Psychological Works of Sigmund Freud. Volume XXI*, ed. by James Strachey, pp. 159–66. London: The Hogarth Press.

Fröhlich, Vincent. 2015. *Der Cliffhanger und die serielle Narration. Analyse einer transmedialen Erzähltechnik*. Bielefeld: Transcript.
Gabriel, Gottfried. 1980. "Familienähnlichkeit." In: *Enzyklopädie Philosophie und Wissenschaftstheorie*. Vol. 1, ed. by Jürgen Mittelstraß, pp. 473f. Tübingen: Metzler.
Gehlen, Arnold. 1988. *Man: His Nature and Place in the World*. New York: Columbia University Press.
Geimer, Peter. 2009. *Theorien der Fotografie zur Einführung*. Hamburg: Junius.
Gell, Alfred. 1998. *Art and Agency: An Anthropological Theory*. Oxford: Clarendon.
Genette, Gérard. 1987. *Paratexte*. Paris: Seul; engl.: *Paratexts. Thresholds of Interpretation*. Cambridge: Cambridge University Press 1997.
Goeres, Ralf. 2000. *Die Entwicklung der Philosophie Ludwig Wittgensteins unter besonderer Berücksichtigung seiner Logikkonzeption*. Würzburg: Königshausen und Neumann.
Grampp, Sven. 2011. *Marshall McLuhan. Eine Einführung*. Konstanz, München: UVK. Grau, Oliver. 2003. *Virtual Art: From Illusion to Immersion*. Cambridge, MA: MIT Press.
Gray, Ann, and Erin Bell. 2013. *History on Television*. London, New York: Routledge.
Greve, Jens, and Annette Schnabel, eds. 2011. *Emergenz. Zur Analyse und Erklärung komplexer Strukturen*. Berlin: Suhrkamp.
Gross, Benjamin. 2018. *The TVs of Tomorrow: How RCA's Flat Screen Dreams Led to the First LCD's*. Chicago, London: University of Chicago Press.
Gruber, Bettina, and Maria Vedder. 1983. "Les Levine." In: *Kunst und Video. Internationale Entwicklung und Künstler*, ed. by Bettina Gruber, and Maria Vedder, pp. 164–6. Köln: DuMont.
Gründler, Hana. 2008. *Wittgenstein. Anders sehen. Die Familienähnlichkeit von Kunst, Ästhetik und Philosophie*. Berlin: trafo.
Gumbrecht, Hans Ulrich. 2004. *Production of Presence: What Meaning Cannot Convey*. Stanford: Stanford University Press.
Günther, Gotthard. 1963. *Das Bewusstsein der Maschinen. Eine Metaphysik der Kybernetik*. Baden-Baden: Agis.
Gupta, P. Sen, Meher H. Engineer, and Virginia Anne Shepherd. 2009. *Remembering Sir J.C. Bose*, p. 106. Bangalore: Indian Institute of Science, World Scientific.
Halbwachs, Maurice. 1992. *On Collective Memory*. Chicago, London: The University of Chicago Press.
Halbwachs, Maurice. n. d. *The Collective Memory*. New York et al.: Harper & Row.
Hall, Stuart. 1996. "Encoding/Decoding." In: *Culture, Media, Language: Working Papers in Cultural Studies, 1972–79*, ed. by Stuart Hall et al., pp. 128–38. London, New York: Routledge, Centre for Contemporary Cultural Studies University of Birmingham.

Hanke, Helmut. 1990. "Umbruch im Fernsehen der DDR." In: *Ästhetik und Kommunikation* 19, no.,73/74: 79–86.
Harman, Graham. 2010. *The Quadruple Object*. Winchester, Washington: Zero Books.
Hartley, John. 1999. *Uses of Television*. London, New York: Routledge.
Hartmann, Frank. 2006. *Globale Medienkultur. Technik, Geschichte, Theorien*. Wien facultas wuv.
Heath, Stephen. 1978. "Notes on Suture." *Screen* 18, no. 4: 48–76.
Heidegger, Martin. 1982. *The Basic Problems of Phenomenology*. Bloomington: Indiana University Press.
Heidegger, Martin. 1992. *History of the Concept of Time. Prolegomena*. Bloomington, Indianapolis: Indiana University Press.
Heidegger, Martin. 1993a. "What is Metaphysics." In: Martin Heidegger. *Basic Writings*, ed. by. David Farrell Krell, pp. 89–110. New York: HarperCollins.
Heidegger, Martin. 1993b. "The Question Concerning Technology." In: Martin Heidegger. *Basic Writings*, ed. by David Farrell Krell, pp. 307–41. New York: HarperCollins.
Heidegger, Martin. 1995. *The Fundamental Concepts of Metaphysics: World, Finitude, Solitude*. Bloomington, Indianapolis: Indiana University Press.
Heidegger, Martin. 2008. *Being and Time*. New York et al.: Harper Collins.
Heßler, Martin, and Dieter Mersch. 2009. "Bildlogik, oder: Was heißt visuelles Denken?." In: *Logik des Bildlichen. Zur Kritik der ikonischen Vernunft*, ed. by Martina Heßler, and Dieter Mersch, pp. 8–62. Bielefeld: Transcript.
Hickethier, Knut. 1998. *Geschichte des deutschen Fernsehens*. Stuttgart, Weimar: Metzler.
Hiebel, Hanns H., Heinz Hiebler, Karl Koger, and Herwig Walitsch. 1999. *Große Medienchronik*. München: Fink.
Holland, John H. 1998. *Emergence: From Chaos to Order*. Oxford, New York: Oxford University Press.
Hollendonner, Barbara. 2009. "Der Zauber der Präsenz. Evidenzproduktion in CSI: Crime Scene Investigation." In: *Zeitschrift für Kulturwissenschaften* 1: 27–40, Topic "Sehnsucht nach Evidenz."
Hollendonner, Barbara. 2015. "Der Blick nach Innen." In: *Medien in Zeit und Raum. Maßverhältnisse des Medialen*, ed. by Ingo Köster, and Kai Schubert, pp. 107–16. Bielefeld: Transcript.
Holmes, Su. 2004. "'All You've Got to Worry About is the Task, Having a Cup of Tea, and Doing a Bit of Sunbathing': Approaching Celebrity in *Big Brother*." In: *Understanding Reality TV*, ed. by Su Holmes, and Deborah Jermyn, pp. 111–35. London: Routledge.
Horkheimer, Max, and Theodor W. Adorno. 2002. *Dialectic of Enlightenment: Philosophical Fragments*. Stanford: Stanford University Press.
Horton, Donald, and Richard R. Wohl. 1956. "Mass Communication and Para-Social Interaction. Observations On Intimacy at a Distance." *Psychiatry* 19: 215–29.

Husserl, Edmund. 1991. *On the Phenomenology of the Consciousness of Internal Time (1893-1917)*. Dordrecht, Boston, London: Kluwer Academic Publishers.
Iser, Wolfgang. 2013. *Emergenz. Nachgelassene und verstreut publizierte Essays.* Konstanz: KUP.
Jakobson, Roman. 1960. "Closing Statements: Linguistics and Poetics." In: *Style in Language*, ed. by Thomas A. Sebeok, pp. 350-77. Cambridge, MA: The MIT Press.
Jantsch, Erich. 1980. *The Self-Organizing Universe: Scientific and Human Implications of the Emerging Paradigm of Evolution.* Oxford: Pergamon Press.
Jenkins, Henry. 2006. *Convergence Culture: Where Old and New Media Collide.* New York, London: The University of New York Press.
Jermyn, Deborah. 2004. "This is About Real People: Video Technologies, Actuality and Affect in the Television Crime Appeal." In: *Understanding Reality TV*, ed. by Su Holmes, and Deborah Jermyn, pp. 71-90. London: Routledge.
Jermyn, Deborah. 2007. "Body Matters: Realism, Spectacle, and the Corpse in CSI." In: *Reading CSI: Crime TV under the Microscope*, ed. by Michael Allen, pp. 79-89. New York: Tauris.
JFK1963NEWSVIDEOS. 2013. *KRLD-TV Footage of The Oswald Shooting.* Accessed July 16, 2019. https://www.youtube.com/watch?v=m5khMFFKslw.
Jörisson, Benjamin. 2007. *Beobachtungen der Realität. Die Frage nach der Wirklichkeit im Zeitalter der Neuen Medien.* Bielefeld: Transcript.
Kapp, Ernst. 2018. *Elements of a Philosophy of Technology: On the Evolutionary History of Culture.* Minneapolis: University of Minnesota Press.
Kava, Misha, and Amy West. 2004. "Temporalities of the Real: Conceptualising Time in Reality TV." In: *Understanding Reality TV*, ed. by Su Holmes, and Deborah Jermyn, pp. 136-53. London: Routledge.
Kawamoto, Hiroshisa. 2002. "The History of Liquid-Crystal Displays." *Proceedings of the IEEE*, 90, no. 4: 460-500.
Kelleter, Frank, ed. 2012. *Populäre Serialität: Narration—Evolution—Distinktion. Zum seriellen Erzählen seit dem 19. Jahrhundert.* Bielefeld: Transcript.
Keppler, Angela. 2015. *Das Fernsehen als Sinnproduzent. Soziologische Fallstudien.* Berlin: de Gruyter.
Keppler, Angela. 1980. *The Concept of Anxiety.* Princeton: Princeton University Press.
Kierkegaard, Søren. 1942. *Repetition: An Essay in Experimental Psychology.* London: Oxford University Press.
Kirchmann, Kay. 1993. "Zwischen Selbstreflexivität und Selbstreferentialität." *Film und Kritik* 2: 23-37.
Kittler, Friedrich. 1993. *Draculas Vermächtnis. Technische Schriften.* Leipzig: Reclam. [war so mal im 1. Kapitel, jetzt nicht mehr]
Kittler, Friedrich. 1999. *Gramophone, Film, Typewriter.* Stanford: Stanford University Press.

Kittler, Friedrich. 2013. *The Truth of the Technological World: Essays on the Genealogy of Presence*. Stanford: Stanford University Press.

Kittler, Friedrich. 2017. "Real Time Analysis, Time Axis Manipulation." *Cultural Politics* 13, no. 1: 1–18.

Kluge, Alexander. 1985. *Der Angriff der Gegenwart auf die übrige Zeit*. Frankfurt/M.: Syndikat/EVA.

Knopp, Guido, and Siegfried Quandt, eds. 1988. *Geschichte im Fernsehen*. Darmstadt: Wissenschaftliche Buchgesellschaft.

Koch, Gertrud, and Christiane Voß, eds. 2009. *Es ist, als ob . . . Fiktionalität in Philosophie, Film- und Medienwissenschaft*. München: Fink.

Korte, Jule. 2020. *Zwischen Script und Reality. Erfahrungsökologien des Fernsehens*. Bielefeld: Transcript.

Kracauer, Siegfried. 1960. *Theory of Film: The Redemption of Physical Reality*. New York: Oxford University Press.

Kracauer, Siegfried. 1995. "Those Who Wait." In: Siegfried Kracauer. *The Mass Ornament: Weimar Essays*, ed. by Thomas Y. Levin, pp. 129–40. Cambridge, MA, London: Harvard University Press.

Kubitz, Peter Paul. 1997. *Der Traum vom Sehen*. Dresden: Verlag der Kunst.

Kühnert, Hanno. 1969. "Die Mondnacht." *Frankfurter Allgemeine Zeitung* 27 (7): 7.

Lacan, Jacques. 1990. *Television: A Challenge to the Psychoanalytic Establishment*. New York, London: W. W. Norton & Company.

Lacan, Jacques. 1998. *The Seminar of Jacques Lacan. Book XI: The Four Fundamental Concepts of Psychoanalysis*. New York, London: W. W. Norton & company.

Lacan, Jacques . 2006a. "Seminar on 'The Purloined Letter." In: Jacques Lacan. *Écrits: The First Complete Edition in English*, pp. 6–48. New York, London: W. W. Norton & Company.

Lacan, Jacques. 2006b. "The Function and Field of Speech and Language in Psychoanalysis." In: Jacques Lacan. *Écrits: The First Complete Edition in English*, pp. 197–268. New York, London: W. W. Norton & Company.

Lacan, Jacques. 2013. "The Symbolic, the Imaginary, and the Real." In: Jacques Lacan. *On the names-of-the-Father*, pp. 1–52. Cambridge, Malden, MA: Polity Press.

Lancioni, Judith, ed. 2009. *Fix Me Up: Essays on Television Dating and Makeover Shows*. New York: McFarland.

Lane, Frederick S. 2000. *Obscene Profits: The Entrepreneurs of Pornography in the Cyber Age*. New York: Routledge.

Lasswell, Harold D. 1948. "The Structure and Function of Communication in Society." In: *The Communication of Ideas: A Series of Addresses*, ed. by Lyman Bryson, pp. 32–51. New York: Harper & Brs.

Latour, Bruno. 1986. "Visualization and Cognition: 'Drawing Thigns Together'" In: *Knowledge and Society. Studies in the Sociology of Culture Past and Present, Jai Press, vol 6 (1986)*, ed. by H. Kucklick, pp. 1–40. Greenwich, CT: Jai Press.

Latour, Bruno. 1993. *We Have Never Been Modern*. Cambridge, MA: Harvard University Press.
Leibniz, Gottfried Wilhelm. 1863. *Mathematische Schriften. Initia Mathematica. Mathesis universalis, vol VII: Die mathematischen Abhandlungen*. Halle: Gerhardt.
Lersch, Edgar, and Reinhold Viehoff, eds. 2007. *Geschichte im Fernsehen: Eine Untersuchung zur Entwicklung des Genres und der Gattungsästhetik geschichtlicher Darstellungen im Fernsehen 1995-2003*. Berlin: VISTAS.
Lessing, Gotthold Ephraim. 1967. "Laocoön or the Limits of Painting and Poetry." In: Gotthold Ephraim Lessing. *Laocön. Nathan the Wise. Minna von Barnhelm*, ed. by William A. Steel, pp. 1–110. London: Dent.
Lewis, Tania. 2009. "Changing Rooms, Biggest Losers and Backyard Blitzes: A History of Makeover Television in the United Kingdom, United States and Australia." In: *TV Transformations: Revealing the Makeover Show*, ed. by Tania Lewis, pp. 7–18. New York: Routledge.
Ludes, Peter. 1991. "Die Rolle des Fernsehens bei der revolutionären Wende in der DDR." *Publizistik* 36, no. 2: 201–16.
Luhmann, Niklas. 1978. "Temporalization of Complexity." In: *Sociocybernetics: An Actor-Oriented Social Systems Approach*, ed. by Felix R. Geyer, and Johannes van der Zouwen, pp. 95–111. Leiden: Nijhoff.
Luhmann, Niklas. 1981. "Über die Funktion der Negation in sinnkonstituierenden Systemen." In: Niklas Luhmann. *Soziologische Aufklärung, Vol. 3: Soziales System, Gesellschaft, Organisation*, pp. 35–49. Opladen: Westdt. Verl.
Luhmann, Niklas. 1990a. "Meaning as Sociology's Basic Concept." In: Niklas Luhmann. *Essays on Self-Reference*, pp. 21–79. New York: Columbia University Press.
Luhmann, Niklas. 1990b. "The Work of Art and the Self-Reproduction of Art." In: Niklas Luhmann. *Essays on Self- Reference*, pp. 191–214. New York: Columbia University Press.
Luhmann, Niklas. 1995. *Social Systems*. Stanford: Stanford University Press.
Luhmann, Niklas. 1996. *Die Wissenschaft der Gesellschaft*. Frankfurt/M.: Suhrkamp.
Luhmann, Niklas. 2000a. *The Reality of Mass Media*. Cambridge: Polity Press.
Luhmann, Niklas. 2000b. *Art as a Social System*. Stanford: Stanford University Press.
Luhmann, Niklas. 2012. *Theory of Society. Volume I*. Stanford: Stanford University Press.
Lury, Karen. 2007. "CSI and Sound." In: *Reading CSI: Crime TV under the Microscope*, ed. by Michael Allen, pp. 107–21. New York: Tauris.
Lynch, Michael. 2013. "Ontography: Investigating the Production of Things, Deflating Ontology." *Social Studies of Science* 43/3: 444–62.
Lynch, Michael. 2019. "Ontography as the Study of Locally Organized Ontologies." In: *Zeitschrift für Medien- und Kulturforschung (ZMK)*, ed. by Lorenz Engell and Bernhard Siegert 10/1: 147–60.

Lyotard, Jean-François. 2003. "Wittgenstein 'After.'" In: Jean-François Lyotard. *Political Writings*, pp. 19–22. London: UCL Press.
Lyotard, Jean-François. 2012. "Philosophy and Painting in the Age of Their Experiment." In: Jean-François Lyotard. *Textes dispersés I: esthétique et théorie de l'art. Miscellaneous Texts I: Aesthetics and Theory of Art*, pp. 147–75. Leuven: Leuven University Press.
Maeder, Dominik. 2013. "Transmodalität transmedialer Expansion. Die TV Serie zwischen Fernsehen und Online-Medien." In: *Der Medienwandel der Serie*, ed. by Dominik Maeder, and Daniela Wentz (=Navigationen, 1/2013), pp. 105–26. Siegen: Universi.
Maye, Harun, and Leander Scholz. 2015 "Einleitung." In: Ernst Kapp. *Grundlinien einer Philosophie der Technik: zur Entstehungsgeschichte der Kultur aus neuen Gesichtspunkten*, ed. by Harun Maye, and Leander Scholz, pp. VII–L. Hamburg: Felix Meiner Verlag.
Malinowski, Eric. 2010. "Dec 7, 1963: Video Instant Replay Comes To TV." In: *Wired*, 20/12/1207. Accessed September 2, 2018. https://www.wired.com/2010/12/1207army-navy.game.first-instant-replay/.
Marschall, Rick. 1987. *The Golden Age of Television*. London: Bison.
Mattenklott, Gert. 1987. "Tödliche Langeweile." *Merkur. Deutsche Zeitschrift für europäisches Denken* 41: 91–103.
McCarthy, Anna. 2001. *Ambient Television*. Durham: Duke University Press.
McLuhan, Marshall. 1964. *Understanding Media. The Extensions of Man*. London, New York: Routledge.
McLuhan, Marshall, and Quentin Fiore. 1967. *The Medium is the Massage: An Inventory of Effects*. New York: Bantam.
Mengue, Philippe. 2003. "Aiôn/Chronos." In: *Le Vocabulaire de Gilles Deleuze*, ed. by Robert Sasso, and Arnaud Villani, pp. 41–7. Nice: Les Cahiers de Noesis, 3 (2003).
Menke, Christoph. 2016. "Breaking Bad. Versuch über die Befreiung." *West End. Neue Zeitschrift für Sozialforschung* 2: 3–24.
Merleau-Ponty, Maurice. 1964. "Eye and Mind." In: Maurice Merleau-Ponty. *The Primacy of Perception: And other Essays on Phenomenological Psychology, the Philosophy of Art, History and Politics*, ed. by James M. Edie, pp. 159–90. n. p.: Northwestern University Press.
Merleau-Ponty, Maurice. 2002. *Phenomenology of Perception*. London, New York: Routledge.
Mersch, Dieter. 2013. *Ordo ab chao—Order from Noise*. Berlin, Zürich: Diaphanes.
Mersch, Dieter. 2018. "Meta/Dia Two Different Approaches to the Medial." In: *Thinking Media and Beyond: Perspectives from German Media Theory*, ed. by Briankle G. Chang, and Florian Sprengler, pp. 102–31. Abingdon, Oxon, New York: Routledge.
Meyrowitz, Joshua. 1985. *No Sense of Place: The Impacts of Electronic Media on Social Behavior*. New York: Oxford: Oxford University Press.

Mody, Cyrus C. M., and Michael Lynch. 2009. "Test Objects and Other Epistemic Things: A History of the Nanoscale Object." In: *British Journal for the History of Science (BJHS)* 1–36. Accessed May 28, 2019. https://depts.washington.edu/ssnet/archive/ModyandLynch_Test_objects.pdf.
Modleski, Tania. 1983. "The Rhythms of Reception: Daytime Television and Women's Work." In: *Regarding Television: Critical Approaches—An Anthology*, ed. by Ann Kaplan, pp. 67–76. Frederick, MD: Univ. Publ. of America.
Morreale, Joanne. 2007. "*Faking It* and the Transformation of Identity." In: *Makeover Television: Realities Remodeled*, ed. by Dana Heller, pp. 95–106. London: Tauris.
Morton, Robert. 1997. *Worlds Without End: The Art and History of the Soap Opera*. New York et al.: Abrams.
Mumford, Lewis. 2010. *Technics and Civilization (1934)*. Chicago: The University of Chicago Press.
Nielsen, Arthur C. 1950. *Television Audience Research for Great Britain*. Chicago: Nielsen Corp.
Nietzsche, Friedrich. 2000. "The Birth of Tragedy." In: Friedrich Nietzsche. *Basic Writings of Nietzsche*, ed. by Walter Kaufmann, pp. 1–144. New York: The Modern Library.
Nietzsche, Friedrich. 2012. *On Truth and Lies in a Nonmoral Sense*. n. p.: Aristeus Books.
Nohr, Ralf. 2014. *Nützliche Bilder. Bild, Diskurs, Evidenz*. Münster: Lit.
Nora, Pierre. 1984. *Les lieux de mémoire. I. La République*. Paris: Gallimard.
Nora, Pierre. 1986. *Les lieux de mémoire. II. La Nation*. Paris: Gallimard.
Nora, Pierre. 1992. *Les lieux de mémoire. III. Les France*. Paris: Gallimard.
Oliva, Mercè. 2013. *Telerrealidad, disciplina e identidad. Los Makeover Shows en Espana*. Barcelona: Editorial UOC.
O'Neill, John J. 1944. *Prodigal Genius: The Life of Nikola Tesla*. New York: McKay.
Oudart, Jean-Pierre. 1978. "Cinema and Suture." *Screen* 18, no. 4: 35–47.
Pasolini, Pier Paolo. 2005. "The Written Language of Reality." In: Pier Paolo Pasolini. *Heretical Empiricism*, ed. by Louise K. Barnett, pp. 197–222. Washington, DC: New Academia Publishing.
Peirce, Charles S. 1906. "Prolegomena to an Apology for Pragmaticism." *The Monist* 16: 492–546; auch in: (CP 4.537).
Peirce, Charles S. 1958. "To Lady Welby." In: *Charles S. Peirce: Collected Papers of Charles Sanders Peirce. Volume VIII. Reviews, Correspondence, and Bibliography*, ed. by Arthur W. Burks, pp. 220–45. Cambridge, MA: Harvard University Press.
Peirce, Charles S. 1960. "How to Make Our Ideas Clear." In: Charles S. Peirce. *Collected Papers of Charles Sanders Peirce. Volume V: Pragmatism and Pragmaticism*, ed. by Charles Hartshorne, and Paul Weiss, pp. 248–71. Cambridge, MA: The Belknap Press of Harvard University Press.

Peirce, Charles S. 1983. *Phänomen und Logik der Zeichen*. Frankfurt/M.: Suhrkamp.
Peirce, Charles S. 1998. "A Syllabus of Certain Topics of Logic." In: *The Essential Peirce: Selected Philosophical Writings, Vol. 2*, pp. 258–99. Bloomington: Indiana University Press.
Peirce, Charles S. 2016a. "Phaneroscopy; Or: the Natural History of Concepts." In: Charles S. Peirce: *Prolegomena to a Science of Reasoning: Phaneroscopy, Semeiotic, Logic*, pp. 65–76. Frankfurt/M.: Peter Lang.
Peirce, Charles S. 2016b. "Phaneroscopy." In: Charles S. Peirce: *Prolegomena to a Science of Reasoning: Phaneroscopy, Semeiotic, Logic*, pp. 77–94. Frankfurt/M.: Peter Lang.
Pfaller, Robert. 2008. *Ästhetik der Interpassivität*. Hamburg: Philo Fine Arts.
Pfaller, Robert, ed. 2000. *Interpassivität. Studien über delegiertes Genießen*. Berlin: Springer.
Pias, Claus. 2002. *Computer-Spiel-Welten*. München: Sequenzia.
Pisters, Patricia. 2012. *The Neuro-Image: A Deleuzian Filmphilosophy of Digital Screen Culture*. Standford: Stanford University Press.
Plessner, Helmuth. 2019. *Levels of Organic Life and the Human: An Introduction to Philosophical Anthropology*. New York: Fordham University Press.
Postman, Neil. 2006. *Amusing Ourselves to Death: Public Discourse in the Age of Show Business*. New York et al.: Penguin Books.
Radiomuseum. n. d. "Mystery Control." Accessed August 28, 2019. https://www.radiomuseum.org/r/philco_mystery_control.html.
Reichertz, Jo. 2006. "Das Fernsehen als Akteur." In: *Medien der Gesellschaft - Gesellschaft der Medien*, ed. by Andreas Ziemann, pp. 231–46. Konstanz: UVK.
Reichertz, Jo. 2016. "Weshalb und wozu braucht man einen 'korporierten Akteur'" In: *CSI. Rechtsmedizin. Mitternachtsforensik*, ed. by Carina J. Englert and and Jo Reichertz, pp. 149–68. Wiesbaden: Springer.
Reichertz, Jo, Lorenz Engell, Carina Jasmin Englert, Natascha Kempken, Dominik Maeder, Jems Schröter, Daniela Wentz. 2014. "Das Fernsehen als Akteur und Agent." In: *Die Mediatisierung sozialer Welten*, ed. by Friedrich Krotz, Cathrin Despotovic, and Merle Marie Kruse, pp. 145–64. Wiesbaden: Springer.
Revers, Wilhelm Josef. 1949. *Die Psychologie der Langeweile*. Meisenheim: Hain.
Rheinberger, Hans-Jörg. 1997. *Toward a History of Epistemic Things*. Stanford: Stanford University Press.
Richtmeyer, Ulrich. 2009. "Vom Bildspiel zum Sprachspiel—Wie viel Kompositphotographie steckt in der Logik der Familienähnlichkeit." In: *A Selection of Papers from the International Wittgenstein Symposium in Kirchberg am Wechsel*, ed. by Volker A. Munz, Klaus Puhl, Joseph Wang n. p. Accessed August 25, 2015. http://wittgensteinrepository.org/agora-alws/article/view/2828/3380.
Scannell, Paddy. 2014. *Television and the Meaning of Live*. Cambridge: Polity Press.

Schmidgen, Henning. 2017. *Horn oder die Gegenseite der Medien*. Berlin: Matthes und Seitz.
Schneider, Birgit. 2014. "Red Futures. The Colour Red in Scientific Imagery of Climate Change." In: *Disaster as Image: Iconographies and Media Strategies across Europe and Asia*, ed. by Monica Juneja, and Gerrit Jasper Schenk, pp. 183–93. Regensburg: Schnell + Steiner.
Schulte, Joachim. 1992. *Wittgenstein: An Introduction*. Albany: State University of New York Press.
Schulz, Martin. 2005. *Ordnungen der Bilder: Eine Einführung in die Bildwissenschaft*. Paderborn: Fink.
Schwaab, Herbert. 2008. "Stanley Cavell, King of Queens und die Medienphilosophie des Gewöhnlichen." In: *Ästhetik und Alltagserfahrung*, ed. by Deutsche Gesellschat für Ästhetik. Accessed December 12, 2019. http://www.dgae.de/downloads/Herbert_Schwaab.pdf.
Schwarte, Ludger. 2011. "Bilder bezeugen, was nicht ausgesagt werden kann. Überlegungen zur visuellen Performanz." In: *Bild-Performanz. Zur Kraft des Visuellen*, ed. by Lena Stölzl, and Ludger Schwarte, pp. 137–60. München: Fink.
Sellars, John. 2007. "Aion and Chronos: Deleuze and the Stoic Theory of Time." *Collapse* 3: 177–205. Also published in: *Academia*. Accessed June 26, 2018. http://www.academia.edu/9816442/Ai%C3%B4n_and_Chronos_Deleuze_and_the_Stoic_Theory_of_T ime.
Serres, Michel. 2008. *The Five Senses: A Philosophy of Mingled Bodies (I)*. London, New York: Continuum.
Shannon, Claude. 1948. "A Mathematical Theory of Information." *Bell System Technical Journal* 27: 379–423 (July), 623–56 (October).
Sieber, Gerald. 2016. *Reenactment. Formen und Funktionen eines geschichstdokumentarischen Darstellungsmittels*. Marburg: Schüren.
Siegert, Bernhard. 2010. "Kulturtechnik." In: *Einführung in die Kulturwissenschaft*, ed. by Harun Maye, and Leander Scholz, pp. 95–118. München: Fink.
Simondon, Gilbert. 1989. *L'individuation psychique et collective*. Paris: Aubier.
Simondon, Gilbert. 2017. *On the Mode of Existence of Technical Objects*. Minneapolis: Univocal.
Sloterdijk, Peter. 2001. *Das Menschentreibhaus. Stichworte zur historischen und prophetischen Anthropologie. Vier große Vorlesungen*. Weimar: vdg.
Sluyterman, A. A. S. and Erik Boonekamp. 2005. "Architectural Choices in a Scanning Backlight for large LCD-TVs." In: *SID05Digest 2005*, pp. 996–9.
Smith, Andrew. 2019. *Smith: Totally Wired: The Rise and Fall of Josh Harris and the Great Dotcom Swindle*. New York: Groove Press, Black Cat.
Souriau, Etienne. 1943. *Les différents modes d'existences*. Paris: Presses Universitaires de France; engl.: *The Different Modes of Existence*. Minneapolis: Minnesota University Press.

Souriau, Etienne. 2015. "Of the Mode of Existence of the Work To-Be-Made." In: Etienne Souriau. *The Different Modes of Existence*, pp. 219–40. Minneapolis: Minnesota University Press, Univocal Publishing.

Spencer, Herbert. 1974. *The Evolution of Society: Selections from Herbert Spencer's Principles of Sociology*. University of Chicago Press.

Spencer, Herbert. 2019. *First Principles of a New System of Philosophy (1867)*, Withorn: Anodos.

Spigel, Lynn. 1992. *Make Room for TV, Television and the Family Ideal in Postwar America*. Chicago, London: University of Chicago Press.

Sprenger, Florian. 2012. "Die Einführung als Medium. Sven Grampp liest McLuhan in seiner Einführung vierfach." *literaturkritik.de*, Nr. 2, Februar 2012. Accessed February 2, 2018. http://literaturkritik.de/id/16298.

Sprenger, Florian. 2013. "Extension Extended—Ernst Kapp, Marshall McLuhan and Their Affiliated Correspondence." In: *McLuhan's Philosophy of Media—Cenbtzennial Conference*, ed. by Yoni van den Eede, Joke Bauwens, Joke Beyl, Marc van den Bossche, Karl Verstrynge, pp. 279–88. Brussels: Koninklijke Vlaamse Academie van Belgie voor Wetenschappen en Kunsten.

Stadler, Michael. 2014. *Was heißt Ontographie? Vorarbeit zu einer visuellen Ontologie*. Würzburg: Königshausen & Neumann.

Stauff, Markus. 2005. *Das neue Fernsehen. Machtanalyse, Gouvernementalität und digitale Meiden*. Münster: LIT.

Sprenger, Florian. 2015. "The Second Screen: Convergence as Crisis." *Zeitschrift für Medien- und Kulturforschung* 6, no. 2: 123–44.

Stehling, Miriam. 2015. *Die Aneignung von Fernsehformaten im transkulturellen Vergleich. Eine Studie am Beispiel des Top-Model Formates*. Wiesbaden: Springer VS.

Stengers, Isabelle. 1995. "The Galileo Affair." In: *A History of Scientific Thought: Elements of a History of Science*, ed. by Michel Serres, pp. 280–314. Oxford, Cambridge, MA: Blackwell.

Stjernfelt, Frederik. 2007. *Diagrammatology: An Investigation at the Borderlines of Phenomenology, Ontology, and Semiotics*. Dodrecht: Springer.

Turnbull, Steven. 2007. "The Hook and the Look. CSI and the Aesthetics of Television." In *Reading CSI: Crime TV under the Microscope*, ed. by Michael Allen, pp. 15–32. New York: Tauris.

US Patent US3834794 (A). 1974. 1974-09-10 (*Liquid Crystal Electric Field Sensing Measurement And Display Device*).

Verna, Tony. 2009. *Instant Replay: The Day that Changed Sports Forever*. New York: Creative Publishers.

Vernet, Marc. 1988. *Figures de l'absence. De l'invisible au cinema*. Paris: Cahiers du cinema, coll. Essais.

Vertov, Dziga. 1984. "Kinoks: A Revolution." In: Dziga Vertov. *Kino-Eye: The Writings of Dziga Vertov*, ed. by Annette Michelson, pp. 11–21. London: University of California Press.

Vogl, Joseph. 2007. "Becoming Media: Galileo's Telescope." *Grey Room* 29: 14–25.

Voß, Christiane. 2008a. "Fiktionale Immersion zwischen Ästhetik und Anästhesierung." In: *IMAGE—Zeitschrift für interdisziplinäre Bildwissenschaft*. Accessed June 6, 2019. http://www.bildwissenschaft.org/image?function=fnArticle&showArticle=126.

Voß, Christiane. 2008b. "Kinästhetische und semantische Dimensionen immersiver Erfahrung." In: *Immersion, Montage/av 17/2*, ed. by. Robin Curtis, and Christiane Voß, pp. 69–86. Marburg: Schüren.

Voß, Christiane. 2009. "Fiktionale Immersion." In: *Es ist, als ob. Fiktionalität in Philosophie, Film- und Medienwissenschaft*, ed. by Gertrud Koch, and Christiane Voß, pp. 127–39. München: Fink.

Voß, Christiane. 2010. "Auf dem Weg zu einer Medienphilosophie anthropomedialer Relationen." *Zeitschrift für Medien- und Kulturforschung (ZMK)* 1/2: 170–84.

Voß, Christiane. 2013a. *Der Leihkörper. Erkenntnis und Ästhetik der Illusion*. München: Fink.

Voß, Christiane. 2013b. "Der dionysische Schalter. Zur generischen Anthropomedialität des Humors." *Zeitschrift für Medien- und Kulturforschung (ZMK)* 1: 119–32.

Voß, Christiane. 2015. "Affekt. Affektverkehr des Filmischen aus medienphilosophischer Sicht." In: *Essays zur Filmphilosophie*, ed. by Christiane Voß, Lorenz Engell, Oliver Fahle, and Vinzenz Hediger, pp. 63–116. München: Fink.

Wang, Haiying, Thomas X. Wu, Xinyu Zhu, and Shin-Tson Wu. 2004. "Correlations Between Liquid Crystal Director Reorientation and Optical Response Time of a Homeotropic Cell." *Journal of Applied Physics* 95, no. 10: 5502–8.

Wehmeier, Klaus. 1979. *Die Geschichte des ZDF: Entstehung und Entwicklung 1961–1966*. Mainz: v. Hase und Köhler.

Wentz, Daniela. 2017. *Bilderfolgen. Diagrammatologie der Fernsehserie*. Paderborn: Transcript.

Wentz, Daniela. 2019. "Existential Graphs as Ontographic Media." *Zeitschrift für Medien- und Kulturforschung (ZMK)* 10/1: 177–89.

Wenzel, Harald. 2000. "Obertanen. Zur soziologischen Bedeutung von Prominenz." *Leviathan* 4: 452–76.

Whitehead, Alfred North. 1978. *Process and Reality: An Essay in Cosmology*. New York: The Free Press.

Williams, Raymond. 1977. *Marxism and Literature*. Oxford: Oxford University Press.

Williams, Raymond. 1992. *Television as Cultural Form (1973)*. Middletown: Wesleyan University Press.

Winkler, Hartmut. 1991. *Switching-Zapping. Ein Text zum Thema und ein parallellaufendes Unterhaltungsprogramm*. Darmstadt: Häuser.

Winkler, Hartmut. 2006. "Nicht handeln. Versuch einer Wiederaufwertung des couch potato angesichts der Provokation des interaktiv Digitalen." In: *Philosophie des Fernsehens*, ed. by Oliver Fahle, and Lorenz Engell, pp. 93–101. München: Fink.

Winston, Brian. 1986. *Misunderstanding Media*. Cambridge, MA: Harvard University Press.
Wired. 2007. "1956: Zenith Space Commander Remote Control." In: *Wired*, October 23, 2007. Accessed August 28, 2019. https://www.wired.com/2007/10/vg-greatestgadget/.
Wittgenstein, Ludwig. 1999. *Philosophische Untersuchungen. Zweite Auflage. Philosophical Investigations*. 2nd edn, trans. by G. E. M. Anscombe. Oxford, Malden: Blackwell Publishers.
Wulff, Hans Jürgen. 1995. "Flow. Kaleidoskopische Formen des Fern-Sehens." *montage a/v*, 4/2: 21–42.
Youngblood, Gene. 1970. *Expanded Cinema*. London: Studio Vista.
Yuste, Antonio Perez, and Magdalena Salazar Palma. 2005. "Scanning the Past from Madrid. Leonardo Torres Quevedo." *Proceedings of the IEEE* 93, no. 7: 1379–82.
Zec, Peter. 1985. "Mana oder die 0_Funktion der Television." In: *Unser Fernsehen! Vom Pantoffelkino zum Terminal*, ed. by Norbert Nowotsch, and Rainer Weißenborn, pp. 17–23. Drensteinfurt: Huba.
Zeigarnik, Bljuma. 1927. "Das Behalten erledigter und unerledigter Handlungen." *Psychologische Forschung*, 9: 1–85.
Zenith: Remote Background. n. d. "Six Decades of Channel Surfing: History of the TV Remote Control." Accessed November 14, 2019. https://www.zenith.com/remote-background/.
Zettl, Herbert. 1978. "The Rare Case of Television Aesthetics." *The Journal of the University Film Association* 30, no. 2: 3–8.
Zielinski, Siegfried. 1999. *Audiovisions: Cinema and Television as Entr'actes in History*. Amsterdam: Amsterdam University Press.
Ziemann, Andreas. 2011. *Medienkultur und Gesellschaftsstruktur. Soziologische Analysen*. Wiesbaden: Springer VS.
Ziemann, Andreas. 2013. "Zu Philosophie und Soziologie der Situation. Eine Einführung." In: *Offene Ordnung? Zu Philosophie und Soziologie der Situation*, ed. by Andreas Ziemann, pp. 7–18. Wiesbaden: Springer VS.
Žižek, Slavoj. 2001. *The Fright of Real Tears: Krzysztof Kieślowski between Theory and Post-Theory*. London: bfi publishing.
Zola, Émile. 1893. *The Experimental Novel and Other Essays*. London: Cassell Publishing Company.
Zubayr, Camille, and Heinz Gerhard. 2017. "Tendenzen im Zuschauerverhalten. Fernsehgewohnheiten und Fernsehreichweiten im Jahr 2016." *media perspektiven* 3: 130–44.
Zupančič, Alenka. 1996. "Philosophers' Blind Man's Buff." In: *Gaze and Voice as Love Objects*, ed. by Renata Salecl, and Slavoj Žižek, pp. 32–58. Durham, London: Duke University Press.
Zweites Deutsches Fernsehen. 1970. *Jahrbuch 1969*. Mainz: Informations- und Presseabteilung ZDF.

# Index

**Concept**

absent, absence  21, 59, 123, 140–1, 143, 155, 157, 207, 318, 322, 325, 331, *see also* present
action-image  38
actor  28, 61, 87, 97, 99–102, 144, 162, 172, 184, 186, 228, 237, 239, 248, 276–7, 282, 289, 295, 324
actor-network theory  97–8, 220
actual, actuality, actualization  31, 36, 60, 80, 83–4, 104, 111, 141, 144, 153, 188, 192, 204–8, 213, 227, 231, 234, 251, 264, 276–7, 285, 287, 297, 312, *see also* virtual, virtuality
actual image  206–8, *see also* virtual image
aesthesis  76
affect, affectivity, affective  13, 49, 52, 55–6, 63, 91, 103–4, 110–13, 115, 119, 126, 138–9, 144, 151, 158, 207, 225, 227, 246, 252, 263, 274, 277, 313–17, 322–5, 327, 330
affect-image  56
agent, agency  3, 63–7, 70–1, 85, 98–100, 102, 104, 107, 111–15, 119, 161, 162, 184, 186, 215, 220, 223, 239, 246, 254, 256, 330
*aion, aionic*  137, 140–4, 156, 158, 208
allness  195–6, 201
ambient television  218–20, 236, 245
AMPEX  127–30, 239
analog  20, 36, 144, 225, 231, 251, 319, *see also* digital
*analogia*, analogy  255–6, 268
analogism, analogistic  225–7, 246–7, 255, 264–5, 280
anchor-images  325–9
animated image  251–2
animation  34, 234, 298
anthropic  325–7
anthropocene  167, 297
anthropography, anthropographic  111–12, 115, 119–20
anthropology, anthropological  111, 165, 213–14, 224, 238, 246
anthropomediality, anthropomedial, anthropo-mediatic  5, 12, 15–16, 21, 31–2, 109–10, 148, 151, 166, 184, 186, 195, 205, 213, 216, 224, 309, 323, 327–8
apparatus  3, 8–9, 12, 19–20, 26, 38, 65, 80, 86, 90, 100, 103–4, 106–8, 111, 127, 136, 161–5, 168, 182, 203, 213, 217, 226, 245, 248, 273, 289, 291, 297–8, 305, 309, 315, 321, 334
appearance, appear  20, 52, 65–6, 68, 72, 75, 134, 154, 184, 205, 219, 228, 239, 255, 288
archive, archival images  6, 27, 34, 43, 59, 127–8, 228, 295, 297–300
arret sur image  134
articulate, articulation  5–6, 33–4, 36–7, 62, 75, 80, 82, 84, 88, 91, 93, 139, 142–3, 155, 158, 184, 190, 195, 197, 201, 208, 217–18, 221–2, 240, 278, 292, 306–7, 313, 330–1
artifact, artifactual  168, 291, 308
audience  52, 97, 101, 130, 148, 161–3, 173, 188–90, 193, 216,

268, 281, 285, 291, *see also* public
autobiography   300

being, nonbeing   9, 11, 21–2, 24–5, 29, 32–4, 39, 65, 71, 99, 104, 115, 135–6, 138–41, 158–9, 163, 197, 203–4, 226, 235, 256, 264, 273, 297–8, 311, 329, 330, 333
being-a-body   87
being-in-the-world   5
Berlin Wall   164
binging   215, 239, 257, 304
blinds   231, 248
body   34, 36, 39, 47, 87–9, 100, 102–7, 110–12, 137, 140–2, 192, 205, 229, 248, 256, 289–92, 299, 305, 308, 323–4, 327–8, 333
boredom   39, 87, 115, 154–9, 167, 329–33
borrowed memory   61
broadcast   4, 13–15, 20, 23–8, 31–4, 38–9, 42–4, 47–54, 57, 60, 64, 75–6, 78, 84–5, 90, 97–8, 101, 119–20, 124–35, 137–8, 141, 144, 148, 150–2, 154–5, 157, 158, 162–4, 166, 172–4, 180, 182, 187, 189–91, 193, 199, 202, 207, 215, 219, 221, 227–8, 231, 234, 236–7, 239, 255, 257, 261–2, 272–4, 277, 280–2, 287–90, 293–5, 299, 304–6, 312, 316, 319–21, 325–6, 333

catastrophe   33–4, 68, 128, 151, 250–1, 275, 278, 325
cathode ray tube   90, 213–15, 224, 225, 229–31, 233, 245, 273, 304–6, *see also* tube
causality   6, 133, 209, 292, 310–13, 332
celebrity   286–8, *see also* prominence
CGI   249

channel hopping   202, 204
chronography, chronographic   137, 141–2, 144, 148, 298
chronophotograph   293
*chronos, chronic, chronocentric*   89, 137–40, 143–4, 156–8, 208
cinema, cinematographic, cinematography   12, 21, 29, 42, 46, 53, 107, 121, 174, 214, 219, 226, *see also* film
cinematographic consciousness   29
cliffhanger   14, 56–8, 64, 100, 259–60, 314–19, 321, 324, 327
coalescence, coalescent   72, 247, 253–4, 257
coherence, cohesion, coherent, cohesive   28, 55–7, 69, 70, 75, 77–8, 100, 157, 171, 195, 199, 225, 306–7, *see also* incoherence, incoherent
cold medium/media   16, 107–9, 111, 166, 213, 224, *see also* hot medium
commercial   13, 23, 50, 76, 80, 85, 124, 181, 199
communicate, communication   9, 55, 60, 65, 80, 97, 100–2, 104, 148, 154, 158, 161, 163, 185–92, 196–8, 200, 236–7, 240, 281, 284
complexity, complex   53–4, 62, 77–9, 83–4, 90, 99, 105–6, 127, 132–3, 152–3, 163, 165, 167–8, 175, 179, 184, 208–9, 214, 223, 231, 234, 247, 251, 258, 264, 291–2
community   58–9, 281, 325
computer, computing   113, 114, 167, 178, 183, 185, 203, 214, 219, 225, 227–30, 236–7, 239–40, 249, 251, 257, 261, 266, 295, 304
*conditio essendi*   112
consensus, consensual   33, 38, 277, *see also* non-consensual

contingent, contingency   24, 28, 46, 81, 162, 192, 195–8, 200–1, 203, 205, 208–9, 223, 294
continuum, continuity, continuous   8–9, 11–12, 14–15, 19–20, 22–4, 27–9, 31–4, 36, 44, 46, 49, 52, 54, 56–8, 61–3, 68–70, 72, 75, 77–9, 81, 86, 89, 100, 120, 126, 128, 130, 133–8, 140–1, 181, 189, 191, 196, 202, 224–5, 227, 231–5, 245–7, 249–51, 253–4, 257–60, 266, 275, 282, 286, 298, 304–8, 310, 313–17, 321–3, 328, 333, *see also* discontinuity, discrete
control   6–7, 31, 50, 62, 65, 85, 87, 91–4, 98–9, 104, 112–13, 131, 140, 154, 157, 161–4, 173, 179, 200, 220, 223–4, 231–3, 238–9, 256, 258, 276, 281, 285, 306, 330, *see also* remote control
Copernican   165, 167, 172
corporate actor   98, 101
correlation   100, 136, 240
cosmos, cosmic   105, 120, 148–9, 151, 155, 165, 267
couch potatoe   220
counter-actualization; counter-present   136, 144–5, 273–4, 278, 292, 299–300, 305, 332
counterfactual   295
crisis   33, 63, 68, 198, 278
cultural studies   82, 91, 102
current (electrical, electromagnetic, signal)   7, 11–12, 19, 21–2, 50, 112, 122, 181, 186, 225, 232, 305, 309, 322

*Darstellung*   292
*Dasein*   98–9, 155–6, 158
definite   32, 62, 233, *see also* indefinite
delay   27, 37, 42, 57, 65, 123, 126, 133, 155, 157, 192, 312–16, 318, 324, 329, 331–2

determinacy, determination, determinate   20, 142, 156, 201, 222, 310–13, *see also* indeterminate
diachrony   213, *see also* synchrony
diagram, diagrammatic   20, 136, 169–70, 173, 233–6, 251, 264–8, 280, 293
difference   48–9, 51–2, 54–5, 64, 66–7, 70, 79, 102, 107–8, 113–14, 119, 137, 158, 216–17, 220–1, 226–7, 232, 235, 246, 249, 253, 268, 272, 284–5, 287, 299, 312–13, 316, 321–2, 333, *see also* identity
*differentia specifica*   79
differentiation   14, 36–8, 52, 70, 109, 140, 191, 219, 295, 312–13, 315, 317, 319, 328, 332–3
differentiation-image   308, 313–14, 317–18, 333
digital, digitalization, digitization   2, 4, 6, 9, 22, 37, 79, 114, 120, 130, 171, 175, 181–3, 193, 199, 207, 210, 214–15, 225–6, 228, 230–1, 236–9, 249, 251, 257, 268, 280, 317, 319, 330, *see also* analog
diode   9–10, 183, 186, 203–4, 321
Dionysian, Dionysian switch   91–4, 100, 119–20, 327–30
direction, directed   104, 107, 138, 141, 150–1, 154–5, 162, 169, 171, 188–9, 208, 210, 229, 245, 265, 281, 284, 307, 312, 326–7, 333
disappear, disappearance   11, 22, 25, 29, 59, 79, 87, 155–7, 193, 201, 203, 206, 214, 228–9, 233, 236, 239–40, 259, 263, 292, 306–8, 318, 320–2, 333, *see also* appear
discontinuity, discontinuous   24, 57, 69–70, 75, 77–8, 152, 190, 199, 224–6, 230–1, 235, 245, 247,

261–2, 264, 297, 306–8, 328, *see also* continuity
display   7, 25, 55, 150, 179, 203, 214, 218, 230–2, 265, 307, 321
*dispositif*   20, 87–8, 161, 165–6, 213–14, 218, 227, 275, 283, 292–3
dream   63, 171, 194–5, 203–4
duplication, duplicate   144, 220, 274, 278
duration   4, 22, 29–30, 34, 36–7, 39, 55, 134, 138, 140, 144, 148, 152, 157, 231, 233, 264, 273, 307, 314, 331–2

early television   4, 23–4, 35, 42–3, 100, 124, 128, 163, 181, 216, 228, 258
earth   7, 148–52, 154, 164–72, 179, 230, 245, 320, *see also* planet
ecology   167
electricity, electric, electromagnetic, electronic   5–9, 11–14, 17, 19–22, 42–3, 50–1, 53, 90, 104–5, 112, 123, 125–7, 160–2, 180–3, 186, 207, 218–19, 224–5, 231–2, 245, 248, 251–2, 288, 305, 319, 322
electrographic   7–8, 12, 21
embody, embodiment   3, 21, 27, 37, 46, 68, 102–3, 148, 220, 254, 265–7, 288, 292
emergence, emergent   22, 24, 27, 28, 55, 78–80, 83, 94, 104, 115, 119, 124, 133, 138, 143–4, 166, 170–1, 179, 199, 204, 213, 219, 232, 255, 259, 261, 286, 293, 305, 307, 311–12, 314, 330, 332
ensembles of opto-phonetic data   179
episodic series, episode   14, 15, 23, 44, 48, 51–2, 54–67, 69–70, 75–6, 79, 83, 100, 124, 137, 152, 191–2, 237, 239, 247–50,
252–4, 258–63, 266, 268, 315, 317, 328, 331
epistemography   160, 234
epistemology, epistemological   16, 106–7, 227, 233, 254, 257
event   12, 14–15, 22–8, 30–9, 42, 44, 46, 50–1, 54, 59–63, 67–9, 71, 75, 77–8, 80–1, 83–6, 90–4, 97–8, 100–1, 103–4, 120, 125–35, 140–5, 148–51, 154–9, 161, 164, 171–2, 180, 182–3, 191, 194–5, 200, 207–8, 220, 225–6, 230–2, 237, 239–40, 247, 250–7, 259, 261, 264, 273–6, 278, 282, 285–6, 289–91, 293–4, 296–9, 304–7, 310, 316, 318, 321, 327, 329–31, 333
experience   24–32, 37, 39, 42, 56, 60–1, 63, 76–9, 81, 86–8, 91–4, 97, 102, 113–14, 132, 137–8, 142, 155–8, 195, 221, 238, 246, 273, 277, 286, 288, 304–5, 314, 321, 324–5, 329–32, *see also* formation of experience; television experience
experiment, experimental   8, 19, 26–7, 42–3, 49, 123, 153, 159–65, 181, 201, 249, 253, 256, 260, 266, 268, 272, 279, 280, 282–4, 290, 295, 297, 308, 322
expert   34, 82, 153, 234, 277, 295, 297–8
extensions of man   104, 288
eye   12, 24, 27, 51, 57, 77, 101, 103, 107, 111–12, 141, 150, 166–7, 169–72, 174, 178, 223–5, 228, 231, 232, 234, 314

family resemblance   253, 257–64, 268, 315
film   4, 6, 8, 15–16, 23, 27, 29, 42, 46–8, 51–2, 54–5, 58, 76–7, 79, 81–2, 90, 101, 112, 121–6, 138,

142, 171, 194, 200, 204, 225, 234, 238–9, 253–4, 257, 262, 272, 274, 277, 281–3, 291, 293, 295, 298, 308, 311, 326
filmed series   51–2, 54, 57
finality   332
finite, finitude   140, 196, 247, 249–50, 254, 259–61, 263, see also infinite
fireplace   320–1, 325, 329
flashback   76, 204–6, 250, 262, 268
flat, flatness   126, 215, 222–4, 227–30, 233–4, 306–8
flow   5, 7, 9–10, 12–14, 21, 24–5, 32, 35–6, 47–8, 50, 58, 66, 75–94, 100–1, 108, 113, 115, 119–20, 126–7, 133–6, 140, 143, 148, 157, 171, 185–6, 190, 194, 196, 199, 202, 213, 225–6, 231–2, 237–40, 245–6, 262, 278–9, 282, 293, 305–8, 310–12, 314–18, 320–1, 328–33, see also neo-flow
forensics   247
forgetting   37, 60–4, 67, 87–8, 100, 119, 120, 300, 317–18, see also remembering
form of existence   193, 216, 286, 308, 328, see also mode of existence, mode of being
format, formatting   4, 23, 39, 43–4, 47, 49–52, 54–7, 76, 82, 85, 90, 110, 119–20, 124–6, 139, 153, 162, 190–3, 198, 216–17, 219–20, 234, 246, 268, 272–3, 277, 280–1, 283–4, 286–90, 293–4, 299, 317, 326, 330
formation of experience   26, 31
fragment, fragmentation   43, 76–7, 167, 171, 188–9, 194, 224, 305
frame   4, 6, 12, 46, 62, 88, 129, 134, 143, 169, 205, 229, 249–50, 260–1, 284, 293, 316, 321, 324, 327, 331

freeze   124, 129, 134, 139, 143, 253, 260, 293, 314, 316, 318, 321, 324, 327
future   10, 29–30, 44, 54–6, 87, 89, 133–4, 137–8, 140–1, 148, 156–7, 175, 228, 266, 294, 310, 313, 331, 333, see also past; present

Gaia   167
gaze   20, 82, 88, 110, 120, 149, 165, 168–75, 245, 275–6, 284, 286, 326
genre   46–51, 53, 58, 76–7, 80, 84–6, 184, 191–3, 236, 258–60, 272, 287, 293–4
German media theory   104
*Gestalt*   24–5, 56
*Gestell*   99
gesture   45, 51, 56, 87–8, 184, 188, 193, 205, 209–10, 324, 326
Golden Age of Television   23, 123
governmentality   114
grazing   201–2, 204, 207
Gulf War   38, 274–5
Gutenberg Galaxy   103

habitat   112, 125, 165–6, 175, 219–21, 230, 236, 240, 289
heterochrony, heterochronic   89–90
heterogeneity, heterogeneous   47, 68, 81–2, 86, 89–92, 98, 221, 273, 331
heterography, heterographic   85–6, 88–90, 93
historiography   128, 198, 294–6
homogeneity, homogeneous   86, 216, 220
hot medium/ media   16, 107–9, see also cold media
house   217, 251, 281, 283–7, 293
household   53, 162, 175, 183, 190, 217
housewife   52–4, 216, 218, 251

housework  54, 88–9
human, humankind, human being  58–60, 68, 90, 93, 97–8, 102–12, 120, 130, 132, 134, 137, 142, 144, 150–1, 155, 165, 167, 169, 171, 174, 186, 193–4, 196, 209, 219, 222, 224–6, 231–2, 249, 276, 279, 282, 284, 288–9, 291, 299, 306, 308–9, 320, 323–5
humor  93–4, 329, 332

icon, iconic, iconicity  131, 167, 169, 208–9, 264–7, 297–8, 309, 327
identity  44, 46, 48–9, 64, 66, 69–70, 253, 262–3, 276, 299, *see also* non-identity
images, animated  251
immaterial  98, 136, 142, 184, 188, 226, 291, 333, *see also* material
immediacy, immediate  16, 25–6, 35–6, 44, 101, 123, 127–8, 165, 183, 248, 312–14, 317, *see also* medium
immersion, immersive  15, 78–9, 88–9, 119, 305, 330
impulse modulation  181
incoherence, incoherent  56, 75–6, 194, 307
indefinite  57, 157, 235, 254, *see also* definite
indeterminate  201, 313, *see also* determinate
index, indexical, indexicality  21–2, 207–10, 252, 264, 292, 296–8, 309, 327
individuation, individuality  222, 277, 288–9
infinite, infinitude  12, 67, 77, 132, 134, 138, 140–1, 156, 165, 233, 247, 249–50, 254, 259–60, 312, 332, *see also* finite
information  11, 33, 60, 67–8, 77, 84, 103, 108, 127, 132, 161, 163, 183, 187–92, 194, 196–7, 199, 210, 232, 234, 237–8, 257, 276, 278, 330
instant, instantaneous  30–2, 34, 37, 39, 134, 140, 165–6, 209, 225, 233, *see also* moment; now
instant composing  24
instant replay  35, 37, 123, 125, 127–45, 157, 213, 239, 245–6, 273, 312, 314, 316–19, 321, 324
intention, intentional  27, 67, 77, 83, 93, 98–9, 105–6, 186, 194–6, 209
intermediate film system  42, 123, 126
internet  9, 35, 183, 214, 219, 236–8, 240, 272, 281–3, 288, 295
interpassive, interpassivity  268
interpersonal  101, 184, *see also* person
interruption  8, 37, 57, 77, 80, 130, 133, 181, 190, 195, 199, 208, 231–2, 235, 286, 290, 306–8, 312–16, 318–19, 321–5, 327–9
interruption-image  312–16, 319, 322–5, 327
irreversibility, irreversible  100–1, 196, *see also* reverse

knowledge  3, 44, 85, 93–4, 99, 103–4, 106–7, 198, 249, 252–4, 256–7, 265–6, 277, 325–6

latency, latent  10–13, 84, 119–20, 186, 194–5, 203–4, 321–2, *see also* manifest; virulent
latency protection  194–5
liquid-crystal display, liquid crystal screen, LCD  214–16, 230–3, 235–6, 246, 260–1, 264–5, 279, 292, 306–7, 311, 314, 331
live, liveness  19, 21–39, 42–4, 46–8, 51–4, 57, 76, 78, 82, 89–90,

97, 119–20, 123–35, 137–9, 144, 148–55, 157, 160, 163–4, 172–3, 180, 187, 189, 193, 213–14, 219, 227–8, 237, 239, 245–6, 252, 267–8, 272–5, 277, 280–5, 287, 289, 297–9, 304, 309, 316, 318–19, 326, 330
location   14, 19–22, 24, 37–8, 46, 59, 62, 71, 82, 128, 130, 157–8, 165, 168–71, 173–5, 179, 186, 191–2, 202, 215, 218, 220–1, 223, 227–8, 230, 237, 239, 245–6, 252, 255, 263–4, 266–7, 280, 285–6, 297–9, 306–7, 318, *see also* place; space
logic of sense   137, 247, 274, 332–3

makeover show   287, 289
malleability   263, *see also* plasticity
manifest, manifestation   10–13, 81, 83–4, 113, 119, 120, 167, 195, 203–4, 261, 298, 321–2, 330, *see also* latent, latency
mass media   53, 102, 114, 155, 180, 188, 276–8, 299
massage   76, 88, 92, 102
material, materialism, materiality   21–3, 29, 34, 39, 42, 50, 89, 92, 109–10, 124, 129, 131, 135–6, 142, 144, 151, 157, 184, 188, 195, 218, 221, 226, 228, 235, 248–9, 252, 264, 291–2, 295, 297–8, 304, 308–9, 311–12, 314, 316–21, 323, 330, 333, *see also* immaterial
material-images   322
matter   29, 55, 308–9, 317, 334
meaning, meaningful, meaningless   25, 28, 33, 46, 68, 71, 75–80, 82–6, 88, 91–3, 102, 112, 115, 132, 142–4, 150–1, 155, 157, 159, 185, 191, 194–5, 199, 221, 238, 294, 305–6, 309, 311, 330, 332–3

media, mediality, mediatic   3, 26, 32, 43–4, 52, 68, 79, 81–2, 84, 86, 92, 101–4, 106–12, 119, 129, 136, 149, 153, 163, 175, 180, 193, 219, 234–8, 240, 257, 263, 268, 272–3, 276–7, 279, 281, 288, 298, 304, 306, *see also* immediacy
media-ontological   108
media philosophy, media-philosophical   3, 5, 87, 91, 101, 107, 112, 143, 260, 329, 334
media sphere   7–8, 12, 14, 17, 21, 320
media theory, media-theoretical   102, 104, 136, 279, 281, 308
medium   5, 8, 16, 22–3, 35–6, 38, 42–3, 47–8, 54–5, 57–8, 67, 76, 89–92, 102, 104, 106–12, 115, 120, 123–4, 127, 132, 138–9, 149, 150, 152, 162, 166, 174, 181–3, 186, 200, 205, 210, 213, 223–4, 235–6, 238, 240, 248–9, 258, 260–3, 273–4, 278, 280, 283, 291, 294, 296, 298–9, 304–6, 321, *see also* form
memory   29, 43–4, 57, 59–62, 67, 100, 103, 105, 125, 129, 206–7, 299–300, 308, 317–19, 322, 328, 330, 334, *see also* borrowed memory; operative memory; storage memory
message   13, 76, 92, 101–2, 104, 166, 185–8, 190, 196–7, 237
metabeing   106
milieu   7, 10
mnemotope   299
mode of being, mode of existence   10–12, 17, 149, 157, 189, 213, 239, 240, 252, 273, 286, 288, 308, 329–30, 332–4

moment, momentum  6, 11–12, 27–31, 33, 36–7, 48, 70, 72, 77, 80, 84–5, 87, 89, 113, 128, 131–6, 138–9, 141–3, 151, 157, 163, 167, 195, 200, 204–7, 218–19, 221, 247, 250, 273, 295, 312, 314, 316, 318, 324, 328, 332–3, *see also* instant; now

narrativity, narrative  44, 51–2, 54–5, 58, 63, 65–6, 69–70, 88, 113, 124, 153, 191–2, 204–7, 234, 249–50, 254, 257, 261–2, 315–16, 324
NASA  151, 173
navigation, navigate  63, 127, 154, 184, 191, 195, 204, 230, 238
neo-flow  308, *see also* flow
neo-series  247, 315
neotelevisionn  198–200, 209, 214, *see also* paleotelevision
neuroimage  112
news, news coverage, news report, news show  13–14, 23–4, 49, 60, 68, 75–6, 79, 81, 84–5, 102, 123, 125, 127–8, 152–4, 175, 189, 191, 199, 201, 215, 218, 223, 227–9, 231, 234, 237, 261, 272, 276, 326
non-consensual  33–5
non-identity  38
nonsense  157, 159, *see also* sense
now  5, 12, 29, 46, 71, 84, 89, 139, 156, 203, 205, 221, 228, 245, 304, 327, 333, *see also* instant; moment

object, objectification  109–10, 115, 148, 160, 162, 165, 166, 168–74, 180, 186, 192, 205, 208–9, 213, 223, 228, 231, 235, 248, 252, 257, 262–5, 278–9, 282, 289, 293, 296, 298–9, 309, 313, 316, 324–5, 328, 333, *see also* subject
object-image  308, 314, 327
object oriented ontology  136
object stability  213
omnipresence, omnipresent  9, 45, 279, 297, *see also* ubiquity
ontic  136, 144, 149, 256
ontogram, ontogrammatic  232–5, 240, 246, 265–7, 279–80, 293, 306, 314, 316, 329
ontography, ontographic  8, 12, 14–17, 22, 24, 27, 44, 49, 79, 86, 93, 111–12, 119–20, 126–7, 131–3, 135–7, 143–5, 148–50, 153–4, 158–60, 180, 187, 189, 193, 199, 213–15, 224–7, 230, 232–3, 235, 240, 245–7, 255–6, 264–5, 272–6, 278–80, 286–7, 289–96, 298, 300, 305–6, 309, 316, 329, 333–4
ontology, ontological  16, 27, 31, 45, 98, 108, 125, 132–3, 136–7, 140, 143, 149, 158, 225–7, 248, 273, 280, 291, 308–10, 329, 333
operation, operate, operational, operative, operativity  3–5, 7–13, 15, 17, 21, 25, 27, 29–30, 32, 36, 38, 43–5, 47, 49, 53, 59–63, 65, 67, 69–70, 75, 77–8, 85–9, 92, 97–100, 102, 111–15, 119–20, 124–7, 130, 132–3, 135–6, 140–4, 148–54, 156–60, 163–4, 174–5, 179–81, 183–90, 195–9, 202–4, 206–7, 209, 213, 215–17, 220–1, 225, 227–8, 231–6, 240, 245–6, 256, 261, 264–8, 272–3, 275, 278, 284, 290–300, 304, 306, 312–13, 316–18, 321–2, 325–8, 330–1, 334
operative memory  43–4, 59–60, 62, 67

optical unconscious   84, 195
order-from-noise   75
organ projection   104-7, 111, see also projection
outer space   7, 59, 81, 148-52, 157-68, 172, 174, 179, 282, 284, 320-1, see also space; space travel

paleotelevision   198, 216, see also neotelevision
panopticon   275, 285
panoramic   58
paradox, paradoxical   32, 34-5, 45, 49, 67, 71-2, 81, 87, 136, 138-9, 153, 169, 171, 179, 235, 247, 249, 254, 262, 267, 276, 278, 295, 332
parody   23, 274, 283
past   23, 27-30, 33, 43-4, 55-6, 59-61, 63, 67, 87, 89, 125-6, 133-4, 137-8, 140-1, 148, 155-7, 206-7, 228, 294, 296, 299-300, 317-19, 326, 333, see also future; present
patient   222-3, 237, 239, see also agent
Perseus' mirror   172
person, personal, personality, personnel, personify   25, 51, 60, 72, 87, 90, 97-8, 101, 141, 153, 183-5, 190-1, 193, 227-8, 253, 256, 263, 276, 281, 286-9, 291, 326-7, 330, see also interpersonal
phaneroscopy   235
phatic   7, 320
phenomenology, phenomenological   16-17, 28, 87, 110, 136, 138, 203, 235, 329
*phenomenotechnique*   159
picture, picture tube, television picture   4-12, 16, 46, 101, 111-12, 123, 143, 161, 166, 169, 172, 175, 213, 225, 229, 233, 249, 293, 306-7, see also television image
pinboard   251, 266-7
pixel   11-12, 19, 36, 108, 113, 199, 207, 224, 230, 279, 291, 306-7, 319, 328
place   16, 51, 59, 71-2, 81-2, 88, 141, 148, 161, 170, 179, 191, 203, 206, 209, 215, 218-19, 223, 255, 259, 284, 297-8, 307, 333, 334, see also location; room; space
planet, planetary   61-2, 120, 148, 150-1, 154-6, 164-8, 171-3, 175, 179, 196, see also earth
plasma screen   224, 226-7, 230-1
plasticity   55, 262-3, see also malleability
playback   42, 123
poetology   84
pragma/paskein   111
presence   6, 10, 24, 28, 32-3, 35, 37-9, 71-2, 75, 82, 84, 89-90, 126, 134, 138-9, 186, 201, 214, 268, 275, 279, 285, 291, 293, 297-8, 325, see also absence
present   4, 6-7, 9-11, 14, 20-1, 24-36, 38-9, 43-4, 46, 55, 59-61, 71, 77, 87, 89-90, 98, 105, 120, 123, 125-7, 129, 132-45, 155-8, 186, 203, 206-7, 220, 225, 227-8, 245-6, 252, 259, 261, 289, 293-6, 298-300, 310, 312, 318, 322, 329, 331, 333, see also absent; future; past
present-at-hand   27, 115
projected image   6
projection   15, 153, 162, 168-9, 173, 220, 293, see also organ projection
proliferation   144, 157, 219, 250-1, 253, 257

prominence, prominent   13, 79, 82, 286–91, *see also* celebrity
proprioception, proprioceptive   88, 110, 322–3
prosumer   181, 237–8, 330
proximity   83, 291, 299
pseudo-event   37–8, 149, 274
psychasthenia   223
public   24, 32–3, 38, 82, 101, 150, 152–4, 158, 161–4, 181, 199, 215, 218–19, 228, 238, 272, 274, 277, 282–3, 285–7, 299, 320, *see also* audience

quiz show   49, 76, 124, 162, 200, 217, 239

radio   7, 25–6, 35, 42–4, 48–9, 51, 53, 88, 100–2, 104, 107, 158, 171, 181, 186
reality   10, 14, 16, 29, 33–5, 38, 50, 90, 92–3, 130, 144–5, 149–50, 158, 171, 187, 193–5, 198, 206, 226, 234–6, 246, 248, 266, 272–80, 284–94, 296, 298, 300, 304–7, 309, 311, 314, 321
reality show, reality TV   236, 272–80, 283–4, 286–90, 293, 304–5
recaps   76, 281, 287, 293
record, recording   6–7, 12, 23–4, 27, 42–3, 51, 59, 76, 90, 119–20, 123–31, 134–6, 139, 144, 151, 154, 159–60, 162, 167, 200, 227, 239, 248, 256, 262, 264–5, 279, 281–2, 295, 297, 299, 312, 320, 325–6
recursion, recursive, recursiveness   17, 33, 60, 66–7, 106, 120, 125, 133, 135, 143, 149, 160, 227, 232, 246, 250, 305, 307, 311, 314, 317, 321, 328, 330, 331
re-enactment   297

reflection, reflexive, reflexivity   10, 16, 25–9, 36, 43–4, 52, 62, 67, 71–2, 82, 85, 87, 102, 106, 135, 149, 168, 172, 190, 192, 200, 209, 219–20, 222, 251, 255, 262–3, 283, 286, 290, 304, 314, 319, 321–32
regressus ad infinitum; infinite regress   67, 254
remembering   60–3, 67, 100, 119–20, 132, 138, 300, 317–18, *see also* forgetting
remote control   88, 94, 100, 120, 179–210, 213, 232, 236–7, 245, 306, 312, 314, 317, 326–8, 331
repeat, repetition   11, 14, 23, 27, 33–4, 43, 45–6, 48, 51–2, 56–7, 63, 69, 87–8, 100, 110, 121, 125, 127–8, 131–2, 134–6, 138, 141, 143–4, 155, 158, 179, 184–5, 193, 196, 208, 214, 219, 226, 246, 249, 251, 261–2, 272, 274, 286, 291, 295, 299, 316–18, 330–1
replay   120, 128–9, 133–4, 141–4, *see also* instant replay; slow motion
representation   23, 25, 28–9, 65–6, 106, 136, 143, 159, 174, 198, 200, 204, 235, 246, 264–5, 274, 279–80, 292, 296–7, 308–9, 311–12, 318–19
res extensa/res cogitans   87
resemblance   253–265, 268, 280, 311, 315
resolution   58, 108, 165, 168, 224–5, 229–30, 291, 319, 321
reverse, reversal, reversible   23, 26, 56, 66, 75, 82, 91, 106, 108, 111, 126, 129, 132, 136, 141, 143–4, 149, 165, 169, 171, 197, 205–6, 221, 236–7, 255, 275–6, 279, 285, 288–90, 293–4, 311, 318–19, 321–2, 324, 330, *see also* irreversible

room   15, 31, 76, 79, 88, 150, 161, 166, 173, 180–1, 203, 214–15, 217–23, 228, 237, 240, 255, 275–6, 281, 285, *see also* location; place; space
ruling   98, 115, 205, 273, *see also* switching

satellite   7, 35, 168, 170, 182, 219, 238, 320–1, 325
scan   30, 36–7, 42, 110, 112, 123–4, 155, 183, 225, 234, 245, 307
scandal   275, 281
screen   4–7, 10–12, 14–15, 22, 24–5, 31, 33, 44, 46, 52, 54, 56, 58, 62, 72, 76, 91, 101, 103, 105, 108, 110–12, 114, 120, 130, 133–4, 166, 170–4, 180, 183, 185, 188, 191, 195, 199–200, 203–4, 209, 213–40, 245–6, 248–53, 255–7, 260–1, 264–8, 273, 279–80, 282–3, 285–6, 290–3, 297, 300, 304, 306–8, 312, 314, 317, 319, 326–7, 330–1
scripted reality   287, 289
search scene   51, 124
second order   32, 219, 278, 283, 290
second screen   213–39, 257, 279, 282, 330
segment, segmentation   69, 81, 231, 246, 267
selection, select, selective   10, 25, 50, 108, 152, 179, 183–204, 206–10, 220, 232, 237, 259, 277, 281, 284–5, 287, 313, 316–17
self-contained   51, 54, 60, 64, 66, 98, 253, 284, 328
self-differentiation   36
self-evidence, self-evident   85, 97, 277
self-experience   88
self-forgetting   88

self-reference, self-referential, self-referentiality   256, 265, 290
self-reflexive, self-reflexivity   82, 87, 135, 209, 286, 290
self-transcendence   91, 214
semantic   4, 83–4, 102, 119, 142–3, 151, 154, 158, 185, 190–1, 194, 199, 264, 309, 312, 314–15, 319, 323–5, 327–8
semiotic   13, 208, 235, 264–5, *see also* sign
sensation, sensational   76, 132, 153, 289–90, 306
sense   85, 222, 251, 306, *see also* logic of sense; nonsense
sense, sensation, sensitive, sensory, sensual   11, 19, 26, 76, 78, 80, 85–9, 91–2, 107–10, 132, 137, 194, 224–5, 247, 308, 318, 322, 325–6, *see also* body; perception
sensor   19, 181–3
sequence, sequential, sequentiality   14–15, 22, 25–6, 29, 33, 42, 44–7, 54, 56–7, 61–2, 65–7, 69, 72, 75–7, 79–81, 83–4, 89, 91–2, 94, 100, 124, 128, 132–3, 136–40, 143, 145, 152–3, 159, 180, 183, 187–9, 192, 194–202, 204, 206, 217, 224–5, 228–32, 234, 240, 245, 248, 251–3, 259, 273, 291, 305–7, 311–12, 315–16, 320, 328–30
series, serial, seriality, serialization   14, 23, 42–72, 75–6, 78–80, 82–3, 85, 88, 99–100, 110, 119–20, 124–5, 127, 129, 137, 139, 141–3, 148, 150, 152–4, 160, 191–3, 195, 202, 209, 213–15, 227–8, 234, 236–9, 246–68, 272, 274–5, 280–1, 288–9, 293, 306, 314–19, 324, 327, 330–3
sex   23, 88, 103, 110, 193, 288
shock   194–5, 205

sign, signifier, signified  7, 9, 12–13, 68–9, 71, 80, 208–9, 234–6, 247, 251–3, 256–7, 264–7, 291, *see also* semiotic
simulation  21, 38, 79, 106, 126, 149, 273–7, 279, 284–5, *see also* dissimulation
simultaneity, simultaneous  14–15, 19–24, 26, 28–32, 35–6, 38–9, 42, 45, 60, 62, 68–9, 75, 82–3, 85–7, 89–90, 103, 107, 111, 115, 119, 126–7, 132–3, 135, 137–9, 144, 150–1, 153, 156–9, 166, 168, 170, 194, 202, 215–18, 222–3, 228, 230, 233–4, 237, 240, 245, 254, 256, 259, 265, 267, 272–3, 283, 286, 291, 296, 298, 304, 315, 321, 324–5, 328–9, 331, 334, *see also* synchronicity
singularity  141, 148, 289
Sitcom  267–8
slow-motion  127, 129–33, 289, 316
soap opera  53–8, 63, 67, 70, 85, 88, 184, 202, 216, 220, 236, 259, 262, 275
sound  3–4, 9, 12, 17, 29, 35, 43, 88, 92, 108–10, 129, 141–2, 151, 154–5, 157–8, 181–2, 187, 248–9, 264, 320
space, spatial  4, 16, 20–2, 25, 34, 36, 38, 45, 48, 53, 55, 68, 70, 80–2, 89, 120, 125, 148–54, 157, 161, 163–8, 172, 174, 179–80, 207, 214, 215, 217–23, 225, 227–30, 233, 236–7, 245–6, 248, 255, 265–6, 282, 284, 299, 307, 318–21, 328, 331, *see also* location; place; outer space; room
space travel  153–4, 182, 320, *see also* outer space
spectator  13, 172, 248, *see also* user; viewer

speculative realism  136, 240, 329
sports  24, 31, 49, 60, 64, 75, 81, 88–90, 123, 129–30, 132, 135, 138, 141, 144, 161, 202, 207, 215, 221, 223, 228, 239, 277, 290, 326
stand by  9–10, 203, 322–3, 334
Stoa  137–8
storage memory  44, 300
subject  15–17, 20, 25–7, 29–31, 45, 53, 60, 65–6, 79, 87, 92, 97–9, 109–10, 112–15, 119, 141, 150–1, 158, 168–71, 174–5, 184, 216, 238–9, 264, 278, 286, 288, 299, 309, 313–14, 318, 324–7, 333–4
subject-image  170, 174, 184
succession, successivity  15, 22, 34, 42, 46, 49, 67–9, 75–6, 138, 181, 225, 234, 253, 265, 315, 331
supertext  82
surveillance  15, 65, 81, 154, 169, 175, 261, 275, 281, 283
suture  82, 326–7
swiping  184, 193
switch image  26, 35–8, 43, 66, 69, 72, 81, 97–100, 102, 115, 119–20, 125, 127, 143–5, 148–51, 154, 158–60, 164, 172–5, 179–80, 184, 186, 190, 193, 197–9, 208, 213–15, 219, 223–4, 230–3, 235–6, 238, 240, 245–6, 264–5, 267, 272, 276, 279, 283, 289–94, 296, 298, 304, 306, 308, 311–20, 322–8, 331, 334
switching (remote control)  88, 94, 100, 120, 179–210, 213, 232, 236–7, 245, 306, 312, 314, 317, 326–8, 331
switching, switchable  3–6, 8–13, 15–16, 21, 23, 25–7, 30–2, 34, 36–7, 42–3, 47, 52, 60, 62,

66, 69, 75, 77, 80–1, 84, 92–4,
  97–100, 112–13, 115, 119–20,
  124, 126, 133, 135, 139, 144,
  156–9, 162–4, 173–4, 179–81,
  183–4, 186, 188–91, 193,
  195–208, 213–14, 219–21, 227,
  231–3, 245–6, 273, 276, 290–3,
  295, 304–7, 311–12, 314–17,
  320–3, 327–34, *see also* ruling
switch-off-image   304–34
symbol, symbolic   84, 114, 210, 264
synchronization, synchronicity   28–
  33, 35–9, 42, 75, 119, 132, 134,
  151, 157, 237–8, 240, 265, 267,
  331, *see also* simultaneity
systems theory   78

tactility, tactile   107, 109–10, 115,
  119, 174, 208, 276, 314, 326–7
*taxis*   326
*techné*   115
technology, technological   19–20,
  35, 37, 46, 51, 62, 65, 81–2,
  89, 93, 98–9, 103–7, 111–12,
  127–8, 130, 162, 181–3, 185,
  188, 210, 214, 219, 223, 227,
  230–1, 236–9, 250, 268, 279,
  286, 289, 296, 299, 320, 326
teleplay, television play   23, 43, 47,
  49–51, 124
teletext   182, *see also* videotext
television aesthetics   90, 277
television experience   81, *see also*
  experience
television history   155, 257, 293–4,
  297, 299–300, 305
television image   4–7, 11–12, 14,
  17, 22, 79, 81, 90, 119–20, 123,
  126–8, 130, 136, 151, 167,
  170–2, 175, 180, 193–4, 198,
  201, 205–6, 209, 215, 220, 224,
  231–2, 234–6, 249, 264, 275,
  277, 321, 329, *see also* picture
television philosophy   16

television theory   24, 76, 78, 92,
  214, 309
televisual, televisuality   12, 16, 22,
  24, 26, 28, 33, 43, 52, 58, 76,
  81–2, 90, 93, 112, 120, 126–7,
  145, 153–4, 158–60, 165, 172,
  198–200, 208–9, 214, 221,
  223, 238, 267, 273, 276–7, 284,
  289–93, 296, 298, 305, 316,
  327–8, 330–1, 333
temporality, temporalization,
  temporal   4, 22–4, 27–8,
  30–1, 33, 36–9, 44–6, 51, 55,
  57–8, 60, 62, 64, 82, 84, 87, 89,
  91, 125–7, 132, 134–5, 137,
  139–40, 148, 157–8, 167, 194,
  208, 225, 228, 235, 240, 250,
  259–60, 262, 267, 289, 293,
  298, 312, 331, 333
temporal object   22–4, 33, 148, 289
time   4–5, 20–3, 28–31, 35–6, 39,
  43–6, 49, 55–6, 75, 84, 89, 91,
  126–8, 131–5, 137–44, 148,
  150–1, 154–8, 196, 206–8,
  227–30, 245, 254, 261–2, 265,
  267, 293–6, 318, 330–3
timeless, timelessness   8, 131–2, 134
token/type   45–8
touch   4–5, 102, 109–10, 180, 200,
  208, 264, 314, 328
trajectory   127, 207
transmedial, transmediality   43,
  52, 247
transmission   4, 7, 13, 19, 21, 23–5,
  28, 31, 35, 37, 49, 77, 102, 104,
  112, 124, 126, 131, 135, 154,
  157, 161, 180–1, 186–7, 214,
  220, 248, 252, 260, 279, 299
transmission-image   180
transparency   150, 215, 229–31,
  261, 295
transvisibility   179, 196
tube   7–12, 19, 22, 36–7, 42, 108,
  110–11, 120, 123, 161, 170,

183, 207, 213, 217, 222, 224, 232, 233, 236, 239, 319, *see also* cathode ray tube

ubiquity, ubitquitous  9, 45, 108, 183, 219, 236, 279, 297, 307, *see also* omnipresence
universality  106, 182–4, 192, 298
univocity  158–9
user  5, 15, 108, 113, 166, 209, 214–16, 220, 223, 238, 257, 261, 291, 330, 334, *see also* spectator; viewer

video, videographic, videography  4, 20, 125–9, 135–6, 141, 154, 161, 191, 199–200, 214, 219, 223, 233, 239, 319
videotext  182, 232, *see also* teletext
view, viewer  5–6, 11, 14–17, 20, 23–5, 29, 31–3, 35, 38, 43, 46–7, 49–50, 52–4, 56–7, 62–3, 68–70, 72, 75–6, 78, 82, 88–92, 94, 98–104, 107, 110–15, 119–20, 124–5, 128–9, 131, 135, 138–9, 141, 148, 151, 155, 157–8, 162–4, 166–7, 170–5, 179–81, 184, 186, 188–95, 198, 200–2, 205–8, 215–20, 224–6, 228–31, 234, 236–9, 245–6, 249, 251–2, 255, 257, 262, 267–8, 277–8, 282, 285, 287, 290–1, 293–4, 296–8, 304–5, 307, 310, 312, 314–16, 319, 323–31, 334, *see also* spectator; user
virtual history  295–7
virtuality, virtual  52–3, 61–2, 71, 84, 128, 132, 165, 204–8, 268, 276, 285, 295–8, 312, 318, *see also* actual
virtual reality  205–8, 318
visual, visualize, visuality  7, 11–12, 20, 24, 65, 71, 76, 82, 100, 112–13, 119, 128, 135, 161, 166–70, 174, 184, 199–200, 214, 220, 232–4, 236, 248, 251–2, 258, 261, 265, 276–7, 290, 297, 305–6, 314, 318–20, 323–4, *see also* televisual, televisuality

war  38, 53, 150, 274–5, 298
witness  15, 24, 297–8
world  4–5, 7–9, 12–17, 25, 31, 33–4, 37–8, 44, 48, 50, 62, 68, 71–2, 79, 87, 99, 102, 107, 109–10, 120, 125, 130, 139, 142, 145, 160, 169–71, 185–7, 191–2, 194–6, 198, 207–10, 213, 225–7, 229–30, 248, 251, 254, 257, 262, 266, 272–3, 275, 279, 281, 283–4, 293, 308–12, 314, 317, 321–2, 327–9, 334

zapping  181, 193, 201–2, 327
Zeigarnik effect  56–7, 318

**TV Stations/Shows/Films**

*24*  250, 267
*77 Sunset Strip*  61, 64

ABC  51, 124
*Alfred Hitchcock Presents*  51
*Ally McBeal*  192, 264
Amazon  238
Apollo project/Apollo program/ Moon landing  120, 148–53, 164, 168, 173, 276, 284, 320
ARD  153
*The Avengers*  61, 64, 70

*The Bachelor/The Bachelorette*  193, 287–8
BBC  293
*The Big Bang Theory*  268
*Big Brother*  193, 275–6, 280–93

*Bonanza* 57, 59, 61, 69–70
*Breaking Bad* 250, 259, 261–4
*Broken Arrow* 58
*Bundespolizei Live* 289

*Candid Camera* 272, 290
CBS 129–30, 154
*Celebrity Big Brother* 288
*I'm A Celebrity-Get Me Out of Here* 288
CNN 191, 200
*Colt .45* 58
*COPS* 289
*Criminal Intent* 267–8
*CSI* 247–54, 259, 261, 266

*Dallas* 61, 63, 70, 72, 259, 261, 268
*Das aktuelle Sportstudio* 228
*Department S* 64, 70
*Deutschland sucht den Superstar* 287
*Die Fußbroichs* 275–6
*Discovery Channel* 293, 295–6
*The Docks of New York* 47

*The FBI* 61
*FishbowlCam* 282
*Flash Forward* 250–1, 261, 266–8
*Friends* 268
*The Fugitive* 72, 254

*Good Morning America* 81
*Grace and Frankie* 268
*The Guiding Light* 259
*Gunsmoke* 57

*History Channel* 293
*Homeland* 261
*House of Cards* 250, 262
*House, MD* 234, 250, 261, 263, 266–7
*How I Met Your Mother* 268

*I Love Lucy* 268

*I Spy* 64
*Ich bin ein Star-Holt mich hier raus* 288
*Ich bin ein Star-Lasst mich hier rein* 288
*The Invaders* 68–9
*Invitation to Love* 255
*It's Always Sunny in Philadelphia* 268

*JenniCam* 282–3

*Kraft Television Theatre* 23, 50

*Law and Order* 267–8
*Lie to me* 251
*Lost* 257, 266

*Mad Men* 53, 129, 262–3, 267
*Man Against Crime* 51, 57
*The Man From U.N.C.L.E.* 64
*Martin Kane* 51, 57
*Maverick* 59
*Miami Vice* 64–6, 70–1, 191–3
*Mission: Impossible* 64, 70, 259
*The Motorola Television Hour* 50
*Mr. District Attorney* 51, 57
MTV 189, 200

*Netflix* 238–9
*Next Top Model* 193, 287
*Nosferatu* 47
*Numb3rs* 266

*Percy Stuart* 254
*The Persuaders* 64
*The Philco Television Playhouse* 23, 50
*Pop Idol* 287
*Private Eye* 51, 57
*Promi Big Brother* 288

*The Queen's Messenger* 49
*Quiet: We Live in Public* 283–4

*Rawhide*  57, 59, 72
RTL  130

*The Seven Year Itch*  23
*Sex and the City*  193
*Sherlock*  234, 266
*The Sopranos*  250, 262
*Star Trek*  59, 61, 69, 150
*Survivor*  193

*Television Department Store*  184
test patterns  319–20, 325, 327, 331
*Trackdown*  59
*The Truman Show*  282–3
*The Twilight Zone*  51
*Twin Peaks*  250, 253–7, 259, 261–2, 264, 267

*The Untouchables*  61

Warner Bros.  51, 124
*We Live in Public*  283–4
*Wünsch Dir was (Make a Wish)*  162

YouTube  215

ZDF  152, 228
*ZDF History*  293

**Names**

Abramson, Albert  7, 8, 11, 42, 123, 127, 161
Adorno, Theodor W.  113, 274, 283
Anders, Günther  4, 44–5, 101–2, 114, 125, 165–6, 172, 216, 230, 253
von Ardenne, Manfred  19
Aristotle  29–30, 75, 138–9
Assmann, Aleida  60, 299
Assmann, Jan  299

Bachelard, Gaston  159
Baird, John Logie  19

Barnouw, Eric  49, 51, 57, 123–4, 129–30, 148, 150, 152, 154, 162
Baudrillard, Jean  38, 90, 101, 149, 155, 274–6, 284–5
Bazin, André  4, 8, 24, 35, 81
Benjamin, Walter  84, 194–5
Bense, Max  99, 187, 235
Bergson, Henri  28, 29, 39, 55, 138, 206, 308–15, 317–19, 322–4, 327, 334
Bogost, Ian  16, 136
Bose, Jagadish Chandra  181
Bourdieu, Pierre  45
Bühler, Karl  185–7
Buxton, David  58–9, 64–5

Caillois, Roger  222–3
Caldwell, John Thornton  200, 214
Canetti, Elias  272–3
Cantor, Muriel  53–5
Casetti, Francesco  198–9
Cavell, Stanley  15, 47, 139, 214, 258, 260, 262, 281, 311, 321, 328–9
Churchill, Winston  295
Claerbout, David  233
Comte, Auguste  310
Crockett, Sonny  64
Czikszentmihaly, Mihaly  86–9, 92, 94

Da Vinci, Leonardo  296
Dayan, Daniel  32, 37, 326
Deleuze, Gilles  36, 45–6, 55–6, 67–72, 80, 82, 86, 112, 133–4, 137–44, 156–9, 204, 206, 208, 221–2, 227, 233, 235, 238, 247, 254, 256, 267, 273–4, 278, 280, 294–5, 308, 311, 332–4
Derrida, Jacques  36, 105
Descola, Philippe  225–7, 255, 280
Dewey, John  24–8, 56, 77
Dienst, Richard  98, 171, 179, 196
Doane, Mary Ann  33–4, 68, 128, 278, 325

# Index

Eco, Umberto   24–8, 31–2, 34–5, 37, 77, 97, 151, 187, 198, 296
Elias, Norbert   78
Englert, Carina   98, 248
Esch, Deborah   35–7, 90
Ewing, Bobby   63, 259, 261
Ewing, J.R.   63

Fahle, Oliver   42, 69, 150, 205, 251–2, 267
Feuer, Jane   35, 81–2, 89–90, 126, 228
Foerster, Heinz von   59–60, 75, 317
Foucault, Michel   114, 238, 254–7, 264, 275–6, 286
Freud, Sigmund   93, 194–5

Galilei, Galileo   165
Galton, Francis   253, 260–1
Gell, Alfred   22, 66, 292
Gramsci, Antonio   102

Halbwachs, Maurice   299
Hall, Stuart   85, 102
Harman, Graham   16, 136, 329
Harris, Josh   283
Hartley, John   102, 161, 216
Heidegger, Martin   5, 25, 30–1, 39, 87, 91, 98–9, 155–6, 158, 332–3
Hitler, Adolf   295–6
Horton, Donald   72

Jakobson, Roman   7, 9, 14, 185–6, 320
Jenkins, Henry   43, 257
Jermyn, Deborah   252, 289

Kandinsky, Wassili   46
Kapp, Ernst   104–7, 111
Katz, Elihu   32, 37
Kennedy, John F.   128–9, 262
Kierkegaard, Søren   30, 62
Kittler, Friedrich   6, 43, 91
Knopp, Guido   294

Lacan, Jacques   67, 84, 113, 169–71, 174
Lasswell, Harold   100, 185–6
Latour, Bruno   20–1, 98, 220
Luhmann, Niklas   31, 33, 48–50, 60, 78, 97, 132–3, 139, 142, 157, 187–8, 196–7, 200–1, 276–9, 290, 294, 317, 325
Lynch, Michael   160, 254
Lyotard, Jean Francois   159–60, 260, 284

McCarthy, Anna   219–23
McDonald, Eugene F.   181
McLuhan, Marshall   15–16, 76, 92, 102–12, 115, 130, 151, 166, 171, 174, 213, 224, 281, 288–9, 309, 328–9
Marconi, Guglielmo   181
Materazzi, Marco   131
Mattenklott, Gert   330
Menke, Christoph   261–2
Mersch, Dieter   75, 106, 265
Meyrowitz, Joshua   216–17
Modleski, Tania   88
Monet, Claude   46
Monroe, Marilyn   23
Mumford, Lewis   45
Murnau, Friedrich Wilhelm   47

Nielsen, Arthur C.   162
Nielsen, Brigitte   288
Nietzsche, Friedrich   91–3

Odin, Roger   198–9, 214
Oswald, Lee Harvey   128, 132

Pasolini, Pier Paolo   273
Peel, Emma   64
Peirce, Charles S.   21, 45, 208–9, 234–6, 240, 264–7, 298
Pias, Claus   161
Pingree, Suzanne   53–5
Polley, Eugene   181

Postman, Neil 304
Preece, William 181

Quevedo, Leonardo Torres 181

Rheinberger, Hans-Jörg 161, 164
Richtmeyer, Ulrich 260
Ringley, Jennifer 282
Roosevelt, Franklin Delano 295–6
Ruby, Jack 128

Schumacher, Michael 131
Senna, Ayrton 130–1, 141
Serres, Michel 16, 22, 329
Siefarth, Günther 153
Sloterdijk, Peter 115
Spencer, Herbert 310
Spigel, Lynn 52–3, 161, 184, 216–18
Stadler, Michael 8, 136
Stalin, Joseph W. 295–6
Stauff, Markus 114, 149, 236–9
Stichweh, Carl Rollie 129

Tubbs, Ricardo 64

Vogl, Joseph 165
Von Sternberg, Josef 47
Voss, Christiane 91, 328

Wentz, Daniela 233–5, 250, 257, 260, 264–6
White, Walter 250, 261–2, 264
Whitehead, Alfred North 251
Williams, Raymond 76–86, 91–2, 94, 102, 113, 305, 306
Winkler, Hartmut 113–15, 155, 188, 194–5, 203, 205
Winston, Brian 123
Wittgenstein, Ludwig 253, 257–8, 260–1, 263–4
Wohl, Richard R. 72
Wulff, Hans Jürgen 77, 83, 85–6

Zeigarnik, Bljuma 56–7, 318
Zidane, Zinedine 131
Zielinski, Siegfried 49, 161

www.ingramcontent.com/pod-product-compliance
Lightning Source LLC
Chambersburg PA
CBHW072119290426
44111CB00012B/1703